THE LAW OF SCHOOLS, STUDENTS AND TEACHERS
IN A NUTSHELL

FOURTH EDITION

By

KERN ALEXANDER

Professor
University of Illinois, Urbana–Champaign

M. DAVID ALEXANDER

Professor
Virginia Polytechnic Institute and State University

WEST®

A Thomson Reuters business

Mat #40760212

COPYRIGHT © 1984, 1995 WEST PUBLISHING CO.
© West, a Thomson business, 2003
© 2009 Thomson/Reuters

    610 Opperman Drive
    St. Paul, MN 55123
    1–800–313–9378

Printed in the United States of America

ISBN: 978–0–314–19539–5

TEXT IS PRINTED ON 10% POST CONSUMER RECYCLED PAPER

OUTLINE

Page

Page

*

TABLE OF CASES

References are to Pages

A

TABLE OF CASES

B

C

D

E

F

G

H

I

J

K

L

M

N

O

P

Q

R

S

TABLE OF CASES

U

V

W

THE LAW OF SCHOOLS, STUDENTS AND TEACHERS
IN A NUTSHELL

FOURTH EDITION

*

INTRODUCTION

This book is designed as a textbook for courses of study for teacher training programs, undergraduate and graduate, and as a handbook for on-the-job teachers and practicing school administrators. In concise and non-technical terms it explains the prevailing law as it governs the operation of America's schools. As we all know, professional personnel in today's public schools are to a great extent reluctant recipients of the legal overburden emanating from our litigious society. Parents and students frequently see the school in a legalistic adversarial context that is obviously contrary to the cooperative community perspective envisioned for the common school. In spite of these diversions endemic to our modern social existence, school teachers and administrators very effectively carry forward the essential school function of conveying worthwhile knowledge and cultural values to each succeeding generation. Sometimes these duties of educators are carried out in spite of the perception by some that the laws and regulations are not always conducive to an efficient system of education. Yet, the overarching mission of the schools in providing for mass universal education to safeguard the democratic form of government moves relentlessly forward with both the assets and liabilities that are engendered in our modern age.

While the encumbrances of the manifold laws and regulations that flow down upon the public schools from both state and federal governments are sometimes excessive and not always necessary, by-in-large these laws have worked to vastly benefit both the children who partake of education and teachers who are the purveyors of a vast store of knowledge and skills. The network of these laws ultimately works to bestow upon the next generation abilities and capacities that enable each fledgling citizen to obtain personal autonomy and to understand, value, and defend our basic liberties and freedoms.

The pages of this book explain in simplified nonlegalese the laws that protect children, enhance their learning opportunities, and assure teachers of the academic freedom and security to pursue the teaching profession without fear of undue restraint. As a practical guide to the legal aspects of public schools, this book includes explanations of laws that govern such important issues as student rights and prerogatives pertaining to compulsory attendance, pupil suspension and expulsion, discipline, child abuse, personal appearance, academic testing and grading, drug testing, search and seizure, freedom of speech, publications, records, and religious observances. Too, considerable attention is given to the federal and state statutes and court cases having to do with education of disabled children and the many aspects of the laws prohibiting discrimination on the basis of race, sex, ethnicity, religion and national origin.

Considerable detail is devoted to the political rights of teachers as protected by various constitutional provisions. The terms and conditions of the teacher's employment relations with the school board are fully explained, encompassing contracts, tenure, and processes for dismissal, including incompetence, insubordination, neglect of duty, moral turpitude, etc. In particular, civil rights legislation is discussed with appropriate attention given to teacher employment rights as required by Title VII and other federal statutes protecting teachers against discrimination due to sex, pregnancy, age, and disability. Further, the current and emerging issues pertaining to search and seizure are expanded upon in some detail. Any book about education law would be remiss if it did not fully explain the potential for civil liability that accompanies employment as a teacher or school administrator; this book pays special attention to that topic. Also, a good reading of the tort chapters will give the practitioner a healthy respect for common law and statutory liability, but will at the same time engender a feeling of confidence in the knowledge that courts are quite cognizant of and sympathetic to the nature of the school and accordingly are willing to extend substantial latitude to teachers and administrators so long as they act with reasonableness and prudence in fulfilling their educational responsibilities.

All projects of this nature are dependent on the support of a few key players. In this instance Shari Hall was the indispensible person who managed the entire undertaking of manuscript preparation. Her scheduling, editing and research skills were essential, indeed critical, to the entire process. Moreover, the speed and accuracy of her typing was beyond comparison. Too, we are very much indebted to Kate Kemball who provided ready assistance and support throughout preparation and production of the book. Without their good works, the book could not have come to fruition.

Kern Alexander, Urbana–Champaign, Illinois

David Alexander, Blacksburg, Virginia

CHAPTER 1

ATTENDANCE IN PUBLIC SCHOOLS

§ 1.1 INTRODUCTION

Legal authorization for the creation and maintenance of free public schools is found in the education clause of state constitutions. Within the boundaries of these constitutional provisions legislatures enact laws which prescribe admission and attendance requirements. Education clauses of state constitutions may designate an age span, such as between six and twenty years of age, for which the state shall provide an education. These constitutional provisions are viewed by the courts as requiring state legislatures to provide for public education covering at least this age group, but do not prohibit the legislatures from expanding educational opportunity beyond the specified ages. For example, courts have held that a legislature has the implied authority to create kindergarten programs for children below the age of six years. *In re Kindergarten Schools*, 32 P. 422 (Colo.1893). Similarly, expansion of vocational education programs for adults has been held to be within legislative prerogative, even though the state constitution defined public education as covering only ages four through twenty years. In this case, the Supreme Court of Wisconsin said that: "The constitutional provision [that] the Legislature shall provide for establishment of district schools and that such schools shall be free to all children between the ages of four and twenty years does not impliedly prohibit free

4

education for persons beyond the age of twenty and under the age of four." *Manitowoc v. Manitowoc Rapids*, 285 N.W. 403 (Wis.1939).

Courts have, generally, acceded to expansion of educational opportunity through reliance on broad implication of either the state constitution or statute. In the famous *Kalamazoo* case, the precedent which helped form public secondary schools in America, the court relied on broad implication of state policy, not explicit statute, to support its conclusion that a local school district could, with consent of the voters, expand its educational program to include high school. *Stuart v. School District No. 1 of the Village of Kalamazoo*, 30 Mich. 69 (1874).

§ 1.2 ADMISSION

As the educational program is expanded, all persons in the particular age group are entitled to attend the public school. A state cannot set up unreasonable attendance classifications for persons within the same age groups. For example, some public schools cannot be closed down and vouchers from public funds given to students to re-enroll in private schools with the result that schools are racially segregated. *Griffin v. County School Board of Prince Edward County*, 377 U.S. 218 (1964). When the state makes the decision to provide an educational program, it must do so uniformly, and denial of attendance cannot be for an unconstitutional discriminatory purpose.

§ 1.21 Age

Statutes setting minimum ages below which a child cannot be enrolled are valid and cannot be construed as denial of a child's right to attend school. In an Illinois case where state statute required a child to be five years of age by September 1, the parents of a child who became five on September 4 filed suit seeking to compel admission by the local school board. The parents maintained that such a cut-off date was arbitrary and therefore unconstitutional. The court ruled that the school board was within its statutory authority to deny admission to the child. According to the court, it was the intent of the legislature to create and strictly enforce a cut-off age below which a child could not attend school. The law was found not to be arbitrary because the statute was based upon good rationale that the age of the child could be reasonably assumed to indicate the readiness of a child for success in school. *Morrison v. Chicago Bd. of Educ.*, 544 N.E.2d 1099 (Ill.App. 1st Dist.1989).

Even though the general rule is that a specified minimum attendance age will be upheld by the courts, there are exceptions. For example, a West Virginia court has held that a state statute requiring a child to attain the age of five years by September 1 implied that local school boards must exercise a reasonable degree of regulatory flexibility in accepting children to kindergarten. Such implied discretion delegated to the local level would require that local school boards give consideration to the intellectual maturity of the child and not rigidly adhere to an "arbitrary cut-off date." *Blessing v. Mason County Bd. of Educ.*, 341 S.E.2d 407 (W.Va.1985).

However, if a child is not entitled to attend school and the parents misrepresent the child's age to the school board, then the school board may recover the costs of the education that had been received by the child under false pretenses. *Board of Educ. v. Marsiglia*, 582 N.Y.S.2d 256 (A.D. 2d Dept. 1992).

§ 1.22 Restrictions

States can impose restrictions on admission to public schools which are reasonably related to the state's purpose of providing a free public education. Such restrictions have been upheld when related to the maintenance of the health and protection of the public welfare. Also, residence requirements for reasonable classifications of children have been upheld. Residence statutes which require children to attend school in one school district rather than in another have been dealt with liberally by the courts. A school district has a right to question the *bona fides* of the residency of its students. Where a student changes guardianship solely to attend school in another school district, the validity of the change in residence may be rejected by the receiving school board. *In the Matter of Proios*, 443 N.Y.S.2d 828 (1981).

§ 1.23 Residence

Most state laws require children to attend school in the district in which the student resides with parents, guardian or person having lawful control of her or him. Because residence and domicile are distinct legal concepts, a child may actually reside in one school district and be domiciled in another; yet, state statutes and case law normally presume that the residency and domicile of an unemancipated minor are where the parent or legal guardian lives. *Craven County Board of Education v.*

Willoughby, 466 S.E.2d 334 (N.C.App.1996) and *Board of Education of the Sewanhaka Central High School District v. Sobol*, 623 N.Y.S.2d 412 (A.D.3d Dept. 1995). If a child lives with a custodian, but his parents are in residence in another school district, he must attend school in the district where his parents reside. The United States Supreme Court has held that a *bona fide* residence requirement which is appropriately defined and uniformly applied furthers the state interest in assuring that educational services of the state are enjoyed only by the state's residents. *Martinez v. Bynum*, 461 U.S. 321 (1983).

"Residence" generally requires both physical presence and an intention to remain. The Supreme Court of Maine provided the best definition over a century ago, "When ... a person voluntarily takes up his abode in a given place, with intention to remain permanently, or for an indefinite period of time; or, to speak more accurately, when a person takes up his abode in a given place without any present intention to remove therefrom, such place of abode becomes his residence." *Inhabitants of Warren v. Inhabitants of Thomaston*, 43 Me. 406 (1857).

Some courts have resolved the residency issue by applying a so-called "best-interest test." A case in point is where a 15–year–old student resided with her grandmother who lived in Arizona and she sought to attend school in the district where her grandmother lived. The grandmother, however, was not the girl's legal guardian. The inevitable question then arose as to whether the girl was to attend public school free or would be subject to a fee. The Arizona Court of Appeals ruled that the "best interest" of the girl was served by tuition-free placement with the relative who resides within the school district, regardless of whether the relative is the legal guardian. According to this court, the best interest rule should apply if the student does not move to the school district for the primary purpose of obtaining educational benefits. *Sleeseman v. State Bd. of Educ.*, 753 P.2d 186 (Ariz.App.1988).

In a decision similar to the Arizona decision above, an appellate court in Illinois held that a student who resided permanently with a maternal aunt was entitled to attend public school tuition-free in the district of the aunt's residence. The court ruled that residence in the school district is sufficient to permit the child to attend school free of charge, so long as residence was not taken solely to enjoy the benefits of the free schools in that district. The court further found that while the child could be required to show that school attendance in the district was not the sole reason for residing there, the school district could not compel the child to prove by third party professional assessment that the parents suffered hardship or were so incapacitated that they could not care for the child. In requiring such a burden of proof, the school district had overstepped its authority. *Israel S. v. Board of Education of Oak Park*, 601 N.E.2d 1264 (Ill.App. 1992). See also *Major v. Nederland Ind. School District*, 772 F.Supp. 944 (E.D.Tex.1991).

§ 1.24 Domicile

The word "domicile" is derived from the Latin "domus" meaning home or dwelling house. The word may be defined by law as the true place of habitation; for example, a Washington statute which was upheld as constitutional by the United States Supreme Court defined "domicile" as "a person's true, fixed and permanent home and place of habitation. It is the place where he intends to remain, and to which he expects to return when he leaves without intending to establish a new domicile elsewhere." *Sturgis v. Washington*, 414 U.S. 1057 (1973). A *bona fide* residence requirement may have the same legal connotation as domicile. Domicile and residence are usually in the same place, but the terms are not identical. A person may have two residences but can have only one domicile. Whether the term "residence" or "domicile" is used, the key is the "intention to remain." A New York state appellate court has ruled that "residence" means "domicile." Residence requires 1) physical and 2) intent to remain. *Longwood Central School District v. Springs Union Free School District*, 806 N.E.2d 970 (N.Y. 2004).

§ 1.241   Homeless Children

Federal law supersedes state law with regard to residence or domicile of homeless children. The McKinney–Vento Homeless Assistance Act has been codified into the No Child Left Behind Act (NCLB). (42 U.S.C. § 11432). The law prohibits school districts from stigmatizing or segregating homeless children from the "mainstream school environment on the basis of their being homeless."

Schools must extend to homeless students the same access, free appropriate public education, as to other children. Education of the homeless student must continue in the student's "school of origin" or the school district must enroll the student in a school that is attended by other students in the same attendance zone. Importantly, the federal law requires that a homeless student must be immediately admitted to the school of the student's choice, pending resolution of a dispute. Schools must notify homeless parents of their child's statutory rights under NCLB's school choice provisions. By virtue of the McKinney–Vento Act, homeless students have a private right of action to enforce its provisions. This means that an action in damages may lie against a school district that denies this statutory right to a homeless student. In addition to legal action under the Act, homeless students and parents can proceed against a school district under the Equal Protection Clause of the Fourteenth Amendment. *National Law Center on Homelessness and Poverty, R.I. v. State of New York*, 224 F.R.D. 314 (E.D.N.Y. 2004).

§ 1.25 Constitutional Classification

Classification of persons by geographical boundaries does not constitute a "suspect" classification requiring strict scrutiny to show a compelling reason to so classify. Domicile requirements are not unconstitutional if the classification is rationally related to a legitimate state purpose. The Supreme Court affirmed a lower federal court decision which held valid a state university regulation which declared that no student could be eligible for resident classification "... unless he had been a *bona fide* domiciliary of the state for at least a year immediately prior thereto...." The rule required that the student show permanent residence and that his presence in the state was not solely for the purpose of attending the state university. *Starns v. Malkerson*, 401 U.S. 985 (1971).

§ 1.26 Irrebuttable Presumption

An "irrebuttable presumption" in this context means that the non-resident or non-domicile status of the student is fixed and cannot be rebutted or altered. Yet, an irrebuttable presumption may be created if there is no way to convert non-residence to residence. State laws that are based on traditional legal criteria for domicile and residency for attending free public schools do not create an "irrebuttable presumption" or a durational residency requirement that violates a student's rights. *Graham v. Mock*, 545 S.E.2d 263 (N.C.Ct. App. 2001). For example, a Connecticut residence requirement for university students was held to be unconstitutional as violating due process because it created an "irrebuttable presumption" of non-residency for all students whose legal addresses were outside the state before they applied for admission. This meant that non-resident students could not gain resident status so long as they were students because the law created a presumption of non-residence for all those who attended the state university. The non-resident students could not rebut this presumption even though they intended to continue to live in the state after graduation. *Vlandis v. Kline*, 412 U.S. 441 (1973).

§ 1.27   Validity of Residence

In *Martinez v. Bynum*, supra, the United States Supreme Court upheld a Texas statute which denied tuition-free admission to minors who live apart from their parent or guardian for the "primary purpose of attending public free schools." In this case, Roberto Morales, who was born in McAllen, Texas, in 1969, a citizen of the United States by birth, was denied tuition-free admission in the McAllen Independent School District because his parents no longer lived in Texas and now resided in Mexico. He moved to McAllen where he lived with his sister who was his custodian but not his legal guardian. The Court held that denial of admission was not violative of equal protection because the State of Texas had a substantial interest in maintaining school quality by imposing *bona fide* residence requirements. The Court said that: "Absent residence requirements, there can be little doubt that the proper planning and operation of the schools would suffer significantly." See: *Graham v. Mock*, 545 S.E.2d 263 (N.C.Ct.App.2001).

§ 1.28 Illegal Aliens

If, however, state law regarding residency works to completely deny school attendance in all districts of a state, the constitution may be violated. Children of illegal aliens have been held to have a right to attend the public schools of Texas when the alternative was that they would receive no public education at all. *Plyler v. Doe*, 457 U.S. 202 (1982). In this case plaintiffs, illegal aliens, challenged a state statute in Texas which withheld state school funds for the education of children who were not legally admitted into the United States and which authorized local school districts to deny their enrollment. The plaintiffs claimed that the statute violated the Equal Protection Clause of the Fourteenth Amendment which states that no state shall "deny to any person within its jurisdiction the equal protection of the laws." The state of Texas in defense maintained that the provision in the clause "within its jurisdiction" excluded consideration of aliens and, further, contended that such a classification was rational because it was in the state's interest to preserve its limited resources for education for those children who were legal residents of the state. In ruling on the first issue, the Court said that the phrase "any person within its jurisdiction" was meant to confirm the understanding that the protection of the Fourteenth Amendment extended to any person, whether they be citizen or not, who is subject to the laws of the state. Since illegal aliens were within the state's boundaries, they were subject to its laws. The Supreme Court pointed out that even though undocumented aliens are not a "suspect class" under the Constitution and that education is not a fundamental right, such a statute would result in a lifetime of hardship for those affected. The Court noted that the children could not be denied services because their parents were illegal aliens and to subject them to such deprivation could not be justified on rational grounds. In arriving at this conclusion, the Court went to great lengths to expound the importance and virtues of public education and, while not declaring it fundamental, apparently elevated it to a level of importance substantially greater than other governmental functions. The Court said that the deprivation of education was not the same as denial of other social benefits of government. Public education plays a pivotal role "in maintaining the fabric of our society and in sustaining our political and cultural heritage"; the denial of education takes an "inestimable toll on the social, economic, intellectual, and psychological well-being of the individual." For the state to impose such an obstacle on a child is to impose a lifetime handicap. In balancing the educational interest of the alien child against the interest of the state, the Court found little contest.

§ 1.3 COMPULSORY ATTENDANCE

An educated citizenry is of paramount importance to perpetuate a democratic society. Experience throughout history has shown that those societies with high levels of illiteracy and ignorance among their people are most susceptible to domination and tyranny. James Madison observed that no nation can expect to have a popular government without popular information, and Jefferson in his *Preamble to a Bill for the More General Diffusion of Knowledge* (1779) admonished that the most effectual means of preventing tyranny is "to illuminate, as far as practicable, the minds of the people."

Mass education is not only the best and surest means of preservation of liberty, but it is also essential to the economic and social welfare of the people. Horace Mann probably expressed it best in 1848 when he said that: "For the creation of wealth, then—for the existence of a wealthy people and a wealthy nation—intelligence is the grand condition.... The greatest of all arts of political economy is to change a consumer into a producer; and the next greatest is to increase the producing power—an end to be directly attained, by increasing his intelligence."

On these grounds the legislatures and the courts have justified universal education for all the people. To accomplish this, compulsory school attendance laws have been enacted throughout the nation. Those who have advanced ideas which would result in deschooling society have been given little serious consideration by thoughtful and forward-looking leaders of society.

§ 1.31 Parens Patriae

Legal rationale for compulsory education is found in the common law doctrine of *parens patriae*, which means that the state is the father or guardian for minors or others "to the end that the health, patriotism, morality, efficiency, industry, and integrity of its citizenship may be preserved and protected." *Strangway v. Allen*, 240 S.W. 384 (Ky.1922). An Illinois court has explained *parens patriae* in this manner, "It is the unquestioned right and imperative duty of every enlightened government, in its character of *parens patriae*, to protect and provide for the comfort and well-being of such for its citizens. . . . The performance of these duties is justly regarded as one of the most important of governmental functions, and all constitutional limitations must be so understood as not to interfere with its proper and legitimate exercise." *County of McLean v. Humphreys*, 104 Ill. 378 (1882).

This power of the state to protect and educate the populace generally supersedes the custodial authority of the parent over the child. Parents have undoubted inherent rights to rear and control their own children, but these rights may be legitimately restricted by the state when parental prerogatives are exercised to the detriment of the child. The courts have long recognized that parents may not always act in the best interest of their children. The United States Supreme Court pointed out in 1962 that ". . . experience has shown that the question of custody, so vital to a child's happiness and well-being, frequently cannot be left to the discretion of the parents." *Ford v. Ford*, 371 U.S. 187 (1962).

The United States Supreme Court clearly enunciated the power of the state in upholding a Massachusetts child labor law in 1943 under which a parent was convicted of contributing to the delinquency of a minor. The parent had continued to force the child to work and would not permit the child to attend school, in spite of the law. In this case, *Prince v. Massachusetts*, 321 U.S. 158 (1944), the Court said: "[T]he family itself is not beyond regulation in the public interest ... acting to guard the general interest in a youth's well-being, the state as *parens patriae* may restrict the parents' control by requiring school attendance, regulating or prohibiting the child's labor and in many other ways."

§ 1.32 Truancy

Compulsory attendance laws provide for enforcement by penalizing parents for their children's absences. When a child is declared a truant or a chronic or habitual truant, the school board may institute legal proceedings which may include criminal penalty of the parent. A typical definition of truant is found in an Illinois law which reads as follows: "A 'truant' is defined as a child subject to compulsory school attendance and who is absent without valid excuse from such attendance for a school day or portion thereof." Ill.–S.H.A. 105 ILCS 5/27–2a

Compulsory attendance laws are enacted for the protection of children. The enforcement of such non-criminal laws is within the traditional authority of the police. Police officers may detain students who are suspected of being truant from school. *Matter of Shannon B.*, 517 N.E.2d 203 (N.Y.1987).

The technical question of whether parents can be punished for their children's failure to attend school has become a more difficult issue as the family structure has broken down and parents are, in many instances, unable to control their children's actions. Two women in Maryland claimed that a compulsory attendance law punishing parents for truancy of children was unconstitutional because it imposed "strict liability" on them for the actions of their children. The court in ruling against the parents explained that the compulsory attendance law imposed an affirmative duty on a person who has control over children to see that a child attends school on a regular basis. Such a requirement is within the proper concern of the state to maintain an educated citizenry. "Passive acquiescence in the child's non-attendance of school is no defense." Thus, where a parent cannot show that he or she attempted to make the child attend school, a conviction of the parent for violating compulsory attendance law will be upheld. *In re Jeannette L.*, 523 A.2d 1048 (Md.App.1987).

Too, parents who pay little heed to the importance of compulsory attendance laws or overtly ignore legal requirements may find themselves subject to prosecution. In a case where parents were rather obviously contemptuous of truancy prohibitions, they withdrew their children from school, without school permission, to take a trip to Europe. The parents had requested school permission for the trip but when the permission was denied, they ignored the denial, and departed anyway. A Superior Court in Pennsylvania upheld a truancy conviction of the parents observing that school boards have the discretionary authority to determine the appropriateness of school absences. *Commonwealth v. Hall*, 455 A.2d 674 (Pa.Super.1983).

State truancy law provisions that punish a parent for failure to send his or her child to school does not violate the constitutional or civil rights of the parent. To fine and incarcerate a parent is the prerogative of a court. Judges and municipalities have immunity from liability in enforcing truancy laws. *Granda v. City of St. Louis*, 472 F.3d 565 (8th Cir. 2007).

Some parents have tried varying approaches to evade compulsory attendance laws by seizing on technicalities of the law. In one such instance a child in Wisconsin was absent eight times in a period of three months and the parents had failed to acknowledge several notices that had been posted to them. The Wisconsin compulsory attendance statute states that any person having control of a school-aged child must "cause the child to attend school regularly ..." When the local school district brought charges, the parent argued before the court that the word "regularly" contained in the statute was vague and therefore unconstitutional. The court ruled against the parent observing that the word was sufficiently definite for a person of average intelligence to grasp its meaning. The parent also asserted the defense that the child, a girl, was uncontrollable, but the court also rejected this assertion, noting that the evidence indicated that the child had a consistent pattern of absences dating back to kindergarten. The court quite rightly concluded that the parent could control a five-year-old child. *State of Wisconsin v. White*, 509 N.W.2d 434 (Wis.App.1993).

Truancy charges, however, must be sustained by the evidence and the school board must be able to present the factual information necessary to enforce a conviction of parents. In one such case where the evidence failed, a Minnesota appellate court ruled that (1) truancy must be proved beyond a reasonable doubt and (2) the student had a right to confront and cross-examine witnesses against him. This court ruled that school attendance records were hearsay and could not be used in court in lieu of a school attendance officer's testimony. Moreover, in truancy cases, the burden of proof is on the state to prove beyond a reasonable doubt that no valid excuse existed for the student's absence from school. Students are not required to prove that their absences were excused; the state must prove that the absences were unexcused. *Matter of Welfare of L.Z.*, 380 N.W.2d 898 (Minn.App.1986), reversed in part on other issues, 396 N.W.2d 214 (Minn.1986). Valid causes for absences may be variously defined by statute as illness, death in the family, family emergency or situations beyond the control of the student.

The importance of a valid doctor's certification is illustrated in an Illinois case where parents took their daughter to several doctors over a two-year period but there was no evidence that any single doctor thought she was unable to attend school and no medical excuse was ever received by the school. Here, the court upheld conviction and fining of parents for permitting chronic truancy of their child. *People v. Berger*, 441 N.E.2d 915 (Ill.App. 1982).

§ 1.33   Education as Compelling Public Interest

In keeping with the *Prince* case, mentioned in § 1.31, education is usually given special constitutional status by the courts when requiring a balancing of constitutional interests. Where parental religious interests conflicted with a compulsory attendance requirement, a Minnesota court found that education constitutes a "compelling interest of the state." *Matter of Welfare of T.K. & W.K.*, 475 N.W.2d 88 (Minn.App.1991).

The fact that education is a compelling "public interest" gives the state, in its sovereign power, the right to make reasonable laws with regard to education even though some parents may believe that such laws encroach on their religious freedom. In a Maine case, the state required that information be submitted to the school board for prior approval before allowing home instruction. The parents refused for religious reasons. The court found that providing such information was reasonable. The court reasoned that even though the parents were motivated by sincerely-held religious beliefs they still had to fulfill the state's prior approval requirements because the state's "public interest in education" outweighed the parents' private religious beliefs. *Blount v. Department of Education & Cultural Services*, 551 A.2d 1377 (Me.1988).

§ 1.34 Limitations on State Power

The legal competence of the state to compel children to attend school is well established, but the power of the state is not unlimited. The state, for example, cannot require attendance solely in public schools. In *Pierce v. Society of Sisters*, 268 U.S. 510 (1925), the United States Supreme Court held an Oregon statute unconstitutional because it sought to compel all children between the ages of eight and sixteen years to attend public schools. Two private schools sued claiming that the law denied them their property without due process of law. The institutions claimed that they owned valuable buildings which were constructed for school purposes and that they acquired income from education programs, the success of which was dependent on long-term contracts with teachers and parents. The Supreme Court held that the law did, in fact, deprive the schools of property without due process. The Court agreed that "the right to conduct schools was property, and that parents and guardians, as a part of their liberty, might direct the education of children by selecting reputable teachers and places." The

Court further said that it was clear that the statute interfered with the liberty of parents to control their children. The "fundamental theory of liberty," the Court said, "excludes any general power of the state to standardize its children by forcing them to accept instruction from public teachers only." *Pierce*, therefore, recognizes and guarantees the private school's property interest and acknowledges a parental liberty interest in education of the child in other than public schools.

§ 1.35   Parental Rights

Prince v. Massachusetts makes it quite clear that the state can require all children to attend school in spite of parental objection. *Pierce v. Society of Sisters*, however, guarantees a parental right of liberty that permits parents to choose whether their children attend public or private schools. But what are the limitations on parental rights to direct and control the public school programs and activities once children are enrolled? This is not an easy question to answer; much of this book deals with this question. In fact, most of education law litigation contends with parents' attempts to force their personal will and beliefs upon the school, in particular, and upon other peoples' children, in general. The overall view of the courts is that once children are enrolled in public schools, the parents must adhere to the statutory and regulatory requirements governing the school. Parents can be banned from a school campus; it's probably not a good public relations move, but it's legal. *Cole v. Montague Board of Education*, 145 Fed. Appx. 760 (3d Cir. 2005). The prevailing view is that school officials can control access to school property and parents who violate the applicable rules can be removed. *Rogers v. Duncan-*

ville Independent School District, 2005 WL 991287 (N.D. Tex. 2005).

The U.S. Court of Appeals, 7th Circuit, has clearly stated that: a) the only constitutional right a parent has, beyond that given by state and federal statute, is the right to choose between a public and a private school; b) parents do not have a constitutional right to participate in a school's management; c) schools have a well-grounded legal interest in limiting the presence of parents on school property. *Crowley v. McKinney*, 400 F.3d 965 (7th Cir. 2005). School officials have not only the authority, but the responsibility to control access to school grounds. The federal courts are very clear, "school officials have the authority and responsibility for assuring that parents and third parties conduct themselves appropriately while on school property." *Lovern v. Edwards*, 190 F.3d 648 (4th Cir. 1999).

With regard to the curriculum of the school, parents have no constitutional right to exercise any control over curriculum content. The issue of curriculum content arises rather frequently where parents claim that their religious beliefs require the school to modify or alter curricular content. The parent does not for religious or other reasons have a right to dictate the content of the school curriculum. *Myers v. Loudoun County School Board*, 500 F. Supp. 2d 539 (E.D. Va. 2007). Examples of parental attempts to control the curriculum are many times hinged on teachings of science versus religion and problems with the teaching of sex education. With regard to these issues much more is said elsewhere in this book. But suffice to say here that parents do not have a fundamental constitutional right based on personal religious beliefs or values to exclusively determine when and how their children will be exposed to the subject of sex. *Fields v. Palmdale School District*, 427 F.3d 1197 (9th Cir. 2005). Parents can be removed from school grounds because of their opposition to school policies and for teachings. *Pisacane v. Desjardins*, 115 Fed. Appx. 446 (1st Cir. 2004).

§ 1.4 HOMESCHOOLING

Homeschooling is not, generally, considered to fulfill the requirements of compulsory school attendance. Statutes which provide for private school instruction as fulfillment of compulsory attendance requirements, as they must under *Pierce v. Society of Sisters*, supra, have not been construed to permit homeschooling. Authority to exempt homeschooling from compulsory attendance laws must be given by express statutory provision. A statute in California which provided for exemption for those "being instructed in a private full-time day school by persons capable of teaching" was held not to implicitly permit home instruction. *People v. Turner*, 263 P.2d 685 (Cal.App.1953). The fact that there is no statutory regulation of private schools does not mean that parents can proclaim that their homes are schools in an effort to avoid enrolling their children in public schools. *State v. M. M.*, 407 So.2d 987 (Fla.App.1981).

Some courts have observed that the attributes of school attendance go beyond merely the instruction of children and include social interaction with other students, appropriate facilities such as libraries, laboratories and other features generally found in formal school settings but absent in homes. Student interaction is an essential ingredient of school, thus, home instruction involving only one's own children cannot constitute the equivalent of a regular school program. *Stephens v. Bongart*, 189 A. 131 (N.J.1937).

A state's refusal to allow home instruction as a valid exemption from compulsory attendance does not violate the Equal Protection Clause of the Fourteenth Amendment. A New Mexico court held that statutory exclusion of home instruction was subject to the rational relationship test of constitutionality. *State v. Edgington*, 663 P.2d 374 (N.M.App.1983). This test requires that the state merely show that the purpose for the law is rational. Plaintiffs had argued that the more rigorous test of strict scrutiny must be applied which would require that the state bear the burden of showing a compelling interest to justify its action. This latter test is very difficult to sustain. In considering the two tests, the court concluded that because the United States Supreme Court had held that education was not a fundamental interest, *San Antonio Independent School District v. Rodriguez*, 411 U.S. 1 (1973), the lesser test was appropriate. Using this test, the court reasoned that requiring children to go to school with other children was a legitimate state interest. The New Mexico court said: "By bringing children into contact with some person, other than those in the excluded group, those children are exposed to at least one other set of attitudes, values, morals, lifestyles and intellectual abilities. Therefore, we hold that the statutory classifications presented in the attendance law rationally relates to a legitimate state interest."

However, compulsory attendance laws must be clear and unambiguous so as not to be unconstitutional because of vagueness in violation of due process of law. A Missouri compulsory attendance law was held to be unconstitutional because of the use of language that could be subject to differing interpretations. The Missouri statute allowed exemption from compulsory attendance in public schools where the child was to be given "substantially equivalent" instruction at home. Without guidelines to interpret what "substantially equivalent" meant, the court found that parents and school officials could only guess at its meaning. *Ellis v. O'Hara*, 612 F.Supp. 379 (E.D.Mo.1985).

§ 1.41   Regulation of Homeschooling

States have the sovereign authority to require all children to attend school, public or private. Parents, nor their children, have a constitutional right to avoid formal schooling. *Prince v. Massachusetts*, 321 U.S. 158 (1944). However, state legislatures also have the authority not to require compulsory attendance or to provide exceptions and punch holes in their own compulsory attendance laws as they like. [See Alexander and Alexander, *American Public School Law, 7th Edition*, (Belmont, Calif.: Wadsworth, Cengage Learning, 2008) pp. 319–324.]

Modifications of compulsory attendance statutes to allow for homeschooling dramatically increased during recent decades. In 1982 only two states, Nevada (1956) and Utah (1957), had statutes that specifically permitted homeschooling. This number had increased to 32 by the end of 1993. In 2009 all states recognized homeschooling, but there is a great difference from state to state in their regulations. Some states have extensive regulations while others are almost non-existent.

Religion is the primary source of contention for parents who do not want their children to attend public schools. They generally object that their particular sectarian brand of religion is not taught and/or that the public schools are secular. The U.S. Supreme Court has, however, maintained that the interest of the state in having an educated citizenry is sufficient to override specific religious objections, save the lone instance of the Amish in the *Yoder* case. *State of Wisconsin v. Yoder*, 406 U.S. 205 (1972). Accordingly religion cannot be used as an excuse to defeat properly prescribed state regulation.

Whether children are compelled to attend school is a matter within the state's prerogative. A state legislature may, if it wished, do away with compulsory education completely if the state constitution permitted. Therefore, a state legislature can prescribe exceptions that allow schooling to take place at home. By the same token, the legislature can determine whether homeschooling will be part-time home and part-time school or must be full-time in one or the other. In the absence of such part-time statutory provisions, school boards can reject part-time "pick and choose" arrangements. The U.S. Court of Appeals, Tenth Circuit, has rejected the claim by parents that a school board rule prohibiting part-time attendance at public school by homeschooled students violated the parents' free exercise of religion. The court said that parents had no right to "pick and choose which courses their children will take from the public school." *Swanson v. Guthrie Independent School District I–L*, 135 F.3d 694 (10th Cir.1998). In addressing an attendant issue, a court in New York ruled that a homeschooled student was not eligible to participate in interscholastic sports. The refusal did not violate due process. *Bradstreet v. Sobol*, 650 N.Y.S.2d 402 (A.D. 3 Dept.1996).

In a similar case, the Pennsylvania Interscholastic Athletic Association did not expressly prohibit participation by homeschoolers in public school athletics, but most local school boards did not allow such participation. The school board refused to allow a homeschooler to play on the public school basketball or baseball team. The Court upheld the school board decision. The court noted that the board also refused to allow parochial students, privately-tutored students, or dropout students attending adult education classes to participate in interscholastic sports. *McNatt v. Frazier School District*, 1995 WL 568380 (W.D.Pa.1995). In a contrary opinion, a Massachusetts court held that a rule requiring public school attendance to participate in sports violated Equal Protection. The court reasoned that the student was attending school, it just happened to be at home. *Davis v. Massachusetts Interscholastic Athletic Association, Inc.*, 1995 WL 808968 (Sup.Ct.Mass.1995). Some states have passed legislation allowing for dual enrollment. Homeschool students attend the public school for part of the school day for certain subjects and the remainder is spent at home.

All courts require that state regulations must be reasonable. A Massachusetts court held a statutory requirement of home visits as a condition of approval of homeschooling was invalid as unreasonable and unnecessary to the attainment of the goals of the state. *Brunelle v. Lynn Public Schools*, 702 N.E.2d 1182 (Mass.1998).

The state's interest in public education may be generally encompassed within two aspects: 1) the attainment of knowledge and 2) socialization. In this regard, states usually defend compulsory attendance laws by requiring some assurance of quality of education and by maintaining that attending public schools with other children from various walks of life promotes tolerance and understanding of others.

Legislatures and courts have been reluctant to permit parents' opting-out to be so complete as to deprive the affected children of access to substantive knowledge. To this end, the legislatures, with the courts acquiescence, have imposed and maintained certain education quality standards for homeschooling. Such standards are usually of two types: 1) teacher certification requirements and 2) testing or output measures.

§ 1.42   Certification for Homeschooling

The majority of the court decisions uphold state requirements that homeschool teachers be certified. Yet, challenges on the religious grounds have been increasingly successful. However, in North Dakota, claims based on religious freedom exercise rights have not prevailed. In upholding the state's authority to require certification of homeschool teachers, the North Dakota Supreme Court provided the most definitive precedent. When parents challenged homeschool certification as a violation of their free exercise of religion, the Court pointed out the importance and validity of certification requirements saying: "While a teaching certificate is no guarantee that the holder is a competent teacher, it does guarantee that the holder has been exposed to the knowledge that a competent teacher should have ... [the] certification requirement for instructors in public, non-public, or homeschools is reasonably justified ... Teacher certification appears to us to be among the least personally intrusive methods now available to satisfy the state's prime interest in seeing that its children are taught by capable persons." *State v. Patzer*, 382 N.W.2d 631 (N.D.1986).

In keeping with this rationale, the North Dakota Supreme Court has ruled that the interest of the state in having an educated citizenry is a legitimate interest that outweighs any perceived religious freedom denial claimed by plaintiff parents in objecting to a certification requirement. *State v. Shaver*, 294 N.W.2d 883 (N.D.1980); *State v. Rivinius*, 328 N.W.2d 220 (N.D.1982); *State v. Melin*, 428 N.W.2d 227 (N.D.1988); *State v. Toman*, 436 N.W.2d 10 (N.D.1989). Agreement with the North Dakota court has come from an Alabama court. Required certification of homeschool instructors was upheld in Alabama to be a valid state interest. *Jernigan v. State*, 412 So.2d 1242 (Ala.Crim.App.1982).

On the other hand, the Michigan Supreme Court has held that the requirement of state certification of homeschool teachers could not be justified as a compelling state interest. To overcome an exercise of religion claim by homeschooling advocates, the state must show that it has a compelling reason for its action. In this light, certification is not of sufficient importance to outweigh the individual's interest in free exercise of religion. *People v. DeJonge*, 501 N.W.2d 127 (Mich.1993). In a companion case, however, the Michigan Court held that such certification requirements did not violate the due process rights of parents. *People v. Bennett*, 501 N.W.2d 106 (Mich.1993).

In Arkansas, a court found a requirement that parents conducting home instruction have college degrees did not violate free exercise. Accordingly, the state's requirement that home instruction be conducted by a qualified teacher did not burden the parent's religious beliefs and did not prevent the parents from otherwise providing religious instruction to their children. *Burrow v. State*, 669 S.W.2d 441 (Ark.1984).

A requirement that home instruction teachers be qualified must be clear enough that the statute or regulation is not constitutionally deficient for vagueness. The words "qualified tutor" have been held not to be vague and therefore do not violate due process. On the other hand, a teacher credential requirement that home instruction be "essentially equivalent" to public school teachers has been held to be invalid for vagueness. *State v. Newstrom*, 371 N.W.2d 525 (Minn.1985).

Even though the precedents are by no means clear and unequivocal, the prevailing view appears to be that states can require instructors at home schools to meet qualification standards as long as the requirements encroach as little as possible on religious beliefs.

§ 1.43 Testing Requirements for Homeschooling

The state can prescribe the conditions tests and other evaluation procedures under which homeschooling will be permitted as an exception to regular school attendance. Homeschooling plans may be required to be submitted to state or local school authorities to ensure that the child is sufficiently protected against ignorance and neglect of parents. Parents who are unwilling to comply with school board rules requiring homeschooled children to submit to educational progress verification reports, may be held in violation of compulsory attendance laws and subject to the school districts invoking of judicial proceedings for the "care and protection" of the children. *In re Ivan*, 717 N.E.2d 1020 (Mass.App.Ct.1999).

State requirements that children in homeschools be tested to assess their academic progress have been generally upheld by the courts so long as the governing statutes are not too vague for reasonable interpretation. *State v. Bowman*, 653 P.2d 254 (Or.App.1982).

Testing was upheld as a reasonable assessment measure in spite of parental objection in Massachusetts. The court there said, "... the superintendent or school committee may properly require periodic standardized testing of the children to ensure educational progress and the attainment of minimal standards." *Care and Protection of Charles*, 504 N.E.2d 592 (Mass.1987). The statute authorizing evaluations to be conducted by local school district officials is not invalid because of unconstitutional delegation.

Neither does a requirement of testing children who were educated at home violate due process or equal protection. In upholding a West Virginia statutory provision making children ineligible for homeschooling if their test scores fell below the 40th percentile, the court said, "The state's interest in education is subject to a balancing process when it impinges on fundamental rights and interests, such as those specifically protected by the Free Exercise Clause of the First Amendment ... (but) when no fundamental right is involved, and only a general Fourteenth Amendment liberty interest is at stake, then parents' liberty interest is subject to reasonable state regulation." *Null v. Board of Education of the County of Jackson*, 815 F.Supp. 937 (S.D.W.Va.1993).

Thus, state requirements that children in home schools be tested as a means to monitor their educational progress serve as a legitimate state interest and will be upheld so long as the statutes and regulations are not vague and are reasonable.

§ 1.5　PRIVATE SCHOOLS

Exemption from compulsory attendance to attend private schools is a right of all parents as protected by the Due Process Clause of the Fourteenth Amendment as applied in *Pierce v. Society of Sisters*, supra. Yet, the U.S. Supreme Court in *Pierce* made it quite clear that parents have no constitutional right of a private school education for their child that is "unfettered by reasonable government regulation." Further, the Court in *Pierce* acknowledged "the power of the State reasonably to regulate all schools, to inspect, supervise and examine them, their teachers and pupils." *Pierce v. Society of Sisters*, 268 U.S. 510 (1925). Litigation frequently arise as to whether a school has the attributes which are required to qualify as a "private school" as contemplated by law. A Washington court in 1912 held that the words "to attend a private school" meant more than home instruction; it means, to be approved for exemption, the school must be "the same character of school as the public school, a regular organized and existing institution making a business of instructing children of school age in required studies and for the full time required by the laws...." *State v. Counort*, 124 P. 910 (Wash.1912).

According to a New Jersey court, whether an instructional program constitutes a "private school" within the meaning of statute is dependent on three tests: first, the qualifications of the parent or instructor; second, the teaching material being used; and third, whether the educational program was commensurate with that provided in public schools. *Knox v. O'Brien*, 72 A.2d 389 (N.J.Super.1950).

Parents and children may be allowed by statute to choose between a "home instruction" and a "private school" exception for exemption from compulsory attendance in public schools. Such choices are, however, normally contained in specific provision of applicable statutes. *Birst v. Sanstead*, 493 N.W.2d 690 (N.D.1992). The burden of proof is on the parent to show that the instructional program is in a "private school" and to be so adjudged, and the school must meet reasonable state regulations.

§ 1.51   Religious Exemption

The general rule of law is that religious objection to education is not a valid reason for keeping a child away from school. The great English jurist Blackstone noted that common law recognized that the most important duty of parents is to give their children "an education suitable to their station in life," and Blackstone further acknowledged the power of the state to take children from the parents to assure that the children's abilities could be developed to "the greatest advantage of the commonwealth." 1 Commentaries 451.

Objection to compulsory attendance cannot be simply justified by parents' claims that they have an inherent right to control their child's religious upbringing. *Prince v. Massachusetts*, supra. In *Commonwealth v. Bey*, 70 A.2d 693 (Pa.Super.1950), Mohammedan parents persistently refused to send their children to school on Fridays, the sacred day of that religion. The court found the parents in violation of the compulsory attendance law and said: "It [the law] permits attendance at private and parochial schools. All that it requires is continuous attendance at a day-school of the kind and character mentioned in the statute, or daily instruction by a private tutor. Since the parents may avail themselves of other schools, including parochial or denominational schools, the statute does not interfere with or impinge upon the religious freedom of parents. . . ."

A number of states have enacted legislation which permits a child to be exempt from compulsory attendance for a *bona fide* religious belief. This is the situation in Virginia where that state's Supreme Court ruled that a compulsory attendance law did not require the school board to state its reasons for denying the religious exemption. *Johnson v. Prince William County School Bd.*, 404 S.E.2d 209 (Va.1991).

§ 1.52   The Amish Exception

The most important exception to the general rule, that religious belief does not exempt one from compulsory attendance laws, is found in the United States Supreme Court's decision in *State of Wisconsin v. Yoder*, 406 U.S. 205 (1972). In this case the Court held that Amish children could not be compelled to attend high school even though they were within the age range of Wisconsin's compulsory attendance statute. The Amish maintained that higher learning beyond that which could be acquired in neighborhood elementary schools tended to develop values which alienated their children from God. The Amish sect believes that its members should reject the competitive spirit, de-emphasize material success and insulate its youth from the modern world.

The Supreme Court, in interpreting the sweep of the First Amendment's Free Exercise Clause, observed that protection of religious beliefs is a basic freedom of such magnitude that the state's interest must be of the "highest order" if it is to overbalance the individual's religious interest. The Court placed the burden of proof on the state to show that universal compulsory education was not merely rational public policy, but, indeed, a compelling state interest.

In attempting to show a compelling interest, Wisconsin maintained that education is necessary to prepare citizens to participate effectively in our democratic system of government. In response, the Court observed that the Amish community is a unique and special case which has been "highly successful as a social unit within our society" and that its members had an exemplary record as productive and law-abiding citizens. With regard to participation in the democratic process, the Court held that the brief period of education from ages fourteen to sixteen, the period in question when the Amish children would be compelled to attend high school, was not a period of time significant enough to justify "severe interference with religious freedom." According to the Court, the Amish alternative to formal secondary education had enabled the Amish to function effectively in day-to-day life of contemporary society as a "separate and sharply identifiable and highly self-sufficient community for more than 200 years in this country." Further, the Court noted that when Thomas Jefferson emphasized the need for an educated citizenry as a bulwark against tyranny, he did not necessarily have in mind education beyond a basic eighth-grade education.

In ruling for the Amish parents, however, the Court so narrowly defined the attributes of the Amish religion in exempting it from compulsory attendance that the use of *Yoder* as precedent by parents of other religions to gain similar exemptions has been generally unsuccessful. The Court set out three criteria for balancing the individual's religious interests against the public interests of the state. The court must determine (1) whether the individual's beliefs are legitimately religious and if they are sincerely held; (2) whether the state regulation unduly restricts the religious practices; (3) whether the state has a compelling interest justifying the regulation and whether the compelling interest is of such importance as to overcome the right to free exercise of religion.

The primary importance of *Yoder* is that it elevates religion to a special constitutional status as a First Amendment right which must be given particular consideration by the courts when parents and students contest state action. Importantly, it requires that the state bear the burden of showing that it has a compelling reason to justify its denial of a religious belief. In the unique case of *Yoder* and the Amish religion, the state was unable to bear this burden.

§ 1.53   Attendance at Religious Schools

The state has a legitimate interest in the quality of the educational program performed in private schools, but as indicated in *Yoder* where freedom of religion is in question the courts will apply strict judicial scrutiny. Yet religious and other private schools have a constitutional right as corporate entities to exist and engage in the business of educating children. The Supreme Court has, however, made it quite clear that the state can reasonably regulate private and religious schools as educational corporations to ensure "that certain studies plainly essential to good citizenship must be taught, and that nothing be taught that is manifestly inimical to the public welfare." *Pierce v. Society of Sisters*, 268 U.S. 510

(1925). The extent of the state regulation to be permitted by the courts will depend on the state's constitution and statutes and how they are applied to the private school.

In a 1979 case, the Kentucky Supreme Court held that the state could not prosecute parents for violation of the compulsory attendance law who enrolled their children in private schools which did not employ certified teachers nor use state-approved textbooks. *Kentucky State Board v. Rudasill*, 589 S.W.2d 877 (Ky.1979). The court decided the case purely on a state constitutional provision which stated in part: " . . . nor shall any man be compelled to send his child to any schools to which he is conscientiously opposed. . . ." This provision, the court observed, was more restrictive on the state than the Free Exercise Clause of the First Amendment of the United States Constitution. In examining the debate at the constitutional convention at which the provision was adopted, the court found the intent of this provision was to allow parents to choose any school for their children as a matter of conscience. The court found nothing wrong with the state mandating that private schools have instruction in several branches of study as was required of public schools, but the court would not allow the state to require the same instruments of education, certified teachers, and state-approved textbooks to be used by private schools.

Parents again prevailed in an Ohio case in which parents were accused of violating compulsory attendance laws because they enrolled their children in a Bible-oriented Christian school which failed to "conform to the minimum standards prescribed by the state. . . ." *State v. Whisner*, 351 N.E.2d 750 (Ohio 1976). The private school had only twenty-three children who were taught by a certified teacher in one room. The state minimum standards in Ohio were highly restrictive regulating virtually to the minute what should be taught in private schools. These standards set forth "[t]he content of the curriculum that [was] taught, the manner in which it [was] taught, the person or persons who [taught] it, the physical layout of the building in which the students [were] taught, the hours of instruction, and the educational policies intended to be achieved through the instruction offered." The court ruled for the parents finding the standards were so excessive as to deny the parents their freedom of religion and the right to direct the education of their children as they saw fit. In following *Yoder*, the court required that the state show a compelling reason to justify the encroachment on individual religious freedom. This burden the state was unable to sustain.

Conviction of parents for violating compulsory attendance laws has, however, been upheld in Nebraska and North Dakota. In *Meyerkorth v. State*, 115 N.W.2d 585 (Neb.1962), the Supreme Court of Nebraska held that statutes requiring that private school instruction be "substantially the same" as that of public schools did not violate the religious freedom of private school parents or the students.

The North Dakota case set a precedent almost precisely opposite that of *Whisner* in Ohio. *State v. Shaver*, 294 N.W.2d 883 (N.D.1980). Here defendant parents were convicted of violating compulsory attendance laws for sending their children to a church-affiliated private school which was not approved by the state. The school had no certified teachers and employed a widely used self-study curriculum made up of a series of Bible-oriented learning packets. The school showed, as was the case in *Rudasill*, that the students of the private school scored higher on achievement tests than did their counterparts in public schools.

The court in applying the three-part test of *Yoder*, balancing the parents' interests against the state's, ruled against the parents. As to the tests: first, the court acknowledged that the defendants had a sincere religious belief; second, the court did not agree that the state rules placed an undue burden on the defendants' religious beliefs but assumed *arguendo* that such a burden did exist in order to apply the third test, holding that the state had a "legitimate and compelling interest ... in educating its people" and the regulation of private schools was within state prerogative.

Therefore, a state may regulate private religious schools so long as the regulations are reasonable and are not so excessive or restrictive as to constitute unwarranted interference with the individual's religious freedom. Where parents, though, are able to show that the state's requirements are too specific, then private school parents may succeed in averting conviction for violation of compulsory attendance laws.

§ 1.6 MARRIAGE

Compulsory attendance laws do not generally apply to married persons. Courts have agreed that the nature and responsibilities of marriage are such that married persons of compulsory attendance age should be exempted. The view of the courts is best expressed in *State v. Priest*, 27 So.2d 173 (La.1946), which said that: "The marriage relationship, regardless of the age of the persons involved, creates conditions and imposes obligations upon the parties that are obviously inconsistent with compulsory school attendance or with either the husband or wife remaining under the legal control of parents or other persons."

In the eyes of the law, then, marriage emancipates the minor from control by either the parent or the state, for purposes of compulsory education.

§ 1.7 VACCINATION

To protect the health and welfare of citizens, states have required school children to be vaccinated. Courts have generally held that if a parent violates a statute requiring vaccination, the parent is subject to arrest or fine, even if he or she claims religious, conscientious, or scientific objections.

In 1905, the United States Supreme Court held that a board of health requirement that all persons in Cambridge, Massachusetts, be vaccinated did not violate personal liberties found under the Fourteenth Amendment. In this case, the Court noted that "the liberty secured by the Constitution of the United States to every person within its jurisdiction does not impart an absolute right on each person to be, at all times and in all circumstances, wholly free from restraint. There are manifold restraints to which every person is necessarily subject for the common good." *Jacobson v. Commonwealth of Mass.*, 197 U.S. 11 (1905). See also *Maricopa County Health Dept. v. Harmon*, 750 P.2d 1364 (Ariz.App.1987).

Although this particular decision challenged the vaccination regulation rather than compulsory attendance laws, the Supreme Court, nevertheless, cited several state court decisions approving state statutes and making vaccination of children a condition of the right to attend public schools.

In *Viemeister v. White*, 72 N.E. 97 (N.Y.1904), the appellant argued that vaccination not only did not prevent smallpox but tended instead to bring on other harmful diseases. The court, while not ruling that vaccination was a smallpox preventive, nevertheless maintained that laymen and physicians alike commonly believed that it did prevent smallpox. The court concluded that the legislature has the right to pass laws based on common belief and the will of the people to promote health and welfare.

When an epidemic is imminent, there is no doubt that the state has the power to protect the citizenry by requiring vaccination. However, when there is no evidence of the imminence of an epidemic, the courts may rule differently.

In *Board of Education v. Maas*, 152 A.2d 394 (N.J.Super.1959), the defendant argued that compulsory vaccination and immunization were not needed because there had been no smallpox or diphtheria in the area for almost a decade. The court disagreed and ruled that the absence of an emergency does not warrant a denial of the exercise of preventive means. The court said, "A local board of education need not await an epidemic, or even a single sickness or death, before it decides to protect the public. To hold otherwise would be to destroy prevention as a means of combating the spread of disease."

States have in recent years started adding legislation that allows students to be exempt from immunization requirements if they violate religious beliefs. A Florida statute provides that if "The parent or guardian of the child objects in writing that the administration of immunizing agents conflicts with his or her religious tenets or practices" then the child is exempt. In a key case in that state, a parent wrote a letter stating, "The administration of immunizing agents ... completely conflicts with my religious tenants [sic] and practices." The request was rejected and the Department of Health sought more information, specifically asking the parent to articulate the specific religious tenets to establish a *bona fide* reason. The Court stated, "The issue which we are called upon to decide implicates two very important social policies—the desire to protect the public health and welfare and the desire to protect a parent's fundamental right to raise his or her child according to the religious tenets that he or she chooses. After considerable reflection, we conclude that the legislature intended that when, as here, the two policies collide, greater protection be afforded to the latter by prohibiting any inquiry by the Department into the *bona fides* of the parent's or guardian's objection." The court ruled that the statute did not require further inquiry, only that a letter be written; the court therefore upheld the parent in excluding her child from immunization. *Department of Health v. Curry*, 722 So.2d 874 (Fla.App. 1 Dist.1998).

In another such case, a mother who was a member of the Congregation of Universal Wisdom objected to the introduction of any foreign material into the body. A New York statute allowed an exception to immunization if the child's parents "hold genuine and sincere religious belief." After questioning the mother, the school district determined that the Congregation was not a genuine religion and the mother's beliefs were a personal philosophy rather than legitimate religion. The Court ruled the exemption did not violate the Establishment Clause. *Tur-*

ner v. Liverpool Central School, 186 F.Supp.2d 187 (N.D.N.Y. 2002).

In a New York case, the parents requested an exemption from immunization due to religious beliefs. The school superintendent found the request insufficient and requested more documentation. Additional information was also rejected by the school as not substantiating a religious exemption. The parent filed suit and the testimony indicated the objection to the vaccination was based on the fear of health risk and not religion. The court found for the school since the beliefs were not genuine and sincere religious beliefs. *Farina v. Board of Education of City of New York,* 116 F.Supp.2d 503 (S.D.N.Y.2000).

A federal court in Arkansas ruled unconstitutional an Arkansas statute that conferred a religious exemption from the immunization requirement on individuals whose religious tenets conflicted with immunization. The statute provided that the religious tenets and practices must be ". . . of a recognized church or religious domination of which [the individual is a] member." The court concluded that the statute violates the Establishment Clause since it was not religiously neutral; individuals can hold sincere religious beliefs and not be a member of an organized religious group. *Boone v. Boozman,* 217 F.Supp.2d 938 (E.D.Ark.2002).

CHAPTER 2

THE INSTRUCTIONAL PROGRAM

§ 2.1 INTRODUCTION

As a general rule, school officials have the authority to prescribe the method of teaching, decide on what curriculum shall be offered, and what books shall be used in the school. Such authority is vested in public schools either expressly or implicitly by state law. However, this authority is not absolute and may be curtailed or modified by the courts if school officials proceed beyond the bounds of their legal authority or act arbitrarily in violation of the constitutional rights of students or teachers. The courts, however, will not intervene in resolution of conflicts which arise from the daily operation of the schools and which do not directly involve basic constitutional values. *Pratt v. Independent School District No. 831*, 670 F.2d 771 (8th Cir.1982).

§ 2.11 Judicial Deference

The judiciary is normally very reluctant to enter the realm of school curricular and instructional matters. Courts have traditionally been uneasy in exercising their authority with regard to nature and content of the curriculum, course offerings and requirements, and the evaluation thereof. By in large, the courts are respectful of the knowledge of professional educators and will give substantial latitude and weight to their opinions. A federal circuit court has stated the court's position in this way: "Decisions on evaluation of the academic performance of students as it relates to promotion are peculiarly within the expertise of educators and are particularly inappropriate for review in a judicial context." This court observed that an expanded judicial presence in the classroom could be deleterious to many of the beneficial aspects of the faculty-student relationship. *Sandlin v. Johnson*, 643 F.2d 1027 (4th Cir.1981).

§ 2.2 CURRICULUM

Local school boards have the power as delegated by statute to enforce reasonable rules prescribing a specific curriculum. *State ex rel. Andrews v. Webber*, 8 N.E. 708 (Ind.1886). Power given to school authorities by state legislatures implies discretion to determine course content. This power may emanate from rules of general authority which allow the local school authorities to establish the curriculum as well as requirements for promotion and graduation. Such power, of course, may be retained by the legislature, and rather than delegating to local school boards, statute may specifically mandate prescribed curricula or graduation requirements.

A case in point is illustrated in Pennsylvania legislation where a local school board passed a rule requiring that all students complete 60 hours of community service during the four years of high school. The objective of the school board was to "help students acquire life skills and learn the significance of rendering services to the community ... [and] gain a sense of worth and pride as they understand and appreciate the functions of community organizations." Parents challenged the requirement claiming it violated the students' First Amendment rights of freedom of speech and Thirteenth Amendment rights of "involuntary servitude" or slavery. The court upheld the requirement holding that it violated neither the First nor Thirteenth Amendments. *Steirer by Steirer v. Bethlehem Area School District*, 987 F.2d 989 (3d Cir.1993).

§ 2.21 Reasonable Rules

The right of every student to attend school is subject to reasonable regulation. Rules have often been invalidated by the courts because they are arbitrary or capricious. By definition a reasonable rule is neither arbitrary nor capricious. As long as the legal authority is appropriately delegated to local school boards and the boards act in good faith in formulating and applying reasonable standards, then their actions will not be overturned.

§ 2.22 The Spectrum of Knowledge

In deciding whether a statute or rule is constitutional, the courts will balance the interests of the parties involved. With regard to the school curriculum, students, parents, teachers, and the state all have interests which must be taken into consideration.

The student's interest is normally one of self-interest which must be accommodated if the educational process is served. As the guardian of the child, the parent has certain expectations for the type of education and the quality and quantity of knowledge his or her child is to acquire. The teacher has freedom to convey knowledge and to exercise those prerogatives which normally flow from the status of being a teacher. Academic freedom bestowed by the First Amendment is part and parcel of the teacher's interests and protections in teaching. The state has an overarching political, social and economic interest in fully developing the abilities of its citizenry. No one rule of law can be prescribed which addresses the problems which may arise from these conflicting interests. The rule which may come nearest to being generally applicable is that the courts will hold in favor of the expansion of knowledge. The party which seeks to "contract the spectrum of knowledge," or restrain the full expanse of human understanding and inquiry will generally be rebuffed by the courts. *Griswold v. Connecticut*, 381 U.S. 479 (1965).

§ 2.23 Marketplace of Ideas

This economic metaphor, "marketplace of ideas," was coined by Justice Oliver Wendell Holmes who argued that truth would not prevail in a democratic society if government suppressed ideas. Competing ideas fully exposed to discussion would ultimately produce the right answers to complex problems. *Abrams v. United States*, 250 U.S. 616 (1919).

The courts have held that to stifle teachers' ardor to investigate and experiment with new ideas is an "anathema" to the idea of education. Imposition of an intellectual straitjacket on teachers or educational leaders would, according to Chief Justice Earl Warren, "imperil the future of our nation." Society is best served when there is wide exposure to truths and an unlimited exchange of ideas. The classroom is, thus, viewed as an intellectual marketplace protected by law.

§ 2.24 Evolution and Creation Science

Charles Darwin's theory of evolution has always bothered some people including conservative legislators, parents, and even a few professional educators. Those who rigidly adhere to the strict constructionist Biblical account of creation express particular dissatisfaction toward school systems which teach science from an evolutionary point of view. Feelings regarding the teaching of evolution have been so strong that several years ago a few states enacted anti-evolution laws making it a criminal offense to teach Darwinian evolution. It was on this issue that the famous "Scopes monkey trial" of Dayton, Tennessee, was contested. This highly publicized confrontation between the great politician William Jennings Bryan and the outstanding lawyer Clarence Darrow ultimately resulted in the conviction (a small fine) of Scopes for teaching the theory of evolution. In the process, however, the Tennessee statute was held in such disdain that the issue lay dormant for over 30 years without a real test of the statute's constitutional validity.

Finally, in 1968, the United States Supreme Court ruled that a 1928 Arkansas law making it unlawful for a teacher in a state-supported institution to teach science from an evolutionary perspective was unconstitutional. By 1968 only two states, Arkansas and Mississippi, had such "monkey laws" on their books. The Court found that the law violated the First Amendment because it proscribed a respected scientific theory from the classroom for no other reason than it was in conflict with a particular religious doctrine in the Book of Genesis. Thus, the court clearly decided that such a state sanction of the Christian doctrine of creation was unconstitutional. *Epperson v. State of Arkansas*, 393 U.S. 97 (1968).

The issue in Arkansas did not, however, fade away. A mixture of religious fundamentalism and political conditions in the late 1970s and early 1980s led to a revival of the evolution question in public schools. On March 19, 1981, the Governor of Arkansas signed a bill which required balanced treatment of "creation-science" and "evolution-science" in the public schools. The federal court in Arkansas ruled that creation-science was not a science at all. Rather, the court said that it was a religious doctrine which was imposed on the youth by the state statute. *McLean v. Arkansas Board of Education*, 529 F.Supp. 1255 (E.D.Ark.1982).

In a similar situation in 1981, the Louisiana legislature passed a law entitled, "Balanced Treatment for Creation–Science and Evolution–Science in Public School Instruction." No school was required to teach the "subject of origin" but if the school chose to teach about "evolution-science," it must give balanced treatment to "creation science." The United States Supreme Court in *Edwards v. Aguillard*, 482 U.S. 578 (1987) ruled the Louisiana act unconstitutional. The Court stated, "The Act impermissibly endorses religion by advancing the religious belief that a supernatural being created humankind."

The conflict has extended into the '90s and beyond. In a recent case, the Tangipahoa Parish Board of Education, Louisiana, passed a resolution that if the scientific theory of evolution is to be presented in schools, it must be accompanied by a disclaimer that informs students that the teaching is "not intended to influence or dissuade" them from belief in the Biblical version of creation. The Fifth U.S. Circuit Court of Appeals ruled that the disclaimer violated the second prong of the *Lemon* test because it was not sufficiently neutral and therefore violated the Establishment Clause. *Freiler v. Tangipahoa Parish Board of Education*, 201 F.3d 602 (5th Cir.2000). The U.S. Supreme Court refused to accept the case, but Justices Scalia and Thomas, wanting to hear the case, filed a dissent. Justice Scalia said that he would accept the case "... if only to take the opportunity to inter the *Lemon* test once and for all." Justice Scalia disagreed with the Fifth Circuit's decision and said, "... today we permit a Court of Appeals to push the much beloved secular legend of the Monkey trial one step further. We stand by in silence while ... [the] Fifth Circuit bars a school district from even suggesting to students that other theories besides evolution—including but not limited to, biblical theory of creation—are worthy of their consideration." *Tangipahoa Parish Board of Education v. Freiler*, 530 U.S. 1251 (2000).

In spite of these clear precedents and Justices Scalia's and Thomas' guile, the matter of the teaching of creationism and/or intelligent design in the public school science class is well settled. Yet, in spite of the prevailing legal precedents, President George W. Bush famously asserted that both evolution and creationism should be taught in science classes. Much publicized lower federal court decisions in Pennsylvania and Georgia, however, show the resiliency of the issue. In both cases, school boards controlled by fundamentalist Christians attempted to circumvent the aforementioned U. S. Supreme Court decisions by various curricular subterfuges. In Dover, Pennsylvania, an overbearing school board president and board sought to compel teachers to use an "intelligent design" reference book and then adopt a biology curriculum that would make students aware of the "gaps/problems in Darwin's theory and other theories of evolution, including but not limited to intelligent design."

The board issued a press release confirming that state standards for biology classes were required to learn about Darwin's theory, but appended the statement that Darwin's theory "was not fact." Further, the press release stated that "intelligent design" was an alternative to Darwin's "natural selection." Suit was filed challenging the board's attempt to change the science curriculum to advance "intelligent design." The federal district court, after a six-week trial, held that the board's intelligent design policy was an attempt to endorse a religious view and, therefore, violated the Establishment Clause of the First Amendment. The court elaborated pointing out that the scientific community overwhelmingly accepted Darwin's theory of evolution and rejected the idea of intelligent design. (*Kitzmiller v. Dover Area School District*, 400 F. Supp. 2d 707 (M.D. Pa. 2005)).

In a later, but similar contest in Georgia, plaintiffs challenged a Cobb County school board action that authorized the school board attorney to draft a statement that was used on stickers placed on each biology textbook, a warning that said: "This textbook contains material on evolution. Evolution is a theory, not a fact, regarding the origin of living things. This material should be approached with an open mind, studied carefully, and critically considered." Parents who believed that the stickers endorsed religion sued the school board. The federal district court held that an informed, reasonable observer would believe the stickers sent a message of approval of Biblical creationism and was opposed to teaching evolution, thus, violating the religion provisions of the First Amendment. On appeal, the federal circuit vacated the decision for technical evidentiary reasons and recommended the lower court issue new findings and conclusions of law. Subsequently, the Cobb County school board voluntarily agreed to remove stickers and any labels that disclaimed evolution. *Selman v. Cobb County School District*, 449 F.3d 1320 (11th Cir. 2006).

§ 2.25 Liberty to Teach and Learn

The power of the state to compel attendance at school and to require all students to take instruction in the English language has been long recognized. Yet, the courts have not condoned the states' overreaching their authority to prohibit the teaching of any other language. In a landmark case rendered in 1923, *Meyer v. Nebraska*, a statute forbidding the teaching of foreign languages to students who had not completed the eighth grade in public, parochial, or private schools was challenged by an instructor in a parochial school who was retained by parents to give their child instruction in the German language. The statute was enacted in 1919 when the thoughts of the nation's legislators were still much influenced by World War I. Constitutional basis for the plaintiff's action was found in the Due Process Clause of the Fourteenth Amendment which provides that "No state . . . shall deprive any person of life, liberty or property without due process of law." In holding for the teacher, the Court said that the state's power was limited where it infringed on the liberty interests of the teacher and the pupil. In so ruling, the Court gave broad definition to the word "liberty" saying "the term . . . denotes not merely freedom from bodily restraint but also the right of the individual to contract, to engage in any of the common occupations of life, to acquire useful knowledge, to marry, establish a home and to bring up children, to worship God according to the dictates of his own conscience, and generally to enjoy those privileges long recognized at common law as essential to the orderly pursuit of happiness of free men."

Where state statute infringes on an individual's liberty, the legislative action may be stricken by the courts. In *Meyer,* the Court said that education of the young is regarded as a high calling, useful, honorable, and, indeed, essential to the public welfare. Becoming knowledgeable about the German language could not be regarded as harmful, meriting state proscription. The Court concluded that the teacher's right to teach and the right of parents to engage the teacher to instruct their children were liberty rights bestowed by the Fourteenth Amendment.

Liberty rights of both teachers and students have been summarized as "the right of the citizen to be free in the environment of his faculties; to be free to use them in all lawful ways; to live and work where he will; to earn his livelihood by any lawful calling," in essence, liberty may be formulated under the phrase, "pursuit of happiness."

§ 2.26　English Language Instruction

State law or school board rule can require that the basic language of instruction in all schools be English. Some states have passed legislation requiring bilingual education. In 1981 Texas passed the Bilingual and Special Language Programs Act which compelled bilingual education in elementary school. See *United States v. State of Texas,* 680 F.2d 356 (5th Cir.1982).

The issue of whether the school district may provide instruction exclusively in English was raised in *Lau v.*

Nichols, 414 U.S. 563 (1974). In *Lau*, the San Francisco school district provided special English instruction for 1000 of 2800 Chinese students. The remaining students were not served because of a lack of funding. The United States Supreme Court ruled that failure to provide methods of bridging the language gap offended Title VI of the Civil Rights Act of 1964, 42 U.S.C.A. § 2000d. The court did not address the issue of deprivation under the Equal Protection Clause of the Fourteenth Amendment. The litigation in *Lau* concerned only Title VI, but the lower federal courts have not found that failure to provide bilingual programs violates the Equal Protection Clause, but of course with *Lau* in place such a ruling is largely obviated.

The Court concluded that "Basic English skills are at the very core of what these public schools teach. Imposition of a requirement that before a child can effectively participate in the educational program he must already have acquired those basic skills is to make a mockery of public education. We know that those who do not understand English are certain to find their classroom experiences wholly incomprehensible and in no way meaningful."

§ 2.27　Academic Freedom

The Supreme Court has discussed the concept of academic freedom on numerous occasions. In *Keyishian v. Board of Regents*, 385 U.S. 589 (1967), the Court said that "Our nation is deeply committed to safeguarding academic freedom, which is of transcendent value to all of us and not merely to teachers concerned. That freedom is therefore a specific concern of the First Amendment. . . ." Justice Brennan in this case in addressing academic freedom said that it was a special concern of the First Amendment. Academic freedom, however, does not bestow upon the teacher and the student "unlimited liberty" to do anything their hearts desire; rather, the concept must be viewed in the total context of the legal purpose and conduct of the school. Although academic freedom and the First Amendment are not synonymous they are closely related. It is well settled that teachers do not relinquish their First Amendment rights because of their public employment. Yet the state as the employer possesses authority to reasonably restrict the speech as it relates to the functioning of their position. Therefore, when an issue relating to an employee's speech arises regarding academic freedom, "a balance between the interests of the employee as a citizen, in commenting on matters of public concern and the interest of the state as an employer in promoting efficiency of public services it performs through its employees," must be taken into account.

In balancing the teacher's speech interest against the school board's interest in conducting the schools, the courts will seek to determine whether the speech involved a protected discussion of a public concern or was merely a matter of private concern. Speech exercised in a public concern is protected, but speech about a private matter is not a protected right and can be regulated by the school. The U.S. Supreme Court in *Connick v. Myers*, 461 U.S. 138 (1983), has said: "We hold only that when a public employee speaks, not as a citizen upon matters of public concern, but instead as an employee upon matters of personal interest, absent the most unusual circumstances, a federal court is not the appropriate forum in which to review the wisdom of a personnel decision taken by a public agency allegedly in reaction to the employee's behavior." See: *Boring v. Buncombe County Bd. of Education*, 136 F.3d 364 (4th Cir.1998).

In a recent Sixth Circuit case that addressed the free speech rights of a teacher, a federal court ruled for the teacher. A tenured fifth-grade teacher teaching a unit on "Saving the Trees," a possible alternative to wood pulp, industrial hemp (marijuana) fibers, was discussed. Television star Woody Harrelson was in Kentucky to speak to the Kentucky Hemp Growers Association. He was invited and accepted to speak to the fifth-grade class with the principal's knowledge. After local news media and CNN coverage, a number of citizens complained to the school board. The Superintendent asked the Kentucky Education Professional Standards Board to investigate the teacher for allowing illegal hemp seeds to be passed around during Harrelson's visit. The board found for the teacher there was an "insufficient basis" for any personnel action. A new policy on "controversial" topics was passed by the school board. The teacher, complying with the policy, had Harrelson return for a second visit. The School Board terminated the teacher. The Court ruled that the teacher's speech touched on a matter of public concern and therefore was constitutionally protected. *Cockrel v. Shelby County School District, et al.*, 270 F.3d 1036 (6th Cir.2001).

Whether a teacher may be disciplined or even dismissed for using a "dirty word" depends on the circumstances surrounding the situation. "Each case must be examined on an independent basis" with the court considering a number of factors such as age of students, context and manner of presentation, and whether a valid educational objective is being met. In a case where a teacher was dismissed because he gave his class copies of an article published in the *Atlantic Monthly* magazine in which the vulgar term for an incestuous son was used, and the teacher explained the word's origin to the class, its context, and why the author had used it, the teacher was subsequently suspended. The teacher sued to recover his position maintaining the article was a valuable discussion of "dissent, protest, radicalism, and revolt" and was in no way pornographic. The court agreed with the teacher in finding that the article was thoughtful and thought-provoking and to delete the offending word would have made it impossible to understand the article or the point of view of the author. *Keefe v. Geanakos*, 418 F.2d 359 (1st Cir.1969).

While the court agreed that some measure of public regulation of classroom speech is inherent in every provision for public education, to deny the teacher use of such words when used in an educational context would be to demean the academic process. Whether language is offensive or inappropriate is dependent on the circumstances in the particular situation. Other circumstances which must also be considered include the educational information being conveyed, the reason for use of the words, and the educational level of the students involved.

Teachers may, however, go beyond their legal bounds in use of offensive terminology. Courts have pointed out that a teacher's academic freedom does not extend to protection of conduct which is "both offensive and unnecessary to the accomplishment of educational objectives ... such questions are matters of degree involving judgment on such factors as the age and sophistication of the students, relevance of the educational purpose, and context and manner of presentations." *Brubaker v.*

Board of Education, School District 149, Cook County, Illinois, 502 F.2d 973 (7th Cir.1974).

The teacher does not have carte blanche in the selection and use of learning materials. Where a school had a learning-material-approval policy, the teacher failed to obtain such approval and showed to his class an R-rated film that depicted nudity, sexual conduct, drug use and violence, the school board dismissed the teacher. The teacher sued claiming a denial of due process and First Amendment free speech rights. The court in finding for the school board, upholding the teacher's dismissal, said that the board's policy was a reasonable method of regulating possibly inappropriate materials, and the board rule was "reasonably related to a legitimate pedagogical concern." *Board of Education of Jefferson County School District R–1 v. Wilder*, 960 P.2d 695 (Colo.1998).

§ 2.28 The Pall of Orthodoxy

School authorities, as public policymakers, have comprehensive powers and broad discretion in discharging their duties to provide public education. In commenting on the extent of these powers, the U.S. Supreme Court said in *Epperson v. Arkansas* that: "By and large, public education in our nation is committed to the control of state and local authorities. Courts do not and cannot intervene in the resolution of conflicts which arise in the daily operation of school systems and which do not directly and sharply implicate basic constitutional values."

School boards, however, do not have an absolute right to remove material from the curriculum. One of the great strengths of the public school in America has been its openness and expansiveness in the conveyance of knowledge.

Of late, there have been increasing attempts by some parents and citizens claiming that public schools have a negative effect on religious or family values to seek to restrict the public school curriculum. In rejecting a parental and student attempt to ban from school the film "The Lottery," a short story in which citizens of a small town select one of their members to be stoned to death each year, a federal circuit rejected the parents complaint and, again, couched the legal logic in the context of protecting the schools against a "pall of orthodoxy." *Pratt v. Independent School Dist. No. 831*, 670 F.2d 771 (8th Cir.1982).

§ 2.3 CENSORSHIP OF TEXTBOOKS

Throughout history, books have been censored and even burned because they were found objectionable by one group or another for reasons usually related to politics or religion. Efforts to control the minds of the people have seen the banning of such great works as *Animal Farm* by George Orwell, *Doctor Zhivago* by Boris Pastermak, *The Rights of Man* by Thomas Paine, and *Uncle Tom's Cabin* by Harriet Beecher Stowe. While the repression of thought for religious reasons has an even more invasive history, such books include *The Age of Reason, Thomas Payne, Oliver Twist, Charles Dickens, Harry Potter, On the Origin of the Species, Charles Darwin, Jude the Obscure, Thomas Hardy*, and various translations of the *Bible*, the *Koran*, and *The Talamud*, and the list goes on. Public schools have become ground zero for many of these book battles as the various ideological and sectarian interests have sought to capture the minds of the youth by sterilizing information or controlled feeding of young minds.

The 1988 Supreme Court decision in *Hazelwood School Dist. v. Kuhlmeier*, 484 U.S. 260 (1988), although involving the school board's ability to control a school-sponsored newspaper, has had an impact beyond student publications. This decision has been applied in a variety of areas inclusive of the school curriculum and academic freedom of teachers. The expansion of *Hazelwood* from a case involving editorial control over a school-sponsored paper to broader application is tied to the following statements by the Supreme Court. "Educators do not offend the First Amendment by exercising editorial control over the style and content of student speech in school-sponsored expressive activities so long as their actions are reasonably related to legitimate pedagogical concerns" and "It is only when the decision to *censor* (emphasis added) a school-sponsored publication, theatrical production, or other vehicle of student expression has no valid educational purpose that the First Amendment is so directly and sharply implicated as to require judicial intervention to protect students' constitutional rights."

The principle enunciated in *Hazelwood* was later applied to a curriculum textbook decision in *Virgil v. School Board of Columbia County*, 862 F.2d 1517 (11th Cir.1989). In this case, a minister whose child was a student in an English class filed a complaint with the school board concerning two books used in the class, Aristophanes' *Lysistrata* and Chaucer's, *The Miller's Tale*. The school board voted to discontinue use of the books because of "sexuality" and "excessively vulgar . . . language and subject matter." In upholding the school board's decision to ban the books, the Eleventh Circuit

Court of Appeals stated, "*Hazelwood* established a relatively lenient test for regulation of expression which may fairly be characterized as part of the school curriculum. Such regulation is permissible so long as it is 'reasonably related to legitimate pedagogical concerns.'" Accordingly, when prescribing learning materials, the school district must take into account the emotional maturity of the audience and the nature and sensitivity of the topics involved.

A case in point was litigated before the U.S. Court of Appeals, Ninth Circuit, where a parent, on behalf of an African–American student, brought suit claiming that the required reading of two works, *The Adventures of Huckleberry Finn* by Mark Twain, and *A Rose for Emily* by William Faulkner, violated the student's rights because the works contain repeated use of the profane, insulting and racially derogatory term 'nigger'. The parent claimed that the required reading violated the Equal Protection Clause and Title VI of the 1964 Civil Rights Act.

The court found for the school board and noted that school boards have wide discretion in deciding which books have educational value. According to the court, for school boards to succumb to the removal of books because of parental threats of litigation would infringe on First Amendment rights of the remaining students. The court stated, "We have no hesitation in concluding, however, that a student's First Amendment rights are infringed when books that have been determined by the school district to have legitimate educational value are removed from a mandatory reading list because of threats of damages, lawsuits, or other forms of retaliation. In this case, the relief that Monteiro's complaint seeks ... would unquestionably restrict the students' First Amendment freedoms and significantly interfere with the District's discretion to determine the composition of its curriculum." *Monteiro v. The Tempe Union High School District*, 158 F.3d 1022 (9th Cir.1998).

In a California case, the court chose to interpret *Hazelwood* in a more narrow light. This court would not accept any pedagogical justification for removing books, and ruled the school board's motives should be examined before accepting their pedagogical reasons as legitimate. In this case the two books, *Grendel* and *One Hundred Years of Solitude*, were removed because of a student complaint based on religious grounds. The court noted that a school board has broad powers to remove and restrict the use of books that may be profane or contrary to the prevailing community moral standards, but ruled that educational unsuitability must be the real reason for excluding a book(s) and not a religious reason. *McCarthy v. Fletcher*, 254 Cal.Rptr. 714 (App.1989).

§ 2.31   Textbooks   Challenged   on   Religious Grounds

Controversy surrounding textbook selection by public school boards has become more frequent and increasingly acrimonious in recent years. The primary cause of this increased dissension has been the rising political strength and activism of fundamentalist religious groups. Various sects have taken great pains to search through textbooks adopted by public schools and ferret out what they consider to be objectionable matter. An example of an attempt by parents to ban certain books because of religious objections is vividly illustrated in a Tennessee case. Here, the parents objected to the use of textbooks, a reading series published by Holt, Rinehart and Winston. The plaintiff, a mother of four children, objected to a story on mental telepathy and claimed that such material violated her religious beliefs as protected by the First and Fourteenth Amendments of the U.S. Constitution. She sought proscription of any teachings that were not circumscribed by the Biblical scriptures. The plaintiff parent testified that she had found at least 17 categories of offensive materials in the books including evolution, pacifism, secular humanism, "futuristic supernaturalism," magic and false views of death. She strongly objected to many specific passages including one that described Leonardo de Vinci as a human with a creative mind that "came closest to the divine touch." The U.S. Court of Appeals, Sixth Circuit, upheld the school board's required use of the textbooks and pointed out the parent had testified that she would "not be tolerant" of religious views other than her own. According to the court, the school board's view and the content of the reading series conveyed a respect and tolerance for the beliefs of others. The court found that the school board had sought to acquaint students with a multitude of ideas and concepts. There was no evidence that the readings prescribed by the school board would lead the plaintiff's children to any conclusions that were contrary to the plaintiff parent's religious beliefs. *Mozert v. Hawkins County Board of Education*, 827 F.2d 1058 (6th Cir. 1987).

While the *Mozert* case was litigated on the Free Exercise of Religion Clause of the First Amendment, another similar textbook case was based on a premised violation of the Establishment Clause. In *Smith v. Board of School Commissioners of Mobile County*, 827 F.2d 684 (11th Cir.1987), a parent claimed that certain textbooks in home economics, history, and social studies violated the Establishment Clause because they were advancing the religion of secular humanism. The plaintiff further claimed that the textbooks inhibited theistic religion. The Sixth Circuit held that the textbooks were secular in nature and as such did not promote secular humanism or inhibit a theistic religion. The court in quoting *Everson v. Board of Education*, 330 U.S. 1 (1947) said, "The public schools in this country are organized 'on the premise that secular education can be isolated from all religious teaching so that the school can inculcate all needed temporal knowledge and also maintain a strict and lofty neutrality as to religion. The assumption is that after the individual has been instructed in worldly wisdom he will be better fitted to choose his religion.' "

However, such efforts to control the adoption of textbooks by religious fundamentalists are not infrequent. In these cases the courts are prone to defer to the established authority of the school board, regardless of its political leanings. An illustration of the deference that courts have for school board authority is illustrated in an Illinois school district case where reading material used in an elementary school contained "scary" stories with ghosts, goblins and witches. A group of parents complained that the readings had the effect of advancing pagan religious views. The court upheld the school board's use of the books finding that the material did not foster any particular religious view. This federal district court noted that these matters were for the school board to decide and observed that the courts cannot sit as reviewers of "educational decisions" made by school boards. *Fleischfresser v. Directors of School District 200*, 805 F.Supp. 584 (N.D.Ill.1992).

In a similar case, a lower federal court ruled that the textbook curricular study series titled "Impressions" did not endorse the religion of witchcraft and/or neopaganism in violation of federal or state constitutions. In this case parents litigated the use of "Impressions," a series of 59 books containing approximately 10,000 literary selections and suggested classroom activities. The parents challenged 32 of the Impression selections saying they promoted witchcraft, which advanced a religion called "Wicca." On appeal to the U.S. Court of Appeals, Ninth Circuit upheld the lower court decision. The parents argued that the resemblance of the challenged selections to the practice of witchcraft causes children to believe that they are engaging in a witchcraft ritual. In viewing the issue from the religious perspective and finding for the school board, the Court observed that the mere resemblance to a religious ritual and the parents' perception that the readings and activities are a religious ritual does not make it so. *Brown v. Woodland Joint Unified School District*, 27 F.3d 1373 (9th Cir.1994).

§ 2.4 CENSORSHIP OF LIBRARY BOOKS

School boards have a significant degree of discretion in the determination of the content of school libraries. That discretion, however, is not without limits and may be abused if exercised in a political or narrowly partisan manner. Because each case must stand on its own factual merits, precedents regarding the authority of the school board to remove books from the school library have not been definitive. The United States Court of Appeals for the Second Circuit held in 1972 that the school board had the discretion to remove books from the library simply because they were without merit either as works of art or science. *Presidents Council, Dist. 25 v. Community School Board*, 457 F.2d 289 (2d Cir.1972). The court observed that administration of a school library "involves a constant process of selection and winnowing based not only on educational needs but financial and architectural realities. To suggest that the shelving or unshelving of books presents a constitutional issue, particularly where there is no showing of a curtailment of freedom of speech or thought, is a proposition we cannot accept."

Whether and to what extent school boards can remove materials from libraries remains a source of contention. The U.S. Court of Appeals for the Second Circuit held in 1980 that books could be removed from the school library because of their vulgar nature. According to this court, school boards could not remove books because of the ideas they contained, but could remove books in applying their own standards and tastes in determining what is vulgar and explicit sexual conduct. *Bicknell v. Vergennes Union High School Bd. of Directors*, 638 F.2d 438 (2d Cir.1980).

On the other hand, other courts have been reluctant to allow the availability of library materials to be contingent upon the tastes and standards of board members. Such unlimited discretion on the part of board members may be so vague as to permit arbitrary administration in such a way to offend due process. Moreover, boards may possibly violate due process if they remove books without adopting procedural safeguards for considering the book's content. *Sheck v. Baileyville School Committee*, 530 F.Supp. 679 (D.Me.1982).

The library censorship issue was addressed by the United States Supreme Court in 1982 in a case in which the school board had removed nine books from the school library. *Board of Education, Island Trees Union Free School District No. 26 v. Pico*, 457 U.S. 853 (1982). The board's justification for removal of the books was that they were irrelevant, vulgar, immoral, and in bad taste, making them educationally unsuitable for junior and senior high school students.

The Supreme Court in *Pico* noted that "local school boards must be permitted to establish and apply their curriculum in such a way as to transmit community values, and there is legitimate and substantial community interest in promoting respect for authority and traditional values, be they social, moral, or political." The Court, however, went on to point out that school boards could not, in exercise of their broad discretion, "strangle the free mind" and limit youth in acquiring important information which will allow them to become responsible citizens.

According to the Supreme Court in *Pico*, the critical issue to be considered is the motivation behind a school board's actions. If the school board members intended the book removal to suppress certain ideas with which they disagreed, then the action was unconstitutional; on the other hand, if the board removed the books because they were "pervasively vulgar" or obscene or solely because they were "educationally" unsuitable, then no right was violated. The evidence in *Pico* showed that the board did not employ regular and unbiased procedures in reviewing the books as to their educational suitability and that, in fact, the books had been removed solely because they had been placed on a list of objectionable books by a conservative organization of parents who had prevailed on the school board for the removal. In ruling against the school board, the Court admonished that its decision was limited to the removal of books from the library and in no way affected a school board's discretion in adding books to the school library. The *Pico* case, however, has not resolved the matter, as school boards have continued to come under pressure to remove books that a particular religious group may find objectionable. While it is generally conceded, as observed above, that in matters of the curriculum, the school board has more direct control, the *Pico* case indicates that the library books are a further reach for the board to assert control.

The critical test, then, that the school board must pass in removal of books from the library is the "motivation of the board." If a school board does remove a book from the school library, then it must be shown that the school board members were not motivated by their personal disagreement with the ideas expressed in the book. *Case v. Unified School District No. 233, Johnson County, Kansas*, 908 F.Supp. 864 (D.Kan.1995). Where books are removed by the school board, the lower court must determine the board member's motivation for the decision. In a Louisiana case where parents, members of the Louisiana Christian Coalition, discovered that a copy of a book in the school library entitled *Voodoo & Hoodoo* described African religions with instructions for casting spells, the school board, after receiving a petition signed by 1600 parents, voted to remove the book from the library. Later, other plaintiff parents sued challenging the removal. The lower federal court granted summary judgment to the plaintiff parents. The U.S. Court of Appeals, Fifth Circuit, upheld the lower court's action, holding the school board's actual "motivation" was for removal of the book. *Campbell v. St. Tammany Parish School Board*, 64 F.3d 184 (5th Cir.1995).

§ 2.5 COURSE CONTENT AND TEACHING METHODS

The school district's authority to decide the course content and to determine the teaching methods to be employed is well established. The weight and importance of the school district's discretion has usually been demonstrated in cases where teaching materials contained matter that was considered to be obscene.

In such cases there has been little doubt about the authority of the school district to regulate the course content. Yet, the courts will examine each circumstance to determine if the magnitude of the teacher's offensive behavior is sufficient to warrant the specific sanctions taken against the teacher. The primary issue to be considered by the courts is the extent and severity of the redress taken against the teacher. Firing of a teacher for unwittingly allowing obscene poetry to be read by students has been held too severe, *De Groat v. Newark Unified School District*, 133 Cal.Rptr. 225 (App.1976), while a nine-month suspension of a teacher for showing cartoons of "Fritz the Cat" in various stages of undress has been held to be appropriate. *DeVito v. Board of Educ.*, 317 S.E.2d 159 (W.Va.1984).

Teaching methods may also be prescribed and regulated by the school district. Teachers do not have a constitutional right to use whatever teaching methodology pleases them if it runs counter to policies of the district. In a case illustrative of this point where two high school teachers claimed their First Amendment rights were violated when a school district refused to allow them to team-teach a history course, the students complained that the teaching technique affected the substance of the course. The Supreme Court of Washington held against the teachers pointing out that while some flexibility in teaching techniques may be employed by teachers, the teachers cannot be allowed to implement a particular technique that will detract from the effectiveness of the course. *Millikan v. Board of Directors of Everett School District*, 611 P.2d 414 (Wash.1980).

In another case yielding similar results, a public high school teacher was reassigned for refusing to teach evolution in the biology curriculum. The teacher claimed violation of the free exercise of religion and due process. The court held that the teacher's rights were not violated. The court stated "... the established curriculum and the [teacher's] responsibility as a public school teacher to teach evolution in the manner prescribed by the curriculum overrides his First Amendment rights as a private citizen." *LeVake v. Independent School District #656*, 625 N.W.2d 502 (Minn.App.2001).

§ 2.6 PROMOTION

Schools are empowered to establish a prescribed level of student performance. Reading attainment may be one criterion for measuring performance for promotion of students from grade to grade. In a case where only one student out of 23 second graders was promoted to the third grade because the others failed to reach a third grade reading level on the Ginn Reading Test, the court in upholding the criterion said, "Decisions by educational authorities which turn on evaluation of the academic performance of a student as it relates to promotion are peculiarly within the expertise of educators and are particularly inappropriate for review in a judicial context." *Sandlin v. Johnson*, 643 F.2d 1027 (4th Cir.1981). Such academic requirements are invalid only if they illegally classify students in a way which is prohibited by statute or by the state or federal constitutions.

The reluctance of the courts to become mired in cases contesting the evaluation of performance of individual students is longstanding. In a 1913 case, the Supreme Court of Massachusetts said that the courts would not intervene "[s]o long as the school committee acts in good faith and their conduct in formulating and applying standards and making decisions ... is not subject to review by any other tribunal." *Barnard v. Inhabitants of Shelburne*, 102 N.E. 1095 (Mass.1913).

§ 2.61   Lack of Scholarship

School boards and teachers have substantial discretion in determining what level of academic attainment will be required of students. School boards set general course requirements and teachers evaluate the students in achieving the objectives. Seldom will courts intervene to overturn a teacher's academic evaluation of a student. Only where school boards or the teachers act in bad faith or are found to be arbitrary or capricious will their actions be overturned. Students, thus, may be placed in alternative classes or retained at a particular grade level depending on their academic performance. (See Student Testing, Chapter 14.)

§ 2.7   DIPLOMA

School boards are empowered to set academic standards required to obtain a diploma. Such requirements, however, cannot be unreasonable and the diploma cannot be withheld except for valid reasons rationally related to the state's interests in public education. A diploma is *prima facie* evidence of educational worth. A student having complied with all the rules and regulations necessary for graduation may not be denied a diploma by arbitrary action of the school board. By establishing and maintaining a public school system, the state creates an expectation, to be reasonably held by the student, that upon successful completion of required courses, he or she will be awarded a diploma. This expectation constitutes a "property interest" on the part of the student which cannot be arbitrarily taken away. The diploma as a property interest cannot be taken away except where the state's interest exceeds that of the individual. Even then the denial can only be valid after the student has had an opportunity to be heard and is provided procedural due process. Thus, to deny the high school diploma because students failed to pass a Florida high school functional literacy examination was held to deny property interests to the student without due process of law. The court found that a test administered at the 11th grade level covered material which had not been taught to students in the public schools of Florida, thus denial of a diploma based on a newly-applied standard, after students had completed all other requirements for graduation, was held to be unfair and violated due process. *Debra P. v. Turlington*, 644 F.2d 397 (5th Cir.1981).

Nothing in federal or state law, however, stands in the way of school boards making reasonable rules to effectuate a legitimate educational purpose. A successful score on a minimal competency test can be required of all students before they can receive a diploma. Those who do not succeed in passing the test may receive only a certificate of program completion. *Rankins v. Louisiana State*

Board of Elementary and Secondary Education, 637
So.2d 548 (La.App.1994).

§ 2.8 GRADE REDUCTION

The issue of reducing a student's grades as punishment for non-academic conduct is not well settled, but
generally the courts have held that grades cannot be
reduced as a disciplinary measure for violation of school
rules. A rule has to pass the test of reasonableness, and
courts have said that reducing the grades for disciplinary
reasons is not reasonably related to academics.

This general rule of law is illustrated in a case where a
student who drank wine on a field trip was suspended
from school for five days, expelled from the cheerleading
squad, prohibited from taking part in school activities
during the suspension and dismissed from the National
Honor Society. The school policy called for a reduction of
grades in all classes by two percentage points for each
day of suspension. The Court held for the student and
ruled the Board may not impose a grade reduction sanction for infractions that was not related to education.
Katzman v. Cumberland Valley School District, 479 A.2d
671 (Pa.Cmwlth.1984).

In another case following the same rationale, three
students left campus to attend a medical biology class at
a medical center and on the way the girls stopped at one
of their homes and drank beer. After admitting to drink-
ing the beer, they were suspended for five days. The
school also reduced their grades by 20% for the semester.
The students sued and argued that the use of academic
sanctions for non-academic misconduct is arbitrary and
capricious. She claimed the penalty was not rationally
related to the offense and moreover was not related to

the disciplinary purpose. The court said, "A student's grade or credit should reflect the student's academic performance or achievement, including participation in class, and presence in class. Reducing grades unrelated to academic conduct results in a skewed and inaccurate reflection of the student's academic performance." This school policy in this case violated the student's substantive due process. *Smith v. School City of Hobart*, 811 F.Supp. 391 (N.D. Ind.1993). (*See In Interest of T. H., III*, 681 So.2d 110 (Miss.1996)).

Yet, if academic penalties have an academic connection, then the school regulation will prevail. Where a school board withheld credit from a student for missing 24 class periods, explicitly stated the purpose was academic and the student's grades were reduced for each unapproved absence, then the court upheld the procedure. Here attendance was closely related to the academic policy. *Campbell v. Board of Education of New Milford*, 475 A.2d 289 (Conn.1984).

§ 2.81 Extracurricular Activities

Increased interest in academics evidenced by a high stakes testing and an equally dramatic continued interest in extracurricular activities has resulted in increased academic standards for athletic participation. The Courts have generally held that there is not a constitutional right to participate in extracurricular activities. Extracurricular activities are generally considered to be a privilege and the board needs only a rational academic policy to deny student participation.

In this regard, the Montana Supreme Court held that a school requirement that a student athlete maintain a 2.0

or C grade average was not unconstitutional (*State v. Board of Trustees of School District*, 726 P.2d 801 (Mont. 1986)). In a similar case, a Louisiana court upheld a rule requiring a 1.6 grade average to participate in cheerleading. The rule was related to academic excellence and did not violate equal protection. *Rousselle v. Plaquemines Parish School Board*, 527 So.2d 376 (La.App.1988).

§ 2.9 HOMEWORK

It is generally assumed that teachers and/or school boards can require students to devote a certain amount of out-of-school time to their studies. In fact, many believe that too little homework is required in schools today. A legal question may, though, arise where a parent objects to homework as an encroachment on parental prerogative and, too, it may be contended that the child should not be held accountable at school for work done at home.

Only a few early cases have been rendered giving guidance on this issue, but the limited precedent available indicates that it is an appropriate exercise of school authority to require homework so long as the requirements are reasonable and are directly related to the student's achievement at school. Teachers may punish students for refusing to do homework assignments. *Mangum v. Keith*, 95 S.E. 1 (Ga.1918). Rules, though, may not be so constrictive as to deprive parental control over the activities of their children. Thus, a school rule setting aside specific hours each night, say between 7 and 9 p.m., during which time the student must be home studying is unreasonable. On the other hand, a rule requiring a student to take math problems home, work them and return them completed to school the next day is a reasonable rule. Too much direction from the school regarding the time and place that the homework is to be performed is apparently the legal determinant. Required homework may be reasonable even though a parent contends that the student time is taken from home chores. *Balding v. State*, 4 S.W. 579 (Tex.App.1887).

§ 2.10   SEX EDUCATION

During the last two decades boards of education have increasingly introduced sex education courses into the public school curriculum. While in most cases the implementation has gone smoothly, in some instances, parents have challenged the efforts as encroachments on religious liberty and privacy. In each instance the courts have rejected the parental claims maintaining generally that such requirements are within the police power of the state.

The rationale for providing sex education is based on the state's interest in the health and welfare of its children. This has been sufficient reason for courts to hold in favor of boards of education establishing such courses. *Aubrey v. School District of Philadelphia*, 437 A.2d 1306 (Pa.Cmwlth.1981).

Mandatory sex education courses have been upheld where students and parents maintained that required sex education courses violated their religious beliefs. A federal district court held in a Maryland case that the interest of the state in "healthy, well-rounded growth of young people" is properly enforced through required sex education courses regardless of the parents' objections based on religious scruples. *Cornwell v. State Board of Education*, 314 F.Supp. 340 (D.Md.1969). The prevailing view appears to be that sex education can be constitutionally defended as a required course of study.

A minority view of some courts is that the compulsory nature of sex education courses may, possibly, make them questionable as an invasion of privacy or an encroachment on the free exercise of religion. The Supreme Court of Hawaii upheld a sex education program promulgated by the state education agency, but in so doing appeared to base its approval on the fact that the program was not compulsory. *Medeiros v. Kiyosaki*, 478 P.2d 314 (Hawaii 1970). No court has ruled, though, that sex education courses are unconstitutional and boards of education appear to be within their rightful authority when they require sex education, and there is little doubt that boards are acting constitutionally when the sex education courses are non-compulsory or have an "excusal" arrangement whereby parents may request that their children not be involved. A state board of education regulation requiring that local school districts develop and implement a family life education course which included teaching about human sexuality did not violate a student's rights of freedom of religion where the regulation provided for the student to be excused from specific portions of the course which the student or parents found objectionable. *Smith v. Ricci*, 446 A.2d 501 (N.J. 1982).

In a recent case, the Court upheld the right of the state to have a mandatory health education course while allowing the students to opt-out of certain family life topics, such as AIDS, family life, personal growth and development. The health class taught health and safety, human growth and development, disease prevention, physical, mental and emotional health. The Court stated "opt-out procedures have been adopted by states and school boards with regard to sex education, as this case shows. However, courts have rejected parental demands to exempt children from mandatory health courses, which although ... value-laden are less so than sex education and closer to basic academic subjects." *Leebaert v. Harrington*, 193 F.Supp.2d 491 (D.Conn.2002).

CHAPTER 3

DUE PROCESS RIGHTS OF STUDENTS

§ 3.1 INTRODUCTION

To deny attendance at public school has always been a method of controlling disruptive student conduct. Although the practice has fallen in disrepute among some educators in recent years, to remove students from public schools remains a disciplinary alternative. Bearing on the issue of exclusion is whether education is of such importance to the individual as to be considered a constitutional interest under the Due Process Clause of the Fourteenth Amendment.

Until relatively recently, decisions to suspend or expel pupils were made on the convenient assumption that to attend public schools was a privilege which could be taken away at the discretion of the school authorities. Students who offended, or were thought to have offended, school rules could be summarily dismissed from school with no redress or opportunity to present their side of the story. The courts have generally held that children have a constitutional interest in attending public schools and cannot be deprived of that interest without due process of law. A state can only deny the benefit of a public school education after providing due process of law. Once the state extends the benefit of education to all persons, education acquires the substantive constitutional status of a property interest and is treated as having the accompanying constitutional due process protections. Liberty interest may also be implicated. Education can be denied, but it can only be taken away after the requirements of procedural due process of law have been fully extended to the child who may suffer a deprivation of education. Thus, the state can take away education as it can life, liberty or property, but it can only do so with strict observance of procedural due process.

§ 3.2   DUE PROCESS

There are two types of due process: one is called *substantive due process* and the other *procedural due process*. To deny substantive due process the state must have a valid legal objective and the means must be reasonably calculated to achieve the objective. Early interpretations by the United States Supreme Court recognized only the procedural aspects of due process of law. It was not until 1923 that the Supreme Court defined due process of law as inclusive of "substantive" protections. *Adkins v. Children's Hospital*, 261 U.S. 525 (1923). Substantive due process means those substantive rights that are implied in the words "liberty" and "property." Substantive due process may be implicated by the rules or regulations written by educators to regulate or control student behavior, such as the student handbook with rights and responsibilities. To deny substantive rights requires procedural due process.

Procedural due process pertains to the actual procedures required to deprive a person of life, liberty, or property. A prescribed constitutional procedure must be followed. The Supreme Court of the United States has said that in order to give an individual procedural due process as required by the federal constitution, three basic factors must be present: 1) the person must have proper notice, 2) must be given an opportunity to be heard, and 3) must be given a hearing that is conducted fairly.

§ 3.21　Substantive Due Process

In 1923 the U.S. Supreme Court created a nexus between acquisition of knowledge and an individual's liberty interest under the Due Process Clause of the Fourteenth Amendment. The due process clause says that "No state . . . shall deprive any person of life, liberty or property without due process of law." According to the Court, the word "liberty" has a substantive aspect which invests each person with a protected interest in acquisition and conveyance of knowledge. *Meyer v. Nebraska*, 262 U.S. 390 (1923). From 1923 until 1961 there was no further development of education as a substantive due process interest. Generally, during that period, the *Meyer* precedent was construed very narrowly, having little implication for education rights, generally.

An important case, however, emerged in 1961 which indicated that education was a substantive interest of such magnitude as to invoke procedural due process if it is to be denied. In *Dixon v. Alabama State Board of Education*, 294 F.2d 150 (5th Cir.1961), a federal court held that attendance at a college was so essential that it could not be taken away without a hearing and attendant due process procedures. Without specifically saying so, this court implied that education was of such importance that it may be implied within the substance of the term property under the Due Process Clause.

Then in *Tinker v. Des Moines Independent Community School District*, 393 U.S. 503 (1969), the Supreme Court explicitly recognized the substantive nature of due process rights of students. In spite of the impact of *Dixon* and *Tinker*, the relationship between education and due process was not clearly defined until 1975 in *Goss v. Lopez*, 419 U.S. 565 (1975), at which time the U.S. Supreme Court pointed out that denial of education for even a short period of time could not be construed as inconsequential. In explaining that the individual's interest in education fell within the substantive scope of "liberty and property," the Court said: "[n]either the property interest in education benefits temporarily denied nor the liberty interest in reputation, which is also implicated, is so insubstantial that suspensions may constitutionally be imposed by any procedure one school chooses, no matter how arbitrary."

More recently the U.S. Supreme Court has said that due process of law is intended to "secure the individual from arbitrary exercise of the powers of government." Due process protects against governmental arbitrariness whether it pertains to physically taking property, the denial of a governmental benefit such as education, imprisonment, or any other exercise of governmental power without reasonable justification. *County of Sacramento v. Lewis*, 523 U.S. 833 (1998).

The Supreme Court has, however, been more reluctant in recent years to expand the concept of substantive due process and has prescribed a standard that requires the invoking of substantive due process only if the governmental action is so invasive and arbitrary as to be "conscience shocking." Following the Supreme Court's standard of "conscience shocking," the U.S. Court of Appeals, Seventh Circuit, upheld a school giving "Fs" to two students in band class who ignored class rules and teacher orders by departing from the planned musical program by interjecting into a band performance impromptu and disruptive guitar solos. Even though assignment of an F to one of the students prevented him from graduating with honors, the court concluded that no substantive due process right had been violated. The court found that the assignment of an F was not constitutionally inappropriate because the school's interest in maintaining order and providing an education was rationally related to its disciplinary action against the students and was not of such a nature as to "shock the conscience." *Dunn v. Fairfield Community High School District No. 225*, 158 F.3d 962 (7th Cir.1998).

§ 3.211 Property

Therefore, education has been determined to have a substantive aspect within the context of property. Property encompasses those individual interests which are created by state statutes that entitle all citizens to a certain benefit. When a state creates a public system of education to which all children are entitled to benefit, each child is vested with a "property" interest.

The Supreme Court has explained the property interest in this way: "Property interests ... are not created by the Constitution; rather, they are created and their dimensions are defined by existing rules or understandings that stem from an independent source such as state law rules or understandings that secure certain benefits and that support claims of entitlement to those benefits." *Board of Regents v. Roth*, 408 U.S. 564 (1972).

In this regard, the federal constitution does not create education as a fundamental right, but rather education becomes a "property" interest when state law establishes a public education system to which all children have a right to attend. Where the right of attendance in public school is extended to all children throughout a state, the state then cannot selectively deny education without procedural due process. Thus, when the state creates a public education system, education is effectively established as a property right or interest for all pupils. The student's property interest in attending school is not absolute and can be denied with proper procedural due process. *Bogle–Assegai v. Bloomfield Board of Education*, 467 F. Supp. 2d 236 (D. Conn. 2006).

§ 3.212 Liberty

As observed above, due process also forbids arbitrary deprivation of liberty, or denial of those interests which are implied by that term. A person's liberty includes his or her "good name, reputation, honor, or integrity." The standard definitions of the substantive breadth of liberty was given in *Meyer v. Nebraska* where the question arose as to whether a teacher in a private school had a liberty interest in teaching the German language, even though teaching German had been prohibited by state statute. The U.S. Supreme Court, in holding for the teacher, asserted the expansive nature of liberty, "While ... [the] Court has not attempted to define with exactness the liberty thus guaranteed, the term has received much consideration and some of the included things have been definitely stated. Without doubt, it denotes not merely freedom from bodily restraint but also right of the individual to contract, to engage in any of the common occupations of life, to acquire useful knowledge, to marry, establish a home and bring up children, to worship God according to the dictates of his own conscience, and generally to enjoy those privileges long recognized at common law as essential to the orderly pursuit of happiness by free men." *Meyer v. Nebraska*, 262 U.S. 390 (1923). For government to take a person's liberty away requires due process of law. In *Goss v. Lopez*, where it was found that procedural due process had not been afforded, the recording of the suspensions in student permanent files effectively attached a stigma infringing on the students' liberty interests. The Supreme Court said, "If sustained and recorded, those charges could seriously damage the students' standing with their fellow pupils and their teachers as well as interfere with later opportunities for higher education and employment."

§ 3.22 What Process Is Due?

When it is determined that due process applies and that a substantive interest is in jeopardy, the question next arises as to what process is due. *Morrissey v. Brewer*, 408 U.S. 471 (1972). The answer is that "The nature of the hearing should vary depending upon the circumstances of the particular case." *Dixon v. Alabama State Board of Education*, 294 F.2d 150 (5th Cir.1961). The hearing should be fair and impartial in keeping with the nature and gravity of the charges. "The nub of the matter is that the student [be] given an opportunity to present his side of the case, including anything by way of denial or mitigation." *McClain v. Lafayette County Board of Education*, 673 F.2d 106 (5th Cir.1982). "Basic fairness and integrity of the fact-finding process are the guiding stars." *Boykins v. Fairfield Board of Education*, 492 F.2d 697 (5th Cir.1974). The principle of fairness, while flexible, requires that the state adhere to the following touchstones of procedural due process. First, notice should be given containing specific charges and grounds, which if proven would justify the prescribed penalty. Second, a hearing should be conducted which gives the school administration the opportunity to hear both sides of the story in considerable detail. The hearing should observe the rudiments of the adversarial process, though full dress judicial hearing is not required. Third, the student should be given the opportunity to present his or her version of the facts. Fourth, the hearing's result and findings should be open for the student's inspection. *Dixon v. Alabama State Board of Education*, 294 F.2d 150 (5th Cir. 1961).

§ 3.23   The Penalty Imposed

The punishment meted out to the student must not be excessive and must be in keeping with the nature of the offense. A prescribed mandatory punishment referring to a particular offense is not unconstitutional simply because it is mandatory. *Clinton Municipal Separate School Dist. v. Byrd*, 477 So.2d 237 (Miss.1985).

It goes without saying that the hearing must precede the punishment, otherwise due process is denied. Where a parent and student were called into the principal's office and the student was given the choice of a ten-day suspension at home or at an alternative school, the U. S. Court of Appeals, Sixth Circuit, held that due process had been denied. There was no evidence that the student had been given the opportunity to tell his side of the story prior to the imposition of the punishment. *Buchanan v. City of Bolivar, Tennessee*, 99 F.3d 1352 (6th Cir.1996).

Expulsion may be an appropriate penalty for certain offenses, but in all such cases strict adherence to standards of procedural due process must be observed. Where a tenth grade student was expelled for leaving school grounds, consuming alcohol, and then returning to school intoxicated, and school regulations provided for suspension or expulsion for "good cause" defined to include use or possession of alcoholic beverages or drugs, the U.S. Supreme Court held that the school board clearly had the authority to suspend and expel the student and that it was beyond the purview of federal courts to substitute their judgment for that of the school board. *Board of Education v. McCluskey*, 458 U.S. 966 (1982). Thus, expulsion is a viable disciplinary option, but can only be instituted after full and careful adherence to requirements of procedural due process.

Another penalty that may be imposed, if permitted by state statute or regulation, is corporal punishment. The U.S. Supreme Court in *Ingraham v. Wright*, 430 U.S. 651 (1977) ruled that corporal punishment did not constitute cruel and unusual punishment under the Eighth Amendment. Because "there can be no deprivation of substantive rights as long as disciplinary corporal punishment is within the limits of common law privilege," procedural due process is not required. The extent and severity of corporal punishment necessary to invoke substantive due process is, however, a developing area of law.

The Supreme Court in *Ingraham* recognized that a child's substantive liberty interests against corporal punishment are not insubstantial, and that the school's disciplinary process may not be totally accurate and unerring, thus there is risk of unjustified intrusion on the child's liberty interest. If the punishment is severe, the child has a "strong" interest in procedural safeguards to "minimize the risk of wrongful punishment."

Ingraham v. Wright, supra. The following statement in *Ingraham* has been interpreted as holding "that, at some point, excessive corporal punishment violates the pupil's substantive due process rights." *Garcia by Garcia v. Miera*, 817 F.2d 650 (10th Cir.1987). According to the *Garcia* court, "the concept of the substantive due process right is implicit in *Ingraham*" where excessive punishment is concerned. Accordingly, corporal punishment of students may violate due process if it amounts "to a brutal and inhumane abuse of official power...." See *Milonas v. Williams*, 691 F.2d 931 (10th Cir.1982).

Other courts, however, have not read into *Ingraham* the extent of substantive due process interest as ascribed by *Garcia*. In *Cunningham v. Beavers*, 858 F.2d 269 (5th Cir.1988), the court found that severe spankings, leaving black and blue marks, on two little girls for the offense of snickering, did not implicate substantive due process so as to require procedural due process. Extension of the *Ingraham* due process was seen to be implicitly limiting by the U.S. Court of Appeals, 5th Circuit, where it held that even though "the infliction of punishment may transgress constitutionally protected liberty interest," that "if the state affords the student adequate post-punishment remedies (such as tort and criminal action alternatives such as assault and battery) to deter unjustified or excessive punishment," then the student receives all the process that is required. *Woodard v. Los Fresnos Ind. School Dist.*, 732 F.2d 1243 (5th Cir.1984).

§ 3.24 Immediate Temporary Suspension

The Supreme Court in *Goss v. Lopez* has explained that there "need be no delay between the time [when] 'notice' is given and the time of the hearing." The court found in *Goss* that "[s]uspension is considered not only to be a necessary tool to maintain order but a valuable educational device"; therefore, immediate suspension is sometimes appropriate to protect other students and to preserve the decorum of the school. "Students whose presence imposes a continuing danger to persons or property or [constitute] an ongoing threat of disrupting [the] academic process may be immediately removed from school." *Goss v. Lopez*, supra. In such circumstances, oral notice, a hearing, and immediate suspension pending more formal proceedings later comports with the requirements of due process. *Tate v. Board of Education*, 453 F.2d 975 (8th Cir.1972); *Vail v. Board of Education*, 354 F.Supp. 592 (D.N.H.1973).

The U.S. Court of Appeals for the Seventh Circuit has upheld an initial suspension after which the school principal had discussed the incident with the student, informed the student of the accusations, and provided him with the opportunity to present his version of the facts. *Lamb v. Panhandle Comm. Unit School Dist. No. 2*, 826 F.2d 526 (7th Cir.1987). Whenever there is an ongoing threat of disruption to the academic process no formal notice is required. *Craig v. Selma City School Bd.*, 801 F.Supp. 585 (S.D.Ala.1992).

§ 3.3 PROCEDURAL DUE PROCESS

As noted above, to take away a substantive liberty or property interest requires procedural due process. Courts are wary of too much discretion residing in the hands of school officials, and have acted to limit this power by establishing standards to ensure due regard for fundamental fairness. Intervention by the courts in matters of justice and fairness is justified on the basis of the ancient concept of "natural justice" and the more modern "due process of law" under the United States Constitution. Judicial developments in this area have had an important impact on public education in the United States and will continue to do so.

§ 3.4   NATURAL JUSTICE AND DUE PROCESS

Due process finds its roots in Clause 39 of *Magna Charta* of England, 1215, which expressed that: "No freeman shall be seized, or imprisoned or dispossessed, or outlawed, or in any way destroyed; nor will we condemn him, nor will we commit him to prison, excepting by the legal judgment of his peers, or by the law of the land." This provision, according to Blackstone, "protected every individual of the nation in the free enjoyment of his life, his liberty and his property, unless declared to be forfeited by the judgment of his peers or the law of the land." W. Blackstone, *The Great Charter and Charter of the Forest* (1759).

The Fifth and Fourteenth Amendments of the United States Constitution provide that neither the federal government nor a state shall "deprive any person of life, liberty or property, without due process of law." Originally, these provisions were interpreted to apply to judicial proceedings only, and not to quasi-judicial or administrative proceedings conducted by governmental ministers or by educational agencies. In early precedents, educators in the United States, by virtue of their standing *in loco parentis*, were not required to adhere to any particular standards of fair play when sitting in judgment over actions of students. Only since the landmark case of *Dixon v. Alabama*, supra, has this changed. *Dixon* manifestly established that procedural due process applied to schools and other governmental agencies and deviations from the minimal fairness required therein may void any disciplinary action taken.

§ 3.5 IMPARTIALITY

Impartiality is the essence of fair judicial treatment. A judge must come to the case with an open mind without previous knowledge of the facts or preconceived notions of the outcome. No connection can exist between the judge and one of the parties involved so as to create a conflict of judicial interest.

Bias in the school setting may not always be so readily recognizable. Seldom do students or teachers sit in judgment over their own cases. If they did, obvious bias would be present. Bias may be charged, though, where an administrator or officer sits in review of challenged policies which he formulated, or in review of executive action which he carried out. Further, it may be that school officers may be forced to sit as tribunals at different levels, possibly reviewing their own decisions on appeal.

A fair trial by an impartial tribunal is a basic tenet of due process, *In re Murchison*, 349 U.S. 133 (1955), just as it is with natural justice, and this applies to administrative agencies as well as to the court. *Gibson v. Berryhill*, 411 U.S. 564 (1973).

§ 3.6 FAIRNESS

The right to be heard as a basic principle of fairness has long been accepted as a tenet of Anglo–American law. Although the right to be heard is a spontaneously acceptable idea, it is not settled as to what it entails or where it applies. Does it require a notice for a hearing, if so what should the notice include? Is there a right to an oral hearing? Can the accused confront witnesses and cross-examine? Can the accused demand legal counsel? Can the hearing be conducted by one body and the decision be rendered by another? Is there a right to remain silent? All of these questions define the parameters of fairness in provision of due process. The discussion below elucidates some of the considerations of fairness.

§ 3.7 ELEMENTS OF PROCEDURAL DUE PROCESS

A hearing is useless if the defendant does not know the charges against him and does not have time to prepare a defense. Where a party is completely unaware of the proceedings, fairness cannot be achieved. Consequently, it is rudimentary that notice is required.

§ 3.71 Notice

Fundamental fairness requires that notice give the specific ground or grounds on which the accused is being charged and the nature of the evidence against him. *Due v. Florida Agricultural and Mechanical University*, 233 F.Supp. 396 (N.D.Fla.1963). According to *Dixon*, supra, the landmark case, no rigid procedural guidelines are required, but notice should contain a statement of specific charges and grounds which if proven could lead to the appropriate disciplinary action.

A notice of charges so vague "that men of common intelligence must necessarily guess at its meaning and differ as to its application" violates the first principle of due process. *Dickson v. Sitterson*, 280 F.Supp. 486

(M.D.N.C.1968). Vagueness is primarily objectionable because it tends toward arbitrary and discriminatory enforcement and fails to provide explicit standards for those who apply them. *Grayned v. City of Rockford*, 408 U.S. 104 (1972). Justice Black observed in *Epperson v. Arkansas*, 393 U.S. 97 (1968), that: "It is an established rule that a statute which leaves an ordinary man so doubtful about its meaning that he cannot know when he has violated it denies him the first essential of due process...." Quite obviously then, if a vague charge is brought against a student or the charge is based on a vague rule or statute, elementary fairness cannot be served.

Notice to a student may be either oral or written as long as it can be documented that the charges against him were clearly conveyed sufficient for the student to present his side of the story. Where a school principal contacted a student's father and the father came to school and discussed the charges with the principal, notice was held to be sufficient. *Atcitty by and through Atcitty v. Board of Education of San Juan County School District*, 967 P.2d 1261 (Ct.App.Utah 1998).

Too, notice that failed to provide the student's attorney with statements of two witnesses in an expulsion hearing did not constitute a due process violation where the attorney did not indicate that the information would have affected his conduct of the student's defense. *London v. Directors of DeWitt Public Schools*, 194 F.3d 873 (8th Cir.1999).

§ 3.711   Miranda Warning

A student is not entitled to a *Miranda* warning prior to being questioned by school authorities. *Boynton v. Casey*,

543 F.Supp. 995 (D.Me.1982); see *Baxter v. Palmigiano*, 425 U.S. 308 (1976). "Schools are not obligated to give Miranda warnings." *Brian A. v. Stroudsburg Area School District*, 141 F.Supp.2d 502 (M.D.Pa.2001).

§ 3.72 Opportunity to Be Heard

The courts have generally held that an accused student must have the opportunity to present evidence in his own behalf. *S. (Charles) v. Board of Education*, 97 Cal. Rptr. 422 (App.1971). Due process fairness, however, may be achieved by giving the student an opportunity to give her side of the story via a telephone conference call with the student's parents. *C.B. by and through Breeding v. Driscoll*, 82 F.3d 383 (11th Cir.1996). The courts have more or less implicitly assumed that such hearings will be oral in nature. The Superior Court of New Jersey has held that witnesses adverse to the accused student must be present and be compelled to testify. *Tibbs v. Board of Education*, 276 A.2d 165 (N.J.Super.1971). Of course, this assumes that school boards have subpoena power which is true in New Jersey and a few other states, but is not uniformly the case in all states. If witnesses may be compelled to appear, then almost certainly one could conclude that the accused himself has a right to appear and testify. In 1914 the U.S. Supreme Court said that: "[T]he fundamental requisite of due process of law is the opportunity to be heard." *Grannis v. Ordean*, 234 U.S. 385 (1914). Here, the court was referring to actual physical appearance and oral testimony.

In its most important due process case involving students, the Supreme Court found that an oral hearing was possibly the only way which school officials in some situations could dismiss a student while allowing for fundamental fairness. *Goss v. Lopez*, 419 U.S. 565 (1975). To say that the student could only convey his side of the story in writing would quite obviously fly in the face of procedural due process. The Court in *Goss* did not decide whether constitutional due process is satisfied where the parent serves as a surrogate for the student in a hearing. The U.S. Court of Appeals, Fifth Circuit, however, has held that due process is satisfied if the student's story is told either directly or indirectly through the parent or a reliable person acting for the parent and student. *Meyer v. Austin Ind. School District*, 161 F.3d 271 (5th Cir. 1998).

While due process is a flexible doctrine, it cannot be construed to be so lax as to deny a student an oral hearing, particularly where the facts are in dispute or where they may be subject to more than one interpretation.

§ 3.73 Access to Evidence

Due process requires that every individual have an opportunity to know the evidence against him or her. The general rule requiring evidence be released to the accused is directly in keeping with the due process standard of *Dixon*. *Dixon v. Alabama State Board of Education*, supra. See also *Goss v. Lopez*, supra; *Esteban v. Central Missouri State College*, 415 F.2d 1077 (8th Cir. 1969); *Soglin v. Kauffman*, 418 F.2d 163 (7th Cir.1969); and *Sullivan v. Houston Independent School District*, 475 F.2d 1071 (5th Cir.1973). The Court in *Dixon* put it succinctly: "The student should be given the names of the witnesses against him and an oral or written report on the facts to which each witness testifies." In *Mills*, a

federal court in Washington, D.C., required the school
board to inform parents of their right to examine the
child's school records before a hearing, including tests,
reports, medical, psychological and educational information. *Mills v. Board of Education of District of Columbia*,
348 F.Supp. 866 (D.D.C.1972).

§ 3.74   Cross–Examination

Cross-examination of witnesses is fundamental to the
criminal trial, but, in school administrative hearings, its
status is less definitive. In *Esteban v. Central Missouri
State College*, supra, the United States Eighth Circuit
Court of Appeals set out procedural safeguards for student disciplinary actions but it excluded cross-examination as a general requirement. *Mills*, supra, contrarily,
specifically required that schools provide the parent or
guardian the opportunity to confront and cross-examine
witnesses.

The United States Supreme Court in *Goss* did not go
so far as to require the confrontation and cross-examination of witnesses for short-term suspensions. The Court
said "[w]e stop short of construing the Due Process
Clause to require ... that hearings ... [or] suspensions
must afford the student the opportunity ... to confront
and cross-examine witnesses...." The issue in *Goss* was
short-term suspensions, but the court left open that for
more serious offenses a more formal procedure might be
required. It has always been recognized that the more
important the rights at stake, the more formal the procedural safeguards. *S. (Charles) v. Board of Education*, 97
Cal.Rptr. 422 (App.1971). Therefore, for a more serious
offense, such as expulsion, fundamental fairness may
require cross-examination. Too, the right of cross-exami-

nation may be necessary for an administrative hearing if the testimony of one witness is the critical factor in determining the outcome of the hearing.

A problem with requiring witnesses to be present is that all school boards do not have subpoena power. With no subpoena power, the student and school officials may ask the witnesses to attend but cannot compel them to do so. Yet, where a board claims that because it lacks subpoena power it has not afforded the accused the opportunity to face his accusers and cross-examine them, to be on the safe side the board should be prepared to show that the witnesses would not have appeared without a subpoena. *Stone v. Prosser Consol. School Dist. No. 116*, 971 P.2d 125 (Wash. App. Div. 3 1999).

The U.S. Court of Appeals for the Sixth Circuit held in 1988 that protecting student witnesses in testifying against fellow students was of paramount importance if order and discipline are to be maintained in the school. The court said a student did not have a due process right to learn the identity of student accusers. The court further discussed in some detail the rationale for differing standards of cross-examination between the criminal courts and public schools. The court stated: "The value of cross-examining student witnesses in school disciplinary cases, however, is somewhat muted by the fact that the veracity of a student account of misconduct by another student is initially assessed by . . . the school principal who has, or has available to him, a particularized knowledge of the student's trustworthiness. The school administrator generally knows firsthand (or has access to school records which disclose) the accusing student's disciplinary history, which can serve as a valuable gauge in evaluating the believability of the student's account.

Additionally, the school administrator often knows, or can readily discover, whether the student witness and the accused have had an amicable relationship in the past. Consequently, the process of cross-examining the student witness may often be merely duplicative of the evaluation process undertaken by the investigating school administrator. The value of cross-examining student witnesses in pre-expulsion proceedings must be set against the burden that such practice would place upon school administration. Today's public schools face severe challenges in maintaining the order and discipline necessary for the impartation of knowledge." *Newsome v. Batavia Local School District*, 842 F.2d 920 (6th Cir. 1988); *Davis v. Alaska*, 415 U.S. 308 (1974); *Caston v. Benton Public Schools*, 2002 WL 562638 (E.D.Ark.2002).

Cross-examination of witnesses may be required, especially if one witness is critical. In an Illinois case, the court stated, "In fact, the only accusing witnesses against [the student] who allegedly observed the entire incident were not even present at the hearing. Here, the outcome of the hearing was directly dependent on the credibility of witnesses whose statements were received by the hearing officer; yet, these statements were conflicting. In such an instance, the opportunity for cross-examination is imperative." *Colquitt v. Rich Township High School District No. 227*, 699 N.E.2d 1109 (Ill.App., 1st Dist., 5th Div.1998).

§ 3.75 Hearsay

The courts have generally held that hearsay evidence is admissible in a formal school disciplinary hearing. In the leading case on the subject, a school principal read before the school board statements made by teachers regarding a student's conduct. *Boykins v. Fairfield Board of Education*, 492 F.2d 697 (5th Cir.1974). The board in using this evidence ultimately suspended eight students for a week and expelled eight for their part in a school boycott. The students maintained that the information was hearsay and could not be used as a basis for dismissal. The court disagreed saying: "There is a seductive quality to the argument—advanced here to justify the importation of technical rules of evidence into administrative hearings conducted by laymen—that since a free public education is a thing of great value, comparable to that of welfare sustenance or the curtailed liberty of a parolee, the safeguards applicable to these should apply to it. . . . In this view, we stand but a step away from the application of the *strictissimi juris* due process requirements of criminal trials to high school disciplinary processes. And if to high school, why not to elementary school? It will not do. . . . Basic fairness and integrity of the fact-finding process are the guiding stars. Important as they are, the rights at stake in a school disciplinary hearing may be fairly determined upon the 'hearsay' evidence of school administrators charged with the duty of investigating the incidents. We decline to place upon a board of laymen the duty of observing and applying the common-law rules of evidence." *Boykins*, supra.

Similarly, hearsay has been allowed in hearings where students have committed serious offenses, *Tasby v. Estes*, 643 F.2d 1103 (5th Cir.1981), and has been allowed by implication in cases involving expulsion. *Linwood v. Board of Education*, 463 F.2d 763 (7th Cir.1972) and *Whiteside v. Kay*, 446 F.Supp. 716 (W.D.La.1978).

Goss did not address the hearsay question directly; the only guidance it provided was the general admonishment that "[l]onger suspensions or expulsions for the remainder of the school term, or permanently, may require more formal procedures." Too, the Supreme Court emphasized in *Board of Curators of University of Missouri v. Horowitz*, 435 U.S. 78 (1978), that due process should provide a "meaningful hedge against erroneous action." This language leaves substantial discretion to the school board in determining the extent of formality to be used in a hearing.

The Supreme Court's intent in *Goss* and *Horowitz* has been interpreted by a Wisconsin court as allowing hearsay statements from teachers or staff members in an expulsion hearing before the school board. *Racine Unified School District v. Thompson*, 321 N.W.2d 334 (Wis. App.1982). This appears to represent the prevailing view of the courts.

§ 3.76 Legal Counsel

Presence of legal counsel is not a fundamental element of fairness but it may well be invoked by the courts if the issues are legally complex or the interests of the accused are of great magnitude. Legal counsel was not required by the U.S. Supreme Court in *Goss* for suspensions of less than ten days, but as with cross-examination, the Court implied that where more severe penalties could be invoked against a student, counsel may be required. *Goss v. Lopez*, supra.

Counsel, then, may probably be denied by tribunals adjudicating relatively minor student disciplinary cases, but, where major detriment may result for the accused, counsel may be elevated as an important aspect of fairness. Thus, for serious offenses that may involve a long-term suspension or expulsion, then full hearing rights would include the right to be represented by counsel. *In re Roberts*, 563 S.E.2d 37 (N.C. Ct. App. 2002), *Buncombe County, North Carolina v. Roberts*, 540 U.S. 820 (2003). On balance, however, representation by legal counsel cannot be said to be, at this time, a fundamental or basic element of due process in the school setting.

§ 3.77 Appropriate Tribunal

Whether the tribunal or hearing committee is an appropriate one depends on at least three issues: (a) the make-up of membership, (b) the *ultra vires* (beyond the scope of powers) doctrine, and (c) due process. Courts are not concerned with whether a tribunal has representation of administrators, teachers or students; the only legal concern is that no conflict of interest or bias exists.

An administrative agency cannot delegate away its quasi-judicial or discretionary functions provided statutorily by a state legislature. *Games v. County Board of School Trustees*, 147 N.E.2d 306 (Ill.1958); see also *State ex rel. School District No. 29 v. Cooney*, 59 P.2d 48 (Mont.1936). Likewise, a local school board cannot delegate its discretionary powers to a subordinate. This does not mean that an administrative committee cannot delegate to a subcommittee the responsibility to collect information, facts, and evidence to be presented to the full official committee for consideration and judgment.

It would be *ultra vires* for a statutorily constituted school board to delegate to a subordinate committee or individual the power to render a decision in a matter which statute required the board, alone, to determine. Similarly, it would contravene due process for a subcommittee to render a decision from a hearing it conducted and then have the superior or full committee to reverse the lower decision in the absence of full and complete hearing documentation. Due process requires, unequivocally, that the decision cannot be made by anyone other than the appropriate tribunal.

In general then it may be said that he who hears the case must also decide it. It is a breach of due process for a member of a judicial tribunal to participate in a decision if he has not heard the evidence presented in the case. Rulings by administrative bodies have been frequently quashed because decisions were given affecting individual rights where oral presentations were made before hearing officers other than those who actually rendered the decision. Bias and ignorance alike preclude fair judgment upon the merits of a case.

§ 3.78   Self–Incrimination

In the United States Constitution, the Fifth Amendment protects the individual against self-incrimination in a criminal proceeding. The Fifth Amendment states in part: "... nor shall [*any person*] be compelled in any criminal case to be a witness against himself...."

There is very little case law addressing whether a student in elementary, secondary or post-secondary may invoke the self-incrimination provision of the Fifth Amendment. But where the courts have ruled, they have generally held that this provision of the Fifth Amendment does not apply in educational disciplinary hearings. In *Boynton v. Casey*, 543 F.Supp. 995 (D.Me.1982), the court said that the student did not have a right to prior advice or right to remain silent before questioning by school authorities. The court in *Boynton* said that since this was for determination of whether an expulsion should take place and not "custodial interrogation" the Miranda warning also was not required.

A complicating factor is added where the charge against the student may also be of such a nature as to violate a criminal statute. Frequently, the student wants to assert the privilege of self-incrimination and postpone the disciplinary hearing until the court determines guilt or innocence in the criminal proceedings, since the testimony may be used against the student in the ensuing criminal trial. In *Gabrilowitz v. Newman*, 582 F.2d 100 (1st Cir.1978), the court said, "[T]he hearing procedures do not place appellee between the rock and the whirlpool. He can, if he wishes, stay out of the stream and watch the proceedings from dry land. But, if he does so, he forfeits any opportunity to control the direction of the current. Appellee must decide whether or not to testify at the hearing with the knowledge that, if he does, his statements may be used against him in the criminal case.... Although the choice facing him is difficult, that does not make it unconstitutional."

Other courts have held that there is no constitutional necessity to postpone a disciplinary hearing until after criminal proceedings. These courts rely on the U.S. Supreme Court decision of *Garrity v. New Jersey*, 385 U.S. 493 (1967). In *Garrity*, the court said the state may not fire police officers for invoking their privilege against self-incrimination during a civil or administrative hearing regarding their conduct, nor may the state use the administrative hearing evidence in a later criminal trial. A school or university may proceed with a disciplinary hearing and not violate a student's privilege of self-incrimination.

At this time, the general rule of law appears to preclude student access to the Fifth Amendment privilege against self-incrimination in a school hearing. Due process does not require it and the school administrator is unaffected by its strictures.

§ 3.781   Character Witnesses

A fair hearing entails the opportunity for the student to be heard and present positive statements on his/her behalf. A school board's refusal to allow a student to call witnesses as to her good character, at a suspension hearing, violated her due process rights. *Nichols v. DeStefano*, 84 P.3d 496 (Colo. 2004).

§ 3.79   Double Jeopardy

Under English common law a second trial and a second punishment for the same offense was prohibited whether the accused was acquitted or convicted. *Ex parte Lange*, 85 U.S. 163 (1874). This is the general rule followed by American courts today. *Kepner v. United States*, 195 U.S. 100 (1904), *United States v. Oppenheimer*, 242 U.S. 85 (1916). The U.S. Supreme Court has, though, held that where the same act is an offense against both state and federal statutes, its separate prosecution and punishment by both governments is not double jeopardy.

The double jeopardy prohibition does not prevent public schools from holding a hearing for the same offense for which the criminal courts have already prosecuted a student. The courts view public school disciplinary matters as issues separate and apart from criminal prosecutions and punishments. A federal court in Texas has explained that "state laws defining criminal conduct and authorizing its punishment are intended to indicate public justice" while a public school board or a public university rule mandating suspension or expulsion is intended to protect "the education goals of the institution from such adverse influence as the offender may wield if he is allowed to remain a student. Thus the two sanctions imposed by the state upon plaintiffs have sufficiently different underlying purposes to permit characterization of the first as 'criminal' or 'punitive' and the second as 'civil,' 'remedial' or 'administrative.' " *Paine v. Board of Regents of University of Texas System*, 355 F.Supp. 199 (W.D.Tex.1972). See also *Clements v. Board of Trustees of Sheridan County School Dist. No. 2*, 585 P.2d 197 (Wyo.1978).

The double jeopardy prohibition was held not to apply in an Arkansas case where a student killed a man off school grounds and then claimed double jeopardy when expelled from school for the offense. *Smith v. Little Rock School Dist.*, 582 F.Supp. 159 (E.D.Ark.1984). Similarly, suspension from school was deemed to be proper where a student in New York assaulted and attempted to stab a person during school vacation period. The court found that off-school grounds offenses were within the cognizance of school authorities and that prosecution in criminal courts did not foreclose school action to suspend for the same charges during the period when the criminal charges were pending. *Pollnow v. Glennon*, 594 F.Supp. 220 (S.D.N.Y.1984).

§ 3.8 IN–SCHOOL SUSPENSION

Is procedural due process required for in-school suspension? Temporary isolation used in school "timeout" has been held to be a *de minimis* punishment not interfering with property or liberty interests. *Dickens by Dickens v. Johnson County Board of Education*, 661 F.Supp. 155 (E.D.Tenn.1987). If the student continues the educational process while serving in-school suspension, then no due process is required, but if the student is serving time in isolation with no educational materials, then due process is probably required. *Orange v. County of Grundy*, 950 F.Supp. 1365 (E.D.Tenn.1996).

§ 3.9   IMPACT OF PROCEDURAL DUE PROCESS

With the evolution of procedural due process as a potent force in the quasi-judicial administrative processes, school boards and school officials are required to formulate guidelines which will protect students. Due process balances the child's interest against corresponding and sometimes contrary school interests. At very least, due process requires school officials to provide the child with a hearing which is impartial and free of bias, and, secondly, to guarantee the student that fairness will prevail. Minimal due process requires that the administrator give the student adequate notice of what is proposed, allow the student to make representations on his own behalf, and/or appear at a hearing or inquiry, and to effectively prepare his case and answer allegations presented.

Courts have maintained that "The touchstones in this area are fairness and reasonableness." *Due v. Florida Agricultural and Mechanical University*, 233 F.Supp. 396 (N.D.Fla.1963); see also *Jones v. State Board of Education*, 279 F.Supp. 190 (M.D.Tenn.1968). The precise boundaries of fairness must be kept reasonably flexible to ensure freedom for school districts to operate. The United States Supreme Court has reminded us that:

"Due process is an elusive concept, its exact boundaries are undefinable, and its content varies according to specific factual contexts.... Whether the Constitution requires that a particular right obtain in a specific proceeding depends upon a complexity of factors. The nature of the alleged right involved, the nature of the proceeding, and the possible burden on that proceeding, are all considerations which must be taken into account." *Hannah v. Larche*, 363 U.S. 420 (1960). But, flexibility cannot be an excuse for denial of proper procedure. Minimal fairness in the words of *Dixon* requires that (a) notice should be given containing a statement of the specific charges and grounds, (b) a hearing should be conducted affording the administrator or board with opportunity to hear both sides in considerable detail, (c) the student should be given the names of the witnesses against him and an oral or written report on the facts, (d) the student should be given the opportunity to present his own defense against the charges and to produce either oral testimony or written affidavits in his own behalf, and (e) if the hearing is not before the Board empowered to make the decision, the results and findings of the hearing should be presented in a report open to the student's inspection. *Dixon v. Alabama State Board of Education*, supra.

Beyond these rudiments of "fair play" various judicial precedents add specificity reducing the school administrator's boundaries of discretion. The following guidelines are suggestive of such boundaries.

§ 3.91 Guidelines: Due Process

§ 3.911 Bias

1. The individual conducting the hearing (the judge) must come to the hearing with an open mind without preconceived notions of the ultimate outcome.

2. No connection can exist between the parties involved and the administrator except through his *ex officio* position as an officer of the school. No decision maker should be disqualified simply because of a position he has taken on a matter of public policy.

3. Committee membership should not be permitted to even approach offending the "real likelihood" of bias standards.

§ 3.912 Fairness

1. Every student has a right to be heard when punishment for an offense is severe enough to deprive him of schooling, even for a few days.

2. Notice should be given conveying the specific ground or grounds with which the student is being charged citing rules or regulations which have been broken. Notice must not be vague or ambiguous.

3. Notice should be delivered to the student, in writing, in sufficient time to ensure ample opportunity to prepare a defense to the allegations.

4. The burden of proof should be borne by the school and not the student.

5. The student should be given the opportunity to testify and present evidence and witnesses in his or her own behalf.

6.   The tribunal should make its decision only on the information presented at the hearing.

7.   With the possible exception of evidence which could be harmful to the child or the parent, all evidence should be made available to the accused child, parent, and legal counsel. *In re Gault*, supra.

8.   To confront and cross-examine witnesses is apparently not basic to due process; however, cross-examination may be required for more serious offenses or to maintain fundamental fairness.

9.   To have legal counsel present is not looked upon by the courts as being essential to fairness; however, the rule appears to be that the "right to have legal counsel present is a function of the complexity of the case" and the potential loss to the student.

10.   Due process requires that the administrator with the quasi-judicial responsibility for rendering a judgment must both hear the case and make the decision. Delegation of decision-making authority is *ultra vires*. An administrator or a board, nevertheless, may delegate the collection of evidence to a subordinate so long as the final decision is made by the lawful authority based on the evidence presented.

11.   Students appear to have no right to remain silent to avoid self-incrimination in a school hearing. This is true even where the student claims that evidence given may tend to incriminate him in a later criminal proceeding on the same charge.

12.   Hearsay may be admissible in either suspension or expulsion hearings.

CHAPTER 4

FREEDOM OF SPEECH AND EXPRESSION

§ 4.1 INTRODUCTION

Freedom of speech and expression are guaranteed by the First Amendment of the U.S. Constitution which says in part, "Congress shall make no law ... abridging the freedom of speech ..." Thus, embedded in the Constitution is the basic and essential freedom to express one's self without fear of reprisal by government, federal or state. Yet, this freedom is not unlimited, and within certain bounds government can exercise restraint of speech. Supreme Court Justice Brandeis spoke of the boundaries of speech to which each person is entitled when he said: "Although the rights of free speech and assembly are fundamental, they are not in their nature absolute. Their exercise is subject to restriction if the particular restriction proposed is required in order to protect the State from destruction or from serious injury, political, economic or moral." *Whitney v. California*, 274 U.S. 357 (1927).

Courts assume that school rules and regulations that affect speech are valid unless there is a clear abuse of power and discretion on the part of the school. A rule or regulation may be challenged on several grounds, the most common are that it is (1) *ultra vires*, beyond the board's legal authority, and (2) vague or overly broad, or (3) violative of one of several constitutional prohibitions

111

such as freedom of expression, religion, privacy, due process, or equal protection. It is the last two of these wherein constitutional challenges to school authority are usually couched.

To raise the *vires* issue simply means that the student maintains that the regulation is beyond the legal power vested in the school board by state law. The question becomes how far does the school's authority extend before it encroaches on the parent's and student's personal prerogatives.

Vagueness, overbreadth, and/or a lack of specificity, delegates excessive authority in application of rules. Courts are suspicious of laws that are imprecise and may be arbitrarily interpreted to reach beyond their more restricted intent. These principles which govern all governmental agencies have been incorporated into constitutional law as the rights and freedoms of students have become more clearly defined. Thus, the rule against vagueness and overbreadth may permit arbitrary administration invoking both substantive and procedural due process of law, as well as free speech, under the First and Fourteenth Amendments of the U.S. Constitution.

School rules and regulations will not stand if they deny individual rights or freedoms which are protected by federal or state constitutions. As observed above, this does not mean that rights and freedoms are without limitation. It does mean, however, that school authorities must have a very good reason to deny a student his or her rights and freedoms. If a school rule is to prevail, there must be a rational relationship between the rule and the purpose for which it is designed. In some instances where a fundamental interest such as race is concerned, the courts have held that the school authorities must have a compelling reason to support rules promulgated to control or categorize students.

§ 4.2 BALANCING THE INTERESTS

At one time it was believed that to attend school was a privilege and that virtually any school rule or regulation constraining a student's conduct was valid. Today, the privilege doctrine is no longer valid, and the courts recognize that students do not "shed their constitutional interests when they enter a schoolhouse door." Having constitutional rights does not mean that a student's conduct can go unregulated. All members of society are subject to reasonable restraints, without which a society cannot adequately function. An environment for learning requires that student conduct be regulated. It is obvious that a student cannot be permitted the personal freedom to come and go at will or to ignore reasonable rules such as to be quiet in a library. In order to balance the constitutional rights of pupils against the necessity for order, peace and quiet, the courts have promulgated the "balance of interests" test. The interests of the school are weighed against the student's loss of a particular freedom or right. This balancing test is the heart of the United States Supreme Court's decision in *Tinker v. Des Moines Independent Community School District*, 393 U.S. 503 (1969). *Tinker* established that school rules and regulations should be based on a determination of the school's legitimate interests. If the purpose for a rule or regulation is unclear or non-existent, then there should be no rule. Teachers and administrators must examine their policies to determine their legitimacy.

§ 4.3   FORECAST OF DISRUPTION

In *Tinker*, the Supreme Court explained the balance of interests in terms of potential for disruption of the school. If a student's exercise of free speech or expression justifies a "reasonable forecast of substantial disruption," then it can be curtailed.

In *Tinker*, certain students and their parents decided to publicize their objections to hostilities in Vietnam and to indicate their support for a truce by wearing black armbands to school. School principals in Des Moines became aware of the plan to wear armbands and two days before the protest passed a rule prohibiting students from wearing an armband to school. Students who refused to remove their armbands would be suspended from school. Students did wear armbands and were subsequently suspended.

After holding that armbands were a manifestation of free speech falling under the ambit of the First Amendment, the Court stated: "School officials do not possess absolute authority over their students. Students are 'persons' under our Constitution. They are possessed of fundamental rights which the State must respect, just as they themselves must respect their obligations to the State. In our system, students may not be regarded as closed-circuit recipients of only that which the State chooses to communicate. They may not be confined to the expression of those sentiments that are officially approved. In the absence of a specific showing of constitutionally valid reasons to regulate their speech, students are entitled to freedom of expression of their views."

With this as the *constitutional* basis of students' rights, the Court then sought to determine if the wearing of a black cloth around the arm could in fact interrupt school activities or intrude on the lives of other students. The Court, in holding for the students, found that the record demonstrated no facts which could have been reasonably construed by school officials as evidencing a "forecast of substantial disruption" or of constituting "material interference" with school activities. The Supreme Court's words were carefully chosen. For a student activity to be proscribed, the school officials must be able to reasonably forecast disruption, and the disruption must be more than minimal, it must be substantial. Too, the disruption must be physical and be deleterious to the intellectual environment of the school program.

Reasonableness of forecast must be for more than mere vague apprehension of disruption, or an "undifferentiated fear or apprehension." There must be evidence to support the expectation of substantial disruption.

In a case where a student showed his teacher a poem he had written which was filled with imagery of violent death and suicide, including shooting fellow students, the principal suspended the student based on family background, past discipline problems, suicidal ideations and reports that he had stalked a girlfriend. The Court upheld the suspension and said, "Forecasting disruption is unmistakably difficult ... *Tinker* does not require certainty that disruption will occur, 'but rather the existence of facts which might reasonably lead school officials to forecast substantial disruption.'" The totality of all relevant facts must be examined; the Court ruled the emergency expulsion did not violate the student's First Amendment rights. *LaVine v. Blaine School District*, 257 F.3d 981 (9th Cir.2001).

§ 4.31   Habits and Manners of Civility

In considering *Tinker*, one may ask what controls, if any, can reasonably be placed on students' conduct. In *Bethel School District No. 403 v. Fraser*, 478 U.S. 675 (1986), the Supreme Court added another constitutional test that supplements *Tinker* and significantly broadens the prerogatives of teachers and school administrators in regulation of student speech. For want of more comprehensive terminology, this standard may be loosely called the "manners and civility" test. In *Bethel*, a student made a lewd speech of sexual innuendos at a student assembly and the school responded by suspending him. The Court drew a line between the freedom of speech or expression to deliver a "political message" and speech or expression that is "lewd and obscene" delivered to an immature audience of school students. The Court asserted that "The determination of what manner of speech in the classroom or in the school is inappropriate properly rests with the school board." *Bethel School District No. 403 v. Fraser*, 478 U.S. 675 (1986). The justices disagreed as to whether there was "disruption" involved. The bottom line was, however, that the Court in *Bethel* did not revert to the *Tinker* "disruption test" and was more concerned with defining the difference between a "political message" and a sexually provocative speech having no particular political message at all. The Court said: "Surely it is a highly appropriate function of public school education to prohibit the use of vulgar and offensive terms in public discourse. Indeed, the 'fundamental values necessary to the maintenance of a democratic political system' disfavor the use of terms of debate highly offensive or threatening to others.... The inculcation of these values is truly the 'work of the schools'

..." The Court further observed that: "The schools, as instruments of the state, may determine that the essential lesson of civil, mature conduct cannot be conveyed in a school that tolerates lewd, indecent, or offensive speech and conduct...." With this case as a new guide, the strictures of *Tinker* were substantially clarified. Nondisruptive political speech is constitutionally protected; lewd, vulgar speech conveying no political message cannot find protection under the U.S. Constitution.

In 1988, the Supreme Court further explained the rights of student expression in *Hazelwood Sch. Dist. v. Kuhlmeier*, 484 U.S. 260 (1988), (discussed later in Chapter 6, Student Publications–Forum Analysis). The principal deleted two articles from the school newspaper, one described three students' experience with pregnancy and the other discussed the impact of divorce. The Court ruled that educators do not offend student expression by exercising editorial control over school-sponsored activities as long as there is a reasonably related pedagogical concern. In other words, should a school have educational concerns about activities involving student expression it need not lend its name or resources to that activity. Thus, freedom of speech and expression in school-controlled student newspapers is not solely determined by the requirements of the "material and substantial disruption" language of *Tinker*.

In *Hazelwood*, the Supreme Court developed what it calls a "forum analysis" by which the courts now view freedom of speech in public schools. According to this analysis, freedom of speech must be classified into the type of forum in which it is delivered. There are three types of public forums: 1) the traditional public forum, open public areas, parks, and sidewalks. In these venues a speech is extensively protected and can only be withdrawn or restrained with a narrowly drawn and compelling government interest; 2) the second type is the "limited public forum" where the state opens its property for public use. A public school is not generally considered to be a "limited public forum" unless school officials have granted use of the school to outsiders for use beyond the curricular interests of the school; and 3) the third forum is the "closed forum," where the public school is not open for general public use by various interest groups not related to school curricular purposes. The forum analysis is further elaborated in Chapter 6 of this book where the *Tinker* analysis is contrasted with the forum analysis. Suffice it to say, the U.S. Supreme Court has considerably modified the free speech rules since *Tinker*. The Court in *Hazelwood* said that the high school paper published by the students did not qualify as a "public forum"; therefore, school officials could impose reasonable restrictions on student speech in the school paper. The Court emphasized that the First Amendment rights of students in public schools are not coextensive with the rights of adults and must be applied in the special circumstances of the school environment. "A school need not tolerate student speech that is inconsistent with its basic educational mission . . . "

Thus, because of *Tinker, Bethel*, and *Hazelwood*, freedom of expression in school can be described as follows: "First, 'vulgar' or plainly offensive speech ([*Bethel*]-type speech) may be prohibited without showing . . . disruption or substantial interference with the schoolwork. Second, school-sponsored speech (*Hazelwood*-type speech) may be restricted when the limitation is reasonably related to legitimate educational concerns. Third, speech that is neither vulgar nor school-sponsored (*Tink-*

er-type) may only be prohibited if it causes a substantial and material disruption of the school's operation or a reasonable forecast of disruption." *Pyle v. South Hadley School Committee*, 861 F.Supp. 157 (D.Mass.1994).

In recent cases, the courts have used *Tinker, Bethel*, and *Hazelwood* in determining the appropriateness of student expression. In one such case, a student wore a "Marilyn Manson" T-shirt to school and the school considered the garment to be offensive and violative of the "Dress and Grooming" policy. The Court stated, "We apply the *Tinker–Bethel–Hazelwood* trilogy to the facts of this case." After reviewing the three cases, the court ruled that "the standard for reviewing the suppression of vulgar, plainly offensive speech is governed by *Bethel*." The school said that the Marilyn Manson T-shirt was "offensive because the band promotes destructive conduct and demoralizing values contrary to the educational mission of the school." The Court found that the school had acted in a reasonable manner in prohibiting the wearing of the T-shirt. *Boroff v. Van Wert City Board of Education*, 220 F.3d 465 (6th Cir.2000).

In another illustrative case, teachers went on strike and the school board employed replacement teachers. Children of the striking teachers arrived at school with buttons and stickers stating, "I'm not listening, scab" and "Do scabs bleed?" and were threatened with discipline. The court used *Hazelwood* to interpret *Bethel* and *Tinker* and ruled that in the absence of disruption, wearing of the emblems was constitutionally protected because the students' actions were related to a political message which was of public concern and therefore fell under the protection of *Tinker*. *Chandler v. McMinnville School District*, 978 F.2d 524 (9th Cir.1992). Another federal court has concluded that the free speech rights of an elementary school child may not be coextensive with the rights of high school students. In this case, an elementary school child objected to the grades assigned to her, and in reaction wore a T-shirt to school proclaiming that the school was racially biased. The wording on the shirt said "unfair grades," "racism," and "I hate Lost Creek" (the school). The school principal imposed disciplinary action. The court ruled for the school, observing that there was no clear and established free speech right of a grade school child to wear an expressive T-shirt. *Baxter v. Vigo County School Corp.*, 26 F.3d 728 (7th Cir.1994).

Some expressions of free speech are clearly political statements of public concern and as such are constitutionally protected. The display of armbands in *Tinker* to protest the war in Vietnam was obviously political. As with Vietnam, the Iraq oil war, justified by the fear of non-existent weapons of mass destruction (WMDs) by the Bush administration has been the source of considerable political ire. As with Vietnam armbands in *Tinker,* the Iraq war issue spilled over to students in the public schools. In one rather high profile case involving a student's T-shirt, both the *Tinker* "material and substantial disruption" test and the *Bethel* "manners and civility" or "plainly offensive or inappropriate" test were applied by a federal circuit court. In this case, a Vermont high school student wore a T-shirt to school that read "George W. Bush, Chicken–Hawk–In–Chief." It showed Bush's face superimposed on a chicken surrounded by pictures of oil rigs, dollar symbols, a razor blade, cocaine and a martini glass. A pro-Bush parent complained to a school staff member who invoked a school rule banning images of drugs and alcohol, and required the student to reverse the T-shirt or tape over the images. The student refused and left school with his father, but returned wearing the T-shirt two days later. He had taped over the word "cocaine" with the word "censored." The school suspended the student and he sued in federal court. The U.S. Circuit Court held that the school had violated the student's right of free expression, applying both the *Tinker* and *Bethel* tests. With regard to *Tinker*, the court said that the T-shirt could not be suppressed. It was not disruptive, nor could the T-shirt be the source of a forecast of material and substantial disruption. With regard to the *Bethel* test, the court said that the T-shirt was not "plainly offensive or inappropriate." The court compelled the school district to permit the student to wear the T-shirt and expunge the suspension from the student's record. *Guiles v. Marineau*, 461 F.3d 320 (2d Cir. 2006). The T-shirt clearly conveyed a personal expression of political belief.

This is quite different from a situation where a student chooses to wear a certain kind of clothing or hair style that is simply a matter of personal expression but is not intended "to convey a particularized message" of public concern. *Land v. Los Angeles Unified School District*, 2007 WL 1413227 (Cal. App. 2007).

The First Amendment does not apply if there is no "particularized speech" being conveyed by the student's speech or dress. A vague, generalized desire to express one's individuality does not rise to the level of free speech protection. In *Blau v. Fort Thomas Public School*, 401 F.3d 381 (6th Cir. 2005), a federal circuit court held that a student's personalized choice of clothing "does not possess the communicative elements necessary to be considered speech-like conduct."

Where students express their free speech rights in such a way as to infringe on another student's rights in a fundamental way, school officials may control and limit the speech. In a school where there developed conflict over sexual orientation, the school permitted a Gay–Straight Alliance group to hold a "Day of Silence" to teach tolerance. In response, a group of students held a "Straight–Pride Day" and wore T-shirts with anti-gay slogans, whereupon fights erupted and an anti-gay student was ordered to remove his T-shirt that stated in large print "I will not accept what God has condemned." A student sued claiming a denial of free speech. The federal circuit court in California chose to follow *Tinker* and noted that the school officials could "reasonably forecast substantial and material interference with the school activities" if action was not taken. Moreover, the court held that school administrators "need not tolerate verbal assaults that may destroy the self-esteem of our most vulnerable teenagers and interfere with their educational development." In following the *Bethel v. Frazer* logic, the court went on to observe that schools had a responsibility to require that students learn civic responsibility and tolerance as a part of the basic educational mission and that such did not permit hateful speech that is injurious to others. *Harper v. Poway Unified School District*, 445 F.3d 1166 (9th Cir. 2006). See: 549 U.S. 1262 (2007) (dismissal of appeal for mootness).

Federal courts following *Bethel v. Frazer* have become rather less prone to expand students' speech rights. The corollary is, of course, that the courts of recent vintage are decidedly more disposed to broaden the discretion of school administrators in exercising control over student behavior. For example, in a case where students were prevented from wearing T-shirts to school that depicted a misshapen boy in a school-sponsored T-shirt contest, the school prohibited the T-shirt as mocking disabled people. The students who designed the offensive T-shirt sued, and the court held for the school, reasoning, first, that the T-shirt did not contain a statement that conveyed any particularized message that was protectable under the First Amendment. The picture and words on the shirt did not express an idea or opinion. Second, interestingly, the court found that a nine-day suspension of an offending student was miniscule and not harmful to the student when the entire length of the school year is considered [see *Goss v. Lopez*, 419 U.S. 565 (1975)]. Third, eighth-grade students have no right to protest at school in a way that would be disruptive and must abide by school rules that prescribe more conventional ways to complain about school activities or policies. Finally, the court blanketed the issue by concluding that the public schools have an interest in reasonable self-management without judicial interference. *Brandt v. Board of Education of City of Chicago*, 480 F.3d 460 (7th Cir. 2007).

That which is "offensive," "inappropriate" or "objectionable" is to some degree in the "eye of the beholder." In this regard, the court becomes the "beholder." A good example is a 2007 case in which students protested a school uniform policy with buttons that said "no school uniforms" with a red slash overlaid by a photograph of hundreds of boys in uniform. The picture of the boys was actually that of Hitler Youth, but no swastikas or symbols were visible. The school banned the buttons as "objectionable" and "offensive." At trial, a federal district court ruled for the students applying the *Tinker* test, concluding that censorship of the buttons violated the students' rights of speech and expression. Evidence indicated that the buttons did not cause disruption nor could the school board show that wearing of the buttons created a fear or forecast of material and substantial disruption. *DePinto v. Bayonne Board of Education*, 514 F. Supp. 2d 633 (D.N.J. 2007).

§ 4.311   Drugs in School Jurisprudence

The Supreme Court is particularly sensitive to the problem of drugs in schools. With an acute awareness of rampant drug use in society, the Supreme Court has notably set forth what some commentators call a kind of "drugs in school jurisprudence." In three important cases, *Vernonia, Earls,* and *Morse*, the Supreme Court has indicated that it will give substantial constitutional leeway to teachers and administrators in dealing with drugs in schools. Whether the issue pertains to searches for drugs as in *Vernonia School District 47J v. Acton*, 515 U.S. 646 (1995) and *Board of Education of Independent School District No. 92* v. *Earls,* 536 U.S. 822 (2002), or to student speech suggesting the condoning of drugs, the Court extends broad control discretion to the school. In the 2007 "Bong Hits 4 Jesus" case, *Morse v. Frederick*, 127 S.Ct. 2618 (2007), the Supreme Court summarized the law in two basic principles that it had earlier laid down in *Bethel*. The Court said, "First, *Bethel v. Frazer's* holding demonstrates that 'the constitutional rights of students in public school are not automatically coextensive with the rights of adults in other settings.' " "Second, *Bethel v. Frazer* established that the mode of analysis set forth in *Tinker* is not absolute." Thus, a showing by the school of a "reasonable forecast of material and substantial disruption" (*Tinker*) is not required if the student's speech is lewd, indecent or offensive and contrary to the "habits and manners of civility."

In *Morse v. Frederick*, a student unfurled a large banner at a school event bearing the phrase: "Bong Hits 4 Jesus." An offending student who had refused to comply with the principal's order to remove the banner was suspended from school for ten days. The principal had interpreted the meaning of the banner to suggest or advocate the smoking of marijuana or use of other illegal drugs. In the alternative, the principal interpreted the meaning to promote the idea that drug use is a good thing. The Court agreed with the principal. Citing *Bethel School District No. 403 v. Fraser*, 478 U.S. 675 (1986), *Hazelwood School District v. Kuhlmeier*, 484 U.S. 260 (1988), *Vernonia School District 47J v. Acton*, 515 U.S. 646 (1995) and *Board of Education of Independent School District No. 92* v. *Earls,* 536 U.S. 822 (2002), the Court observed that to condone such an exercise of speech by the student could be construed as bearing the agreement or the *imprimatur* of the school itself. The Court concluded that "student speech celebrating illegal drug use at a school" was an offense that did not require the forecast of material and substantial disruption. The "danger here is far more serious and palpable" because of the present harm to students from illegal drug use.

§ 4.312   True Threats of Violence

Teachers and school administrators must be constantly on guard to recognize and prevent harm to students. The fact that student speech is protected complicates the problem of discerning an utterance of harmless speech from dangerous menace and warning of actual impending peril. Columbine, Paducah, Virginia Tech and other tragedies are constant reminders. An utterance may with some certainty portend injury, or an utterance, itself, may inflict outrage or harm. Such speech by students can be restrained and prevented by actions of teachers and school administrators, without offending constitutional rights of the offending student. True threats of violence, racial epithets, or "fighting words" are not protected speech. In such instances, prior restraint preventing the speech is within the prerogative of a teacher or school administrator. Appropriate conduct of the school and preservation of the school's learning environment is good legal cause to prevent "fighting words" and racial epithets.

True threats are considered to be of a different genus of offense from "fighting words" and racial epithets. Fighting words and epithets elicit a response that may disrupt the school. True threats, on the other hand, may not elicit a response, but is a sword of Damocles with some certainty that it will fall. A "true threat" is not protected speech. Yet, how does the teacher or administrator determine if there is a "true threat" or is merely loose talk? A federal court in the case of *Doe v. Pulaski County School District*, 306 F.3d 616 (8th Cir. 2002), has set forth criteria by which a threat may be evaluated: "(1) the reaction of those who heard the alleged threat; (2) whether the threat was conditional; (3) whether the person who made the alleged threat communicated it directly to the object of the threat; (4) whether the speaker had a history of making threats against the person purportedly threatened; and (5) whether the recipient had reason to believe that the speaker had a propensity to engage in violence. For example, courts have held a true threat to have occurred when a student told a high school guidance counselor, "If you don't give me this schedule change I'm going to shoot you," *Lovell v. Poway Unified School District*, 90 F.3d 367 (9th Cir.

1996) and when a student wrote a poem about death, suicide, and shooting 28 people to cleanse his soul. *La-Vine v. Blaine School District*, 257 F.3d 981 (9th Cir. 2001). A true threat may emanate external to school grounds. In a case where a notepad, with pictures of large scale war armaments and weapons was found at home by the brother of a student who then brought it to school, and the student was later searched revealing a box cutter, notebooks referring to death, drugs, sex, and gangs, and a fake ID, the court ruled that such constituted a "true threat" justifying expulsion and subsequent assignment to an alternative school. *Porter v. Ascension Parish School Board*, 393 F.3d 608 (5th Cir. 2004).

Another example of a true threat was in the instances of a high school student who wrote a passage in her notebook under the heading of "Dream" where she expressed loathing of her math teacher "with every bone in my body." The "dream" culminating with her shooting him and then her seeing a "bullet rushing at me." The school suspended her and she sued. The court held for the school indicating a strong concern about the increase of school violence and the need for school officials to have the discretion to deal with incidents that may result in grave consequences. *Boim v. Fulton County School District*, 494 F.3d 978 (11th Cir. 2007). Review of "threat of violence" cases usually utilize the judicial criteria from *Bethel, Morse,* or *Hazelwood*; however, the courts appear to most frequently rely on the *Tinker* "disruption" standard.

§ 4.32 Wearing Insignia and Gang Attire

The foregoing precedents establish the guidelines that schools must follow in addressing good conduct in the schools today. Keeping order in schools has never been easy, but with the increase in drugs, weapons, and gangs, maintenance of a proper educational environment has become increasingly difficult. One of the most persistent areas of concern that touches on free expression is the regulation of gang symbols and dress. Because such symbols have an intimidating effect on non-gang members, schools have developed student dress codes that attempt to temper their use. One district, the San Jacinto Unified School District School Board, adopted a dress code which prohibited clothing identifying any professional sport team or college. When the rule was challenged, the court found the policy violated the free speech rights of elementary, but not of high school students. Evidence indicated that the presence of gangs in the high school resulted in intimidation which could lead to disruption of school activities. *Jeglin II v. San Jacinto Unified Sch. Dist.*, 827 F.Supp. 1459 (C.D.Cal.1993).

School policies, however, must be specific enough not to permit room for arbitrary or capricious interpretation. A school district rule prohibiting wearing of "gang symbols" by students without defining "gang symbols" has been held to be invalid and void because of vagueness. *Stephenson v. Davenport Community School District*, 110 F.3d 1303 (8th Cir.1997). Yet, more carefully defined rules prohibiting certain kinds of dress are reasonable exercise of school authority; thus, a school dress policy that was aimed at discouraging gang activity has been upheld as constitutionally permissible. *Long v. Board of Education of Jefferson County, Kentucky*, 121 F.Supp.2d 621 (W.D.Ky.2000).

§ 4.4 SIT–INS/PROTESTS

The precedent set out by the U.S. Supreme Court in *Tinker* has been followed in many federal court decisions that remain as guideposts for school administrators. For example, prohibition of student sit-ins and non-attendance at classes has been upheld by the courts because they were obviously disruptive of the schools. Where a group of students assembled on school grounds outside the principal's office to protest an earlier suspension of eight students, refused to return to class, and 35 were arrested for unlawful trespassing, the court noted that students have constitutional rights as enunciated by *Tinker*, but such rights do not extend to disruption of school. According to the court, the principal "... had the right and duty to take reasonable measures to restore order." The *Tinker* standard of material and substantial disruption was obvious in this circumstance. *Pleasants v. Commonwealth*, 203 S.E.2d 114 (Va.1974).

§ 4.5 FLAGS

School prohibitions of the Confederate flag have been upheld where racial tension was fueled by use of the flag. *Smith v. St. Tammany Parish School Board*, 448 F.2d 414 (5th Cir.1971) and *Melton v. Young*, 465 F.2d 1332 (6th Cir.1972). Yet, in a northern state where no *de jure* segregation had previously existed, the courts have declined to force school districts to remove the Confederate flag as a symbol of the school. *Banks v. Muncie Community Schools*, 433 F.2d 292 (7th Cir.1970).

In a decision that followed the *Tinker* rationale for forecasting disruption, a student was suspended for three days for drawing a Confederate flag during class. The school official reasoned that the act violated a school-based harassment policy against racial harassment or intimidation of another student by name calling, "using racial or derogatory slurs, wearing or possessing items depicting or implying racial hatred or prejudice." Examples of prohibited items included clothing, and various materials, including Confederate flags. The court ruled for the school board finding that student violated the policy, and that the policy was warranted because of a history of racial tension at the school. Moreover, the court found that in balancing the interests involved, the interest of the school in avoiding racial disputes outweighed the students' rights of free speech. *West v. Derby Unified School District No. 260*, 206 F.3d 1358 (10th Cir.2000).

The Confederate flag symbol worn on clothing has been a source of contention in some school districts, most obviously in the South. In a South Carolina case where a student refused to refrain from wearing a jacket with a Confederate flag depicted on the back, the student was suspended for three days. The family and the boy filed suit in federal court claiming denial of the boy's First Amendment right to free expression. The Federal district court held for the school relying on *Tinker*. Evidence was submitted to the court showing that Confederate flags on clothing had precipitated or escalated five earlier incidents of school disruption; therefore, there was reasonable basis for the school to believe that the wearing of the jacket could cause disruption of the school. *Phillips v. Anderson County School District Five*, 987 F.Supp. 488 (D.S.C.1997). Thus, the wearing and exhibition of items, such as the confederate flag, at school by students may be prohibited if such is likely to cause disruption, per the *Tinker* material and substantial disruption test.

§ 4.6 PERSONAL APPEARANCE

Under the general principle that school authorities may make reasonable rules and regulations controlling student conduct, student dress and personal appearance may be regulated. It has been said that it is in the interest of the school to divert the students' attention from the hemline to the blackboard, or from beards to books. Whether or not a particular mode of dress or appearance detracts from the learning environment is influenced by the standards of the particular community. That which is not acceptable in a rural Midwestern town may be quite normal in a major eastern metropolis. If dress or personal appearance is so different and noticeable that it takes away from the ongoing educational program, school authorities have a valid interest in intervening.

Some early courts held that it is a proper function of the school to require students to wear uniforms to school, and to prohibit the wearing of cosmetics, certain types of hosiery, low-necked dresses, or any style of clothing which may tend, according to community norms, to be immodest. *Pugsley v. Sellmeyer*, 250 S.W. 538 (Ark.1923).

§ 4.61 Uniforms

In recent years, policies requiring students to wear uniforms have been justified as a way to reduce violence in the public schools. The courts recently have upheld such policies even if they have no opt-out provision. In New York where a parent objected to such a policy alleging several constitutional violations, even in view of the fact that the policy allowed students to opt-out, the court ruled against the parent and the student, noting that such an intrusion on a student's rights is not unreasonable in view of the school's interests, particularly where there existed an opt-out provision. *Lipsman v. New York City Board of Education*, 1999 WL 498230 (S.D.N.Y.1999). Similarly, an Arizona court upheld a dress code requiring students to wear white shirts and navy blue pants, shorts or skirts. The reasons for the mandatory dress code were clearly set forth by the schools, all of which had to do with fostering a more effective school learning climate. Students and parents sued challenging the code as violating the students' First Amendment rights even though the policy stated that a child not wishing to follow the dress policy could transfer to another school. The appeals court in Arizona found for the school district holding that the dress code was not intended to restrict speech but rather to further the interests of education in the school and, as such, was a "content-neutral" policy that promoted the goals of the school. *Phoenix Elementary School District No. 1 v. Green*, 943 P.2d 836 (Ariz.App. Div. 2 1997).

The Fifth Circuit, in upholding a mandatory uniform policy, held "that the uniform policy, even assuming that it regulated expressive conduct to constitutional protection, did not violate [the] student's First Amendment free speech rights." The policy furthers the district's important and substantial interest in improving the educational process. *Littlefield v. Forney Independent School District*, 268 F.3d 275 (5th Cir.2001). Also see *Canady v. Bossier Parish School Board*, 240 F.3d 437 (5th Cir. 2001).

A high school instituted a dress code that required students to dress in solid black, solid white, or a combination of black and white clothing. The court upheld the dress code, used *Hazelwood* rationale, finding that the dress code fostered a legitimate pedagogical concern. See *Vines v. Board of Education of Zion School District No. 6*, 2002 WL 58815 (N.D.Ill.2002) and *Lowry v. Watson Chapel School District*, 540 F.3d 752 (8th Cir. 2008).

Some dress codes have, however, been stricken by the courts when it has been shown that the rules were too broad, vague, ambiguous, or did not relate to legitimate educational purpose. Thus, the prevailing view of the court is that standard school uniforms can be required if the school documents and supports the requirement with reasonable and "content neutral" educational rationale that advances the educational interests of the school.

§ 4.62 Other Manifestations of Expression

Of late, the piercing of their ears, noses, tongues, and other parts of their anatomy has become quite popular. Whether this is any particular manifestation of speech or expression is open to debate and whether schools permit or deny these practices depends on the ability of the school to show that the decorum of the school is in some way harmed. School policies prohibiting earrings at the elementary school level may be more successful than in middle or high schools because such practices are relatively foreign to small children, and because it is uncommon, may tend to disrupt the school. Such was found to be the situation in two cases, one in Louisiana and one in Indiana. In the Louisiana case a second-grade child wore an earring to school in violation of grade school policy. The court upheld the rule saying that the wearing of an earring by a male student in elementary school could possibly cause disruption. *Jones v. W.T. Henning Ele-*

mentary School, 721 So.2d 530 (La.App. 3d Cir.1998). In a similar case in Indiana, where a fourth-grade student wore a gold stud earring to school, the student refused to dispose of the earring, and after a hearing, a five-day suspension was imposed. The court accepted the schools justification for denying male students the wearing of earrings which was the policy to discourage rebellious-ness. Accordingly, the school policy prohibiting males wearing earrings served a valid educational purpose of instilling discipline and creating a positive educational environment. *Hines v. Caston School Corp.*, 651 N.E.2d 330 (Ind.App.1995).

Tattoos have become inordinately popular among students. Tattoos may be used by students to innocently decorate themselves, but sometimes tattoos have more ominous connotations as indications of gang associations, a kind of tribal display of signals, signs and colors. This issue was discussed at length by U.S. Court of Appeals, Eighth Circuit, where a girl was required by the school to have a tattoo removed, leaving a scar, and the girl sued the school. The court found that the school's policy prohibiting signs and insignia of gangs was unconstitu-tionally vague leaving too much discretion in the hands of school administrators as how to define gang symbols and insignia. From this decision, one can conclude that school policy can prohibit tattoos if they manifest an identity of a gang or organization, the propagation of which could result in material and substantial disruption to the conduct and decorum of the school. *Stephenson v. Davenport Community School Dist.*, 110 F.3d 1303 (8th Cir.1997). See *Bar-Navon v. Brevard County School Board*, 290 Fed. Appx. 273 (11th Cir.2008).

§ 4.63 Hair Codes

The number of hair cases has declined in recent years, but this decline only occurred after several years when the courts were deluged with student long hair questions. Historically, the style of hair has been a contentious issue between schoolmasters and students. Students with generally more radical behavior have tended to deviate from what the teachers thought was acceptable in hair styles. Even today the law is not well settled, in fact, the federal courts of appeals are split on the issue.

Where the students have prevailed, the federal courts have elevated personal appearance to a fundamental interest, and have placed the burden on school boards to show why the school's interest is of such magnitude as to restrain this basic freedom. Several United States constitutional provisions have been used in these cases, the First Amendment's guarantee of free expression, the Fourth Amendment's guarantee of the right to privacy, and the Fourteenth Amendment's guarantee of due process and equal protection. Each has been used to successfully strike down various hair codes. In jurisdictions where personal appearance is elevated to a fundamental interest, school systems must present evidence to show that long hair creates "substantial and material disruption" in the school, or causes health or safety hazards, or, in some other way impinges on the educational program and other students' freedoms. Such evidence is usually very difficult to obtain, and in these jurisdictions the students usually prevail.

In the federal circuits where personal appearance has not been held to be a fundamental interest, the school systems need only show that hair code is rationally related to a legitimate educational purpose. For example, in the Fifth Circuit, school grooming codes are presumed to be *prima facie* constitutional. The burden is placed on the student to state a cause of action designed to show that the code is discriminatory and is arbitrarily or capriciously enforced. In a recent case where the school had established a dress code which prohibited having long hair beyond the bottom of the collar, the rationale for the policy was ". . . [to] teach grooming and hygiene, instill discipline, prevent disruptions, avoid safety hazards and teach authority," the court in upholding the policy pointed out that judicial deference was the best policy in trivial matters of this sort. *Colorado Independent School District v. Barber*, 864 S.W.2d 806 (Tex.App. 1993).

More recently, the courts appear to lend less relevance to student claims of constitutional interests as manifested in hair length or other aspects of personal appearance. There appears to be a tendency for the courts to ask, "What does hair length have to do with speech or expression as a protected constitutional right?" In this regard, a Texas court held that a school's grooming policy did not deprive students of equal educational opportunity or impose improper barriers on their access to an education. Moreover, the haircut policy was not discriminatory on the basis of sex. *Board of Trustees of Bastrop Ind. School Dist. v. Toungate*, 958 S.W.2d 365 (Tex.1997).

Courts in recent years have given yet less attention to hair styles as manifestations of speech or expression and are likely to hold for the school board on a motion to dismiss the plaintiff student's claim. As an example, a school board in a Louisiana parish had a dress code rule that required students to wear uniforms and prohibited any student hair style that was detrimental to student performance and school activity. The rule stated that students must "wear their hair in a standard, acceptable style." The rule permitted African–American female students to wear braids, but prohibited African–American male students from wearing their hair in braids, spiked, or in a style distracting to other students. An African–American male sued claiming denial of his equal protection, free exercise of religion and free speech rights, and further claimed gender discrimination. The court held against the student on each of his claims except gender discrimination. Later, the school board revised its school code to be consistent for males and females. With this change in school policy and on reconsideration, the court also denied the African American male's claim of gender discrimination. *Fenceroy v. Morehouse Parish School Board*, 2006 WL 39255 (W.D.La. 2006). The court cited as precedent the older federal fifth circuit case, *Karr v. Schmidt,* 460 F.2d 609 (5th Cir. 1972), that ruled "there is no constitutional right to wear one's hair in a public high school in the length and style that suits the wearer."

On the other hand, where the length of hair holds implications for one's heritage, religion, race or nationality, then the courts may view the situation differently. Where Native American students filed suit in federal court complaining that a school hair length policy for male students violated their tribal customs and identity and denied them their freedom of religion, the federal court held for the students. The school did not show how the wearing of long hair by Native American students could lead to material and substantial disruption of the school. *Alabama and Coushatta Tribes of Texas v. Trustees of Big Sandy Ind. Sch. Dist.*, 817 F.Supp. 1319 (E.D.Tex.1993).

There is no U.S. Supreme Court precedent generally applicable to the fifty states on haircuts, and it is impossible to reconcile the conflicting decisions of the lower federal courts. The best advice for teachers and school boards is to ascertain the rule of law governing hair for their own jurisdictions and follow the precedents of those courts specifically. In each instance the school district should be prepared to show how a particular hair style or cut is detrimental to the processes and proper workings of the school and how the educational function is diminished by such.

§ 4.7   STUDENT PREGNANCY

In earlier years when unmarried students became pregnant the school rid itself of the issue by simply suspending or even expelling the girl. Usually, pregnancy for an unmarried student meant that her formal education was at an end. This was the unfortunate situation until the late 1960s and early 1970s, at which time more enlightened educators began to wonder about the consequences of such exclusions. At the same time, the courts became more sensitive of legal rights to attend school and the plight of pregnant girls. Courts in a series of cases concluded that such exclusions violated the Equal Protection Clause of the Fourteenth Amendment. *Perry v. Grenada Municipal Separate School District*, 300 F.Supp. 748 (N.D.Miss.1969).

This issue was further statutorily addressed when the U.S. Congress passed Title IX of the Education Amendments of 1972. Title IX prohibits discrimination based on sex. 20 U.S.C.A. 1681(a). Regulations promulgated pursuant to Title IX prohibited gender discrimination on the basis of pregnancy, parental status, and marital status and prohibited discrimination against any student. The Act also prohibited exclusion of girls from extracurricular activities when affected by childbirth, false pregnancies, or termination of pregnancy. Too, even though, the Pregnancy Discrimination Act of 1979 [42 U.S.C. § 2000 e(K)], an amendment to Title VII of the Civil Rights Act, is to prohibit discrimination in employment only, and does not apply to students in school, it nevertheless indicates the strong disfavor with which Congress views any debilitation that a government agency may visit upon a woman because of pregnancy.

In *Wort v. Vierling*, the U.S. Court of Appeals, Seventh Circuit, held that Title IX and Equal Protection were violated when a student was dismissed from the National Honor Society because of her pregnancy. On the other hand, in *Pfeiffer v. Marion Center Area School Dist.*, 917 F.2d 779 (3d Cir.1990), the Third Circuit Court upheld the dismissal of a student from the National Honor Society because she had engaged in premarital intercourse. The premarital sexual intercourse was deemed to be sufficient grounds for dismissal because it was determined to be contrary to qualities of leadership and character required by the school. The court in *Pfeiffer* distinguished *Wort*, saying that in *Wort* the dismissal from the NHS was for pregnancy, while *Pfeiffer* was premarital sex; therefore, the action in *Wort* violated Title IX and Equal Protection. The court in *Pfeiffer* remanded the case to hear evidence that a male student who was a member of the Honor Society had had premarital sex. The court said "We are troubled ... that ... testimony of a male" concerning his premarital sex was excluded. The issue of sex discrimination was a spectre that concerned the court. *Wort v. Vierling*, 778 F.2d 1233 (7th Cir.1985).

Thus, it appears that exclusion from school benefits such as the National Honor Society can be justified on the grounds that such conduct is contrary to the qualities of character that are advanced by the school, based on the *Pfeiffer* case. But exclusion from school or school benefits based on pregnancy will not be condoned by the Courts.

§ 4.8 IMMORALITY

Immorality is a broad term, encompassing wickedness, lying, cheating, stealing, sexual impurity, or unchastity. Immorality is not necessarily confined to sexual matters; instead, it may be acts which are *contre bonos mores*, that which is considered to be inconsistent with the moral rectitude of the community. Synonyms are corrupt, indecent, depraved, dissolute, while its antonyms are decent, upright, good, and right. A student who so flagrantly violates the norms of the school and community as to be immoral under these definitions can be dismissed from school. Also, the selling of drugs or liquor to other students, fraud or plagiarism, sexual promiscuity and lascivious conduct may all constitute immorality.

Pregnancy of an unwed student is not necessarily immoral, but how the pregnancy occurs may be. Sexual intercourse at school may certainly be considered immoral conduct. For a minor to undress for another student or for an adult for the purpose of satisfying sexual desires is immoral conduct violating not only school rules but may offend delinquency statutes as well. *Holton v. State*, 602 P.2d 1228 (Alaska 1979). Such activities on the part of students, in violation of school rules, may be punishable by dismissal from school.

§ 4.9 MARRIAGE

In early cases, courts were inclined to uphold school rules denying participation in extracurricular activities by married students. Today, because the courts do not view education as being merely a privilege, educational activities offered to one student must be offered to all students regardless of whether the student is married. As with all rules, there are some exceptions. For example, the United States Court of Appeals for the Tenth Circuit has held that school attendance could not be denied without necessary procedural safeguards, but that similar constitutional protections did not apply to each component of the educational process, indicating that participation in extracurricular activities may be denied without due process. *Albach v. Odle*, 531 F.2d 983 (10th Cir.1976). The weight of authority, though, appears to support the position that both students' rights of marital privacy, *Moran v. School District No. 7*, 350 F.Supp. 1180 (D.Mont.1972), and equal protection, *Hollon v. Mathis Independent School District*, 491 F.2d 92 (5th Cir.1974), are violated by prohibiting participation in extracurricular activities.

§ 4.10 DRUGS, TOBACCO, AND ALCOHOL

School authorities may prohibit drugs, alcohol, and guns (or other weapons) on school grounds or in off-campus activities which bear on the conduct of the school. Most states have statutes against the possession of drugs on school grounds, but in the absence of such laws school boards may promulgate their own regulations. Students may, of course, be expelled from school for violation of drug regulations. (See Chapter 7, Search and Seizure).

Schools may, too, control or prohibit the use and possession of tobacco and alcoholic beverages in school. Dismissal has been held to be appropriate punishment even though spiking of punch at school was so light as to be barely chemically detectable. So long as procedural due process is properly carried out, dismissals have been upheld. *Wood v. Strickland*, 420 U.S. 308 (1975).

In an illustrative case in point, a student who attended an off-campus party where there was alcohol was suspended from extra-curricular swimming activities, and pursuant to school board policy prohibiting possession of alcohol, the student was disciplined. The court here had ". . . no difficulty concluding that illegal consumption of alcohol has direct affects on the welfare of the schools." Therefore, the regulation was found to be rationally related to the school board's interest in deterring alcohol consumption among minor students. *Bush v. Dassel–Cokato Board of Education*, 745 F.Supp. 562 (D.Minn. 1990).

Several states now have modified their laws governing suspension and expulsion of students to require that offending students be placed into alternative public education programs apart from the regular school program, rather than complete exclusion from school. In a case where a student was suspended from school for violation of alcohol policy, the court found that the school board's refusal to place the student in an alternative education program violated the student's constitutional rights. *In the Interest of T.H., III*, 681 So.2d 110 (Miss.1996).

§ 4.11 WEAPONS

Weapons possession on school campuses has in recent years become a problem of daunting proportions.

The school killings in Columbine, Colorado, Paducah, Kentucky, and similar tragedies elsewhere have dramatically escalated the concerns for safety in the schools. A Pennsylvania court has held that where a student talked about bringing a gun to school and the school interpreted such a threat to create terror, the student was placed on informal probation and required to receive counseling. The student sued. The court found that such talk by the student could not be construed as idle "chit-chat" and could be interpreted as an inference of intent to create terror; therefore, the discipline imposed by the school was appropriate. *In the Interest of B.R.*, 732 A.2d 633 (Pa.Super.1999). Weapons can, of course, be excluded from school, but at times legal complications may occur. In one such instance, a student was charged with criminal possession of a switchblade knife found in her bag during an administrative search with metal detectors at a high school. The student sought to have the evidence suppressed. A team of special police officers from the Central Task Force for School Safety had posted signs at the high school announcing the search. The court determined that the knife could be used as evidence and the search was minimally intrusive, considering the compelling need for security in the schools. *People v. Dukes*, 580 N.Y.S.2d 850 (1992).

With the great concern for student safety, school boards have implemented zero tolerance policies. The courts have upheld these policies while at times disagreeing with their wisdom. Where a 13–year–old student was told by a classmate that she had been contemplating suicide by slitting her wrist, and also told that she had inadvertently brought a knife to school, an Assistant Principal had learned of the knife and took possession of it. The student was expelled and the court upheld the expulsion. The court wrote, "However harsh the result in this case, the federal courts are not properly called upon to judge the wisdom of a zero tolerance policy of the sort alleged to be in place at Blue Ridge Middle School or of its application to [the student]. Instead, our inquiry here is limited to whether [the student's] complaint alleges sufficient facts which if proved would show that the implementation of the school's policy in this case failed to comport with the United States Constitution. We conclude that the facts alleged in this case do not so demonstrate." *Ratner v. Loudoun County Public Schools*, 2001 WL 855606 (4th Cir.2001).

The wording of a school policy or a statute as to the definition of a weapon can be very important as to whether a student is found to be in possession. Thus, a starter pistol used at track meets was held not to be a weapon since it was not deadly or dangerous. *State of Washington v. C.Q.*, 979 P.2d 473 (Wash.App.1999). Three single-edged razor blades found in a student's possession were found not to be a weapon under the state school safety act. The state statute had provided quite specifically as to which weapons are prohibited in school, but the law did not mention razor blades. *In the Interest of R.F.T.*, 492 S.E.2d 590 (Ga.App.1997).

CHAPTER 5

RELIGION IN PUBLIC SCHOOLS AND STATE FUNDING OF RELIGIOUS SCHOOLS

§ 5.1 INTRODUCTION

Education is very important to virtually all religions. Doctrines and dogmas of religious groups are spread and church membership is increased by teaching to youth and non-believers. It is natural that as sectarian beliefs are advanced they will come in conflict with beliefs of other sects and with the non-sectarian purposes of the state. Very early in this country education was conducted almost exclusively by the churches for the purposes of advancing their religious beliefs. Where the state provided tax funds to support schools, one of the justifications was to teach the youth to read the Bible. In fact, the first governmental effort to establish tax-supported schools in this country was in 1647 when the colony of Massachusetts provided by statute for general taxation for the purpose of keeping men knowledgeable of the Scriptures in order that they might not fall into the grip of the "old deluder, Satan."

The concept of public education "divorced from denominational control was foreign to the colonial mind." Leo Pfeffer, *Church, State and Freedom*, Boston: Beacon Press, 1967, p. 321. Later, Justice Frankfurter in the *McCollum* case explained: "Traditionally, organized education in the Western world was Church education. It could hardly be otherwise when the education of children was primarily the study of the Word and the ways of God. Even in Protestant countries where there was a less close identification of Church and State, the basis of education was largely the Bible, and its chief purpose, inculcation of piety." The creation of public schools, the Age of Reason, and the ascent of science were dependent on the removal of education from the control of the Church. Brian L. Silver, *The Ascent of Science* (Oxford: Oxford University Press, 1998) p. 67. (See also: Charles Freeman, *The Closing of the Western Mind* (New York: Vintage Books, 2005), Charles R. Morris, *American Catholic* (New York: Vintage Books, 1997), and Susan Jacoby, *Freethinkers, A History of American Secularism* (New York: Henry Holt and Company, 2004). To the extent that the State intervened, it used its authority to further the aims of the Church. "The immigrants who came to these shores brought this view of education with them. Colonial schools certainly started with a religious orientation." *People ex rel. McCollum v. Board of Education*, 333 U.S. 203 (1948).

The pervasiveness of the early religious influence on public schools is illustrated by the primer used to teach public school pupils to read in New England in the latter part of the 17th century. The book entitled *The New England Primer* taught the alphabet using letters and pictures with Biblical connotations; for example, "A—in *Adam*'s fall we sinned or P—*Peter* denies His Lord and cries." Because of these origins of religious involvement in public education, it has been difficult to keep public schools from becoming inundated with religious strife and discord.

The struggle to establish educational systems based on reason and science rather than on myth and mysticism has permeated each generation since Galileo and Newton. The era of the Enlightenment, the late 18th century, was marked by a great intensification of the conflict between religious control of learning and secular rationalism and scientific exploration. Adam Smith, the great Scottish economist and philosopher, in his classic book, *An Inquiry Into the Nature and Causes of the Wealth of Nations* (1776), said, "Science is the antidote to the poison of enthusiasm and superstition."

Over the decades many conflicts have developed between the clergy and the proponents of public schools. In the 1830s when Horace Mann provided the leadership in the establishment of the first state system of public schools in Massachusetts, his chief opposition came from clergymen who sought to prevent him from creating what they called "Godless" institutions. Mann had insisted the public schools should have no sectarian religious motivations and the state should "abstain from subjugating the capacities of children to any legal standard of religious faith."

Later, contrary to Mann's belief that the public schools should be secular, religious activities were permitted in public schools in most states, including prayer, Bible reading, and other religious exercises. By the 20th century, all but a few states had regular morning religious services. The practices were generally supported by opinion of the state courts and were, except in a few states, held to be consistent with state constitutions.

The public school system envisioned by Mann was founded on three basic assumptions: "First, that the legislature has the power to tax all—even the childless and those whose children attend private schools—in order to provide free public education for all; second, that the legislature has the power to require every parent to provide for his children a basic education in secular subjects; third, that the education provided by the state in the free schools must be secular." *Pfeffer*, supra, p. 327

Each of these basic premises of public education continues to be attacked today by those who seek to impose on public school teachings their own particular brand of religiosity. Some parents of private school children maintain they are entitled to tax credits because of what they consider to be double taxation. Other parents contest compulsory attendance laws, state regulation of private schools, and home instruction (see Chapter 1); and continuing efforts are made by some to teach religious doctrines in the public schools ranging from religious exercises to teaching creation-science (see Chapter 2).

§ 5.2　FREE EXERCISE AND ESTABLISHMENT

The controversy between advocates of religious sectarianism and secularism in the public schools is a part of a larger conflict which tends to permeate most governments and societies, the unending struggle between Church and State. Today, a casual glance at a newspaper reminds one that the Middle East, with Christian against Muslim, Muslim against Jew, is a torrent of religious bigotry and persecution. Ireland, Afghanistan, Azerbaijan, Armenia, Kazakstan, not to mention the problems of the Balkans and the Philippines, are among the current conflicts with critical religious overtones. And the United States is not without its own problems where the rapid rise of religious fundamentalism has created increasing community strife and litigation. Today's religious conflicts are merely descendants of the great religious quarrels of Europe and Asia which have resulted in millions of deaths from wars and persecutions over the centuries.

The European experience of embattled Church and State was fresh on the minds of founding fathers in America when the First Amendment was drafted. The basic antecedents to the religion clauses of the First Amendment were found in James Madison's *Memorial and Remonstrance Against Religious Assessments* and Thomas Jefferson's *Act for Establishing Religious Freedom*. Both were documents written in response to attempts to establish religion in Virginia and to encroach on individual religious liberty. Madison admonished that all persons had a right to "free exercise of their religion according to the dictates of their conscience;" and Jefferson asserted that it was time to do away with the "impious presumption of legislators and rulers, civil and ecclesiastical who ... have assumed dominion over the faith of others"; and that a person's "civil rights should have no dependence on [his] religious opinions."

When finally promulgated and ratified in 1791, the religion provisions of the First Amendment of the Bill of Rights provided: "Congress shall make no law respecting an establishment of religion, or prohibiting the free exercise thereof; ..."

§ 5.3 WALL OF SEPARATION

John Adams interpreted the free exercise and establishment clauses of the First Amendment to mean that "Congress will never meddle in religion ..."; and Jefferson explained the intent was to create a "wall of separation between Church and State." It had been from Jefferson's urging while serving in France in 1787 that Madison proceeded to champion the promulgation and ratification of the Bill of Rights (first ten amendments of the U.S. Constitution).

Interpretations of the meaning of the First Amendment have carried forward to today. Time and again the United States Supreme Court has delineated the boundaries between Church and State only to have Congress, state legislatures and school boards open new cracks and fissures requiring further interpretation. To Justice William O. Douglas there was little debate over the intent of the Amendment. He said, "... [T]here cannot be the slightest doubt that the First Amendment reflects the philosophy that Church and State should be separated." And so far as interference with the "free exercise" of religion and an "establishment of religion are concerned, the separation must be complete and unequivocal." *Zorach v. Clauson*, 343 U.S. 306 (1952).

§ 5.4   CONSTITUTIONAL STANDARD, THE *LEMON* TEST

In the large number of religion and public school cases which have come before the United States Supreme Court over the years, the one principle of law which appears to be consistent throughout is that the state must be "neutral" and cannot enhance or inhibit religion. As stated in *Zorach*, the government should show "no partiality to any one [religious] group" and should let "each [group] flourish according to the zeal of its adherents and the appeal of its dogma." This neutrality of government means, according to Justice Black's opinion in *Everson,* that: "The establishment of religion clause of the First Amendment means at least this: 'Neither a state nor the Federal Government can set up a church. Neither can pass laws which aid one religion, aid all religions or prefer one religion over another.... No tax in any amount, large or small, can be levied to support any religious activities or institutions, whatever they may be called, or whatever form they may adopt to teach or practice religion.' "

The majority of the church-state cases in education have involved the Establishment Clause of the First Amendment while a few cases have had the Free Exercise Clause as the main issue. Prior to 1970 in measuring whether a state action had violated the Establishment Clause, the Supreme Court sought to determine separation with a two-part test which required that: (1) the purpose of the action of the state not be to aid one religion or all religions and (2) the primary effect of the program be one that "neither advances nor inhibits religion." In 1970 the Supreme Court added a third prong to the test, that the state must not foster "an excessive government entanglement with religion." *Walz v. Tax Commission*, 397 U.S. 664 (1970).

Thus, stated in the negative, this three-part constitutional standard for separation of church and state as prescribed by the "Establishment Clause" of the First Amendment actions by government means that: (1) Legislation or governmental action must not have a religious purpose; (2) Legislation or governmental action must not have the primary effect of either enhancing or inhibiting religion; and (3) Legislation or governmental action must not create excessive entanglement between church and state.

The *Lemon* test was applied to all establishment clause cases through the 1980s with the exception of two non-school cases: *Marsh v. Chambers*, 463 U.S. 783 (1983) and *Larson v. Valente*, 456 U.S. 228 (1982). Later, in *Lynch v. Donnelly*, 465 U.S. 668 (1984), the Court, in a dramatic change of direction, stated that the *Lemon* test has never been binding on the Court.

The Supreme Court did not use the *Lemon* test in deciding *Board of Education of Kiryas Joel Village School District v. Grumet*, 512 U.S. 687 (1994), rather it applied a "neutrality" standard, saying "A proper respect for both the Free Exercise and the Establishment Clauses compels the State to pursue a course of 'neutrality' toward religion." In this case the state legislature created a separate special education school district for a religious educational enclave. "The New York Village of Kiryas Joel is a religious enclave of Satmar Hasidim, practitioners of a strict form of Judaism. Its local incorporation intentionally drew its boundaries under the state's general village incorporation law to exclude all but Satmar." The state then carved out a special school district exclusively for the Satmar Hasidic sect. In declaring the act unconstitutional, the Supreme Court stated: "Because this unusual act is tantamount to an allocation of political power on a religious criterion and neither presupposes nor requires governmental impartiality toward religion, we hold that it violates the prohibition against establishment."

More recently the U.S. Supreme Court, under the hand of Justices Rehnquist, Scalia, and Thomas, have rather conclusively leveled the historic wall of separation between church and state held to be a basic principle of rights and liberties as seen by Adams, Madison, Jefferson, and Washington. In a series of cases, today's Supreme Court has negated most of the meaning of the Establishment Clause. The Court has apparently decided to abandon the third prong of *Lemon*, excessive entanglement, thereby permitting public funds to flow to religious schools if the Congress and state legislatures decide to distribute tax funds for that purpose.

In *Mitchell v. Helms*, 530 U.S. 793 (2000), Justice Clarence Thomas, writing for the majority of the Supreme Court, said we have "pared" the *Lemon* factors, thereby reducing the effects of the "excessive entanglement" test clearing the way for the distribution of public funds to parochial schools. Later, in *Zelman v. Simmons–Harris*, 536 U.S. 639 (2002), with the modified and reduced constitutional criteria, the Supreme Court upheld the school voucher program in Cleveland, Ohio, permitting public funds to flow to parochial schools. More will be said below in § 5.6 about the Court's changing philosophy regarding the separation doctrine to permit tax funds to go to church schools.

With regard to the Free Exercise Clause and religious activities in public schools, it should be remembered that the Supreme Court distinguishes between the freedom of individual *beliefs*, which are absolute, and the freedom of individual *conduct*, which is not. The Free Exercise Clause protects an individual "from certain forms of governmental compulsion; it does not afford an individual a right to dictate the conduct of Government's internal procedures." Maintaining an ordered or organized society that guarantees religious freedom to such a vast variety of religious beliefs, as are held in this country, requires some religious practices to yield to the common good. Religious beliefs must be accommodated, but accommodation of certain conduct may restrict the operation of government and encroach on others' religious beliefs. In such instances, religious conduct must be restrained for the good of all.

The Free Exercise Clause is violated when one is compelled to perform an act which violates his or her religious belief or foregoes a benefit bestowed by the government. *Mozert v. Hawkins County Board of Education*, 827 F.2d 1058 (6th Cir.1987), *Sherbert v. Verner*, 374 U.S. 398 (1963), *Hobbie v. Unemployment Appeals Commission of Florida*, 480 U.S. 136 (1987). Section 5.5 below explains how the Court assiduously enforces secularization of the public schools even though it has endorsed the use of public funds for parochial schools.

§ 5.5 RELIGIOUS ACTIVITIES IN PUBLIC SCHOOLS

§ 5.51 Release Time

Many different schemes have been devised by religious groups for using the public schools as a supportive device for teaching religion. A common practice by the turn of the century in many school districts was for a portion of the school day to be set aside for religious instruction in the public school building. This went on without serious challenge until the *McCollum* case in 1948, a case in which the United States Supreme Court held unconstitutional a release-time situation in which Protestant preachers, Catholic priests, and a Jewish rabbi taught religion classes in the school each week. Students who wanted to attend religious classes were *released* from their regular classes, and those students who did not went to another location in the public school building to pursue their secular subjects. The school district defended the practice maintaining that the students were not compelled to attend the religious classes and that one religion was not favored over another. *People ex rel. McCollum v. Board of Education*, 333 U.S. 203 (1948).

The Supreme Court in striking down the practice said that state tax-supported facilities could not be used to disseminate religious doctrines whether it aided only one or all religions. Too, the Court noted that the state's compulsory attendance law provided a valuable aid to religion in that it brought the children to a central location at which the churches could capture the students' attention. According to the Court, there existed too close a cooperation in that (1) the weight and influence of the public school was cast behind a program for religious instruction, (2) public school teachers provided the attendance accounting and policed the process, (3) the school kept track of students who were released, and (4) the normal classroom activities came to a halt. For these reasons the practice was held to violate the First Amendment.

Following *McCollum*, the City of New York devised another release-time program in which students were released from public schools during the school day to attend religious services off school grounds. A period was set aside each week when students could leave the public school grounds to go to a church or church school to attend religious services. The program was entirely optional, the school authorities were neutral, and teachers did no more than release the students when so requested by parents. In upholding this plan the United States Supreme Court said that the state could accommodate religion without aiding religion, and it would too severely "press the concept of separation of Church and State" to condemn this New York law where the state assistance was so minimal. Accordingly, in this instance, for government to fail to accommodate this type of release-time plan would constitute callousness toward religion which is not required by the First Amendment. *Zorach v. Clauson*, 343 U.S. 306 (1952).

In 1990, a federal district court ruled that a release-time program was constitutional using the *Zorach* model. But the court concluded that members of the religious organization in question could not enter the school. The facts of the case indicated that not only were the members of the organization entering the school, but they were offering bags of candy trying to recruit children to join the religious program. *Doe by Doe v. Shenandoah County School Board*, 737 F.Supp. 913 (W.D.Va.1990).

§ 5.52   Prayer and Bible Reading

Prior to 1962 some states required each school day to begin with a prayer and the reading of verses from the Bible. This practice was contested when the New York State Board of Regents composed a prayer which they recommended be used in the public schools. The prayer stated: "Almighty God, we acknowledge our dependence upon Thee, and we beg Thy blessings upon us, our parents, teachers, and our Country." The United States Supreme Court determined that the prayer violated the Establishment Clause. "[W]e think that the constitutional prohibition against laws respecting an establishment of religion must at least mean that in this country, it is no part of the business of government to compose official prayers for any group of the American people to recite as

a part of a religious program carried on by government."
Engel v. Vitale, 370 U.S. 421 (1962).

Then in 1963 came companion cases, *School District of
Abington Township v. Schempp*, 374 U.S. 203 (1963) and
Murray v. Curlett, 83 S.Ct. 869 (1963), that challenged
state practices in Pennsylvania and Maryland school
districts of having prayer and Bible reading at the beginning of each day. Children who did not want to stay in
the room were excused while the exercises proceeded.
The reading of the Bible and Lord's Prayer was challenged as a violation of the First Amendment. The Supreme Court determined that the exercises violated the
Establishment Clause of the First Amendment. But the
Court went on to say, "It certainly may be said that the
Bible is worthy of study for its literary and historic
qualities. Nothing we have said here indicates that such
study of the Bible or of religion, when presented objectively as a part of a secular program of education, may
not be effected consistently with the First Amendment.
But the exercises here do not fall into those categories."
Therefore, the Bible may be used in appropriate study of
history, civilization, ethics, and comparative religion; but
such Bible study classes must be taught in a manner that
is secular and does not promote religion. If the classes
are not objectively taught in a secular manner as an
academic subject, then they are unconstitutional. *Wiley v.
Franklin*, 497 F.Supp. 390 (E.D.Tenn.1980).

These free exercise issues have not subsided as various
religious groups seek to insert their doctrines into the
public schools. The Louisiana legislature, under religious
political pressure, passed an act that allowed for a "brief
time in silent prayer or meditation." Seven years later in
1999 the legislature deleted the word "silent" from the

legislation. The Court ruled that this violated the Establishment Clause. Using the *Lemon* test, the court ruled
that the 1999 Amendment was motivated by a "wholly
religious purpose" and therefore violated the first prong
of the *Lemon* test that legislation must be secular. *Doe v.
School Board of Ouachita Parish*, 274 F.3d 289 (5th
Cir.2001). The Supreme Court in *Santa Fe Independent
School District v. Doe*, 530 U.S. 290 (2000), stated, "...
nothing in the Constitution interpreted by this Court
prohibits any public school student from voluntarily
praying at any time before or after the school day. But
the religious liberty protected by the Constitution is
abridged when the state affirmatively sponsors the particular religious practice of prayer." See *Doe v. Porter*,
188 F.Supp.2d 904 (E.D.Tenn.2002) (religious instruction
in public school by Bible College students violates Establishment Clause).

§ 5.53 Silent Meditation

In an effort to circumvent the U.S. Supreme Court's
proscription of state-sponsored prayer in the public
schools, some states have exercised exceptional creative-
ness. One such example is found in Alabama where in
1981 the legislature enacted a statute authorizing a
period of silence "for meditation or voluntary prayer" in
all Alabama public schools. When the Court examined
the legislative history of the statute, it was found that
the prime sponsor of the statute had stated the purpose
of the Act to be "an effort to return voluntary prayer to
our public schools...." The Supreme Court concluded
this obviously did not constitute a "secular legislative
purpose," and the Act therefore violated the Establish-

ment Clause of the First Amendment. *Wallace v. Jaffree*, 472 U.S. 38 (1985).

The basic question that must be asked is whether the period of silence that is set aside in school is motivated to promote religion or is it simply to have the students sit quietly for a few moments to think about something, anything. Students can, of course, contemplate religion if they want to, but if they do, it cannot be state initiated and promoted. State-initiated religious worship has assumed many forms: "silence," "reflection," and "contemplation" are devices state legislatures and school boards have used to attempt to imbue the public school classroom with certain sectarian religious beliefs and tenets.

The legislature in Georgia managed to prevail in a "silence" case by enacting a statute that provided for a "moment of quiet reflection" in which each public school teacher was required to conduct a period of "quiet reflection" for not more than 60 seconds at the start of each school day. The U.S. Court of Appeals, Eleventh Circuit, upheld the constitutionality of the act, finding that it was secular because it expressly disclaimed religious purposes and, secondly, it did not affirmatively authorize any religious activity. *Bown v. Gwinnett County School Dist.*, 112 F.3d 1464 (11th Cir.1997).

In 2000, the Virginia legislature passed a law which required every school to provide for a minute of silence. During the mandatory minute of silence pupils could "... in the exercise of his or her individual choice, meditate, pray or engage in any other silent activity which does not interfere with, distract, or impede other pupils in the like exercise of individual choice." The United States Fourth Circuit Court of Appeals ruled the statute constitutional and distinguished it from the Supreme Court's decision in *Wallace*. The Circuit Court quoted the U.S. Supreme Court "that enacting a statute solely for a religious purpose is quite different from merely protecting every student's right to engage in voluntary prayer during an appropriate moment of silence during the school day." *Brown v. Gilmore*, 258 F.3d 265 (4th Cir.2001).

Moments of silence in the classroom, as indications of serious and thoughtful scholarly pursuit, are always welcome in the schools; however, when state officials attempt to convert such moments into proselytizing for religion, the U.S. Constitution is offended. The law is consistent in this regard.

§ 5.54   Prayer at Graduation Ceremonies

Insistence by various religious groups that religious exercises be included in public schools has assumed many shapes and definitions over the years. Various interpretations of the law have concluded that the constitutional application is only pertinent to the classroom while ancillary activities, such as commencement exercises, baccalaureate, and athletic events, are beyond the scope of constitutional consideration. The United States Supreme Court has, however, not drawn such definitive lines between curricular and after-curricular activities. In one such case, the U.S. Supreme Court invalidated prayer at high school graduation ceremonies. Here, in *Lee v. Weisman*, 505 U.S. 577 (1992), the public school principals in Providence, Rhode Island, were permitted to invite the clergy to give invocations and benedictions at graduation ceremonies. The school principal invited a Rabbi to offer prayers and provided him with guidelines to follow in the composition of "public prayers" for civic ceremonies and advised him that the prayers should be nonsectarian. The Supreme Court concluded that "state officials [were] direct[ing] the performance of a formal religious exercise" which is prohibited by the First Amendment. This conclusion was based on the fact that a school official, the principal, decided (a) that an invocation and benediction should be given, (b) whom should be chosen to present the prayers, and (c) the content of the prayer. These conditions made it clear that the prayer was state sponsored. The Court rejected the argument that the prayer was a kind of "non-sectarian prayer" legitimately conveyed by the state to advance a "civic religion." The Court said that "While some common ground of moral and ethical behavior is highly desirable for any society, for the state to advance a Judeo–Christian religious doctrine under the mantle of some perceived civic religious motivation is clearly in conflict with the religious clauses."

After *Weisman*, some schools decided that it would be constitutional if remarks such as prayer were student-initiated, student-written and student-delivered. Therefore, this would not have pervasive involvement condemned in *Weisman*. A federal court ruled student-initiated prayer at graduation unconstitutional and said, "The graduating class in Loudoun County certainly could not have voted to exclude from the ceremonies persons of a certain race. To be constructively excluded from graduation ceremonies because of one's religion or lack of religion is not a great deal different." *Gearon v. Loudoun County School Board*, 844 F.Supp. 1097 (E.D.Va.1993).

§ 5.55   Prayer at Other School Activities

The variations on the prayer issue appear to be virtually unlimited. Where a high school band teacher created a "new tradition" of mandatory prayer sessions before rehearsals and performances, a federal circuit court found the practice in violation of the Establishment Clause of the First Amendment. *Steele v. Van Buren Public School District*, 845 F.2d 1492 (8th Cir.1988). See also *Breen v. Runkel*, 614 F.Supp. 355 (W.D.Mich.1985).

Prayers before and after athletic contests are common and often little is said about such exercises. One such instance emerged in Texas where school football games were preceded by carefully orchestrated religious invocations. The activities were designed to skirt constitutional prohibitions. The U.S. Supreme Court, in this case, confronted the issue of whether student-led and -initiated prayers at the games violated the Establishment Clause of the First Amendment. The students who initiated the prayers before school football games were elected by the student body by an election process instituted by school officials. At trial the school district defended the practice by asserting that the election allowed the majority of students to prevail, and if the majority decided to have pre-game prayer, then it was their prerogative. The U.S. Supreme Court, however, looked behind the scene and observed that the practice still had the *imprimatur* of the school, and regardless of the process, the prayers were still a student initiative. The Court concluded that such pre-game religious invocations were, therefore, unconstitutional. *Santa Fe Independent School District v. Doe*, 530 U.S. 290 (2000). The court in this case used the *Lee v. Weisman* coercion test. The Court stated, "For some students, such as cheerleaders, members of the band, and the team members themselves, attendance at football games is mandated, sometimes for class credit ... The constitution demands that schools not force on students the difficult choice between attending these games and avoiding personally offensive religious rituals."

A school choir activity where religious music is performed has also come into question; however, the prevailing view of the courts is that such does not offend the Constitution. In a Utah case the performance of the school choir at graduation, the content of which included two Christian devotional songs, was upheld. The school district defended the practice pointing out that a substantial amount of choral music is religious in nature; the court accepted the school's justification as a secular purpose. *Bauchman v. West High School*, 132 F.3d 542 (10th Cir.1997). In another similar case involving a school choir and its use of music with sacred themes, the court upheld the practice and noted that religious songs by the school choir do not constitute an endorsement of religion. *Doe v. Duncanville Independent School Dist.*, 70 F.3d 402 (5th Cir.1995).

The U.S. Sixth Circuit Court of Appeals ruled that prayer at school board meetings violated the Establishment Clause. *Coles v. Cleveland Board of Education*, 171 F.3d 369 (6th Cir.1999).

§ 5.56　Equal Access Act of 1984 (20 U.S.C. § 4071–4074)

In 1984 the U.S. Congress passed the Equal Access Act. Under this law a school district that has created a limited open forum must allow student organizations to use public secondary school facilities for religious clubs. A limited open forum exists where student groups have been permitted to meet for non-curricular purposes on school grounds during non-instructional time. The constitutional rationale for the law emanated from *Widmar v. Vincent*, 454 U.S. 263 (1981). In *Widmar*, the United States Supreme Court ruled that the University of Missouri's refusal to allow religious groups access to its public facilities while allowing other groups access to the same facilities violated the free speech provision of the First Amendment. In that case the Court ruled that the grounds and facilities of a public university were a "public forum," the use thereof was protected by constitutional free speech rights.

The Equal Access Act prohibited public school districts receiving federal money and allowing non-curricular activities and club meetings to deny secondary school students the right to meet in public school facilities for religious and/or other purposes. The Equal Access Act states in pertinent part: "It shall be unlawful for any public *secondary* school which receives federal financial assistance and which has a limited open forum to deny equal access or a fair opportunity to, or discriminate against, any students who wish to conduct a meeting within that limited open forum on the basis of the religious, political, philosophical, or other content of the speech at such meetings (emphasis added)." Thus, according to this statute, when a school district allows clubs and organizations that are not directly curriculum related to meet in school facilities, then the school has created a *limited open forum*. When such a forum is created the school district cannot deny other student-initiated groups, whether religious, political, or philosophical, from holding meetings in the facilities of the public school.

§ 5.57 Limited Open Forum

The constitutionality of the Equal Access Act was decided in the case of *Board of Education of Westside Community Schools v. Mergens*, 496 U.S. 226 (1990). Two questions were raised. The first was whether the Equal Access Act prohibited the Westside High School from denying a student religious group permission to meet on school premises and, secondly, whether the Act violated the Establishment Clause of the First Amendment. In response, the Supreme Court held against the school and for the student religious group and, further, ruled that the federal statute was not violative of the First Amendment. According to the Court, a "limited open forum" exists whenever a public school "grants an offering to or opportunity for one or more non-curriculum related student groups to meet on school premises during non-instructional time." The statutory reference to "non-instructional time" means "time set aside by the school before actual classroom instruction begins or after actual classroom instruction ends."

In this regard the Supreme Court found that the obligations under the Act are triggered even if the public secondary school allows only one non-curriculum related student group to meet. A "non-curricular-related student group" was interpreted broadly to mean "any student group that does not directly relate to the body of courses offered by the school." A French or a Latin club would directly relate to a French or Latin course offered as a planned part of the curriculum. While a checkers club, chess club, or community service club would be non-curriculum related. If such non-curriculum clubs are permitted, then the school is considered to have a "limited open forum" and religious and other student-initiated clubs have equal access to the school premises.

Therefore, where the school creates a "limited open forum" for non-instructional activities, religious clubs and religious organizations can use the premises for meetings and activities as assured by the Equal Access Act.

For the public school to remain neutral under the Act, however, means that the non-instructional activity (1) must be voluntary on the part of the students; (2) have no sponsorship by the school, the government, or its agents or employees; (3) have no employees or agents of the public school or government present at religious meetings except in a non-participatory, custodial capacity, (4) must not materially or substantially interfere with the orderly conduct of educational activities within the school; and (5) non-school persons may not direct, conduct, control, or regularly attend activities of student groups. 20 U.S.C.A. § 4071(c). Where students wanted to form a religious club and the school had one policy for religious clubs and another for other clubs and refused to recognize the religious club, the court ruled that under equal access, all clubs must be treated the same. *Prince v. Jacoby*, 303 F.3d 1074 (9th Cir. 2002).

Thus, where a school permits the use of school facilities for various non-curricular clubs, religious and civic organizations, access must be provided to all without regard to content of their messages. The EAA, in tandem with Supreme Court interpretations of the Free Speech Clause of the First Amendment, effectively utilizes the access theory to override earlier tenets of separation of church and state that had prohibited use of public school facilities for inculcation of religion. The Equal Access Act

(EAA), however, by its very breadth, has resulted in certain unintended consequences that the conservative Congress that enacted the law probably did not foresee. One example is a case where a student group, Straight and Gays for Equality (SAGE), sought access to school facilities, including the school's public address system, yearbook, and other forms of communication. In spite of the fact that the EAA does not require a school to provide a forum for student groups whose purposes do not directly relate to the school curriculum, the federal court ruled that SAGE was entitled to the same school avenues of communication that had been provided to other student groups. *Straights and Gays for Equality v. Osseo Area Schools–District No. 279*, 471 F. 3d 908 (8th Cir. 2006).

Similarly, a federal court in California has said that: "In order to comply with the Equal Access Act ... the members of the Gay–Straight Alliance must be permitted access to the school campus in the same way that the district provides access to all clubs, including the Christian Club and the Red Cross/Key Club." *Colin v. Orange Unified School District*, 83 F.Supp.2d 1135 (C.D. Cal. 2000).

§ 5.58   Use of Facilities

After *Widmar* and *Mergens*, the courts began to use the free speech test more frequently when dealing with church-state issues. As noted in *Widmar* and *Mergens*, if the school allowed one group to use a facility, religious groups could not be denied equal use since it would violate free speech. The free speech test has recently been applied to the use of school facilities. In the past, courts ruled that school boards could have policies that allowed different groups to use the facility. In other words, for example, the school board could allow use of facilities by the boy scouts and girl scouts but could deny religious groups access.

With the use of the public forum rationale applied to free speech, schools must now be "viewpoint neutral." An aspect of viewpoint neutrality was litigated by the U.S. Supreme Court in *Lamb's Chapel v. Center Moriches Union Free School District*, 508 U.S. 384 (1993). In this case, Center Moriches School District in New York denied Lamb's Chapel Church the after-hour use of school facilities for showing a series of films concerning "child-rearing, family values, family relationships, abortion, pornography, and loving God." The school district had acted in accordance with New York state law that allowed after-hours use by all outside groups except religious groups. The state law excluded religious groups from school premises in order to reduce the possibility of school districts enhancing religion of a particular church in preference to another religious group. In this way the state sought to remain neutral.

The Supreme Court ruled such an exclusion effectively violated the church's freedom of speech because evidence was presented to show that the school district had created a "limited public forum" by opening the school premises for "social, civic, and recreational" purposes such as the Salvation Army Band, Center Moriches Quilting Bee, Center Moriches Drama Club, Girl Scouts, Boy Scouts, and Center Moriches Music Awards Association, among others. According to the Court, to open school premises for other groups but to close them to religious groups was not to remain viewpoint neutral. The Supreme Court said "there would have been no realistic danger that the community would think that the District was endorsing religion or any particular creed" by opening the school premises for church use. Accordingly, the Supreme Court dismissed the concern of the school district that permitting use of school premises for such religious proselytizing would violate the Establishment Clause of the First Amendment.

The Supreme Court again addressed this issue in *Good News Club v. Milford Central School*, 533 U.S. 98 (2001). The Milford Central School enacted a policy allowing citizens to use the school facilities for "among other things, (1) instruction in education, learning, or the arts and (2) social, civic, recreational and entertainment uses pertaining to community welfare." Residents requested to use the facilities after school and their petition was rejected by the school board because the residents proposed ". . . to sing songs, hear Bible lessons, memorize scripture and pray." The school board says this was equivalent to religious service which was prohibited by the policy. The U.S. Supreme Court found against the school board and said, "that exclusion is indistinguishable from the exclusions held violative of the [Free Speech] clause in *Lamb's Chapel* . . . The exclusion was not viewpoint neutral, therefore violating the free speech clause; but at the same time, permitting everyone to be treated the same did not violate the establishment clause."

§ 5.59 Posting Ten Commandments

The Establishment Clause of the First Amendment prohibits the posting in public schools materials that inculcate religion. This general rule of law was specifically applied when the U.S. Supreme Court struck down a

Kentucky statute that required the posting of the Ten Commandments on the wall of each classroom in the state. The posters were to be purchased with private donations. At the bottom of each poster the statute required the printing of the following statement: "The secular application of the Ten Commandments is clearly seen in its adoption as the fundamental legal code of Western Civilization and the Common Law of the United States." The United States Supreme Court ruled that this disclaimer at the bottom did not change the pre-eminent purpose of the Ten Commandments which was plainly not neutral but patently religious in nature. Therefore, the statute violated the Establishment Clause of the First Amendment. *Stone v. Graham*, 449 U.S. 39 (1980).

Since the posting of the Ten Commandments was ruled to be unconstitutional, litigation has continued. Local schools and governmental agencies have posted the Ten Commandments as part of the "Foundations of American Law and Government." In an Ohio case, the school board displayed the Ten Commandments in the high school. Only after litigation commenced did they add other documents for the Foundation of American Law and Government displays. The Court, using the *Lemon* test, ruled displaying of the Ten Commandments was unconstitutional. *Baker v. Adams County/Ohio Valley School Board*, 310 F.3d 927 (6th Cir.2002). See also *Doe v. Harlan County School District*, 96 F.Supp.2d 667 (E.D.Ky.2000). (Multiple displays with Ten Commandments violated Establishment Clause.)

§ 5.6 PUBLIC TAX FUNDS FOR RELIGIOUS SCHOOLS

This section explains how the Supreme Court created a series of precedents that were later used to justify the use of public tax dollars to finance religious schools by means of vouchers and other forms of funding. The evolution of providing governmental aid to support parochial elementary and secondary education started in 1986 with *Witters v. Washington Dept. of Services for the Blind*, 474 U.S. 481 (1986). The Supreme Court in this case began a wholesale reinterpretation of the Establishment Clause regarding financial support to religious schools. In *Witters*, a blind person sought state vocational rehabilitation assistance for study to become a pastor, missionary or church youth director. The Supreme Court of the State of Washington applied the *Lemon* test and determined that such aid would violate the Establishment Clause, having a primary effect of advancing religion. The U.S. Supreme Court reversed the Washington Court. Using the *Lemon* test, the U.S. Supreme Court determined that the aid had a secular purpose. The second prong of the *Lemon* test was as the court stated, "more difficult." The Court said, "It is well-settled that the Establishment Clause is not violated every time money previously in the possession of a state is conveyed to a religious institution." "[T]he Washington program [assistance] is paid directly to the student, who then transmits it to the educational institution of his or her choice." If the aid flows from the government to an individual and then that individual gives it to a religious entity, the Establishment Clause is not violated. This was the beginning of judicial support for private choice for the flow of government funds.

The second case providing judicial support for public aid to parochial schools came seven years later in 1993. In *Zobrest v. Catalina Foothills School District*, 509 U.S. 1 (1993), a deaf student transferred from a public school to a Roman Catholic high school. While in the public school he had a sign-language interpreter, according to Individuals with Disabilities Act (IDEA). His parents requested the interpreter be assigned to him at the Catholic school; the district and appellate court ruled this would violate the Establishment Clause, "as a conduct for the child's religious inculcation...." In finding that placing the public paid interpreter in a religious school did not violate the Establishment Clause, the court stated: "Government programs that neutrally provide benefits to a broad class of citizens defined without reference to religion are not readily subject to an Establishment Clause challenge just because sectarian institutions may also receive an attenuated financial benefit.... The service in this case is part of a general government program that distributes benefits neutrally to any child qualifying as disabled under the IDEA without regard to the sectarian-nonsectarian or public-nonpublic nature of the school the child attends. By according parents freedom to select a school of their choice, the statute ensures that a government-paid interpreter will be present in a sectarian school only as a result of individual parents' private decisions.... The fact that a public employee will be physically present in a sectarian school does not by itself make this same type of aid" unconstitutional. Here again the parent's choice to take public monies to Catholic schools was approved as constitutional; the court cited *Witters* to support this proposition.

In 1997 the United States Supreme Court took another giant step in totally revising the law as it pertained to providing tax money to religious schools. In that year the Court handed down *Agostini v. Felton*, 521 U.S. 203 (1997). This case overruled *Aguilar v. Felton*, 473 U.S. 402 (1985), which had barred New York City Board of Education teachers from providing services to parochial school students in the private schools under Title I of the Elementary and Secondary Education Act. The Court did not stop there, they also overruled *School District of Grand Rapids v. Ball*, 473 U.S. 373 (1985). In *Grand Rapids* the Supreme Court had held that two programs were unconstitutional, violating the Establishment Clause. One program involved hiring public school teachers and placing them in classrooms that were leased from the religious schools by the local school board. The second program that had been ruled unconstitutional was funding community education programs taught by religious personnel in religious schools. The Court said that *Ball* and *Aguilar* were based on three erroneous assumptions: "(i) any public employee who works on a religious school's premises is presumed to inculcate religion in her work, ... (ii) the presence of public employees on private school premises creates an impermissible symbolic union between church and state, ... and (iii) any public aid that directly aids the educational function of religious schools impermissibly finance religious indoctrination, even if the aid reaches such schools as a consequence of private decision making." Since the decision in *Witters* and *Zobrest* had been handed down, the three assumptions were no longer valid law. The court noted that the Supreme Court had the prerogative "... of overruling its own decisions."

In the march to justify state money for religious schools, the U.S. Supreme Court in 2000 handed down *Mitchell v. Helms*. Here an action was brought challenging the constitutionality of state and federal school aid to parochial schools. The Court held that Chapter 2 of Title I of the Elementary and Secondary Education Act which provides educational materials and equipment to public and private schools did not violate the Establishment Clause. Too, the Court overruled other previous church/state decisions which had prohibited aid to parochial schools. One case that was overruled was *Meek v. Pittenger*, 421 U.S. 349 (1975) that had prohibited the same sort of materials and equipment as provided by Chapter 2 in *Helms* as unconstitutional. The second case to be overruled was *Wolman v. Walter*, 433 U.S. 229 (1977). The Court had originally held in *Wolman* that public monies for the purchase of instructional materials and equipment for private school students and using public money for transportation of parochial school students on field trips was unconstitutional.

The constitutional question raised in *Helms* was whether under Chapter 2 of the Education Consolidation and Improvement Act of 1981 lending materials and equipment, such as library and media materials, computers, etc., to church schools violated the Establishment Clause. Justice Thomas wrote that Chapter 2 is not a law respecting an establishment of religion simply because church schools receive the aid. Justice Thomas recast the *Lemon* test as only the first (secular purpose) and second (primary effect of advancing or inhibiting religion), with the third factor in *Lemon,* excessive entanglement, as "not a separate third test, but rather ... simply one criterion relevant to determining the statute's effect."

These precedents gradually negating the effects of the Establishment Clause, permitting state funding of parochial schools, were the precursors of the Court's ultimate goal of constitutional approval of school vouchers. The voucher case arrived in 2002 in *Zelman v. Simmons–Harris*. In this case, the Supreme Court ruled that Ohio Pilot Scholarship Program, voucher program, did not violate the Establishment Clause. The tuition is distributed to parents who in turn convey the funds to the parochial school of their choice. In the 1999–2000 school year 96% of the children receiving vouchers enrolled in religious schools.

In *Zelman*, the Supreme Court said: "This Court's jurisprudence makes clear that a government aid program is not readily subject to challenge under the Establishment Clause if it is neutral with respect to religion and provides assistance directly to a broad class of citizens who, in turn, direct government aid to religious schools wholly as a result of their own genuine and independent private choice.... Under such a program, government aid reaches religious institutions only by way of the deliberate choices of numerous individual recipients."

Based on these court cases, state aid may be provided for religious schools. The U.S. Supreme Court's interpretation of the Federal Constitution appears to allow any aid with the possible exception of direct general aid. However, the rationale of the court in *Helms* and *Zelman* indicates that there is probably no constitutional limit existing that would deny the use of public funds for church schools or churches. The only prohibition would be whether such aid to a church school is prohibited by the state's constitution.

§ 5.61   Textbooks

In 1928 the Louisiana legislature passed an act which allowed the purchase and supply of textbooks for school children throughout the state, including private school children. The United States Supreme Court upheld the act as not violative of the Fourteenth Amendment and based its reasoning on what became known as the "Child Benefit Theory." *Cochran v. Louisiana State Board of Education*, 281 U.S. 370 (1930). Accordingly, the Court said that if the benefit could be justified as benefiting the child, then the law would be upheld.

The state of New York later passed legislation which allowed the lending of textbooks to parochial school children free of charge. In so doing, the New York legislature took constitutional refuge in the child-benefit concept. The United States Supreme Court in *Board of Education of Central School District No. 1 v. Allen*, 392 U.S. 236 (1968) determined that the Act was constitutional and did not violate the Establishment Clause of the First Amendment. Therefore, the loaning of textbooks to private school children does not conflict with the First Amendment. Under the same theory, loans of textbooks were subsequently upheld in *Meek v. Pittenger*, 421 U.S. 349 (1975) and *Wolman v. Walter*, 433 U.S. 229 (1977). Although a state legislative act providing textbooks to private school children may not violate the federal Constitution, it may very well violate a state's constitution. A number of states have more restrictive separation provisions in their constitutions than does the federal Constitution. See *In re Advisory Opinion Re Constitutionality of 1974 Pa. 242*, 228 N.W.2d 772 (Mich. 1975); *California Teachers Association v. Riles (Wilson)*, 632 P.2d 953 (Cal.1981). Yet, of course, now following

Helms and *Zelman*, textbooks as well as more direct aid to parochial schools is constitutionally permissible.

§ 5.62 Public Transportation of Parochial School Students

Transportation of parochial school students at public expense has been upheld by the Supreme Court under the rationale that a "public purpose" or "child benefit" is effectuated. In the leading case establishing this principle, the state of New Jersey authorized reimbursement of bus transportation expenses to parents of private school children, and the practice was challenged as a violation of the New Jersey Constitution and the Federal Constitution. The New Jersey Supreme Court decided the provision violated neither the state nor Federal Constitution. The case was appealed to the United States Supreme Court contending a violation of the First Amendment. The Court ruled that there was no violation of the Establishment Clause. Since the statute was justified on the child benefit theory, the Court said "... we cannot say that the First Amendment prohibits New Jersey from spending tax-raised funds to pay the bus fares of Parochial School pupils as a part of a general program under which it pays the fares of pupils attending public and other schools." *Everson v. Board of Education*, 330 U.S. 1 (1947).

This New Jersey decision, the famous *Everson* case, established that the First Amendment is not offended if transportation aid is provided to private school children. Approximately 30 states now provide aid in a variety of ways, such as transportation expense reimbursement or direct grants to private schools for private school transportation. As with the textbook precedents, *Helms* and

Zelman make the *Everson* discussion superfluous because now there is no general constitutional prohibition to giving parochial schools public tax dollars.

§ 5.63   Tax Credits and Deductions for Students in Parochial Schools

The issue of aid to parochial schools in the form of tax credits or tax deductions is not a new idea. In 1972, a lower federal district court invalidated Ohio's Parental Reimbursement Grant, which provided a tax credit to non-public school parents, a decision that was summarily affirmed by the U.S. Supreme Court in 1973. *Kosydar v. Wolman*, 353 F.Supp. 744 (S.D.Ohio 1972). The Supreme Court also addressed the tax benefit question in *Nyquist* and found a New York statute for nonpublic school parents was unconstitutional. *Committee for Public Education and Religious Liberty v. Nyquist*, 413 U.S. 756 (1973). Again, in 1979, the Supreme Court confronted the tax benefit issue at which time it summarily affirmed the Third Circuit Court of Appeals decision invalidating a tax benefit program for non-public school parents in New Jersey. This program allowed non-public school parents a $100 tax deduction for each dependent child's attendance at a tuition-charging non-public school. *Public Funds for Public Schools v. Byrne*, 590 F.2d 514 (3d Cir.1979). In yet another case, the U.S. Court of Appeals, First Circuit, ruled in 1980 in *Norberg*, a Rhode Island case, that a statute allowing non-public school parents a state income tax deduction for textbooks and transportation expenses was unconstitutional, violating the Establishment Clause. *Rhode Island Federation of Teachers AFL–CIO et al. v. Norberg*, 630 F.2d 855 (1st Cir.1980).

The leading case on the subject of tax credits resulted from a Minnesota statute that allowed all parent taxpayers to deduct from their income taxes a legislatively specified amount. In approving this scheme of aid to private schools, the U.S. Supreme Court appeared to chart a new direction of even greater leniency in provision of public monies for parochial schools. In validating the Minnesota plan, the Court distinguished its rejection of the earlier tax deduction or credit plans by noting that each of those limited tax benefits were available only to parents of private school children, while the Minnesota deduction was available to parents of all children in both private and public schools. The Court did not seem to be concerned that tax deduction benefits to public school parents for tuition, transportation fees and textbooks would be virtually nonexistent. The primary benefits did, of course, accrue largely to the advantage of parochial school parents. Justice Rehnquist, in applying the three-part *Lemon* test for the 5–4 majority, held that the statute had a secular purpose because "A state's decision to defray cost of educational expenses ... regardless of the type of schools ... evidences a purpose that is both secular and understandable." The second prong of the *Lemon* test, the primary effect of advancing religion, was not violated since the tax deduction was available to all and therefore "facially neutral." The government entanglement standard was quickly dismissed by the Court. The Court stated "... we have no difficulty in concluding that the Minnesota statute does not 'excessively entangle' the state in religion." *Mueller v. Allen*, 463 U.S. 388 (1983). Various forms of public aid to parochial schools appear to buttress the rationale of the *Mueller* case; therefore, tax credits (*Mueller*), vouchers (*Zelman*), and materials and supplies (*Helms*) as means of state funding for parochial schools all appear to be permissible under the Establishment Clause. The former "wall of separation" prohibiting public funding of church schools appears to have been eradicated.

CHAPTER 6

STUDENT PUBLICATIONS

§ 6.1 INTRODUCTION

Numerous court decisions have dealt with student publications. The famous *Tinker* case rendered by the U.S. Supreme Court, while not a free press case itself, nevertheless, established that students have constitutional rights and do not abandon those rights at the schoolhouse door. Over the years, the *Tinker* rationale as extended to student publications was not well settled. The court decisions concerning school-sponsored publications were not consistent, and those decisions that dealt with non-school or underground publications were similarly indecisive.

This uncertainty as to publications in schools as to the meaning of precedents, however, did not extend to the freedom of press, generally, beyond the school. Freedom of press is a cornerstone of the basic freedoms found in a democracy. In the Pentagon papers case, the United States Supreme Court stated the importance of freedom of the press. "In the First Amendment, the Founding Fathers gave free press the protection it must have to fulfill its essential role in our democracy; the press was to serve the governed, not the governors. The Government's power to censor was abolished so that the press would remain forever free to censure the Government." *New York Times Co. v. United States*, 403 U.S. 713 (1971).

Accordingly, it would be unthinkable for government agencies to have the legal authority to censor the press; yet, school districts are government agencies and as such have been given special leeway to exercise limited controls over student publications. This authority derives from the historical special legal relationship between the school and the student. The Supreme Court in *Bethel* explained, "... [T]he First Amendment rights of students in the public schools are not automatically coextensive with the rights of adults in other settings and must be applied in light of the special characteristics of the school environment." *Bethel School District No. 403 v. Fraser*, 478 U.S. 675 (1986).

§ 6.11 Types of Publications

In recent years, litigation concerning student publications and their distribution have fallen into three categories: (1) school-sponsored newspapers; (2) non-school or underground newspapers written and distributed by students; and (3) materials distributed by students at school but written and published by non-students. The majority of the cases in the third category concerned the distribution by students of non-student written religious materials. The actions in this last group have resulted in a substantial amount of litigation regarding free speech versus Establishment Clause restrictions and what the courts call forum analysis.

§ 6.12 Forum Analysis and School Newspapers

As discussed above in *Tinker v. Des Moines*, students have constitutional rights including freedom of expression. But as noted in *Bethel v. Fraser*, there is a distinction between the political "message" of the *Tinker* arm-bands and the sexual innuendo that was manifested in *Bethel*. A political message, which may be a matter of public concern, may only be curtailed if it has the proba-bility to "materially or substantially" disrupt the school. This "material or substantial" disruption standard of *Tinker* has been applied to the distribution of non-school publications in school. In other words, students may express their viewpoints in publications unless there is disruption or the reasonable forecast of disruption can be predicted from their publication. More frequently, though, the courts are applying the forum analysis of free speech to student publication issues, a standard different from that of *Tinker*.

Since the Supreme Court identified the notion of a "public forum" in *Hague v. C.I.O.*, 307 U.S. 496 (1939), the precedent has been subject to continuous refinement. Such refinement by the courts has enunciated three types of forums and the restrictions that may be imposed upon each. The three categories are:

First, the traditional public forum, ". . . which [has] immemorially been held in trust for use of the public and . . . [has] been used for the purposes of assembly, com-municating thoughts between citizens, and discussing public questions." *Hague*, supra. This forum has general-ly been applied to areas such as sidewalks and parks. In this forum, a speaker's free speech may be withdrawn only because of a compelling state interest, and the reason must be narrowly drawn and must pass muster under strict scrutiny analysis.

The second category is a limited public forum. This type of forum is found where the state intentionally creates or opens its property for public use. A school is generally assumed to be a closed or non-public forum, but the school may purposely be opened by school officials and therefore created as a limited public forum. A limited forum will not be found to exist in a public school unless (1) there is a government interest in creating such a forum or (2) outsiders seek access to the school and there is evidence that wide access has been otherwise granted. The state is not required to create this type of forum, but once created, it is subject to the same regulations as a public forum and must pass the strict scrutiny analysis.

The third forum is the non-public or closed forum. This forum exists when the state does not open public property for indiscriminate public expression. "Control over access to a non-public forum can be based on subject matter and speaker identity so long as the distinctions drawn are reasonable in light of the purpose served by the forum and are viewpoint neutral." In a non-public forum, the only applicable regulations are time, place, and manner of distribution. The government agency must apply the content neutral standard; in other words, all content must be treated the same. *Slotterback v. Interboro School District*, 766 F.Supp. 280 (E.D.Pa.1991). See also *Gregoire v. Centennial School District*, 907 F.2d 1366 (3d Cir.1990).

Whether the school is a public forum was the heart of a controversy precipitated by a school election in which one of the candidates campaigned by handing out condoms with stickers bearing his slogan. The school had a rule that required prior approval of all campaign flyers and posters used in school elections. Upon complaint the school principal disqualified the student for not obtaining prior approval of the condom campaign tactic. In reviewing the case, the federal court ruled that the school election took place in the context of a non-public forum that was part of the school curriculum, and therefore the school could limit student speech in such school activities that were integral to legitimate pedagogical interests. Even though some other students had campaigned by distributing candy and gum, the court distinguished the condom tactic because the school legitimately did not want to give the impression that it approved such a tactic. *Henerey v. City of St. Charles School Dist.*, 200 F.3d 1128 (8th Cir.1999).

§ 6.13 School–Sponsored Publications

In 1988, after years of litigation involving school's attempts to regulate and control school-sponsored newspapers, the Supreme Court decided *Hazelwood School Dist. v. Kuhlmeier*, 484 U.S. 260 (1988). The *Hazelwood* decision allows the school administration to control or censor a school-sponsored paper, but also gives school officials broad authority regarding other types of expression as well.

The *Hazelwood* litigation involved a challenge of a high school principal's deletion of two articles written by students on the subjects of student pregnancy and divorce. One article described the pregnancy experience of three students while the other discussed the impact of divorce on students at the high school. The principal refused to allow the articles to be printed in the high school newspaper. "The court ... undertook a forum inquiry, [and] concluded that the newspaper was a non-public forum, and held that the school officials had reasonably regulated the contents of the newspaper, thus satisfying the standard of review for state regulation in a non-public forum."

The Court in *Hazelwood* concluded that the First Amendment is not offended if school administrators exercise control over school-sponsored publications or activities. Such include ". . . publications, theatrical productions, and other expressive activities . . ." that may be considered to have the *imprimatur* of the school. The action to exercise editorial control must be ". . . reasonably related to [a] legitimate pedagogical concern." Also, the Court said that school officials had broad discretion to prohibit student articles that are "ungrammatical, poorly written, inadequately researched, biased or prejudicial, vulgar or profane, or unsuitable for immature audiences."

Some states have passed legislation that to a degree counteracts *Hazelwood*. The California Education Code states ". . . students of the public school have the right to exercise freedom of speech and of the press . . . in official publications . . . supported financially by the school." (Cal. Ed. Code § 48907). In *Lopez v. Tulare Joint Union High School District Board of Trustees*, 40 Cal.Rptr.2d 762 (App. 5 Dist.1995), the court decided that the statute protecting student expression did, however, permit school officials to require profanity be deleted in school-sponsored films. The *Lopez* court, citing a previous California case (*Leeb v. Delong*, 243 Cal.Rptr. 494 (App. 1988)), said, "that the broad power to censor expression in school-sponsored publications for pedagogical purposes recognized in *Hazelwood* is not available to California's educators," but California statute does permit school officials to censor expression from official school publications which it reasonably believes to contain an actionable defamation. Other states that have passed similar legislation relating to student newspapers are Colorado, Massachusetts and Iowa.

As stated above, *Hazelwood* reaches beyond the school newspaper. In *McCann v. Fort Zumwalt School District*, 50 F.Supp.2d 918 (E.D.Mo.1999), the superintendent prohibited the school band from performing "White Rabbit" by Jefferson Airplane. He said the lyrics referred to drugs and this would be counter to the school anti-drug programs. The Court acknowledged the playing of "White Rabbit" was protected speech, but *Hazelwood* allows school officials to regulate student expression for a legitimate educational concern. The superintendent's perception that this promoted drugs was reasonable and therefore fell under restriction of *Hazelwood*.

§ 6.14 Non–School Publications

Hazelwood, thus, determined that school authorities may control school-sponsored activities. At the same time, it distinguished between those publications that are not connected officially or appear not to be a school publication. While the school-sponsored activities may be censored for educational reasons, non-school publications enjoy greater freedom and would generally fall under the rationale of the *Tinker* case.

In *Burch v. Barker*, 861 F.2d 1149 (9th Cir.1988), students distributed a student-written four-page newspaper entitled *Bad Astra*. The paper was critical of the school administration but included *no* profanity, obscenity, defamatory statements, etc. School policy required that all non-school publications be submitted to the principal for prior approval. Since this was not a school-sponsored publication, *Hazelwood* did not apply; therefore, the paper was "... not within the purview of the school's exercise of reasonable editorial control." Using *Tinker* as precedent, the court ruled that the prior approval aspect of the policy violated the Constitution by suppressing speech. "... [S]uppressing speech before it is uttered, as opposed to punishment of individuals after expression has occurred, is prior restraint, which generally comes before a court bearing a 'heavy assumption' of unconstitutionality." *Burch*, supra.

Elementary schools by tradition are not public forums where free speech rights are afforded maximum constitutional protection. In elementary schools, administrators may reasonably restrict student expression where it is required to preserve proper decorum, discipline and a desirable school learning environment. Thus, a school principal acted within his prerogative when he halted the distribution of a publication by a fourth grader containing insults, and obscene, libelous language. *Muller by Muller v. Jefferson Lighthouse School*, 98 F.3d 1530 (7th Cir.1996).

§ 6.15   Prior Restraint

A number of student publication cases have been litigated testing the constitutionality of school policies that do permit prior restraint. These policies usually require any student who wishes to distribute material to present that material to the school principal for prior review. The Supreme Court has identified two "evils" which will not be tolerated when considering regulations with prior restraint provisions. "First, a regulation that places 'unbridled discretion' in the hands of a government official constitutes a prior restraint and may result in censorship." The second is prior restraint regulations that do not place time limits within which the official must make a decision as to whether the proposed publication is allowable. Prior restraint is not *per se* unconstitutional and can be justified in situations illustrated by *Hazelwood* where the school is the publisher. *Burch v. Barker*, 861 F.2d 1149 (9th Cir.1988); *Fujishima v. Board of Education*, 460 F.2d 1355 (7th Cir.1972). Other courts have found prior restraint to be constitutional only if accompanied by specific standards and procedural safeguards. *Bystrom v. Fridley High School*, 822 F.2d 747 (8th Cir.1987); *Quarterman v. Byrd*, 453 F.2d 54 (4th Cir.1971).

A school can regulate non-school publications as to time, place, and manner of distribution. There, the school principal can designate the times, locations and means by which non-school literature can be made available at the school. Too, the school principal or teacher in charge can review the materials to be distributed with regard to time and scope of distribution but cannot exercise prior restraint as to content of the materials. *Pounds v. Katy Independent School District*, 517 F. Supp. 2d 901 (S.D. Tex. 2007).

Content can be controlled if it falls within the "disruption" definition of *Tinker*. *Tinker v. Des Moines Independent School District*, 393 U.S. 503 (1969). Moreover, prior restraint can be presumably exercised by the school if the publication violated "fundamental values of habits and manners of civility," within the definition enunciated by the U.S. Supreme Court in *Bethel School District v. Frazer*. In *Bethel,* the court upheld punishment of a student who made a speech that the school officials deemed offensive and in bad taste. The Court said that schools are not required to tolerate "lewd, indecent or offensive speech and conduct" and "evasive sexual innuendo." Thus, even though the courts are particularly protective of publications and frown on prior restraint, school administrators would not be incorrect in applying the *Bethel* speech precedent to non-school publications. *Bethel School District No. 403 v. Fraser*, 478 U.S. 675 (1986).

A policy that required at least 48–hours notice to the principal when 10 or more copies of written material was to be distributed by a student did not constitute prior restraint. *Harless by Harless v. Darr*, 937 F.Supp. 1351 (S.D.Ind.1996). It, of course, goes without saying that the school district should have established school board policies carefully delineating whether the school newspaper is a school-sponsored publication or a non-school publication. If the student newspaper is school sponsored and is not to be considered an open public forum, then school control should be well-defined and uniformly administered. The importance of such a school board policy was illustrated in a New Jersey case where the court agreed that a school newspaper was not a public forum and that editorial control could be exercised by school officials as to both style and content; however, the school district lost the case because it was unable to document by legitimate school board policy that the publication fell under the government of school officials. School publications cannot be governed by vague school board policy. *Desilets v. Clearview Regional Board of Education*, 647 A.2d 150 (N.J.1994).

§ 6.16 Distribution of Religious Materials

A number of recent cases have concerned the distribution of religious material on school campuses. In these cases, the students have attempted to distribute religious newsletters written by non-students. One court has ruled students may not distribute the Gideon Bible in school (*Berger v. Rensselaer Central School Corp.*, 982 F.2d 1160 (7th Cir.1993)), but other court decisions have not been uniform when it comes to distributing other religious materials, such as newsletters. These cases have juxtaposed free speech protections and establishment clause restrictions with some uncertainty as to the prevailing precedent.

This uncertainty has been fed by federal courts permitting religious groups to claim free speech rights as constitutional justification for their proselytizing in public schools. The U.S. Supreme Court in several cases has implicitly encouraged the aggressiveness of these religious groups by holding that a public school cannot deny religious dogma and opinion to be spread (see Equal Access Act) if the school is considered to be an open public forum or a limited public forum. Moreover, the Supreme Court has weighted the constitutional balance against public schools that wish to avoid government establishment of religion, and various Supreme Court opinions have favored religious groups that wish to use public schools to expand their doctrinal beliefs. In this regard, the Supreme Court has said that public schools cannot deny religious speech in schools on the basis of the defense that such religious activity establishes religion. (See *Good News Club v. Milford Central School*, 533 U.S. 98 (2001); *Rosenberger v. Rector and Visitors of University of Virginia*, 515 U.S. 819 (1995). As pointed out above, the Supreme Court has held that where public schools are considered forums open to students and the public, to deny religious speech, the school must show that it has a compelling reason to support such denial; a legal burden that is practically impossible for the public school to carry. *Widmar v. Vincent*, 454 U.S. 263 (1981). Therefore, to prevent religious groups from proselytizing in public schools by speech or distribution of religious materials, the school must declare itself a closed forum or in the alternative must consider religious speech on equal terms and conditions with non-religious speech. Denial cannot be "content based," yet, of course, Bibles (and Korans, et al.) are valued principally by their respective religions for their content.

In a 2007 case a Missouri local school superintendent by the name of M. Homer Lewis, an educational profile in courage, stood against his board and sought to prevent Gideons from coming into the school classrooms to distribute Bibles to fifth graders. The Board sided with the Gideons and Superintendent Lewis had to resign. In the ensuing legal wrangle over the validity of a temporary injunction to prevent the Bible distribution, the U.S. Court of Appeals, 8th Circuit, upheld the injunction and highlighted the schizophrenia of the U.S. Supreme Court decision that on one hand prohibited prayer and Bible reading in public schools as violating the Establishment Clause and on the other hand prohibited schools, in the name of free speech, from making "content-based" decisions on what religious incursions into public schools are permissible. The Eighth Circuit in quoting a *Widmar* dissent observed that, "The Court's Establishment Clause decisions prohibiting, for example, school prayer or posting the Ten Commandments in public schools are inherently based upon content-based distinctions; apart from its content, a prayer is indistinguishable from a biology lesson." See: *Doe v. South Iron R–1 School District*, 498 F.3d 878 (8th Cir. 2007). (*Widmar*, 454 U.S. 285, 102 S.Ct. 269 White, J. dissenting).

Recent cases have largely been decided on the basis of the public forum analysis. According to *Hazelwood*, if school officials have opened the school to "indiscriminate use," then the school becomes a public forum, and a "limited public forum" may be created. If this is the situation, then denial of the right to distribute religious materials may be unconstitutional. *Hedges v. Wauconda Community School District No. 118*, 9 F.3d 1295 (7th Cir.1993).

Thus, school officials may exercise editorial control over school-sponsored publications if they have a legitimate pedagogical reason. If there are non-school publications and the school has created a "limited public forum," then the school officials may control only the time, place, and manner of distribution, but not content. If a school policy requires that students submit materials before distribution, then strong due process procedures must be in place, or the policy is vulnerable to prior restraint challenges.

§ 6.17 Leaflets

Leaflets, brochures, handbills, circulars, flyers or other types of material that are not school sponsored may become an issue of speech and expression in schools. Regardless of the type of materials distributed, the rule of law described above, the "forum analysis," applies. It bears repeating that a public school is not normally a "traditional" public forum nor a government designated one. Most public school districts have done nothing to indicate that their schools are traditional public forums such as parks, byways, or street corners. *Hazelwood School District v. Kuhlmeier*, 484 U.S. 260 (1988). A public elementary school is not a traditional public forum; *Muller v. Jefferson Lighthouse School*, 98 F.3d 1530 (7th Cir. 1996) nor is a public junior high school. *Peck v. Upshur County Board of Education*, 155 F.3d 274 (4th Cir. 1998). The U. S. Constitution "does not require government to freely grant access to all who wish to exercise their right of free speech regardless of the nature of the use of the property or to the disruption that it may cause." *Cornelius v. NAACP Legal Defense and Educational Fund, Inc.*, 473 U.S. 788 (1985).

Public schools are therefore generally considered to be "limited public forums" or "closed forums," not traditional open public forums. School policy may require that leaflets be pre-approved by school officials before distribution. Approval or disapproval must be decided within a reasonable time and must be content neutral. Disapproval may be legal and proper if, as noted above, one could reasonably forecast that the material would cause disruption (*Tinker*). Too, as *Bethel School District No. 403 v. Fraser*, 478 U.S. 675 (1986) indicates, a leaflet can also be disapproved by school authorities if it depicts inappropriate sexual conduct, violence, morbidity or use of obscene language, is libelous, violates another's right of privacy, is false or misrepresents facts, is demeaning of another's race, religion, sex, ethnicity, and constitutes a threat of violence or violates the law. *M.A.L. v. Kinsland*, 543 F.3d 841 (6th Cir. 2008).

Moreover, the school district can regulate time, place and manner of distribution. For example, leaflet distribution can be required to be orderly or posted on particular bulletin boards in hallways, cafeterias or other specified areas. One cannot glue leaflets on walls, lamp posts, or anywhere he or she pleases. What the school cannot do is regulate "content." School policy must be "content neutral" and viewpoint neutral. *M.A.L. v. Kinsland*, 543 F.3d 841 (6th Cir. 2008).

§ 6.18 Guidance for Administration and Teachers

In spite of the fact that most public schools are considered to be limited open forums for speech purposes, school authorities still have considerable discretion as to processes and procedures over distribution of literature and materials by students and others. In way of guidance for public school administrators and teachers, in the face of the U.S. Supreme Court's rather confused signals, the following may be helpful for regulation of the distribution of literature (religious or otherwise) on school premises or at times and places when students are under the jurisdiction of the school:

1. "The First Amendment speech provision does not guarantee the right to communicate one's views at all times and in all places or in any matter that one desires." (*Doe v. South Iron R–1 School District*, 498 F.3d 878 (8th Cir. 2007).

2. "Nothing in the U.S. Constitution requires the government (public schools) to give access to all who desire to exercise their right to free speech on government property without regard to the use of the property or to the disruption that might be caused by the speaker's activities." (*M.A.L. v. Kinsland*, 2008, op cit.)

3. If the school is considered to be a "limited open forum," and not a "closed forum," then "content-

based" censorship cannot prevail unless the school can show a compelling state interest in controlling the content.

4. Even with a "limited open forum," the school authorities can regulate speech as to "time, place and manner" of distribution. The school district's restrictions may be constitutionally valid so long as the restraints are "viewpoint neutral" and reasonable in pursuit of the school's purpose of good conduct of the school.

5. School policy may require students to submit materials to the school administration for approval prior to distribution. The administrator, or designee, must respond within a reasonable time his/her approval or disapproval. If disapproved, reasons should be given. Disapproval may be justified if the literature or material:

   a) could be reasonably foreseen to cause disruption or material interference with the normal operation of the school (*Tinker*);

   b) is potentially offensive to a portion of the school community due to depiction of sexual conduct, violence, morbidity or use of language or pictures that are profane, vulgar or obscene (*Bethel*);

   c) is libelous or violates another's right of privacy;

   d) is false, misleading, or misrepresents facts;

   e) is disparaging or demeaning as to race, religion, gender or ethnic group;

   f) includes true threats or implied threats of harm to anyone;

g) suggests or encourages violation of law, federal, state, or local.

6. Disapproval must provide for appeal to a higher level in the school and finally to the school board.

7. The meaning of the term "distribution" must be defined and clearly set forth.

8. The place of distribution should be specified, such as hallway or cafeteria, tables or bulletin boards, and must be set forth as well as time at which the distribution can occur. Manner should be prescribed; for example, materials should not be scattered and the distribution area should be free of trash and clutter.

9. Finally, the policy should be formally adopted by the school board and included in school policy manuals and student handbooks. Students should be made aware of the policy and there should be documentation of such. (See *M.A.L. v. Kinsland*, 543 F.3d 841 (6th Cir. 2008) and *Doe v. South Iron R–1 School District*, 498 F.3d 878 (8th Cir. 2007)).

CHAPTER 7

SEARCH AND SEIZURE

§ 7.1 INTRODUCTION

Teachers and principals have frequently found it necessary to search students and remove from their possession items which may be harmful to them or to others. Several years ago most searches were found to be necessary to remove slingshots or pocketknives from a student's possession, or to detect and retrieve the fruits of minor thievery. Such searches remained almost entirely an affair internal to the school and seldom, if ever, involved outside authorities. Today, however, the prevalence of drugs, handguns, bombs, and/or bomb threats have broadened the importance of school search and seizure to include offenses which may subject the student to criminal prosecution. A majority of the student search and seizure cases are initiated during criminal proceedings by students who are seeking suppression of evidence obtained at school that is being used against them by the prosecution.

§ 7.11 Right of Privacy

The courts have ruled that students have a right to privacy which is protected by the Fourth Amendment, and this right cannot be invaded unless the intrusion can be justified in terms of the school's legitimate interests. The right of privacy is not absolute but is subject to reasonable school regulation within the bounds of reasonable suspicion. The Supreme Court in *New Jersey v. T.L.O.* and again in *Vernonia School District 47J v. Acton* stated that students in the school environment have a lesser expectation of privacy than the general population.

The right of privacy itself is predicated on two factors being present: first, whether the person in question "exhibited an actual (subjective) expectation of privacy," and, second, whether the "expectation of privacy be one that society is prepared to recognize as 'reasonable.'" The Supreme Court has said that: "The Fourth Amendment protects people, not places. What a person knowingly exposes to the public, even in his own home or office, is not a subject of Fourth Amendment protection.... But what he seeks to preserve as private, even in an area accessible to the public, may be constitutionally protected." *Katz v. United States*, 389 U.S. 347 (1967).

§ 7.2 FOURTH AMENDMENT

The Fourth Amendment of the United States Constitution provides: "The right of people to be secure in their persons, houses, papers, and effects, against unreasonable searches and seizures, shall not be violated, and no warrants shall issue, but upon probable cause, supported by oath or affirmation, and particularly describing the place to be searched, and the persons or things to be seized."

The Fourth Amendment has five important components. First, it enunciates and protects the *right* of people "to be secure in their persons, houses, papers and effects." Second, it protects persons from *unreasonable* searches and seizures. Third, a search cannot be institut-

ed without government showing *probable cause* or giving
evidence that a search is necessary. Fourth, the search
must be *specific*, describing the place to be searched and
the articles to be seized. Last, a *magistrate* or *judge* is
interposed between the individual and the government,
requiring that the government justify with evidence the
necessity of the search.

Application of three of these five components is easily
made to student searches in public schools. Students
have a right of privacy—to be secure in their persons,
papers and effects—and this right protects them against
unreasonable searches and seizures. Moreover, any
search must be specific as to what is sought in the search
and the location where it is secreted. The courts do not,
however, require that school officials be able to provide
evidence constituting probable cause or that they obtain
a warrant from a judge justifying a search.

The Supreme Court in *New Jersey v. T.L.O.*, 469 U.S.
325 (1985) established the prevailing precedent regarding
school searches and seizures. The Court held that the
Fourth Amendment does apply to schools, and in order
for searches to be constitutionally valid, reasonableness
must prevail. The Court stated that "the legality of a
search of a student should depend on the reasonableness,
under all circumstances, of the search." According to the
Court in *T.L.O.*, the constitutional validity of a search is
to be determined at two levels. The first level involves
consideration of whether the search is justified at its
inception. The inception of the search is the point at
which reasonable suspicion comes into play. Was the
motivation for the search reasonable in light of the
information obtained by the school official? The second
level concerns the reasonableness of the search itself; the

"measures adopted for the search must be reasonably related to the objectives of the search and not excessively intrusive in light of the age and sex of the student and the nature of the infraction." A search is not reasonable if it lacks specificity, or if it excessively intrudes on the student's privacy. (See Chapter 13.)

§ 7.21 Reasonable Suspicion

Reasonable suspicion is a standard less rigorous of proof than the requirement of probable cause. Probable cause requires more than mere suspicion or even reasonable suspicion. Probable cause is the standard required of police to obtain a warrant from a magistrate or a judge before a search can be legal. School officials need only have "reasonable suspicion," not the more stringent "probable cause." Reasonable suspicion is a belief or opinion based on the facts or circumstances. Although the standard of "reasonable suspicion" is a lower standard than that of the "probable cause" required for police to obtain a warrant, it is not so unrestrictive as to place no constraints on school personnel.

A student's freedom from unreasonable search and seizure must be balanced against the need for school officials to maintain order and discipline and to protect the health and welfare of all the students. For example, in a case where a student's car was searched revealing cocaine, after an assistant principal observed that the student had glassy eyes, a flushed face, slurred speech, smelled of alcohol, and walked with an unsteady gait, the court found this condition to be ample evidence to support reasonable suspicion. *Shamberg v. State*, 762 P.2d 488 (Alaska App.1988). "Reasonable suspicion of wrong doing is a common-sense conclusion about human behavior upon which practical people, including governmental officials, are entitled to rely." *United States v. Cortez*, 449 U.S. 411 (1981).

"A number of courts have held that information provided by an informant can serve as a basis for a reasonable suspicion that a student may be engaged in illegal activity." *Singleton v. Board of Education*, 894 F.Supp. 386 (D.Kan.1995). In *C.B. v. Driscoll*, 82 F.3d 383 (11th Cir.1996), a high school principal searched a student's coat based on another student's tip. The tip was that the student had drugs, and the court ruled that a reliable tip with some additional corroboration constituted reasonable suspicion.

§ 7.22   Inception of Search

The facts leading to the initiation of a search must indicate that the suspicion was reasonable from the inception. In a case where a student was observed in an office where items had been stolen and was also found to have unauthorized objects in his possession, the court concluded that reasonable suspicion was established for a search of the student's locker. *R.D.L. v. State*, 499 So.2d 31 (Fla.App.1986).

§ 7.23   Intrusiveness of Search

Whether a search is reasonable is a subjective determination, and the court's decision will be based on the individual facts of each case. It is clear, though, that excessively intrusive searches must be supported by a strong degree of suspicion by the school officials. The courts will require a corresponding relationship between the extensiveness of grounds supporting reasonable suspicion and the degree to which a search intrudes on a student's privacy. A more extensive and intrusive search, however, may require more evidence to establish reasonable suspicion.

§ 7.24 Suspicionless Searches and Special Needs

The ultimate measure of the constitutionality of a government search is "reasonableness." "Reasonableness" of a search is dependent on a fact-specific balancing of the intrusion on a child's Fourth Amendment rights against the promotion of a legitimate governmental interest. The U.S. Supreme Court in recent years has been inclined to permit greater school prerogative in search situations. In *Vernonia School District 47J v. Acton*, the U.S. Supreme Court explained that a search unsupported by probable cause can be constitutional when "special needs" beyond the normal need for law enforcement make the "warrant and probable-cause requirement impracticable." Such a "special needs" situation exists in a public school context where strict adherence to the requirement of probable cause "would undercut the substantial need of teachers and administrators for freedom to maintain order in the schools."

The question, therefore, arises as to whether the reasonable suspicion criterion for schools forecloses any possibility of suspicionless searches. The answer is "no." As noted above, the reasonable suspicion standard for schools, while far less stringent than probable cause, nevertheless, does require a showing that the suspicion was generated by some specific evidence that something harmful is secreted in the plan to be searched. In other words, reasonable suspicion, as explained by the court in *T.L.O.*, to be a legal search, had to be reasonably specific and could not be random or suspicionless. *T.L.O.*, however, is not the end of the story. As the U.S. Supreme Court's thinking has evolved on the matter and the exigencies of school safety have become more pronounced, the Court has permitted greater school prerogative and control. Subsequent to *T.L.O.*, the U.S. Supreme Court approved random or suspicionless searches in the aforementioned *Vernonia* case (1995) and later in *Board of Education of Independent School District No. 92 of Pottawatomie v. Earls*, 536 U.S. 822 (2002). Both *Vernonia* and *Earls* permitted suspicionless searches because the special need for a random search of a specific population of students in the school student body was greater than the privacy interests of the students. Thus, the Supreme Court in *Vernonia* and *Earls* concluded that the requirement of reasonable suspicion was not a hard-and-fast constitutional rule and that a search could be reasonable even though specific suspicion did not exist at the time. The real test of reasonableness of a search must ultimately be determined in the conduct of a fact-specific balancing of the children's Fourth Amendment rights against the promotion of governmental interests. Both *Vernonia* and *Earls* suggest that the governmental interests of the school are substantially weightier in an era when guns, bombs, and drugs may threaten the safety of children in school.

Neither *Vernonia* nor *Earls*, however, suggests that school administrators have open-ended authority to conduct random or suspicionless searches of all the students in a school. Moreover, as the interests are balanced, the courts will be very much concerned with whether a search was conducted for school disciplinary reasons solely internal to the conduct of the school or for purposes of criminal prosecution of students. *Vernonia* and *Earls* involved random drug testing of students who participated in athletics (*Vernonia*), extracurricular activities (*Earls*), and not classes internal to the educational process. It must be noted that extracurricular activities are not viewed by the courts as a property or liberty interest whereas curricular matters and classes are viewed quite differently by the courts.

§ 7.241 Validity of Searches Under State Constitutions

While *Vernonia* and *Earls* prescribe search protections under the federal constitution, they do not define the protections under state constitutions. State constitutional provisions guarding the rights of privacy may be stronger in shielding an individual against government intrusion than does the federal constitution. This extra strength is sometimes referred to as "independent vitality." A good example of this superior safeguard is illustrated in a 2008 case rendered by the Supreme Court of the State of Washington. In this instance, that court ruled that the Washington state constitution providing "no person shall be disturbed in his private affairs, or his home invaded, without authority of law" effectively, contrary to *Vernonia* and *Earls*, prohibited suspicionless, random drug testing of student athletes. In applying this state constitutional provision to a school policy requiring that a student athlete must go to a bathroom stall and provide a urine sample intrudes on the student's reasonable expectation of privacy. The Washington court said, "Indeed, we offer heightened protection for bodily functions compared to the federal courts." In so holding, the court observed that a person's privacy is a fundamental right that cannot be overcome except by law where warrants are issued or in narrow exceptions where a search is in plain view, incident to arrest or for automobile investigative stops. The Washington court rejected the federal exception for drugs in schools as a category of "special needs" as discussed above. The court said, "We have not created a general special needs exception ... that would allow the State to depart from the warrant requirement whenever it could articulate a special need...." Further, this court stated emphatically that "We cannot countenance random searches of public school student athletes ..." It concluded, "We decline to adopt a doctrine similar to the federal special needs exception in the context of randomly drug testing of student athletes." *York v. Wahkiakum School District No. 200*, 178 P.3d 995 (Wash.2008).

Therefore, while random suspicionless searches of student athletes may be permissible under the federal constitution as a special needs exception to a requirement of a warrant, the same may not be true under state constitutions that have higher standards in protection of privacy rights.

§ 7.25 Exclusionary Rule

School officials should be primarily concerned with removing contraband from the school environment for the betterment of other students and not for use in the criminal prosecution of students. Because materials seized in public schools are frequently illegal and may be turned over to law enforcement officials, the "exclusionary rule" has often been raised where the student is ultimately tried in a court of law. The question thus arises: Can illegal materials seized by school officials be used in criminal prosecutions or must they be excluded as evidence?

In 1914, in *Weeks v. United States*, 232 U.S. 383 (1914), the Supreme Court established that evidence seized without a warrant could not be used in federal courts for federal prosecution. This doctrine, the *Weeks Doctrine*, thereafter excluded evidence obtained illegally by federal officials from use in federal trials. In *Mapp v. Ohio*, 367 U.S. 643 (1961), the Supreme Court expanded the *Weeks Doctrine* or "exclusionary rule" to ban illegally-seized evidence in state courts. This extension of the exclusionary rule has been litigated numerous times in public education cases.

The Supreme Court in *T.L.O.* noted the courts have ". . . split over whether the exclusionary rule is an appropriate remedy for Fourth Amendment violations committed by school authorities." The Court further observed that the issue was not resolved by *T.L.O.* ". . . our determination that the search at issue in [*T.L.O.*] did not violate the Fourth Amendment implies no particular resolution of the question of the applicability of the exclusionary rule." A majority of the courts have ruled that materials seized by school officials may be used as evidence in a criminal prosecution.

§ 7.26 Liability for Illegal Search

One may wonder what the consequences are of an illegal search of students by teachers or school administrators. What redress is available for the student? As discussed above, if the search is illegal, its fruits may or may not be excluded from prosecution of the student should a criminal trial ensue. Beyond this, the student may possibly bring an action under Title 42 U.S.C.A., Section 1983. (See Chapter 12, Civil Liability.) As discussed elsewhere in this book, a student may seek damages under Section 1983 if school officials maliciously deny his or her constitutional rights. The Sixth Circuit in the *Williams* case, infra, noted, "government officials performing discretionary functions generally are shielded from liability for civil damages insofar as their conduct does not violate clearly established statutory or constitutional rights of which a reasonable person would have known." It is important to note that if school officials deny constitutional rights, but do so in the good faith fulfillment of their responsibilities and not in ignorance and disregard for established indisputable principles of law, then no liability will occur. This immunity is accorded only within the bounds of reason. When school officials, in *Doe v. Renfrow*, infra, strip searched a child "without any individualized suspicion and without reasonable cause," the court said: "We suggest as strongly as possible that the conduct herein described exceeded the 'bounds of reason' by two and a half country miles. It is not enough for us to declare that the little girl involved was indeed deprived of her constitutional and basic human rights. We must also permit her to seek damages from those who caused this humiliation. . . ."

A police officer may also be liable for damages under § 1983. Where a police officer at school searched 30 students for missing money by having them remove their shirts and/or lower their pants for visual inspection, the court ruled the search was unreasonably intrusive; it was not justified at its inception because there was no individual suspicion. *Bell v. Marseilles Elementary School*, 160 F.Supp.2d 883 (N.D.Ill.2001).

§ 7.27   Police Involvement

School officials, therefore, may be held liable for damages for violation of a student's civil rights for illegal searches; however, as a general rule, qualified immunity shields school officials who perform their discretionary duties in a reasonable manner. In order for liability to accrue, there must be a clear violation of the student's rights. The Supreme Court in *T.L.O.* gave the school wide discretion in order to operate a well-managed school. *Jenkins by Hall v. Talladega City Board of Educ.*, 115 F.3d 821 (11th Cir.1997).

Because school officials may on the basis of reasonable suspicion search students without a search warrant, police will on occasion seek school assistance from a school principal or other school official in searching students. The stronger probable cause standard to which police must adhere makes it more advantageous and opportune for police to merely convince a school principal that a search is needed. If this is done, the court must decide whether the school official was, in fact, conducting the search based on his/her own initiative or whether the search was really conducted at the instigation of the police. A number of courts have ruled that where police are involved and in charge, the full complement of Fourth Amendment rights applies, and the higher standard of probable cause must prevail. Simply because a student is on school grounds does not mean the police officers are not bound by appropriate constitutional duties. The lesser "reasonable suspicion" standard is not available to school officials if the search is carried out at the behest of the police. *In Interest of F.P. v. State*, 528 So.2d 1253 (Fla.App.1988). If a school official does not act on his/her own initiative and follows the request of the police, then the school officials would be acting as an agent of the police. In this capacity school officials would need consent from the student in order to search.

Police school liaison officers who are under the control of school officials may conduct searches at the request of school officials without first obtaining a warrant. Where a police liaison officer was contacted by the assistant school principal and given information regarding the possible secreting of a knife in a backpack of a female student, conducted a search and found the knife, the court held the search valid even though the evidence was used by the state against the girl in juvenile court proceeding. The court reasoned that the liaison officer acted under the authority of the school for the welfare and safety of students and the search was no more intrusive than necessary. Probable cause and a warrant were not required because the search was directed by the school with reasonable suspicion sufficient to justify the search. *In the Interest of Angelia D.B.*, 564 N.W.2d 682 (Wis.1997).

§ 7.271 School Resource Officers (SROS)

School liaison officers are now commonly referred to as school resource officers (SROs). School resource officers are defined by the federal Omnibus Crime Control and Safe Streets Act of 1968 (Part Q, Title I) as "a career law-enforcement officer, with sworn authority, deployed in community-oriented policing, and assigned by the employing police department or agency to work in collaboration with school and community-based organizations." Duties of SROs usually include patrolling school grounds, parking lots, hallways, restrooms, assistance in handling disruptive students, preventing trespassing, and investigating criminal complaints.

With regard to search and seizure, a question arises as to whether SROs are actually school employees, or, in fact, municipal police. If the latter, the contraband or personal "effects" that they discover in searches can be suppressed in a criminal proceeding.

Critical questions arise, therefore, as to whether the SRO is actually a municipal police officer. Lawrence cites four essential questions in this determination:

1) What are the terms of employment of the SRO? If school employees, then they should be considered school personnel comparable to teachers and school administrators.

2) What is the purpose of the search? If the search is instituted as a matter of school control and discipline, then only reasonable suspicion is required of the SRO, school administration or teacher. If the purpose is to discover information for a criminal investigation and prosecution, then probable cause and a warrant is required.

3) What is the role of the SRO in the search? If the SRO is merely a school safety employee, then reasonable suspicion is the test; but if he/she is considered a municipal police officer, then a search requires probable cause and a warrant.

4) What is the emanation of the search? If the search originates with a school administrator, teacher or a SRO school employee, then reasonable suspicion is all that is required. However, if the SRO is a municipal police officer and the search emanates from him/her, then probable cause and a warrant is

required. (See: Richard Lawrence, *School Crime and Juvenile Justice, 2d ed.* Oxford, Oxford University Press, 2007, pp. 206–208.)

In an Illinois case brought to determine whether cocaine should be suppressed as evidence in a criminal prosecution of a student, the court said that there are three main factors to be considered as to school searches and the involvement of municipal police officers: 1) whether the school administrators or teachers initiate the search and the police involvement is minimal and secondary; 2) whether the municipal police officer is acting on his/her own authority, and 3) whether the municipal officer causes the search to be undertaken. (*People v. Dilworth*, 661 N.E. 2d 310 (Ill. 1996).

Courts will consider the facts and will give the school administrator or teacher "flexibility" in engaging the assistance of a municipal police officer if there is some danger to the school. *In re Alexander B.,* 220 Cal.App.3d 1572 (1990).

The Supreme Court of New Hampshire has put the issue rather succinctly, saying that school administrators and teachers and school SROs should not assume the role of "criminal investigators." If they do so, then they exceed their privilege of search of only "reasonable suspicion." On the other hand, the municipal police cannot assume the protective mantle of school personnel to legitimize a search under the lesser reasonable suspicion standard where the facts indicate that the purpose of the search is for criminal prosecution. *State of New Hampshire v. Heirtzler*, 789 A.2d 634 (N.H. 2001).

Fourth Amendment protection against government intrusion on the privacy of a student may possibly apply to the interrogation of a student by police in the investigation of a commission of a crime. Search procedures by police are covered by what is known as "Miranda warnings" which emanate from U.S. Supreme Court requirements that police inform all persons under interrogation of their constitutional rights not to incriminate themselves. Miranda warnings do not apply to school official's interrogation of students regarding the breaking of school rules even though the offense may produce evidence that could be used against a student in a criminal prosecution. *In re Harold S.*, 731 A.2d 265 (R.I.1999).

§ 7.28 Consent

School authorities do not need the consent of the student in order to conduct a search. If municipal police participate in the search, they must have a warrant or obtain the student's consent. Consent, though, must be given freely and willingly without coercion. The police cannot lawfully ask a school official to influence the student's decision to permit a search. Thus, authority of the school cannot be validly converted by police to acquire the student's consent in order to forego the necessity of a warrant.

If SROs are considered municipal police officers and not school employees, then students are entitled to *Miranda* rights (*Miranda v. Arizona*, 384 U.S. 436 (1966), to have charges read as to their right to remain silent and to have legal counsel in criminal investigations. With regard to *Miranda* rights, a secondary issue emerges as to whether a minor can give consent to a search or interrogation by police without an attorney present. The U.S. Supreme Court has held that a juvenile can waive the right to an attorney if he/she understands the "totality of circumstances" involved. *Fare v. Michael C.*, 442

U.S. 707 (1979). On the other hand, if SROs are considered to be school employees and not municipal police officers, then the *Miranda* warning is not required.

Lawrence summarizes the *Miranda* issue in four main points:

> 1) Did the juvenile student make a voluntary or informed consent as to a confession or statement?
>
> 2) Was the student told by his/her parents to cooperate with police? If so, consent may not be valid.
>
> 3) Was the questioning of the student/ juvenile initiated in order to get information to support taking him/her into "custody"?
>
> 4) Was the school resource officer involved a municipal police officer or a school personnel resource officer?

Richard Lawrence, *School Crime and Juvenile Justice, 2d edition* (Oxford: Oxford University Press, 2007) p. 217.

§ 7.29 Dragnet Searches

Random suspicionless searches are sometimes referred to as dragnet searches whereby school officials attempt to clear the schools of harmful substances or dangerous weapons. As discussed elsewhere in this chapter, such searches are usually of three types: a) urinalysis detection for drugs, b) drug-sniffing dogs, and c) metal detectors for weapons. The key to the validity of such searches is the "intrusiveness" of and "reasonableness" of the search. Where a search was conducted that revealed a hunting knife when all students in class were required to stand and empty their pockets to determine which student had a disruptive cell phone that kept playing music, the court ruled that the search was not "unreasonable and overly intrusive" even though the hunting knife was used as evidence in a criminal prosecution. *In re Elvin G.*, 851 N.Y.S.2d 129 (1st Dept. 2008).

The U.S. Court of Appeals, Eighth Circuit, in a Little Rock, Arkansas case, ruled that in spite of today's extraordinary need to protect students at school from drugs and weapons, the schools cannot employ "highly intrusive" random, dragnet searches that encroach upon "students' legitimate privacy interests." *Doe ex rel. Doe v. Little Rock School District*, 380 F.3d 349 (8th Cir. 2004). This court distinguished this situation from that of the *Vernonia* and *Earls* searches that were upheld by the U.S. Supreme Court, the departing line being that in this instance the school district could not show any immediate governmental need for the searches, and the fruits of the searches were routinely turned over to the police for criminal prosecution. The federal court elaborated saying that these "[f]ull-scale searches that involve rummaging through personal belongings concealed within a container are manifestly more intrusive than searches effected by metal detectors or dogs." This federal court acknowledged that "the line separating reasonable and unreasonable school searches is sometimes indistinct," yet reasonableness and the intrusiveness of the search provides good judicial guideposts. Moreover, the court observed that a more subjective but important condition is that the school undertakes the search to provide a safe school environment and not for the singular purpose of obtaining evidence for the criminal prosecution of students.

§ 7.3 CANINE SEARCHES

In recent years, officials have used dogs to sniff out contraband. Canine searches have been viewed by the courts with mixed reactions.

The Tenth Circuit Court of Appeals in *Zamora v. Pomeroy*, 639 F.2d 662 (10th Cir.1981) upheld the use of dogs in the exploratory sniffing of lockers. The court noted that since the schools gave notice at the beginning of the year that the lockers might be periodically opened, the lockers were jointly possessed by both student and school. With joint possession either party can obtain entry. The court further stated that since the school officials had a duty to maintain a proper educational environment, it was necessary for them to inspect lockers. Similarly, the Seventh Circuit Court in *Doe v. Renfrow*, 635 F.2d 582 (7th Cir.1980) held that school officials stood *in loco parentis* and had a right to use dogs to seek out drugs because of the diminished expectations of privacy inherent in the public schools.

However, a contrary conclusion was reached in a federal district court case, *Jones v. Latexo Independent School District*, 499 F.Supp. 223 (E.D.Tex.1980). The school district in *Jones* used dogs to sniff both students and automobiles. The court ruled, in the absence of individualized suspicion, that the sniffing of the students was too intrusive and not reasonable. Moreover, because the students did not have access to their automobiles during the school day, the school's interest in having dogs sniff the cars was minimal and was, therefore, also unreasonable.

In another dog case, *Horton v. Goose Creek Independent School District*, 690 F.2d 470 (5th Cir.1982), the court wrote, "The problem presented in this case is convergence of two troubling questions. First, is the sniff of a drug-detecting dog a 'search' within the purview of the Fourth Amendment? Second, to what extent does the Fourth Amendment protect students against searches by school administrators seeking to maintain a safe environment conducive to education?" In response to the first question, the court stated, "We accordingly hold that the sniff of the lockers and cars did not constitute a search ..." Concerning the second question, the court ruled that school officials may search students if they have "reasonable cause" but "the intrusion on dignity and personal security that goes with the type of canine inspection of the student's person involved in this case cannot be justified by the need to prevent abuse of drugs and alcohol when there is no individualized suspicion; and we hold it unconstitutional." It should be noted that these canine search cases pre-date the U.S. Supreme Court case of *New Jersey v. T.L.O.*. We do know that in a post-*Vernonia* and pre-*Earls* decision, the U.S. Court of Appeals, Ninth Circuit, held that random suspicionless sniff searches of students by dogs was unreasonable, in particular where the school officials could produce no evidence that would suggest that the school had a drug problem prior to the search. *B.C. through Powers v. Plumas Unif. School District*, 192 F.3d 1260 (9th Cir. 1999). Using the standards in *T.L.O.* and assuming that the dogs were not used to sniff the belongings of a certain school population such as band members or athletes, then it would appear that individual suspicion or a very high risk to the health and safety of the student body would be required to justify a canine search.

§ 7.4 STRIP SEARCHES

The courts have allowed school officials to search students if they have reasonable suspicion that the student is in possession of something illegal or in violation of school regulations. Strip searches of students are permissible if they are justified at their inception and are performed with reasonableness and in the least intrusive manner possible.

The U.S. Court of Appeals, 9th Circuit, in a 2008 case, explained that "under ordinary circumstances, a search of a student by a teacher or school official will be justified at its inception when there are reasonable grounds for suspecting that the search will turn up evidence that the student has violated or is violating either the law or the rules of the school; reasonableness depends on context." The operative words are "inception," "reasonableness" and "context." *Redding v. Safford Unified School District No. 1*, 531 F.3d 1071 (2008). Where a nude search may be justified for reasonable suspicion of marijuana, cocaine or other illegal drugs, a strip-search may not be justified in search for lesser drugs such as Ibuprofen or aspirin. (*Redding v. Safford Unified School District No. 1*, 531 F.3d 1071 (2008).

Reasonable suspicion to support a search at its inception may concern what information is acquired and from what source. If a fellow student is the informant and that student has a questionable record of trust, then a strip-search may well be unreasonable. Courts do not treat all informants' tips with equal veracity and weight in establishing reasonable suspicion. The U.S. Court of Appeals in *Redding* points out that there cannot be valid reasonable suspicion without taking into account the "totality of the circumstances." For example, a fellow student informant who provides a tip about hidden drugs may not be reliable if the informant does so to exculpate herself from suspicion and is, in fact, seeking to unload suspicion on another student. Therefore, such information may fall well short of reasonable suspicion to justify the inception of a strip search. To justify a strip search, the school official must consider that the "experience of disrobing and exposing one's self for visual inspection by a stranger ... can only be seen as thoroughly degrading and frightening." (*Redding v. Safford Unified School District No. 1*, 531 F.3d 1071 (2008). Therefore, because of the intrusiveness of strip searches, maximum care should be taken to verify and validate the reasonable suspicion supporting the inception of a nude search. What is the "totality of the circumstances" involved is the key.

However, the courts have generally been more lenient in allowing strip searches where drugs are involved. The Sixth Circuit Court of Appeals concluded in one case that a strip search was valid because school officials were searching for drugs. In that case, after talking with concerned parents and students, school officials believed a student possessed a "white powdery substance" and the student was requested to remove her t-shirt and lower her jeans to her knees. In spite of this high degree of intrusiveness the court held that the search complied with *T.L.O.* standards and was "... not unreasonable in light of the item sought (narcotics) in conducting a search so personally intrusive in nature." *Williams by Williams v. Ellington*, 936 F.2d 881 (6th Cir.1991).

In another drug-related-search case, a 16–year–old student who was enrolled in a behavioral disorder program was known to use drugs and to hide them in his crotch. School personnel observed that the student appeared "too well endowed" and reported this to school administrators. The following day two school administrators took the student to the boy's locker room and required him to remove his clothes. The student was requested to change into gym clothes while the administrators stood approximately ten to twelve feet away and visually inspected him. Previously, the student told a teacher he crotched drugs, and a policeman told the Dean of Students earlier he had information the student was selling marijuana and had failed a urine test for cocaine; therefore, reasonable suspicion was cumulative. Because these incidents were reported by various individuals, there was sufficient reasonable suspicion to conduct the strip search, and, given the circumstances, the method of search was the least intrusive under the circumstances. *Cornfield by Lewis v. Consolidated High School District No. 230*, 991 F.2d 1316 (7th Cir.1993).

Strip searches to find stolen money have generally not been upheld by the courts. The court in *Konop v. Northwestern School District*, 26 F.Supp.2d 1189 (D.S.D.1998) ruled that the strip search of eight students to find $200 stolen was unreasonable, and the principal and teacher were not entitled to qualified immunity.

In *Bellnier v. Lund*, 438 F.Supp. 47 (N.D.N.Y.1977), the court ruled that a teacher who strip-searched the entire class trying to locate three dollars violated the Fourth Amendment. The court noted that the relative slight danger of the missing money had to be considered, and if something more dangerous were present, the result might be different.

In a case of similar factual nature, but with different results, a West Virginia court ruled a strip search for missing money was unreasonable. The court stated that stealing "... should never be condoned or encouraged in our schools, but in evaluating the nature of the situation in terms of the danger it presents to other students, it does not begin to approach the threat posed by possession of weapons or drugs." *State of West Virginia v. Mark Anthony B.*, 433 S.E.2d 41 (W.Va.1993).

Thus, the object of the search is very important as to the "totality of the circumstances" and the reasonableness of the search. The discovery of drugs, weapons, or items that may be harmful to health and safety weigh more heavily than searches, the objects of which are of lesser importance to the health and welfare of the students.

When strip searches take place, the following procedures are in order: (1) have members of the same sex perform the search, (2) use a room where only the participants are present to conduct the search, and (3) limit the search to exclude body cavities. *Rudolph v. Lowndes Co. Bd. of Ed.*, 242 F.Supp.2d 1107 (M.D.Ala. 2003).

§ 7.5 LOCKERS

Since the *T.L.O.* case, most courts have concluded that no expectation of privacy exists for the search of school lockers. Lockers are made available to the students for the limited purposes of storing legitimate materials needed for educational purposes. Some courts have held there is no reasonable expectation of privacy at all if school officials have an announced policy that lockers are not private property. One court stated, "School administrators may adopt a locker policy retaining ownership and possessory control of school lockers and give notice of that policy to students." Such policy permits school searches. *In Interest of Isiah B.*, 500 N.W.2d 637 (Wis. 1993). The Supreme Court of Wisconsin in this case held constitutional a random search of student lockers. In this case, the school was having considerable problems with weapons. Guns on school buses, guns in school, and multiple gunshots at a school dance were found to be justifiable reasons to have a random search of lockers as a "preventive measure." Because of a written policy stating that the school retained ownership of the lockers, the court found that: "... students had no reasonable expectation of privacy in those lockers." The court further observed "our holding is an example or adaptation of constitutional principles to a modern crisis." *In Interest of Isiah B.*, supra.

In Maryland where state law permitted reasonable searches of a student based on reasonable belief that a student had in his possession something that would constitute evidence in a criminal offense, the court held that school lockers could be searched by school officials. The state law made it clear that a student could not have had an expectation of privacy in the school locker that was temporarily assigned to him. *In re Patrick Y.*, 746 A.2d 405 (Md.2000). As this case and others indicate, the school or school district policy and/or state statute regarding the nature of lockers should clearly state that the student is not in sole possession of the locker, and that it is not a private place as against the school (against the world) but, rather, the school is the owner and reserves right of entry to its own property at anytime. With such a clear right of entry to lockers, school officials can require that all lockers be emptied if they fear that something is hidden there that may be harmful to students.

§ 7.51 Surveillance Cameras

Schools may utilize surveillance cameras in classrooms, hallways, school grounds, and school buses without encroaching on the right of privacy of students; however, cameras in locker rooms present a more complicated issue, even if the school's purpose is to catch locker room thieves. The U.S. Court of Appeals, Sixth Circuit, has ruled that school locker rooms where students undress and shower are of elevated personal privacy, and it is clearly judicially established that the personal privacy of students prohibits school administrators from surreptitiously videotaping students when they are changing their clothes. *Brannum v. Overton County School Board*, 516 F.3d 489 (6th Cir. 2008).

This court further elaborated, saying, "Teenagers have an inherent personal dignity, a sense of decency and self-respect, and a sensitivity about their bodily privacy that are at the core of their personal liberty and that are grossly offended by their being surreptitiously videotaped while changing their clothes in a school locker room." (*Brannum*, op cit.)

The primary constitutional rationale to make judgments regarding surveillance cases is found in *Katz v. United States*, 389 U.S. 347 (1967), and is couched in the notion of the individual's "reasonable expectation of privacy." According to *Katz*, a reasonable expectation of privacy exists when:

1) "The individual [has] manifested a subjective expectation of privacy in the object of the challenged search," and

2) "society [is] willing to recognize that expectation is reasonable."

Applying the first *Katz* standard to surveillance of school locker rooms, one can easily see how a student's expectation of privacy would be very high and inviolate under normal circumstances. Concerning the second *Katz* requirement, society would, of course, normally look upon a locker room as a place secured for personal privacy. A locker room would be presumed by its users to be a place of confidentiality, giving a person a reasonable expectation of privacy. (See: *California v. Ciraolo,* 476 U.S. 207 (1986).

§ 7.6 AUTOMOBILE SEARCH

Few cases are available to define the law governing searches of students' automobiles in school parking lots. The precedents which do shed light on the subject suggest that there is no difference in the school official's prerogative in searching autos; as with other searches, reasonable suspicion is required before such a search can be undertaken.

In an illustrative case, a reliable student informant told the vice principal that a student was selling marijuana in the school parking lot; the student was searched whereupon a large amount of cash and a telephone pager were found. The offending student's locker was then searched and nothing else was discovered. The school officials then searched his car and a locked briefcase inside the car. Marijuana was found. The court ruled the search was reasonable and observed that school officials were confronted with exigent circumstances that warranted an immediate search because the car could have been removed from school grounds. *State v. Slattery*, 787 P.2d 932 (Wash.App.1990).

In another case the court upheld the search of a student's car and stated, "... the suspicion that marijuana was to be sold to high school students justified the intrusiveness of the search of the [student's] person, locker, and car." *People in the Interest of P.E.A.*, 754 P.2d 382 (Colo.1988).

In yet another case, a student who was attempting to "skip school" was stopped, patted down, made to remove his shoes and socks, and required to pull his pants down to his knees. The court ruled that the principal "had reasonable grounds to investigate why [the student] was attempting to leave school and was justified in 'patting down' ... for safety reasons." The principal then searched the student's car. This, the court felt, went too far and was unreasonable because of excessive intrusion. The car search was not sufficiently connected to the inception of the search and therefore not justified. *Coronado v. State*, 835 S.W.2d 636 (Tex.Crim.App.1992).

Thus, student automobiles on school grounds are quite obviously more private than school lockers, and the expectation of privacy by the student is far greater than is the case with school lockers and desks, etc. that are in possession of the school.

§ 7.7 FIELD TRIP SEARCHES

Many schools have established the practice of searching all the baggage of students who are participating on school field trips. The courts are currently split as to whether such searches can be conducted without specific reasonable suspicion. In one pre-*T.L.O.* ruling, school officials' authority to search student baggage before a band concert tour was challenged. The purpose of the search was to deter disruptive conduct. The court ruled the search was unreasonable because it was not "particularized with respect to each individual searched." *Kuehn v. Renton School District No. 403*, 694 P.2d 1078 (Wash. 1985).

On the other hand, in a post-*T.L.O.* case, the court ruled that hand luggage searched prior to a field trip was justified under the Fourth Amendment. This decision was based on the presence of a legitimate interest of school administrators to prevent students from taking contraband on field trips. *Desilets v. Clearview Board of Education*, 627 A.2d 667 (N.J.Super.1993).

An illustrative case arose in Florida where a high school took a school-sponsored field trip to Disney World. The students were notified prior to the trip that they were subject to "room checks." A chaperone passed a large number of students in the hotel hallway at which time he detected a strong odor of marijuana. A search of the rooms uncovered marijuana and alcohol, whereupon the students were sent home and subsequently suspended from school. The court ruled the search was constitutionally reasonable. The court wrote: " . . . this case impels us to conclude that in a school-sponsored trip, where the students have signed waivers promising not to use drugs or alcohol, where they have been specifically informed that room checks will be conducted, where the school staff travels far from home with these students and thus is acting *in loco parentis*, and where a school official smells marijuana around a cluster of students outside one of their rooms and, thus, has strong reason to believe that his wards are engaging in illegal activity, it is reasonable to ask hotel security to open the students' rooms and to search them." *Rhodes v. Guarricino*, 54 F.Supp.2d 186 (S.D.N.Y.1999).

§ 7.8   DRUG TESTING

The private sector, beyond state and federal government agencies, is now resorting to drug testing as a means to deter drug use and ensure job health and safety. Where governmental agencies are concerned, the collection and testing of urine constitutes a "search" within the meaning of the Fourth Amendment. Any procedure used to collect samples invades a personal function "traditionally shielded by great privacy."

The United States Supreme Court in 1989 ruled on two cases concerning search of governmental employees: one railway workers and the other customs officials. The Court upheld drug testing of these employees because the government was found to have a compelling interest in protecting the public's health and safety. Because customs officials carry firearms and railway workers operate dangerous machinery, they must always be alert and sharply cognizant of their immediate physical situation. The Court ruled individual suspicion was not required before drug testing. The Court did note that in the absence of health and safety of the general public, governmental officials must have reasonable individualized suspicion before testing for drugs or other searches. *Skinner v. Railway Labor Executives' Assoc.*, 489 U.S. 602 (1989); *National Treasury Employees Union v. Von Raab*, 489 U.S. 656 (1989).

The problem of drugs in today's society continues to be a major concern of teachers and officials in public schools. As the above mentioned cases involving government employees indicate, the taking of urine samples to test for drugs constitutes a search under the cognizance of the Fourth Amendment. The question, thus, arises as to whether school officials can search individual students, and, secondly, can the school search several students or groups of students? Previous cases mentioned above, including *T.L.O.*, clearly indicate that individual student's persons and things can be searched if there is reasonable suspicion that drugs are secreted there. As *T.L.O.* explains, there must be reasonable suspicion at the inception of the search. Thus, searches of individual students are permissible if there is individualized reasonable suspicion.

Yet, the second and broader question is whether school officials can conduct random searches of groups of students without individualized suspicion. The U.S. Supreme Court has answered this question rather emphatically. In *Vernonia*, mentioned above, the U.S. Supreme Court observed that the Fourth Amendment does not protect all "subjective expectations" of privacy; what constitutes a legitimate expectation must be determined by the context of the search. For example, expectations of privacy in a home are different from that of a car, and much different from that of a public park. In this light, the expectation of privacy of a child attending school is in yet another context. Moreover, the court will ask, "What is the individual's legal relationship with the state or the public school?" With regard to children in school, the Court said in *Vernonia* that while students don't shed their rights when they enter the school house gate, those rights must of necessity be more narrowly defined. Accordingly, the Court noted that the "reasonableness" of a search cannot disregard the schools' "custodial and tutelary responsibility for children." With this in mind, the Supreme Court in *Vernonia* ruled that a drug search conducted by means of a random urine analysis was permissible and did not violate the students' rights under the Fourteenth Amendment.

In *Vernonia,* the search policy of the school applied to students participating in interscholastic athletes and not to the general student body. That participation in such athletic programs was voluntary and the fact that student athletes were looked upon differently than the regular students of the school was a decisive factor. Moreover, the context is quite different in that when athletes choose to go out for the team, they voluntarily subject themselves to a greater degree of regulation than the regular student. They must, therefore, expect and accept certain intrusions on their rights and privileges beyond those to be expected by other students. Finally, the Court felt that the status of student athletes as "role models" creates yet a greater need for the school to be sure that this group is drug free. The random, suspicionless search was therefore justified and constitutionally valid.

The U.S. Supreme Court, itself, in *Board of Education of Independent School District No. 92 of Pottawatomie County v. Earls*, 536 U.S. 822 (2002), expanded the reach of the *Vernonia* rationale to permit random drug searches of students in the school band and other extracurricular activities. In this case, the school district required all middle and high school students to consent to drug testing if they wished to participate in extracurricular activities. In practice, the school district applied the policy only to groups such as band, choir, Future Homemakers of America, and cheerleading. Under the policy, students were required to take drug tests before participating and, thereafter, submit to drug tests when required. The tests were to be both and/or either random, suspicionless, and/or upon reasonable individualized suspicion. As in *Vernonia*, the Court upheld the policy, and in so doing reasoned that the urine testing policy constituted only a "negligible" intrusion on Fourth Amendment rights for several reasons.

The circumstances and the reasoning of the Supreme Court in both the *Vernonia* and *Earls* cases indicate that a school policy of random, suspicionless, drug testing does not violate the Fourth Amendment if:

1) the students volunteered for the extracurricular activity,

2) the testing procedures constituted a "negligible" intrusion on the student's privacy,

3) the test results were kept confidential,

4) the testing results were not used to invoke school academic, curricular, disciplinary measures or to provide evidence in a criminal proceeding.

In sum, these rulings indicate that the Supreme Court has shifted the balance of interests, to a substantially greater weight, toward discretion of school officials and a diminished liberty interest for the students.

§ 7.9   METAL DETECTOR SEARCHES

In each circumstance of a search, the court will determine whether the search was reasonable. The Fourth Amendment permits reasonable searches, and in the case of the school, as we learned in *T.L.O.*, the school needs only to have reasonable suspicion. The use of metal detectors to search students is reasonable where the context of the search is justified due to violence in the school or there are threats of harm to students. The use of metal detectors was upheld in Pennsylvania because of the history of violence in Philadelphia public schools citing *T.L.O.* as precedent. *In re F.B.*, 658 A.2d 1378 (Pa.Super.1995). Use of metal detectors as a reasonable screening device is justified and reasonable in the face of the reality of violence in the schools. *People v. Pruitt*, 662 N.E.2d 540 (Ill.App. 1st Dist.1996). Similarly, search of students by means of a metal detector has been found to be reasonable when the degree of intrusion on a student's privacy is overbalanced by the school's compelling need for security.

In a New York case, the Board of Education established guidelines for the use of metal detectors in high school that required a team of special police officers from the Central Task Force for School Safety to set up a scanning post in the school's main lobby. All students entering the school were subject to the search although the officers could choose to limit the search by any random formula if the waiting lines became too long. A student was searched with the metal detector whereupon a switchblade knife was found with a 4– to 5–inch blade, and she was charged with criminal possession of a weapon, a Class A misdemeanor. The court found the metal detector search satisfied the balancing test and was not unreasonable because the school's need for security was compelling. *People v. Dukes*, 580 N.Y.S.2d 850 (1992). See also 75 Opinion California Attorney General 155, 1992 WL 469726.

CHAPTER 8

STUDENT DISCIPLINE

§ 8.1 INTRODUCTION

Courts have long recognized that if schools are to be properly conducted, teachers and principals must be given authority to maintain an orderly and responsible learning environment. This requires that students live and study in a relationship of mutual accord with other students and with the school faculty. Disruption of the school social setting will undoubtedly have deleterious effects on the quality of the educational program. Recognizing this, courts have uniformly held that student conduct is under the reasonable control of school officials.

Parents, by law, acquiesce in this control when they place their children in the charge of the school. Thus, the teacher and principal are said to stand *in loco parentis*, in the place of the parent, in the performance and exercise of those functions necessary to operate the schools. As one court has explained, "school discipline is an area which courts enter with great hesitation and reluctance—and rightly so. School officials are trained and paid to determine what form of punishment best addresses a particular student's transgression. They are in a far better position than is a black-robed judge to decide what to do with a disobedient child at school. They can best determine, for instance, whether a suspension or an after-school detention will be more effective in correcting a student's behavior. Because of their expertise and their closeness to the situation—and because we do not want them to fear court challenges to their every act—school officials are given wide discretion in their disciplinary actions." *Donaldson v. Board of Educ.*, 424 N.E.2d 737 (Ill.App.1981). See also *Smith v. School City of Hobart*, 811 F.Supp. 391 (N.D.Ind.1993).

§ 8.2   *IN LOCO PARENTIS*

To stand *in loco parentis* means that the teacher has the authority and the duty to guide, correct, and punish the child in the accomplishment of educational objectives. The teacher is the substitute for the parent while the child is in school and for those endeavors which bear directly on the school. The teacher, however, does not have unlimited control over the student and, of course, neither does the parent for that matter. Child abuse is prohibited whether it is committed by a parent or a teacher. To stand in the place of the parent, though, means that the teacher can control the conduct of the student in various ways, including corporal punishment where permitted by state statute. Blackstone, the great jurist, in summarizing the law of England in 1788 wrote that the schoolmaster had only that portion of parental powers necessary for the conduct of the school. Authority to control students is not necessarily vested in the teacher through affirmative school board policy; it, instead, is derived from the common law relationship between teacher and pupil. In other words, a teacher is assumed to stand *in loco parentis* unless state law or school board policy removes that authority. It has historically been held by the courts that there exists, on the part of students, the obligation of civil deportment, obedience to reasonable commands, and a respect for rights of other pupils. Students must submit to these requirements, and teachers have an inherent duty to see to it that good order is carried out. These obligations on the part of both students and teachers constitute the common law of the school.

Implicit in common law authority is the power of the state to control student conduct for the welfare of the school. Statutes or regulations may place limits on the teacher's authority to discipline students. Where statute or rule limits the teacher's discretion, the teacher must act accordingly. The authority of school officials acting within their state-prescribed powers has been consistently reaffirmed by the courts. "School officials are afforded broad discretion in enforcement of school codes because of the important interests and responsibilities affiliated with school administration." *Wiemerslage v. Maine Township High School Dist. 207*, 824 F.Supp. 136 (N.D.Ill.1993).

§ 8.21　Reasonable Rules

If students break school rules, they may be held accountable. The broken rule, though, must be a reasonable one. Courts are relatively vague as to what constitutes reasonableness but have generally held that a rule must, first, be motivated by reason and humanity premised on accomplishment of some desirable educational result, and, second, the teacher must act in good faith in enforcing the rule. By standing *in loco parentis* teachers have a legal presumption in favor of the correctness of their actions. To exceed this presumption, a teacher must have been motivated by malice and with disregard for the pupil's welfare.

That which constitutes reasonableness is often litigated. For example, in a case where a student was expelled for having approximately 100 pills that contained caffeine and later claimed in court that the punishment was "arbitrary, unreasonable and excessive," the court said the punishment was neither arbitrary, unreasonable, capricious, nor oppressive because rules prohibiting such conduct were in the best interest of the school. *Wilson v. Collinsville Community Unit School District No. 10*, 451 N.E.2d 939 (Ill.App.1983).

§ 8.3 CORPORAL PUNISHMENT

Corporal punishment for many years was a widely-accepted medium for disciplining school children. This tradition has historic roots in Western culture. The great Samuel Johnson, the famous lexicographer, lamented the decline in corporal punishment in the English schools of the 18th century and said, "There is now less flogging in our great schools than formerly, but then less is learned there; so that what the boys get at one end they lose at the other."

Corporal punishment has been defined as "the infliction of bodily pain as a penalty for disapproved behavior." *Daily v. Board of Education of Morrill County School District, No. 62–0063*, 588 N.W.2d 813 (Neb. 1999). The Supreme Court in *Ingraham v. Wright*, 430 U.S. 651 (1977), observed that: "At common law a single principle has governed the use of corporal punishment since before the American Revolution: teachers may impose reasonable but not excessive force to discipline a child. . . . The basic doctrine has not changed." The U.S. Supreme Court further explained what the words "reasonable" and "excessive" meant in the context of student discipline; the Court said that among the most important considerations are: 1) seriousness of the offense, 2) the attitude and past behavior of the child, 3) the nature and severity of the punishment, 4) the age and strength of the child, and 5) the availability of less severe but equally effective means of discipline.

In spite of the Supreme Court's approval of the common law justification for corporal punishment in the schools, the public's acceptance of corporal punishment in the public schools has apparently declined rather dramatically. During the recent past there has been substantial debate about the appropriateness of corporal punishment in schools. During the 1970s, two states prohibited corporal punishment, and during the decade of the 80s other states enacted legislation abolishing such punishment. Today over one-half of the states prohibit corporal punishment. Those states that have no statutes regarding corporal punishment are governed by the common law right of school personnel to reasonably punish students. The theory is that the individual interests of the parent and the child may be subordinated to the interests of the state in good conduct and decorum in the schools. Parental permission is not necessarily required. In the absence of state statutes to the contrary, teachers or administrators may paddle students in spite of opposition of the parents. Where school officials spanked a pupil over the parent's protest, the federal court held for the school, saying that even though the parents maintain general control of their child's discipline, nevertheless, the public school "has a countervailing interest in the maintenance of order in the school sufficient to sustain the right of teachers and school officials to administer reasonable corporal punishment." *Baker v. Owen*, 395 F.Supp. 294 (M.D.N.C.1975).

§ 8.31 Assault and Battery

Corporal punishment may invoke a charge against the teacher of assault and battery. Such actions may be brought either in criminal law or in tort. If the criminal action is successful against a teacher, the teacher may be subject to a fine or imprisonment. In a tort action, the unsuccessful defendant may suffer monetary damages. Torts are discussed in more detail in a later chapter of this book.

Actions against teachers for criminal assault and battery are relatively infrequent. One court has said that whether such an action is successful depends on the circumstances and the severity of the punishment. Some of the factors to be considered are: the prior conduct of the student, whether there was malice on the part of the teacher, the motivation for punishment, the pupil's size and strength, and the effect of the pupil's conduct on other pupils in the school. *People ex rel. Hogan v. Newton*, 56 N.Y.S.2d 779 (1945).

Prior conduct of the pupil is an important factor for the court to consider. Punishment may be permissibly more severe if the student has a long history of rule infractions. In a case where a teacher was convicted at trial of criminal assault and battery for whipping a pupil who had dropped a book from the school auditorium balcony, the state appeals court reversed the decision because the student's prior misbehavior had not been taken into account in considering the reasonableness of the punishment. *People v. Mummert*, 50 N.Y.S.2d 699 (1944).

Teachers and administrators have a privilege that permits them to discipline students; however, they can by excess exceed their privilege, opening themselves up to liability. The Supreme Court in *Ingraham* pointed out that, "Public school teachers and administrators are privileged at common law to inflict only such corporal punishment as is reasonably necessary for the proper education and discipline of the child; any punishment going beyond the privilege may result in both civil and criminal liability ..." Thus, for teachers and administrators in states where corporal punishment is permitted, the standard that must be adhered to is common law "reasonableness."

§ 8.32   Cruel and Unusual Punishment

The only United States Supreme Court case directed to corporal punishment is the aforementioned *Ingraham v. Wright*, 430 U.S. 651 (1977). It involved an action by students who claimed corporal punishment constituted "cruel and unusual" punishment as proscribed by the Eighth Amendment. The case also addressed whether the Fourteenth Amendment required due process before paddling. In this case, the school principal and an assistant had whipped two students so severely that one suffered a hematoma requiring medical attention. The Court, while admitting that the punishment was possibly too severe, nevertheless, denied the students relief under the Eighth and the Fourteenth Amendments.

In commenting generally on corporal punishment, the Court said that even though professional and public opinion is sharply divided on the practice, at common law a single principle has governed the use of corporal punishment: "Teachers may impose reasonable but not excessive force to discipline a child.... The prevalent rule in this country today privileges such force as a teacher or administrator reasonably believes to be necessary for [the child's] proper control, training and education." Further, the Court observed that to the extent that the force used by the teacher is unreasonable or excessive, virtually all states provide the student with a possible criminal law remedy and additionally a possible claim for damages may lie in a tort action. Therefore, the law provides redress to the student in both tort and criminal law.

In considering the constitutional question, the Court gave a thorough analysis of the intent of the "cruel and unusual" provision of the Eighth Amendment finding that the prohibition was meant to apply to criminal cases where, historically, persons were punished by being maimed in various ways. Historical antecedents to the Eighth Amendment led the Court to conclude that public school spankings were not envisioned as falling within the amendment's proscriptions. The Court concluded by saying, "The openness of the public school and its supervision by the community afford significant safeguards against the kinds of abuses from which the Eighth Amendment protects the prisoner. In virtually every community where corporal punishment is permitted in the schools, these safeguards are reinforced by the legal constraints of common law...."

With regard to a plaintiff's assertion that procedural due process must be given each student before punishment the Court disagreed. Even though the Court found that physical punishment fell within the scope of "liberty" as a substantive due process interest, the need to have notice and a hearing prior to a spanking was obviated by the longstanding common law tradition which gives the teacher a privilege to administer moderate punishment.

§ 8.33 Substantive Rights

The federal Circuit Courts of Appeals have not been in agreement as to whether the U.S. Supreme Court in *Ingraham* meant to encompass protection against corporal punishment as a substantive constitutional right.

The U.S. Courts of Appeals for the Fourth and Tenth Circuits have sought definitive standards with regard to punishment. Both have maintained that punishment may be so severe as to constitute a denial of a substantive due process interest. The U.S. Appeals Court for the Fourth Circuit, in *Hall v. Tawney*, 621 F.2d 607 (4th Cir.1980), said that the scope and magnitude was of a different level than commonly considered in tort law, whether "ten licks rather than five licks" is excessive; rather, the court observed that "substantive due process is concerned with violation of personal rights of privacy and bodily security of so different an order of magnitude" and that an overly simplistic application, such as counting of licks, is not necessarily appropriate.

The U.S. Court of Appeals for the Tenth Circuit, in *Garcia v. Miera*, 817 F.2d 650 (10th Cir.1987), has followed the rationale of *Hall v. Tawney*. This court concluded "that grossly excessive corporal punishment may indeed constitute a violation of substantive due process rights." In *Jones v. Witinski*, 931 F.Supp. 364 (M.D.Pa. 1996), a teacher became angry at a disruptive student. The teacher grabbed the student's arm and pulled him across a desk with the student ending up on the floor. The Court said that "pulling a student by the arm is not a brutal and inhuman abuse of official power literally shocking to the conscience."

In a case where the court found a teacher/coach action was a violation of substantive due process, a student on the varsity football team was slapped by a fellow teammate. The student told the coach who replied, "You need to learn how to handle your own business." Later, the student took a weight lock and struck his teammate. The teammates started fighting again with the coach not attempting to stop the fight. The coach shouted, "If you hit him then I am going to hit you." The coach struck the student, knocking the student's eye out of the socket, leaving it "destroyed and dismembered." Yet even after the coach struck the blow, the fight did not stop. The court ruled that this was corporal punishment that violated substantive due process "shocking the conscience." *Neal v. Fulton County Bd. of Ed.*, 229 F.3d 1069 (11th Cir.2000).

"Government officials are justified in using force, even deadly force, in carrying out legitimate governmental functions, but, when force is excessive, or used without justification or for malicious reasons, there is a violation of substantive due process." A principal who hit a student in the mouth, grabbed and squeezed the student's neck, punched student on chest, and threw student head first into lockers violated substantive due process. *P.B. v. Koch*, 96 F.3d 1298 (9th Cir.1996).

§ 8.34   Conscience Shocking

Whether punishment is unreasonable, of course, may have to do with punishment other than corporal punishment. A constitutional interest of substantive due process could be implicated if the school's action against the student is "conscience shocking." Such would normally be rare circumstances, yet, such situations do occur. Arbitrary actions by school officials may lead a court to conclude that a certain disciplinary action is "conscience shocking." A case in point occurred where a student was disciplined by in-school isolation in a text-book storage closet for an entire school day with no advance notice of punishment. The school justified the disciplinary action because one student had left school without permission for a medical emergency and the other student claimed that she had to leave school for a dental appointment. On hearing, the federal court denied the school board's motion for summary judgment, observing that the arbitrary action by the school, no hearing and no prior warning to the students, coupled with the daylong isolation in a closet could constitute "conscience shocking" action by the school. *Orange v. County of Grundy*, 950 F.Supp. 1365 (E.D.Tenn.1996). See *Neal v. Fulton County Sch. Bd.*, supra.

The Alabama Supreme Court ruled that where a school principal beat a student about the head, ribs, and back with a metal cane, such constituted such excessive force as to implicate substantive due process rights. *Kirkland v. Greene County Board of Education*, 347 F.3d 903 (11th Cir. 2003). However, for a constitutional substantive due process claim to prevail, the plaintiff must show that the "force applied causal injury so severe, was so disproportionate to the need presented, and was so inspired by malice or sadism rather than a merely careless or unwise excess of zeal, that it amounted to a brutal and inhuman abuse of official power literally shocking to conscience." *Ellis v. Cleveland Municipal School District*, 455 F.3d 690 (6th Cir. 2006).

Where a principal grabbed a student's neck and threw him on a bench, the court held that such was not "conscience shocking" as to bring into play a valid claim that the corporal punishment was "conscience shocking" in violation of substantive due process. *Golden ex rel. Balch v. Anders*, 324 F.3d 650 (8th Cir. 2003). The Fifth Circuit Court of Appeals has taken a reluctant stance in invoking federal Fourteenth Amendment substantive due process into corporal punishment situations. The court has held that excessive corporal punishment does not implicate substantive due process regardless of the severity so long as there are state, civil, and criminal law remedies available to the student. *Moore v. Willis Ind. School District*, 248 F.3d 1145 (5th Cir. 2001).

In the final analysis, however, the precedents indicate that teachers and school administrators are entitled to considerable deference in performing their duties and in their efforts to maintain decorum and discipline in the school.

§ 8.4 CHILD ABUSE

While the sad inhuman state of child abuse and neglect are ageless, only recently have they been given national attention. Commencing in 1962, state legislatures began enacting legislation designed to deal with problems of child abuse and neglect, and in 1974 a federal statute, the Child Abuse Prevention and Treatment Act was enacted. The purpose of this legislation was to provide federal financial assistance to the states that had implemented programs for identification, prevention, and treatment of instances of child abuse and neglect. Currently, all 50 states plus the District of Columbia, Puerto

Rico, and the Virgin Islands have enacted various forms of child abuse and neglect statutes. A component of the 1974 act was the creation of the National Center of Child Abuse and Neglect, which developed the Model Child Protection Act (Model Act). The Model Act has been used extensively throughout the nation for development of individual state child abuse legislation.

§ 8.41 Corporal Punishment/Child Abuse

Corporal punishment as a common law prerogative of the school may run counter to most child abuse statutes. This conflict between corporal punishment and child abuse statutes has not gone without litigation. In one such case where an assistant principal paddled students for smoking, a parent reported the administrator's action to the appropriate state agency and charged child abuse. Since the child had marks from the paddling, the case worker ruled the charges were "substantiated" because the child abuse law prescribed that markings after paddlings was evidence of abuse. The administrator's name was placed on the State Central Registry for Child Abuse. The administrator appealed to have her name removed, whereupon the court ruled the paddling was not abusive. The court observed that reasonable paddling may be legal but excessive punishment may be abuse. This scenario has been played out numerous times in courts. *Arkansas Dept. of Human Services v. Caldwell*, 832 S.W.2d 510 (Ark.App.1992).

Where allowed, punishment administered must be moderate, with a proper instrument taking into account the age, sex, size and overall physical strength of the child. Within these broad limits a teacher must balance the gravity of the offense with the extent of the punishment to be meted out. Because teachers are usually present when student mischief transpires and normally know the manner, look, tone, gestures, language, setting and general circumstances of the offense, courts will allow teachers considerable latitude in their exercise of discretion. Yet, punishment which is cruel and excessive will not be tolerated by the courts. Cruel and excessive punishment is evidence of malice which will override the teacher's *in loco parentis* privilege.

§ 8.42 Child Abuse Definition

The federal Model Act includes the following succinct definition of child abuse and neglect: "*[C]hild abuse and neglect* means the physical or mental injury, sexual abuse, negligent treatment, or maltreatment of a child under the age of 18 by a person who is responsible for the child's welfare under circumstances which indicate that the child's health or welfare is harmed or threatened thereby, as determined in accordance with regulations prescribed by the Secretary."

Commonly contained within state child abuse and neglect statutes is a purpose statement that outlines the intent of the legislation. Typically, the primary purpose of child abuse and neglect statutes is to identify children who are being abused or neglected so that state protection may be provided. A commonly enunciated purpose of child abuse laws, as stated in the Virginia law, is the state's desire to preserve "the family life of the parents and children, where possible, by enhancing parental capacity for adequate child care."

Nearly all states have accepted the federal definition of a child as a person under the age of 18, but such statutes vary widely in regard to definitions of abuse and neglect.

Some states provide their own individualized definitions, yet a number of states attempt to distinguish between child abuse and child neglect.

§ 8.43 Child Abuse Reporting

An essential part of state child abuse and neglect statutes is the mandated reporting of suspected instances of child abuse and neglect. Statutes protect teachers who report parental abuse from counteractions in court.

All states have enacted legislation granting immunity to persons who report child abuse and neglect from actions for criminal and civil liability if the report *is made in good faith*. For example, the Virginia immunity statute states: "A person making a report ... shall be immune from any civil or criminal liability in connection therewith unless it is proven that such person acted with malicious intent."

A 1985 Oregon case, *McDonald v. State, By and Through CSD*, 694 P.2d 569 (Or.1985), serves to illustrate the effect of statutory immunity granted reporters of child abuse and neglect. In this case, a teacher observed scratches on the neck of one of her pupils and had him examined by a child development specialist. When questioned about how he had acquired the scratches, the child told two stories. One version attributed the scratches to his kitten, and the second version suggested that the child's mother had made the scratches by choking him, as the child said she had done on several occasions. The principal was informed, who in turn instructed the child development specialist to report the incident to the state's Children's Services Division. The child was removed from parental custody and placed in a foster home. Subsequently, the parents appeared in court where the allegations of child abuse were ruled groundless and the child was reinstated with his parents. The parents brought suit against Children's Services Division, principal, teacher, and others. The court dismissed the parents' complaint and indicated that although two versions of the derivation of scratches were told and that the principal relied only upon the opinion of the child development specialist, both the principal and teacher had acted in good faith and had reasonable grounds to report suspected child abuse.

§ 8.44 Child Abuse: Penalty for Failure to Report

In order to gain compliance from those persons, including teachers, who are required to report instances of child abuse and neglect, most states permit the assessment of penalties for knowing and willful failure to report. These states have enacted criminal penalties for those persons guilty of not reporting suspected cases of child abuse and neglect. Other states have legislated both criminal and civil penalties, and a few states have provided for only civil remedies.

§ 8.45 Child Abuse: Defenses for Failure to Report

Included in child abuse statutes that provide criminal penalties for failure to report child abuse are terms such as "reasonable cause to believe," "cause to believe," or, as in the case of Oklahoma, "reason to believe." Within these terms rest the nucleus for a teacher's discretion in reporting or not reporting child abuse. These terms may also serve to defend a teacher who is accused of not reporting. Such terms are considered to provide an objective standard on which to determine compliance. Less rigorous terms, such as "knows or suspects" are considered to provide a subjective standard and one that may permit mandatory reporters to shield their own poor judgments. Regardless of whether the standard is objective or subjective, a teacher charged with failure to report suspected child abuse under the criminal code of a state will attempt to show that there was not "reasonable cause to believe" that child abuse and neglect had occurred.

§ 8.5 DISCIPLINE FOR OUT–OF–SCHOOL ACTIVITIES

The teacher has no general right of discipline over students after school hours and off school grounds, but this rule has its limitations. The school has the responsibility to discipline students going to and from school; such authority extends to any student misconduct which has a direct or immediate tendency to harm or subvert the proper performance of the educational function. When children fight and misbehave it is likely that these actions will carry over to their performance in school. A classic case is where one boy intimidates another by announcing that he will "meet him after school" to settle affairs. In such instances, the welfare of the child and the school are intertwined.

In this regard, Mechem has summarized the rule of law as follows: "The authority of the teacher is not confined to the school room or grounds, but he may prohibit and punish all acts of his pupils which are detrimental to the good order and best interests of the school, whether such acts are committed in school hours or while the pupil is on his way to or from school or after he was returned home." Mechem on Public Officers, 730.

The most explicit case demonstrating this point of law is *O'Rourke v. Walker*, 128 A. 25 (Conn.1925), an old Connecticut case, wherein a principal administered moderate corporal punishment to two young boys for abusing and annoying two small girls while on their way home from school, after school hours. The mother of one of the boys sued the school principal maintaining that he had no legal right to administer punishment for any misconduct of the pupil which did not occur in school hours, or for misbehavior which did not take place in the school building or on the school grounds. The lower court concluded and the appellate court affirmed: "(1) that the conduct of the plaintiff boys had a tendency to demoralize the other pupils of the school and to interfere with the proper conduct of the same; (2) that the acts of the plaintiff were detrimental to the good order and best interests of the school; (3) that the defendant, as the principal of said school, in the absence of rules established by the school board or other proper authority, had a right to make and enforce all necessary and proper rules for the regulation of the school and pupils during school hours and afterwards; (4) that said punishment administered by the defendant was reasonable and proper."

In a case where a school rule placed off-limits an area just off school property and students were punished for loitering there, the court ruled that the school was only exercising "... its power *in loco parentis* to guide student behavior...." *Wiemerslage v. Maine Township High School District 207*, 824 F.Supp. 136 (N.D.Ill.1993).

Even though schools can discipline students for inappropriate conduct while not on school grounds, reasonable school regulations should be in place to govern and justify such discipline. The extension of the school's disciplinary hand beyond school grounds is particularly important and justifiable where safety of children is involved. The importance of the school's off-campus prerogative is vividly illustrated in a case where students in a jeep and a pickup truck impeded the progress of a school bus loaded with school children. School officials took disciplinary action against the students, and the parents and offending students challenged the school's authority to mete out such punishment. The court ruled for the school and said: "It matters little that the proscribed conduct occurred on a public highway. It is generally accepted that school authorities may discipline students for out-of-school conduct having a direct and immediate effect on the discipline or general welfare of the school." *Clements v. Board of Trustees of Sheridan County School District No. 2*, 585 P.2d 197 (Wyo.1978); see also 53 A.L.R. 3d 1124; 68 Am. Jur. 2d, Schools §§ 256, 266

The court in *Flynn–Scarcella v. Pocono Mountain School District*, 745 A.2d 117 (Pa.Cmwlth.2000), upheld the school in excluding a student from graduation ceremonies because he possessed alcohol at an off-campus location where the school prom was being held.

The safety of students requires that the school protect students against physical violence or drug dealing in and around school grounds. See *Nicholas B. v. School Committee*, 587 N.E.2d 211 (Mass.1992) and *Howard v. Colonial School District*, 621 A.2d 362 (Del.Super.1992).

§ 8.51   Internet Disruption of School

The ubiquity of the Internet may pose special problems for teachers and administrators in preventing disruption of the school. Yet, aside from the practical problem of users of the Internet hiding their identities behind anonymous names and thereby creating difficulties in finding and punishing the culprits, the law governing the use of the Internet in disrupting the school is the same as disruption by any other means. The *Tinker v. Des Moines* disruption test applies to all circumstances whether on or off campus. If means of the Internet is used to harm, disturb, or disrupt the school, then the perpetrator can be disciplined by the school. A case in point was a 2007 New York case where a student sent messages to friends via Internet computer software that depicted a pistol firing a bullet at a person's head with dots representing blood with the caption worded "Kill Mr. VanderMolen," the English teacher. The student was suspended for a year and sued. The court upheld the suspension saying that the fact that the speech originated off school grounds did not insulate the student from school discipline. The court cited *Tinker* as precedent. Off-campus like on-campus misconduct can create a foreseeable risk of material and substantial disruptions. *Wisniewski v. Board of Education of Weedsport Central School District*, 494 F.3d 34 (2d Cir. 2007).

In *Killion v. Franklin Regional School District*, 136 F.Supp.2d 446 (W.D.Pa.2001), a student created a web page at home with a "top ten" list that offended school officials. The student was suspended. The court ruled the document did not disrupt the school environment or anyone's rights. Likewise, in *Beussink v. Woodland R–IV School District*, 30 F.Supp.2d 1175 (E.D.Mo.1998), the website created at home did not materially and substantially interfere with school discipline, the *Tinker* test. In other words, there was no nexus between the outside activity and the school.

In contrast, a court affirmed the expulsion of a student in *J.S. v. Bethlehem Area School District*, 757 A.2d 412 (Pa.Cmwlth.2000), who created a website titled "Teacher Sux." The website contained derogatory comments about teachers and administrators. It also had a picture of the severed head of a teacher and a picture of her face morphing Adolph Hitler. There was a request for funds to hire a hit man for the teacher's execution. Given the website's disruption of the school, the expulsion did not violate the student's First Amendment rights.

MySpace.com has become a favorite means for students to communicate regarding activities and persons at public schools. The standard by which the school must abide in controlling such communication is normally the *Tinker* disruption test and alternatively Internet issues may fall under the *Bethel v. Frazer* "civility" standard. In a well-publicized case in Pennsylvania, a high school student used his grandmother's computer in non-school time to construct and transmit a parody showing a picture of the school principal stating that he was "too drunk" to remember his birth date. There was no lewd or profane speech used in the parody. The school suspended the student, and the student was banned from graduation ceremonies and other school events. The federal circuit court, applying *Tinker,* found that there was no disruption and held for the student. The court did observe that school officials had a qualified privilege against individual liability in such matters. *Layshock v.*

Hermitage School District, 496 F. Supp. 2d 587 (W.D.Pa. 2007).

In another case involving MySpace.com, discipline of a student was upheld because of in-class clandestine video-taping of a male student pelvic thrusting toward a female teacher who was bending over. The student had linked a YouTube video to MySpace.com. Even though the editing and posting was done off-campus, the filming was on-campus and was done in violation of school student code on sexual harassment and possession of electronic de-vices. The court upheld the discipline of the student. This case is instructive in that a school may have en-forceable rules regarding electronic recording of anything at school, the violation of which can result in discipline for the student. In this light, the matter is not one of free speech, but rather the more mundane aspects of failure to follow school regulations. In summary, the rule re-garding Internet use by students to create problems with the conduct and decorum of the school rests squarely on the disruption test of *Tinker* or possibly on the "civility" test of *Bethel*.

§ 8.52 Cell Phones

Possession and use of cell phones in school during school hours can be regulated by school officials. There is no "constitutional right to bear cell phones" in school. *Price v. New York City Board of Education*, 837 N.Y.S.2d 507 (2007). A regulation forbidding cell phones can be justified on the basis of a school's interest in reducing disruption of the learning process. Neither does denial of student's possession of cell phones in school violate any alleged constitutional right of parent-to-student commu-nication. A school rule that forbids student's to have cell phones in school only addresses one mode of communication between the student and parent. (*Price v. New York City Board of Education*, 837 N.Y.S.2d 507 (2007)).

However, the cell phone situation has potential for complications involving privacy of the student. In a case where a cell phone was confiscated by a teacher in a classroom, in accordance with school policy, and while the teacher was in possession of the phone, a text message appeared on the screen from another student requesting marijuana; a complex legal scenario unraveled. The student sued alleging, among other things, that the teacher's and principal's access to the cell phone information violated the Pennsylvania Wiretapping and Electronic Surveillance Control Act. The court ruled the Act did not apply because the plaintiff student was the receiver of the message, not the caller, as protected by the Act. However, the court found that there was a privacy issue involved regarding whether there was "reasonable suspicion" or "probable cause" for the school to access other messages on the cell phone. *Klump v. Nazareth Area School District*, 425 F. Supp. 2d 622 (E.D. Pa. 2006).

As one can see, the entire field of communication law can be a thorny one for school officials with many aspects and complications. Suffice it to summarize, however, that at this time, school officials can ban the possession and use of cell phones in schools, but the use of confiscated cell phones to derive further information about a student's possible violation of school regulations, or violation of criminal laws, requires a high degree of circumspection and reference to the prevailing law of privacy and search and seizure. (See other sections of this book.)

§ 8.6 ACADEMIC DISCIPLINE

Challenges to school grading policies have usually been couched in due process of law. A Michigan court has said that a student has no vested interest in a particular grade and the school board has the authority to set grading policy. The court's rationale is based on the assumption that grading concerns academic standards and is not a discipline measure.

If students violate school academic rules or teachers' classroom academic requirements, then a reduction in grades or, even, a denial of promotion may be justified. In a case where four students submitted a paper for a history project that had to be largely copied verbatim from reference sources, the students were given a grade of zero. The parents sued claiming the teacher's instructions had been unclear. At a hearing, the school superintendent found that the teacher had explained plagiarism and its consequences. The court held for the school district finding that the assigned grade was not inappropriate. The process afforded the student was reasonable and the assignment of a grade of zero was fair. *Zellman v. Independent School Dist. No. 2758*, 594 N.W.2d 216 (Minn.App.1999). Similarly, where students stole copies of an algebra test, the school, after a hearing, assigned Fs to the students. Three of the students were given 10–day suspensions in addition to the Fs. The court held for the school district. *Reed v. Vermilion Local School Dist.*, 614 N.E.2d 1101 (Ohio App. 6th Dist.1992). The U.S. Court of Appeals, Seventh Circuit, has held that giving students an F in band class for violating band performance rules did not implicate substantive due process and did not shock the conscience even though the grade of F prevented one student from graduating with honors. *Dunn v.*

Fairfield Community High School District No. 225, 158 F.3d 962 (7th Cir.1998). Thus, academic discipline for academic offenses will normally be upheld by the courts so long as there is evidence that the school conducted at least a rudimentary hearing on the matter, and did not act arbitrarily.

Yet, attendance at school and academic performance may be reasonably connected, and failure to attend school may affect the overall educational process. If a school board decides that attendance is essential to fulfill academic requirements and rules are so promulgated relating attendance to academic performance, then the courts are not likely to intervene. *Slocum v. Holton Board of Education*, 429 N.W.2d 607 (Mich.App.1988). In *Slocum*, the court said, "School authorities may determine that attendance, class participation and similar factors are proper educational values bearing on a student's academic achievement." (See Chapter 2 Grade Reduction.)

Thus, while school authorities have broad authority in the evaluation of students, the exercise of the authority cannot be so broad and indiscriminate as to permit unreasonable or improper exercise of discretion. What constitutes appropriate use of discretion largely depends on how well the school documents its rationale and how closely that rationale relates to the desirable educational end that the rule is designed to achieve.

§ 8.61 Zero Tolerance

The highly publicized violence in public schools has produced a legislative and regulatory reaction of more restrictive discipline measures governing the conduct of students, referred to as "zero tolerance" policies. These strict rules limiting administrative discretion in punishment of students are usually imposed for possession of weapons or offenses related to drugs and alcohol. Zero tolerance policies are of the same genre as mandatory prison terms in criminal courts that restrict sentencing discretion of prosecutors, judges and juries. As in the criminal courts, zero tolerance in schools does not deny due process of law, but does prescribe non-negotiable penalties. After guilt is established, the penalty is swift and certain. Proponents argue for the necessity of zero tolerance while opponents maintain that such "one-strike-and-you're-out" policies are unfair in that there is no latitude for school administrators to consider the punishment in light of the gravity and nature of the offense. (117 A.L.R. 5th 459, 2004).

For example, zero tolerance punishment for "possession" may not take into account whether the offense was "unknowing" or "knowing" and there was "intent" to harm. For example, in the case where a middle school student took a binder containing a knife from a suicidal fellow student and put the binder in his locker, discovered by school officials, the student was given a long-term suspension under a zero tolerance policy. Testimony by the school dean indicated that the student had acted in the suicidal student's best interest and had no intent to possess a weapon to harm anyone. The rescuing student claimed that the long-term suspension violated his fundamental equal protection and due process rights. The federal court disagreed and ruled for the school district, reasoning that the rule was valid even though "intent" to "possess" or "intent" to harm another was not essential to the validity of the zero tolerance policy. (*Ratner v.*

Loudoun County Public Schools, 16 Fed. Appx. 140 (4th Cir. 2001). In a case where a student claimed that he did not know that a machete was in his toolbox and the school failed to show a culpable mental state to justify punishment, the court ruled *scienter* was not a requirement of the school's policy; *scienter* could be assumed and imputed from the student's possession. *Scienter* is a legal term for "knowing," or "guilty knowledge." (*Bundick v. Bay City Independent School District*, 140 F. Supp. 2d 735 (S.D. Tex. 2001). Yet, "knowledge of possession" or "intent to possess" a weapon or a harmful substance has been given credence by some courts where zero tolerance penalties have been exacted. A court in Florida ruled on this point holding that the term "possession" of controlled substances as used in law and regulation required proof that of the student's knowledge of possession. (*D.T. v. Harter*, 844 So.2d 717 (Fla.App. 2003). The prevailing view, however, is that knowledge or *scienter* is not required for a zero tolerance policy to be valid.

Another constitutional matter is whether zero tolerance regulations have a rational relationship with the state's interests in the good conduct of the school and safety of students. Such a relationship has been found to be valid where there is potential of harm to other students. (*Hill v. Sharber*, 544 F. Supp. 2d 670 (M.D. Tenn. 2008). Zero tolerance rules and the attendant punishments have been upheld for offenses other than weapons and drugs and alcohol, such as verbal threats, gangs, and fighting. Such regulations have been challenged as violating the student's rights of speech and liberty; however, the courts have upheld the policies. (*A.G. v. Sayreville Board of Education*, 333 F.3d 417 (3rd Cir. 2003); *M.M. v. Chesapeake City Schools*, 2000 WL 33261105 (2000);

T.H. v. San Diego Unified School District, 19 Cal.Rptr.3d 532 (4th Dist. 2004).

Additional aspects that are of relevance to the validity of zero tolerance policies are: first, the policy must be clearly stated and adopted by the school district, and, second, students should be made aware of the policy. The school should be able to show that the zero tolerance policy is for clearly specified offenses, and that students throughout the school were made aware of the policy by student handbooks and/or other means of documented communication. (See: *Vann ex rel. Vann v. Stewart*, 445 F. Supp. 2d 882 (E.D. Tenn. 2006).

CHAPTER 9

RACIAL SEGREGATION

§ 9.1 INTRODUCTION

Governments have the inherent authority to classify persons in reasonable ways and for legitimate purposes. Reasonableness of classification and legitimate purposes are, however, difficult to define. The regretful history of racial discrimination in the United States and its immoral consequences make all classifications in American society highly suspect. Racial discrimination is, as a result of that history, particularly noxious to American sensitivities of right and wrong and justice and injustice. The American tradition of relying on mass public education as the means by which persons gained social and economic mobility naturally resulted in the public schools being a primary battleground on which the racial discrimination issue was to be contested. Thus, the most important court decisions involving the racial discrimination in American history have been educationally related.

§ 9.2 SEPARATE–BUT–EQUAL

The pernicious doctrine of separate-but-equal emanated from an 1850 Supreme Court of Massachusetts decision that legalized the concept in permitting racial segregation in the public schools of Boston. *Roberts v. City of Boston*, 59 Mass. 198 (1850). In this case an African–American child was compelled by school board rule to attend an elementary school designated for black children even though other elementary schools were closer to her home. The court concluded that this infinite variety of circumstances which may justify school segregation can be found in societal standards which separate the races. Thus, according to this court, separation of races in schools was not discriminatory so long as the school facilities were not unequal. The court made it clear that it did not consider segregation of the races to be unequal *per se*.

The *Roberts* case was decided under the Constitution of Massachusetts, because the United States Constitution, at that time, contained no prohibition against racial discrimination and had none until the Fourteenth Amendment was enacted.

§ 9.21 Equal Protection Clause

It was not until 1868 when the American people adopted the Fourteenth Amendment that a constitutional basis existed for racial discrimination to be held impermissible at the federal level. The Fourteenth Amendment provided that "... no state shall ... deny any person within its jurisdiction the equal protection of the laws."

In spite of this amendment, racial segregation persisted as courts failed to enforce its intent. Many states enacted Jim Crow laws which extended segregation to most aspects of public life, including separate waiting rooms in railroad stations, train cars, telephone booths, separate storage for textbooks used by black school children, separate elevators, and separate Bibles for swearing in African–American witnesses in some southern courts, and, of course, separate schools. The federal government's practices were as discriminatory as many of the southern states since federal laws and regulations also allowed and even provided for segregation, including the maintenance of racially separate schools in the District of Columbia.

Segregation gained legal credence through the adoption of "separate-but-equal" from the aforementioned Roberts case in *Boston*, which was adopted by the United States Supreme Court in applying to the Fourteenth Amendment in the infamous case of *Plessy v. Ferguson*, 163 U.S. 537 (1896). Justice Harlan dissented in *Plessy* maintaining that the separate accommodations contributed to creation of a racial caste system excluding blacks from association with whites. *Plessy,* however, was the precedent that prevailed until 1954 when the Supreme Court, in *Brown v. Board of Education*, 347 U.S. 483 (1954), held the separate-but-equal doctrine to be inherently unconstitutional.

§ 9.22 Demise of Separate-but-Equal

The United States Supreme Court was never able to clearly enunciate what constituted "equal" in the context of "separate-but-equal." It was, though, generally understood that the entire absence of facilities would violate equal protection. As a result, states made some provision, though in most cases quite modest, for black students to have some type of facility. Educational facilities at the graduate and professional school levels were, generally, not available in southern states for black students. Where this was the case, the state legislatures usually provided some type of tuition assistance for black students to attend colleges in other states. In *Missouri ex* rel. Gaines v. Canada, 305 U.S. 337 (1938), an African–American plaintiff who did not want to attend law school in another state challenged the State of Missouri because it had no law school for black students. Justice Hughes, writing for the majority of the United States Supreme Court, ruled that Missouri must either permit plaintiff to attend the white law school or that the state must establish a black law school. At the next session of the Missouri legislature a statute was enacted to create a law school for blacks.

It was not until twelve years after *Gaines*, however, that the Supreme Court was asked to rule on the quality of the separate facilities. The inferiority of the black institutions was obvious, but no court decision had established a standard of comparison until 1950 when the Supreme Court, in *Sweatt v. Painter*, 339 U.S. 629 (1950), held that the black law school in Texas was so inferior to the University of Texas Law School that it could not be construed as a "separate-but-equal."

§ 9.3　THE *BROWN* CASE

A frontal attack was launched on the doctrine of separate-but-equal by the NAACP in the decade between 1940 and 1950 led by Thurgood Marshall and a battery of African–American lawyers, law professors, historians, and sociologists who had analyzed both the legal and social ramifications of segregation. *Brown v. Board of Education of Topeka*, supra, was the first cited case of five cases which were carefully selected to present the complete issue of school segregation to the Supreme Court. Initial arguments were made on December 9, 1952, two and one-half years after the *Sweatt* decision, but the Court reached no decision based on these first briefs and arguments. The case was reargued on December 8, 1953, after which the *Brown* decision was rendered and the doctrine of "separate-but-equal" was nullified.

The basic legal issue propounded by the Court was whether the Fourteenth Amendment contemplated abolishment of school segregation. This was the essential question, whether the constitutional intent was to prohibit state statutory or regulatory segregation of the public schools. The Court rendered its decision saying: "We conclude that in the field of public education the doctrine of 'separate-but-equal' has no place. Separate educational facilities are inherently inequal."

The potential societal effects of *Brown* were so pervasive that the Court was forced to carefully evaluate alternative enforcement measures. Suddenly, the dual system of public education in seventeen states which had been legal under "separate-but-equal" was now unconstitutional. Because of these immense ramifications on the rendering of the *Brown* decision, the Court charged plaintiffs, defendants and friends of the Court to return and present alternatives for implementation. The plan that was finally adopted by the Court in *Brown II* in 1955 said that the lower courts should act "with all deliberate speed" in desegregating the public schools. *Brown v. Board of Education*, 349 U.S. 294 (1955).

Because *Brown* dealt only with state-enforced segregation, no guidelines were established for the courts to follow in bringing about desegregation. *Brown* extended only to the erasure of state segregation laws and their enforcement, but did not provide guideposts for abrogation of the continuing effects of segregation.

§ 9.31 With All Deliberate Speed

A plethora of lower federal court decisions dominated the actions of school boards in the south during the 15 years after *Brown*. Almost immediately, upon remand to a lower federal court, in a companion case to *Brown*, *Briggs v. Elliott*, 132 F.Supp. 776 (E.D.S.C.1955), the issue of desegregation versus integration was addressed. Here the federal judge was asked to determine whether *Brown* merely meant to abolish state-sanctioned segregation or did it intend that the courts force the states to act affirmatively to integrate the schools. The judge concluded that "all that is decided is that a state may not deny to any person on account of race the right to attend any school that it maintains.... The Constitution, in other words, does not require integration. It merely forbids segregation." Accordingly, for several years thereafter, this case stood as precedent for school districts which did not want to take affirmative action to mix white and black children in the same schools.

§ 9.32 Vouchers for Whites

One device used to circumvent the effects of *Brown* was to close the public schools and to provide vouchers for students to attend private schools. When this method of maintaining segregation was challenged, the Supreme Court held that the ill effects of such a system bore more heavily on African–American students because the white students had access to accredited private schools while the African–American children did not. Thus, the Court concluded that to close public schools and contribute tax funds for students to attend segregated private schools was a violation of equal protection. *Griffin v. County*

School Board of Prince Edward County, 377 U.S. 218 (1964).

§ 9.33   Freedom of Choice

Whether the Equal Protection Clause required that states merely eradicate state enforced segregation or act affirmatively to integrate, the issue addressed in *Briggs* persisted as a major question. The United States Office of Education (now U.S. Department of Education) in the mid–1960s issued guidelines for desegregation of school districts in southern states which, if not followed, could result in the withholding of federal funds. The guidelines initially permitted freedom of choice plans to be submitted in order to qualify for the federal funds; but after a time it was concluded that freedom of choice would not bring about desegregation in many districts. It was found that black parents for many reasons, including community coercion, would not choose to send their children to schools which were formerly all white. Freedom of choice and voucher schemes in Virginia only perpetuated the segregation.

When the "freedom of choice" issue finally reached the United States Supreme Court, the Court concluded that if freedom of choice plans actually worked to desegregate the schools, then they constituted acceptable legal alternatives; but if they failed to integrate the schools, then the state and school districts must devise new schemes that would place black children in schools with white children and vice versa. According to the Court, a "freedom of choice" plan must "effectuate a transition" to a "unitary system." *Green v. County School Board of New Kent County*, 391 U.S. 430 (1968).

§ 9.34   Desegregate at Once

The "all deliberate speed" standard which was attributed to Justice Felix Frankfurter ultimately proved to be unworkable. After 15 years of attempting to implement the standard, the United States Supreme Court reconsidered the entire question in *Alexander v. Holmes County Board of Education*, 396 U.S. 976 (1969). The Court concluded that the "all deliberate speed" terminology was a legalized term that allowed too much discretion and resulted in action so deliberate that schools would remain segregated indefinitely in many districts of the South. The Court concluded that " . . . continued operation of segregated schools under a standard of allowing 'all deliberate speed' for desegregation is no longer constitutionally permissible." The Court ordered all school districts in the seventeen southern states to "terminate dual school systems at once and to operate now and hereafter only unitary schools." From the date of this decree, all school districts in the south were required to become unitary without further delay.

§ 9.4   THE *SWANN* CASE

Even though *Alexander v. Holmes County Board of Education* required that every school district operating dual school programs for blacks and whites was to immediately terminate the practice and to establish unitary schools, the Supreme Court did not clearly define what unitary meant, nor did it prescribe the standards to be used by school authorities to disestablish dual school systems. The Supreme Court undertook to accomplish this in *Swann v. Charlotte–Mecklenburg Board of Education*, 402 U.S. 1 (1971). *Swann* addressed the issues in four contexts: (1) the use of racial quotas, (2) the elimination of one-race schools, (3) racial gerrymandering of attendance zones and (4) the use of busing for remedial purposes.

§ 9.41   Racial Quotas

Several earlier lower court decisions had used ratios of black to white in the total school population to establish racial quotas for each school. A federal district court had established that racial imbalance could not be justified at substantial variance from a 71–29, white to black, ratio for schools in Charlotte–Mecklenburg County, and ruled that no school could be operated with an all black or predominately black student body. The Supreme Court said that if it was, in fact, the lower court's intent to establish a "mathematical racial balance reflecting the pupil constituency of the system" then the approach would be disapproved and the lower court would be reversed. The Supreme Court said: "The constitutional command to desegregate schools does not mean that every school in every community must always reflect the racial composition of the school system as a whole."

§ 9.42   One–Race Schools

A second question necessary to define a unitary system is whether one-race schools are to be permitted at all. The Court answered this question affirmatively, but admonished that such schools required close judicial scrutiny to determine whether the assignment of pupils was a part of state-enforced segregation. Where a school district's desegregation plan permits such schools to continue, the district has the burden of showing that pupil assignments are "genuinely non-discriminatory."

§ 9.43 Remedial Altering of Attendance Zones

Racial gerrymandering of districts as required by courts is a permissible device to overcome segregation. Pairing, clustering, and grouping may also be validly required by the lower courts. The Supreme Court said that no rigid rules could be set because of varying local conditions such as traffic patterns and availability of good highways, but that pairing and grouping of non-contiguous school zones may be feasible alternatives. The Court said: "All things being equal, with no history of discrimination, it might well be desirable to assign pupils to schools nearest their homes. But all things are not equal in a system that was deliberately constructed and maintained to enforce racial segregation." Thus, where *de jure* segregation has prevailed, the school district must reassign students to bring about integration whether or not the reassignments result in breaking up neighborhood school attendance patterns.

§ 9.44 Busing

The use of busing to alleviate segregation has long been a volatile issue. Until *Swann,* the Supreme Court had not directly sanctioned busing as a remedial measure to effectuate integration. In *Green,* supra, the freedom of choice case, the Court had remained vague on the issue saying merely that measures must be taken which are "workable," "effective," and "realistic." With regard to busing, the Supreme Court said in *Swann* that: "Bus transportation has been an integral part of the public education system for years, and its use is not novel nor are the people unaccustomed to use of buses." "Desegregation plans," the Court said, "cannot be limited to the walk-in school."

§ 9.5 *DE FACTO* AND *DE JURE* SEGREGATION

With the *Alexander* case, supra, it was well decided that school districts in states with legal segregation, *de jure,* before *Brown,* had an affirmative duty to integrate, but it had not been clearly decided whether schools that were *de facto* segregated because of housing patterns were required to integrate. President Nixon summarized the law in 1969 saying that "There is a fundamental distinction between so-called '*de jure*' and '*de facto*' segregation: *de jure* segregation arises by law or by the deliberate act of school officials and is unconstitutional; *de facto* segregation results from residential housing patterns and does not violate the Constitution."

Earlier, the United States Court of Appeals for the Seventh Circuit had said that "There is no affirmative United States constitutional duty to change innocently arrived at school attendance districts by the mere fact that shifts in population either increase or decrease the percentage of either Negro or White pupils." *Bell v. School City of Gary*, 324 F.2d 209 (7th Cir. 1963).

§ 9.51 Implicit Intent to Segregate

Thus, if segregation is *de facto* and not *de jure,* no affirmative duty exists to integrate. In the 17 southern states, all segregation was *de jure,* but in the North, *de jure* segregation could only be present if the plaintiffs could show that states or local school boards had acted either explicitly or implicitly to bring about segregation. In explaining the requirement for northern states, the Supreme Court said in *Keyes,* a Denver case, that "... we have held that where plaintiffs prove that a current condition of segregated schooling exists within a school district where a dual system was compelled or authorized by statute at the time of our decision in *Brown* ..., the state automatically assumes an affirmative duty to 'effectuate a transition to a racially non-discriminatory school system.' " In states where dual systems of education did not exist, the plaintiffs must show that there was official purpose or intent to segregate. *Keyes v. School District No. 1, Denver*, 413 U.S. 189 (1973).

De jure segregation has, though, been found to exist within several school districts in northern states. For example, both the Columbus and Dayton, Ohio, school systems were held to have been segregated by discriminatory acts of public officials and, thus, an affirmative duty was required to eradicate the vestiges of such *de jure* segregation. *Columbus Board of Education v. Penick*, 443 U.S. 449 (1979); *Dayton Board of Education v. Brinkman*, 443 U.S. 526 (1979). To desegregate, the court required that a "balanced" school system be attained; the Court said: "[T]he measure of the post-*Brown* conduct of a school board under an unsatisfied duty to liquidate a dual school system is the effectiveness, not the purpose, of the actions in decreasing or increasing the segregation caused by the dual system." Thus, a school board in a *de jure* situation must not only abandon its discriminatory practice, but it must establish policies and procedures which will integrate the schools. The prevailing view remains today that there is a legal distinction between *de facto* and *de jure* segregation. The basic distinction is that in the states which had legal segregation before 1954, the burden is on the school district to overcome vestiges of past discrimination. If the effect is to segregate, then it must be addressed with affirmative action to erase the racial imbalance. On the other hand, in other states, plaintiffs must show that there was an official intent to segregate before remedial measures will be required by the courts. As time passes, however, there are now hopefully few districts that still retain the trace of intentional or *de jure* segregation.

§ 9.6 A UNITARY SYSTEM

A dual school system becomes unitary when the vestiges of past legal (*de jure*) segregation are erased. The Supreme Court has defined a unitary system as the status a school system achieves "when it no longer discriminates between school children on the basis of race," *Columbus Board of Education v. Penick*, 443 U.S. 449 (1979), or when no person is "effectively excluded from any school because of race or color." *Alexander v. Holmes County Board of Education*, 396 U.S. 976 (1969). In *Flax v. Potts*, 915 F.2d 155 (5th Cir. 1990), a federal circuit court ruled that a school district is unitary if schools are not identifiable by race and students and faculty are assigned in a manner that eliminates the vestiges of past segregation.

Over a quarter of a century ago the U.S. Supreme Court held, in *Green v. County School Board of New Kent County, Virginia*, 391 U.S. 430 (1968), that the courts must look to six areas of the educational program to determine whether a district is unitary: 1) student assignment, 2) faculty, 3) staff, 4) transportation, 5) extracurricular activities, and 6) facilities. Subsequently, as the courts applied these criteria, the question arose as to whether all measures had to be met at once or whether they could be achieved incrementally. This "incremental approach" did not, however, have a consensus among the federal courts. Another view advanced by the U.S. Court of Appeals for the Eleventh Circuit, *Pitts v. Freeman*, 887

F.2d 1438 (11th Cir.1989), added a potential seventh criterion, "quality of education," and ruled that all criteria had to be met simultaneously. This court said, "If the system fulfills all six factors *at the same time* for several years, the court should declare that the school system has achieved unitary status. If the school system fails to fulfill all six factors at the same time for several years, the federal district court should retain jurisdiction" (emphasis added). Finally, in 1992 the U.S. Supreme Court settled the question by upholding the "incremental approach." In so holding, the Supreme Court reversed the lower *Pitts*, and held that a workable plan may be effectively achieved if some of the six criteria are successfully addressed and the others are left to further consideration. Thus, by this ruling the Court substantially reduced the strictures on school boards in accommodating conditions of unitariness. *Freeman v. Pitts*, 503 U.S. 467 (1992).

§ 9.61   Unitariness and Burden of Proof

How, though, can one know when this erasure has been achieved? Experience has shown that there may be substantial difficulty in ferreting out the causes of segregation, whether it is *de facto* or *de jure*. The actual condition of the school district at the time of trial is perhaps the most crucial consideration in a unitariness determination. The plaintiff bears the burden of showing the existence of a current condition of segregation.

The school district must show that no causal connection exists between past and present segregation not merely that it did not intend to cause current segregation. *Brown v. Board of Education of Topeka* (Brown), 892 F.2d 851 (10th Cir. 1989).

The Supreme Court in *Freeman* had made it clear that the school district bears the burden of showing the current racial imbalance is not traceable to the original *de jure* segregation. *Brown v. Board of Education*, 892 F.2d 851 (10th Cir. 1989). See also *Board of Education of Oklahoma City v. Dowell*, 498 U.S. 237 (1991).

Whether the vestiges of past discrimination have been eradicated and unitary status has been achieved is, thus, vital to an equal protection case. As noted above, after the declaration of unitariness, the burden of proof borne by the plaintiffs to relitigate the case is much heavier in subsequent actions to prove that a school board actually had the underlying intent to discriminate. If unitariness has not been declared, discriminatory intent is presumed by virtue of the fact that earlier *de jure* segregation existed.

According to the U.S. Supreme Court, the key to unitariness is whether the school district has complied in good faith and eliminated "the vestiges of past discrimination." *Board of Education of Oklahoma City Public Schools v. Dowell*, 498 U.S. 237 (1991).

§ 9.7 INTERDISTRICT DESEGREGATION

In reversing a lower court decision which had found that *de jure* segregation existed in Detroit and its suburbs, creating a constitutional requirement to integrate several of the suburban districts with the Detroit School System, the United States Supreme Court said that before boundaries of school districts can be changed to effectuate integration it must be shown that "racially discriminatory acts of the state or local school districts, or of a single school district have been a substantial cause of interdistrict segregation." *Milliken v. Bradley*, 418 U.S. 717 (1974). The Supreme Court could not find in the record of the Detroit case any evidence that would suggest discriminatory acts, explicit or implicit, by the state of Michigan or by suburban districts that would cause the districts themselves to be segregated.

§ 9.8   REMEDIES

During the later years of the 1960s and the decade of the 1970s the federal courts fashioned remedies for school segregation by moving students from school to school to achieve desegregation. The hypothesized social benefits from such integration have been very difficult to achieve or prove, however, because white flight to the suburbs and to private schools had rendered such integration largely ineffectual.

Possibly the most definitive enunciation of the various means of remediation are given in *Milliken II* in which the U.S. Supreme Court set out guidelines that must govern lower court consideration of remedial options. *Milliken v. Bradley*, 433 U.S. 267 (1977). The guidelines are three: First, the remedy should be commensurate with the nature and scope of the constitutional violation. Second, the court's decree should be remedial in nature, fashioned as nearly as possible "to restore the victims of discriminatory conduct to the position they would have occupied in the absence of such conduct." Third, in formulating a decree, the courts "must take into account the interest of state and local authorities in managing their own affairs, consistent with the Constitution."

The lower courts, in abiding with these strictures, however, have substantial latitude, and more recent cases have seen new measures of substantial innovation.

Moreover, these measures are relying less and less on student reassignment and more on educational program remedies, some of which, in addition to those referred to above, include reduction in class size, provision for summer school, full-day kindergarten, pre- and post-school day tutoring, early childhood education, magnet schools, and facilities improvements.

The major issue of costs and whether federal courts can require expensive programs to be instituted as remedies has been of great importance. Can the federal courts require the school district to levy taxes to raise sufficient revenues to implement such plans? Can the federal courts levy the taxes themselves? In a case where a federal district court imposed taxes on the Kansas City School District sufficient to pay the local share of the costs for desegregation initiatives, the U.S. Supreme Court held that the federal district court had exceeded its authority by imposing the increase in local taxation. According to the Supreme Court, the district court had abused its discretion in levying the tax itself. Thus, the end result was that a federal district court could fashion remedies that had substantial cost consequences and could require the school district to levy the necessary taxes to achieve the desired end, but would not itself intervene into a local prerogative and actually levy taxes. *Missouri v. Jenkins*, 495 U.S. 33 (1990).

Therefore, in answer to the general question as to whether federal courts have the authority to require costly remedial measures, the answer is in the affirmative. The courts can within their judicial prerogative require a whole range of alternative programs to erase the vestiges of racial discrimination, including very expensive ones. The courts, however, cannot usurp taxing authority and in fact levy taxes themselves to raise the revenues.

§ 9.9   AFFIRMATIVE ACTION AND DIVERSITY

Immediately after the *Brown I* decision, some Southern courts sought to distinguish between the words "desegregation" and "integration." The argument was that Southern states that were segregated by statute merely had to abrogate those laws to come into conformity with the requirements of the Equal Protection Clause of the Fourteenth Amendment. As explained above, the U.S. Supreme Court, however, in developing a new kind of bifurcated jurisprudence with regard to school segregation, decided that the 17 southern states and the District of Columbia must be required to overcome past vestiges of discrimination by taking affirmative steps to rectify the misdeeds of segregation. This led to the *de jure* versus *de facto* definitions of segregation, discussed above, or separation of situations that required different judicial remedies. Dworkin, the eminent legal theorist, in commenting, observed that "the courts developed a distinct jurisprudence of racial integration, neither entirely successful nor entirely coherent, but nevertheless largely a credit to law." Ronald Dworkin, *Law's Empire* (Cambridge, Mass.: Harvard University Press, 1986), p. 391.

This bifurcated system of judicial rationale drew the remedy line between obvious, explicit intradistrict southern segregation and the more subtle northern segregation of interdistrict segregation. Thus, if there existed vestiges of past legal segregation, the courts would require affirmative measures such as busing and redrawing of school attendance zones; in short, affirmative action must be taken by the effected school boards. "Affirmative action," thereby, entered the vocabulary and the psychology of the American people. The federal courts subsequently blurred the lines between southernness and northernness of remedies by holding that school districts in states that were not segregated in 1954 must also take affirmative steps to overcome past segregation if their schools had become segregated by commission, either implicit or explicit, latent or potent, that led to the schools being segregated. The U.S. Supreme Court, however, effectively stopped in its tracks northern interdistrict integration or affirmative action in its 1974 Detroit decision, *Milliken v. Bradley*, 418 U.S. 717 (1974). The increasingly conservative Supreme Court observed that plaintiffs bore the burden of proof to show that interdistrict segregation among the hundreds of small suburban school districts around northern cities was created with intent to racially segregate. After *Milliken,* cross-district affirmative action remedies were not generally available to plaintiff African–American children who witnessed the increasingly obvious and dramatic phenomenon of "white-flight" from the northern cities.

The issue of affirmative action became most prominent as a national issue stoking the imagination and political ire of increasingly conservative voters and their correspondingly conservative elected federal officials. The *Bakke* decision was a critical point of ignition regarding affirmative action. *Regents of the University of California v. Bakke*, 438 U.S. 265 (1978). Bakke had been twice rejected by the medical school at the University of California at Davis. The admissions committee used a two-part method whereby whites were considered in one group and minority applicants were considered in another. The U.S. Supreme Court, in a divided and unclear set of five opinions, concluded that a quota system based on race violated Title VI of the Civil Rights Act in states and institutions where there had been no previous legal segregation. Although there were five votes, the justices differed on the reasoning; therefore, the *Bakke* decision was a plurality without cohesive and clear reasoning. In *Bakke*, Justice Powell observed that "preferring members of any one group for no reason other than race or ethnic origin is discrimination for its own sake." Significantly, however, Justice Powell did give judicial credence to the social concept of diversity as a defensible and even compelling goal for educational institutions that was to come later in *Grutter* and *Gratz*. One of the four justices who dissented, Justice Brennan, said that "race had often been used by those who would stigmatize and oppress minorities" and that here "color blindness" would result in oppression.

After *Bakke*, the Supreme Court followed-up saying, "Distinctions between citizens solely because of their ancestry are by their very nature odious." *Adarand Constructors, Inc. v. Pena*, 515 U.S. 200 (1995). Having earlier established that, a plaintiff's complaint of racial discrimination, whether invoked by a black or a white, requires strict scrutiny by the courts to determine if a policy with regard to race creates unconstitutional discrimination. As in *Bakke*, the strict scrutiny analysis has been utilized by whites claiming reverse discrimination. Under the strict scrutiny analysis the Supreme Court will ask whether, (1) the racial classification of the policy serves a compelling government interest, and (2) is it narrowly tailored to achieve the goal. Therefore, racial classifications may be used by states and school districts to remediate past legal segregation.

If, however, a school district has never had legal segregation of the races and then creates racial classifications for non-remedial purposes, such as diversity, then the courts will exercise strict scrutiny and require that the school district's rationale be compelling and that the policy be narrowly tailored to achieve the envisioned end. Narrow tailoring of race policies requires that the school district show (1) the efficiency of alternative race-neutral policies, (2) the planned duration of the policy, (3) the relationship, the numerical goal, and the percentage of minority group members in the relevant population, (4) the flexibility of the policy, and (5) the burden the policy places on innocent third parties. *United States v. Paradise*, 480 U.S. 149 (1987). In applying these standards, the courts have increasingly rejected affirmative action policies in elementary and secondary education. See: *Tuttle v. Arlington County School Board*, 195 F.3d 698 (4th Cir.1999), and *Eisenberg v. Montgomery County Public Schools*, 197 F.3d 123 (4th Cir.1999). *Boston's Children First v. Boston School Committee*, 183 F.Supp.2d 382 (D.Mass.2002).

The upshot is that the courts will not now permit racial classifications by school districts and institutions where remediation for past discrimination is not the objective, and the goal is to capture and achieve the benefits of diversity of student body. Thus, the issue arises as to whether diversity is of such transcending value as to amount to a compelling state interest.

§ 9.10 DIVERSITY

Is diversity an educationally compelling state interest? The answer is "yes." In sanctifying Justice Powell's approval of "diversity" as a constitutionally valid rationale for educational institutions to pursue, the U.S. Supreme Court in 2003 in *Grutter*, (*Grutter v. Bollinger*, 539 U.S. 306 (2003), Justice O'Connor writing for the Court, quoted with approval Powell's view that the "nation's future depends upon leaders trained through wide exposure to the ideas and mores of students as diverse as this Nation." (*Bakke* 1978 and *Grutter* 2003) However, she wrote that diversity as a constitutional concept is not to be focused on race or ethnicity alone, but rather on "all factors that may contribute to student body diversity." (*Grutter v. Bollinger*, 539 U.S. 306 (2003)).

In *Grutter,* in further clarifying the concept of diversity, O'Connor said, "it is not an interest in simple ethnic diversity in which a specified percentage of the student body is in effect guaranteed" ..., but, " 'a far broader array of qualifications and characteristics of which racial or ethnic origin is but a single though important element, ...' " (*Grutter v. Bollinger*, 539 U.S. 306 (2003)). Diversity is desirable and viewed as "part of a broader effort to achieve exposure to widely diverse people, cultures, ideas, and viewpoints," (*Grutter v. Bollinger*, 539 U.S. 306 (2003)). The objective of diversity is, thereby, elevated by the Court to a rarified position of being constitutionally compelling. When analyzing racial classifications there are only two: First, racial classifications will only be permitted as a compelling interest in remedying past intentional, *de jure*, segregation of schools. (*Freeman v. Pitts*, 503 U.S. 467 (1992). Second, the government interest in diversity may be a compelling interest, but, as such, diversity cannot be defined as solely on the basis of racial or ethnic balancing. (*Seattle* and *Louisville* cases, 2007, *Parents Involved in Community Schools v. Seattle School District No. 1,* 551 U.S. 701 (2007)). Therefore, the issue is settled. Diversity is a valid compelling interest of the state. To achieve diversity, however, the process and remedial measures must be designed in a broad context using several characteristics including culture, ideas, viewpoints, language, income, achievement, and a host of other identities, of which race is but one aspect of the composite.

§ 9.11 NARROW TAILORING

Narrow tailoring is terminology that has come into more frequent usage by the U.S. Supreme Court when it examines state action that might impinge on a constitutional interest. The objective is to permit government latitude to achieve a particular objective without diminishing individual constitutional rights or interests. With regard to race, the Court, as explained in *Bakke*, was troubled by affirmative action policies that favor one person over another simply because of the color of their skin. As the Supreme Court has become more conservative with the appointees of Reagan and the Bushes, there has become discernibly less concern for the correction of historical racial discrimination that earlier so negatively affected the social condition in America. The Supreme Court today effectively discourages governmentally prescribed affirmative action policies, but does acknowledge that diversity is a permissible goal of school districts if it is not simply pursued to mix the races, and if the policies used to promote diversity are "narrowly tailored." What legal rules then must a school board accommodate if it desires to encourage diversity among students, teachers and staff?

The diversity policy of the school must be based on an amalgam, composite, or blend of related attributes calibrated to enhance learning experiences of students—a mosaic if you will. While race and ethnicity can be considerations in that mosaic, they cannot be the *raison d'etre* nor the criterion on which the movement of students among schools is based. In short, the Supreme Court has said in the controlling *Seattle* and *Louisville* cases (551 U.S. 701 (2007)) that constitutional policies must be narrowly tailored and designed to achieve their "asserted goal of fostering educational and broader socialization benefits through a racially diverse learning environment." School districts cannot constitutionally justify policies that simply move children around based on racial classifications.

In *Grutter*, the University of Michigan case, with reference to higher education admissions, the Court said that: "To be narrowly tailored, a race-conscious admissions program cannot use a quota system . . ." and further, the Court said that race and ethnicity can be used as "plus" factors in narrow tailoring for diversity, but they cannot be used as fixed, inflexible, primary, mechanical percentages, numbers or quotas. (*Grutter v. Bollinger*, 539 U.S. 306 (2003)). The Court will not permit racial balancing as the means to achieve diversity in school districts that have never had legal segregation or have been declared by the courts to be unitary. Diversity cannot be constitutionally achieved by quotas for racial or ethnic classifications.

Narrow tailoring, according to the Court in the *Grutter* case, must include a more "holistic" view than just race or ethnicity. Racial classifications must be a part of a "broader assessment of diversity and not simply an effort to achieve racial balance." (*Grutter v. Bollinger*, 539 U.S. 306 (2003). See also *Gratz v. Bollinger*, 539 U.S. 244 (2003). Thus, if diversity is the goal, the school district should seek to achieve a student body in each school that reflects "talents, experiences and potential," not just race of the entire student population. Some of these "holistic" elements might be grades, travel, language, and/or income level of family. Income is not a suspect class as is race and ethnicity; therefore, there is no constitutional prohibition on balancing student enrollments based on the students categorized by percentages of free and reduced-price lunches. Therefore, if a school district desires to create greater student body diversity in each of its schools, then it must not by reassigning students based on race or ethnicity but by creating a mosaic of student attributes that it wishes to define as an enrollment.

CHAPTER 10

EDUCATION OF DISABLED CHILDREN

§ 10.1 INTRODUCTION

Provision for education of disabled children has historically been far from adequate. Until the mid to late 1960s, most states did not have uniform standards for education of the disabled, and many states did not provide state financing for such purposes. Disabled students were systematically excluded from educational programs because their emotional or physical disabilities tended to disrupt the continuity of the everyday school program, or the costs of their education were beyond that which the taxpayers were willing to undertake.

Today the situation is much different, both state and federal statutes guarantee educational opportunity for children with disabilities, and court decisions have mandated that the civil rights of these children be protected.

§ 10.2 RIGHT TO ATTEND SCHOOL

Although a number of states already had statutes requiring educational services to disabled children, two cases provided impetus to other state legislatures and the Congress to form new legislation guaranteeing educational opportunity for disabled children. The first case, *Pennsylvania Association for Retarded Children* (PARC), was brought by the parents of 17 children who claimed that Pennsylvania laws enacted prior to 1972 were unconstitutional. *Pennsylvania Association for Retarded Children v. Commonwealth*, 334 F.Supp. 1257 (E.D.Pa.1971) and *Pennsylvania Association for Retarded Children v. Commonwealth*, 343 F.Supp. 279 (E.D.Pa.1972). The laws allowed for exclusion of disabled children from public school if they were certified by psychologists as "uneducable and untrainable." The parents claimed that: (1) the law did not provide for appropriate due process measures to be taken before exclusion, such as notice to parents and a proper hearing; (2) the children were denied equal protection because they were declared to be uneducable without a rational factual basis for such determination; (3) the state constitution guaranteed education for all children; and (4) the law which excluded handicapped children was arbitrary and capricious. The federal district court held that exclusion of handicapped children was, indeed, unconstitutional, that: "having undertaken to provide a free public education to all its children, including its exceptional children, the Commonwealth of Pennsylvania may not deny any mentally-retarded child access to a free public program of education and training." The court gave the parties involved an opportunity to agree on procedures acceptable to both sides. A consent decree was issued which required a "free public program of education and training appropriate to the child's capacity within the context of a presumption that, among the alternative programs of education and training required by statute to be available, placement in a regular public school class is preferable to placement in a special public school class i.e., a class for 'handicapped' children (only), and placement in a special public school class is preferable to placement in any other type of program of education and training. . . ."

Shortly following *PARC* which required services to mentally-retarded children, another court action, the *Mills* case, emerged that further accentuated the issue of educating the disabled. The *Mills* case extended the rights not only to mentally-retarded children but also to all disabled children. *Mills v. Board of Education of District of Columbia*, 348 F.Supp. 866 (D.D.C.1972). Because this case arose in Washington, D.C., it gained substantial notoriety having a great impact on both state and federal legislation. Here, parents challenged exclusionary practices which had resulted in nearly 18,000 disabled children going without public education in 1972–73. Law in the District of Columbia mandated a free public education for all children between the ages of 7 and 16. Parents of disabled children claimed that denial of education violated the constitutional right of due process. In defense, school officials argued that to educate the disabled children would cause a great financial burden for which there was not adequate funding.

The federal district court held that equal protection was implicit in the Due Process Clause of the Fifth Amendment, applying to the District of Columbia, and that through this provision a right existed to attend public schools. While the substantive aspects of due process gave these students a right to attend public schools, the procedural aspects of due process entitled the students to a fair hearing before they could be excluded or placed in alternative classes within the school system.

In answer to the school district's financial concerns, the court bluntly stated, "If sufficient funds are not available to finance all of the services and programs that are needed and desirable in the system, then the available funds must be expended equitably in such a manner that no child is entirely excluded from a publicly-supported education consistent with his needs and ability to benefit therefrom. The inadequacies of the District of Columbia Public School System, whether occasioned by insufficient funding or administrative inefficiency, certainly cannot be permitted to bear more heavily on the 'exceptional' or handicapped child than on the normal child." In the decree the court established due process procedures which included step-by-step detail on how notice was to be given to parents when placement of a child was contemplated, who should serve as hearing officers, and the requirements for the actual hearing. Many of these procedures were later adopted in state and federal legislation to protect the interests of disabled children.

§ 10.3   THE ORIGINAL PUBLIC LAW 94–142 AND SECTION 504

With an awareness created by *PARC* and *Mills* and emergent cases in other states, the Congress moved rapidly to provide federal legislation and funding which would assist in educating disabled children. The federal law entitled Education for All Handicapped Children Act of 1975, 20 U.S.C.A. § 1401, initially applied to all children between the ages of 3 and 21. In order to receive federal funds under the Act, states were required to abide by the Act and regulations made pursuant thereto.

Congress, a year earlier in 1973, had addressed the needs of disabled individuals when it had passed the Vocational Rehabilitation Act of 1973 which applies to all agencies receiving federal funds for any purpose. These funds may be forfeited if charges of agency discrimination against disabled people are sustained. Section 504 of this act states: "No otherwise qualified handicapped individual in the United States ... shall, solely by reason of his handicap, be excluded from the participation in, be denied the benefits of, or be subjected to discrimination under any program or activity receiving federal financial assistance."

Although § 504 is concerned with the discrimination of disabled individuals in work situations, it also addresses the problems encountered by disabled children in seeking equal educational opportunity. Five mandates are encompassed in § 504 that pertain directly to the educational needs of disabled children: "(a) location and notification, (b) free appropriate public education, (c) educational setting, (d) evaluation and placement, and (e) procedural safeguards." These provisions of § 504 have been used successfully in obtaining desirable school programs and services for disabled students. Moreover, this Act has been used to obtain services for disabled children who do not meet the IDEA definition. For example, the provision for a free appropriate public education in a proper educational setting enabled a child with cystic fibrosis to attend regular classes while receiving supportive services for a daily suctioning procedure and was instrumental in assisting children with Acquired Immunodeficiency Syndrome (AIDS) to remain in school. Also, Section 504 is not as prescriptive as IDEA.

§ 10.31   Individuals With Disabilities Education Act (IDEA)

The original Act, the Education for All Handicapped Children Act (EAHCA), signed on November 29, 1975, by President Gerald R. Ford, was amended in 1978 and in 1986 and was incorporated into a new law in 1990, the

Individuals with Disabilities Education Act (IDEA), 20 U.S.C.A. §§ 1400–1485. The Act was again reauthorized and amended in 1997 and in 2004 with several important changes. Little of substance was added in the 1990 legislation except a limited expansion of the definition of disabilities, such as inclusion of head trauma, autism, etc., and a provision to prevent states from using the Eleventh Amendment as a shield against liability in actions by disabled children.

In 1997 Congress enacted Public Law 105–17 entitled the *Individuals with Disabilities Education Act Amendments of 1997*. The amendments included a revised funding formula based on the state's population of children and on the child poverty levels modified requirements for the least-restrictive environment for student placement, and the new Act generally advanced an outcome-based approach for determining adherence to the requirements for children as well as expanding the guarantee of access to educational services. (*See* 20 U.S.C.A. § 1401(3) and 34 Code of Federal Regulation Part 300.7).

Additionally, the 1997 Amendments affected several other aspects of the IDEA, including special provisions for evaluation and placement of children with disabilities when carrying firearms or involved in illegal drugs. The 1997 Amendments also allow school districts to reduce or deny payments to parents for tuition costs when the parents unilaterally place their children in private schools, without notice, referral or consent of the public schools. Further, the parents cannot expect reimbursement if they did not make the child available to the public school for assessment and evaluation prior to removal of the child to a private school or facility.

The IDEA defines disabled children as those who are mentally retarded, hard of hearing, deaf, speech and language impaired, visually impaired, seriously emotionally disturbed, orthopedically impaired, autistic, traumatically brain injured, or otherwise health impaired. In addition, the definition includes children with specific learning disabilities who require special education and related services. The Act also requires the development of services for disabled students to ease their transition into the world of the adult. Provisions for such transitional services must be included in the IEPs of all students 16 years of age and older.

Importantly, the IDEA assures that all disabled children have access to "a free appropriate public education and related services designed to meet their unique needs." The appropriate educational program must be tailored to each disabled child's educational needs. Under the law, an "individualized education program" (IEP) must be designed for each child, and re-evaluation of the plan must be conducted annually. Another provision mandates that disabled children be educated in the "least-restrictive" environment appropriate to their needs. This requires disabled children be mainstreamed and included in regular classes where possible. A regular class with appropriate supplemental services is considered to be preferable to special classes, special classes are considered to be preferable to separate special schools, and special schools are considered to be preferable to homebound instruction. If no public facilities are available, then private schools may be used in the alternative and public funds may be used to defray the costs.

Evaluations of children to establish IEPs and determine the least-restrictive environment is to be conducted by the school district at least every three years and upon request by a parent or teacher. Federal regulations, 34 C.F.R. § 300.534(b), give the school district the prerogative of conducting a triennial re-evaluation by persons selected by the district. Such a re-evaluation can be conducted in the absence of a parental request for a hearing and without parental consent. *Johnson by Johnson v. Duneland School Corp.*, 92 F.3d 554 (7th Cir. 1996). Too, the decision as to the placement of the child seeking special education services allows the public school district to conduct its own evaluation, and the district cannot be compelled to rely solely on an independent evaluation by persons of the parents' exclusive choosing. *Andress v. Cleveland Independent School District*, 64 F.3d 176 (5th Cir.1995).

The IDEA requires that courts give "due weight" to administrative decisions by the school district regarding student placement. The courts will defer to the school districts so long as the precise procedural requirements of IDEA are followed and the educational expertise on which the school district depends is directly relevant to the disability of the child and the IEP. *Burilovich v. Board of Education of Lincoln Consolidated Schools*, 208 F.3d 560 (6th Cir.2000).

Judicial deference to decisions by educators regarding the appropriate methodologies utilized in IEPs is predicated on the assumption that the child is in fact benefiting from her education. *E.S. v. Independent School Dist. No. 196*, 135 F.3d 566 (8th Cir.1998).

The IDEA contemplates an IEP that contains such specific instructional elements as to enable a child to receive passing grades and to progress in school. In a case where a student had been classified as gifted but had fallen down in grades, failed to turn in written assignments and was reported as bored in class, seven different evaluators analyzed him, four of whom recommended an IEP that reduced handwriting assignments replaced through the use of computers and tape recorders, and tests were also modified to minimize the need for writing, the Court found the IEP was appropriate even though the student continued to struggle academically. The Court held for the school district finding that the IEP contained specific goals, means of assessment, and identified objectives for tests and writing performance. *D.B. v. Craven County Board of Education*, 210 F.3d 360 (4th Cir.2000).

Some of the procedural safeguards provided for in the Act are: (1) access by parents to relevant school records, (2) prior notice to parents of any proposed change in their child's educational placement, (3) opportunity for a fair and impartial hearing, including right to be represented by a lawyer or advisor, right to present evidence, to subpoena, confront and cross-examine witnesses and obtain a transcript of the hearing and written decision, (4) opportunity to appeal to court, (5) right of child to remain in current placement during pendency of hearing proceedings, and (6) parents may be eligible for legal fees if they prevail.

§ 10.311   IDEA Amendments in 2004

In 2004 IDEA was reauthorized by H.R. 1350, and several key provisions were added; among these were: (1) Schools can conduct an evaluation of a child who transfers from out-of-state before becoming required to fulfill the IEP; (2) Where parents repeatedly refuse to cooperate with a school in the conduct of an individual evaluation of a child, the school is relieved of the obligation to convene and involve the parents in an IEP meeting; (3) Parents have a two-year limitation for filing of IDEA complaints; (4) Parents or the school district has 90 days under federal law to appeal an adverse decision of a hearing officer, or the time as stated in state law; (5) School districts must provide parents with notice of their and their child's rights once a year, including the procedure for filing a due process complaint; (6) Rules for the placement of disabled students in alternative settings have been changed to allow schools to "consider any unique circumstances on a case-by-case basis when determining whether to order a change in placement," for disabled students who violate school conduct codes. 20 U.S.C. § 1415; (7) A new provision was added that for "special circumstances" a school may remove a student to an interim educational setting for up to 45 days even without a determination of a "manifestation of disability." The "special circumstances" are weapons possession, the sale, use, or possession of drugs, and/or infliction of serious bodily injury to another while at school, on school grounds, or at a school-sponsored event. 20 U.S.C. § 1415 (k)(G); (8) In the case of a disciplinary removal, the hearing officer may return the student to the original placement or may place the student in an alternative placement setting for up to 45 days; (9) An evaluation of a student must take place within 60 days of obtaining the consent of parents or in keeping with the time limits established by the state; (10) The school district does not need to abide by the 60–day rule for students who transfer into the school district if the parent "repeatedly fails or refuses to produce the child for evaluation"; (11) Eligibility determinations for IDEA cannot be based on lack of English proficiency, or lack of instruction in math or reading, nor can the school district consider discrepancies between achievement and ability in oral expression, listening comprehension, written expression, basic reading skill, reading comprehension, mathematical calculation, or mathematical reasoning; (12) The school district is not required to seek an evaluation before terminating the IDEA eligibility of a disabled student who graduated from high school with a regular diploma or who becomes too old to be eligible for a free appropriate public education; (13) The 2004 amendments emphasized the importance of transition services for disabled students. Transition services are defined as educational programs that are "results-oriented," that focus on "improving the academic and functional achievement" of disabled children.

§ 10.32   A Right to Special Education

By virtue of the IDEA, a disabled child has a right to an education and does not need to show that he or she will benefit from an education in order to attend public school. Whether such a right exists was one of the primary issues emerging from the enactment of the Individuals with Disabilities Education Act (IDEA). The issue was whether the severity of handicap can be so great as to render the child incapable of benefiting from education. The theory is that if a child cannot benefit from the educational process, then the state is not required to provide an educational service to the child. Indeed, the question as to whether a showing of benefit is required at all was the subject of litigation of primary importance for education of disabled children. The court answered very clearly and held that IDEA does not require a child to demonstrate a benefit from the education as a condition precedent to participation.

In the defining case on the subject, *Timothy W.*, the child had been born two months premature with severe respiratory problems and had shortly thereafter suffered intracranial hemorrhage, subdural effusions, seizures, hydrocephalus, and meningitis. As a result, the boy was multiply handicapped and profoundly mentally retarded. These extensive handicaps specifically included complex developmental disabilities, spastic quadriplegia, cerebral palsy, seizure disorder, and cortical blindness. Expert testimony indicated that the boy had virtually no brain cortex and, therefore, had no capacity to learn. Other expert testimony was to the effect that he was aware of his surrounding environment, attempted on occasion purposeful movement, responded to tactile stimulation, recognized familiar voices and noises, and could part his lips when spoon fed.

In considering the extensiveness of the handicap and the intent of the federal statute, the court concluded the meaning of the law was that "*all* handicapped children should be included," and, in fact, the Act gives priority to the most severely handicapped. Furthermore, the Act does not in any provision place the burden on the child to demonstrate that he or she can "benefit" from the educational program. The court pointed out emphatically that the Act made it clear it intended a "zero-reject" policy; that is, no child, "regardless of the severity of his or her handicap," is to be deprived of education. This court summed up its opinion by saying: "Public education is to be provided to all handicapped children, unconditionally and without exception." *Timothy W. v.*

Rochester, New Hampshire School District, 875 F.2d 954 (1st Cir.1989).

§ 10.33   Eleventh Amendment Immunity Abrogated

Importantly, too, the 1990 IDEA amendments abrogated state immunity for liability that could be claimed under the Eleventh Amendment. The amendments responded to a loophole in the original Act that had not specifically rendered states liable for reimbursement to parents of disabled children for tuition and other necessary costs they incurred in educating their children. The Supreme Court had ruled that even though the Congress had the authority under Section Five (5) of the Fourteenth Amendment to specifically abrogate state immunity under the Eleventh Amendment, the wording of the original 1975 legislation (P.L. 94–142) had not done so, thus depriving parents of the reimbursement. The IDEA legislation of 1990 provided language in "unmistakably clear" terms, stating "[a] state shall not be immune under the Eleventh Amendment to the Constitution of the United States from suit in Federal Court for a violation of this chapter."

§ 10.34   Child Find

An issue that has been an ongoing problem in the provision of special education has been the difficulty in identifying or finding the children that qualify as disabled. Early in the implementation of IDEA, there were wide variations among school districts in percentages of children that were thought to have special needs. As a result, there was reason to believe that many disabled children were going undiscovered and were not provided with a free appropriate public education. To help remedy this problem, a "child find" provision was included in IDEA. 20 U.S.C. § 1415 (k)(5)(b). The law requires a hunt or a quest to find such children and prescribes procedures to do so. Under this part of the Act, local education agencies (school districts) are required to "identify, locate, and evaluate all children with disabilities residing within their boundaries." A school district is thereby obligated to seek out disabled students; and if the district has "knowledge" of a disabled child, then it must provide appropriate services. This obligation to seek extends to children enrolled in private schools and to homeless children.

The statutory duty to provide special services to a child becomes incumbent on a school district that has "knowledge" of the child's condition. A school district, by IDEA rationale, is determined to have knowledge that a child has a disability where: (a) the child's parent "has expressed concern in writing" to a teacher or school official that the child is in need of special education or related services; (b) the child's parent has sought an evaluation to ascertain whether the child has a disability; or (c) the child's teacher or school official "has expressed specific concerns about a pattern of behavior demonstrated by the child, directly to the director of special education of such agency or to other supervisory personnel of the agency." (20 U.S.C. § 1415 (k)(5)(b).

A part of the school district's obligation for "child find" is fulfilled by a publicity campaign, and the public school is not obligated to pursue the parents of a child enrolled in a private school to make them respond to the educational opportunity. *Doe v. Metropolitan Nashville Public Schools,* 9 Fed.Appx. 453 (6th Cir. 2001).

§ 10.4   LITIGATION PURSUANT TO IDEA

Much litigation has emerged during the last few years which clarifies several of the provisions of the Act. Most of these cases have to do with interpretation of appropriateness of program, placement, and costs of treatment.

§ 10.41   Impartial Hearing

Implicit in the due process provision of the Act is that there should be an impartial tribunal (see Due Process, Chapter 3). The IDEA specifically provides for extensive procedural due process protections. These procedures must be strictly adhered to by the school district in evaluation and placement of disabled children. One aspect of the due process afforded a child is the "stay-put" provision requiring that a child's status cannot change until the required due process procedures are completed. Then, and only then, can the child's placement be changed. With regard to the "stay put" requirement, the U.S. Supreme Court has said, "The language of Subsection 1415(e)(3) (of IDEA) is unequivocal. It states plainly that during pendency of any proceedings initiated under the Act, unless the state or local educational agency and the parents or guardian of a disabled child otherwise agree, 'the child *shall* remain in the then current educational placement.' " § 1415(e)(3) (emphasis added). *Honig v. Doe*, 484 U.S. 305 (1988).

§ 10.42   Stay–Put

The IDEA contains a pendency of review provision that prohibits school authorities from unilaterally excluding a disabled child from school during review proceedings to determine the placement of the student. Section 1415(e)(3) of the act states that "the child shall remain in the then current educational placement" until proper placement can be determined. This so-called stay-put provision raises the question as to whether a child can be excluded from school for an indefinite period of time for dangerous or disruptive conduct growing out of a disability. In *Honig v. Doe*, 484 U.S. 305 (1988), the U.S. Supreme Court resolved the issue by making it clear that the EAHCA (1) confers a substantive right to education on disabled students, (2) prohibits school officials from unilaterally excluding a disabled student from the classroom for dangerous or disruptive conduct for an indeterminate period of time where conduct grows out of a disability, and (3) permits school officials to temporarily suspend a student for up to ten days to protect the safety of others and to provide a "cooling down." This does not violate "stay-put." During a period of temporary suspension an IEP process can be initiated to review the child's placement.

In *Texas City Independent School District v. Jorstad*, 752 F.Supp. 231 (S.D.Tex.1990), the court issued an injunction allowing the school more time to find an appropriate placement for a child who was a danger to himself and others; he struck teachers and other students, tore a wooden door off its hinges and jumped out of a second floor window, among other things.

The "stay-put" requirement is, therefore, an essential component of the law. There are, of course, extenuating circumstances that may modify the school district's obligations under this provision. For example, the "stay-put" provision, to stay in the current educational placement, does not apply to the new school district where a parent and child move to another state. The receiving state is not obliged to abide by the former state's placement decisions and the former IEP. *Michael C. v. Radnor Township School District*, 202 F.3d 642 (3rd Cir.2000).

Some courts have described the stay-put provision of the IDEA as an "automatic injunction" against the school district's moving the student in an alternative education placement. The U.S. Court of Appeals has said that "the stay-put order is sufficiently clear and definite to be enforceable by the usual sanction for violating an injunction—civil or criminal contempt—so that the order has not only the form of an injunction but also the bite that a real injunction has." *Board of Education of Oak Park v. Illinois State Board of Education*, 79 F.3d 654 (7th Cir.1996).

§ 10.421   Manifestation Determinations

Manifestation determinations are essential to "stay-put" considerations when discipline is an issue. In cases of discipline the decision as to whether the offense by a student is a manifestation of a disability is essential. A manifestation review by a team, parents and IEP team members, is required if a school wants to remove a student to an alternative educational setting for over 10 days. If the team decides that the offending behavior is not a manifestation of a disability, the discipline action taken against the disabled student can be the same as that applied to the nondisabled student. Offenses related to drugs and weapons are a special category as provided under IDEA. A disabled student guilty of such offenses can be suspended up to 45 days without a manifestation determination. *A.P. v. Pemberton Twp. Board of Education*, 2006 WL 1344788 (D.N.J. 2006); *S.W. v. Holbrook Public Schools*, 221 F. Supp.2d 222 (D.Mass.2002).

Under IDEA, see *Honig* case above, disciplinary removal of a student that exceeds ten days constitutes a "change of placement." The Act does, however, provide for placement in alternative educational settings. Schools are allowed to "consider any unique circumstances on a case-by-case basis when determining whether to order a change of placement" for students with disabilities who break codes of student conduct. Congress acted in 2004 to modify the law with a provision for special disciplinary circumstances. 20 U.S.C. § 1415 (K)(G). Under this part schools may remove students to an interim alternative educational setting for up to 45 days. The movement of students to an interim alternative setting will be permitted whether or not the offending behavior by a disabled student is a "manifestation" of a disability. Various aspects of manifestation considerations are clearly described in the 2007 New York case. (*Coleman v. Newburgh Enlarged City School District*, 503 F.3d 198 (2d Cir. 2007).

§ 10.43 Least–Restrictive Environment

An overriding objective of the IDEA is to normalize the education of disabled children and place them in the regular classroom setting whenever possible. Federal regulations promulgated pursuant to IDEA state "... that separate schooling, or other removal of handicapped children from the regular educational environment, [should] occur only when the nature of severity of the handicap is such that education in regular classes with the use of supplementary aids and services cannot be achieved satisfactorily." 34 C.F.R. § 300.551; 20 U.S.C.A. § 1412(5)(B).

Under this regulation the disabled child is to be given the broadest educational opportunity available, and the option with the "least-restrictive environment" must be chosen in order to minimize to the greatest extent possible harmful effects on the child. In considering alternative placements a continuum is envisaged that has on one end the regular classroom, the least-restrictive environment, and at the other end, the hospital, the most restrictive. See Laura F. Rothstein, *Special Education Law* (New York: Longman, 1990), p. 112.

"Integrating children with disabilities in regular classrooms is commonly known as 'mainstreaming.' " The least-restrictive environment should result in mainstreaming the child as frequently as possible. Although mainstreaming is not always required, a number of courts have interpreted sections of IDEA which relates to mainstreaming as so requiring. The specific statement in IDEA that establishes mainstreaming is "procedures to assure that, to the maximum extent appropriate, children with disabilities ... are educated with children who are not disabled, and that special classes, separate schooling, or other removal of children with disabilities from the regular educational environment occurs only when the nature of severity of the disability is such that education services cannot be achieved satisfactorily ..." 20 U.S.C.A. § 1412(5)(B). *Mavis v. Sobol*, 839 F.Supp. 968 (N.D.N.Y.1993). This provision appears to reflect

Congress' strong preference in favor of including or integrating disabled children in regular classrooms.

In determining whether a child should be mainstreamed, some of the federal circuits have used what is known as the *Daniel R.R.* test. *Daniel R.R. v. State Board of Education*, 874 F.2d 1036 (5th Cir.1989). This test has a two-part inquiry. "First, we ask whether education in the regular classroom, with the use of supplemental aids and services, can be achieved satisfactorily for a given child.... If it cannot and the school intends to provide special education or to remove the child from regular education, we ask, second, whether the school has mainstreamed the child to the maximum extent appropriate."

Other federal circuits apply the *Roncker* test. The *Roncker* test provides "[W]here the segregated facility is considered superior, the court should determine whether the services which make the placement superior could be feasibly provided in a non-segregated setting. If they can, the placement in the segregated school would be inappropriate under the Act." *Roncker v. Walter*, 700 F.2d 1058 (6th Cir.1983).

What constitutes the least-restrictive environment is yet so uncertain that litigation continues to proliferate. The courts have generally held that where disputes arise over appropriate educational methodology, the court will defer to the judgment of school officials. *Lachman v. Illinois State Board of Education*, 852 F.2d 290 (7th Cir.1988). "The primary responsibility for formulating the education to be accorded a handicapped child, and for choosing the educational program most suitable to the child's needs, was left by the Act to state and local educational agencies in cooperation with the parents and guardians of the child." *Board of Education of Hendrick Hudson Central School District v. Rowley*, 458 U.S. 176 (1982).

The court in *Lachman* concluded that parental discretion in the matter of placement must defer to the judgment of the professional educators of the public school district. This court said that "... parents, no matter how well-motivated, do not have a right under EAHCA (IDEA) to compel a school district to provide a specific program or employ a specific methodology in providing for education of their handicapped child...." *Lachman v. Illinois State Board of Education*, supra. *See also Kruelle v. New Castle County School District*, 642 F.2d 687 (3d Cir.1981).

Today, the IDEA in seeking the least-restrictive environment for children with disabilities creates a presumption in favor of inclusion in regular education classes. Such inclusion, however, may be inappropriate if satisfactory progress cannot be achieved due to the nature or severity of the child's disability. *Hartmann v. Loudoun County Board of Education*, 118 F.3d 996 (4th Cir.1997). Placement of the student in the least-restrictive environment does not always mean that the nearest neighborhood school is the appropriate location for the child. Parents' contention that implementing regulations of the IDEA created a presumption that the child should be placed in the nearest neighborhood school has been rejected by the courts. *Murray v. Montrose County School District*, 51 F.3d 921 (10th Cir.1995).

§ 10.44   Inclusion

The terms "inclusion," "full inclusion" and "integrated services" are not found in Public Law 94–142 (EAH-

CA, 1975) or Public Law 101–476 (IDEA, 1991) or regulations for these acts. The inclusion rationale came out of the U.S. Department of Education in the early 1980s under the "regular education initiative." Regular education initiative advocates criticized special and regular education because disabled children were not being placed in regular education classes frequently enough. Although not classified in the statute or regulations, these terms are now being used by the courts when addressing the child's "least-restrictive environment."

Thus, even though the terminology continues to evolve, there appears to be sustaining general agreement that disabled children should be placed in regular classrooms whenever possible. The congressional desire for disabled children to attend school in the regular classroom is given substantial new support in the 1997 amendments. The statutory language now requires that the IEP include "an explanation of the extent, if any, to which the child will not participate with non-disabled children in the regular class...." This is different from the earlier IDEA regulations which required the child's IEP to state "the extent that the child will be able to participate in regular educational programs." This change effectively shifts the burden to the school district to show why the disabled student should not participate in a regular classroom, not why he or she should. Implicit in this placement objective is the overriding and most important concern that all children benefit from the socialization processes that are inherent in being educated with one's peers. It is this attribute of commonality and mutual participation so important to the learning process that advances the time-honored idea of public schools—all should attend school in common, rubbing shoulders with the non-disabled and the disabled—that best expresses the abiding spirit of public education.

§ 10.45   Free Appropriate Public Education

IDEA gives children with disabilities the right to a free appropriate public education (FAPE). The key to meeting the requirements of IDEA is to determine what constitutes an appropriate education. In the most authoritative statement yet made in interpretation of IDEA, the United States Supreme Court in *Board of Educ. of Hendrick Hudson Central School District v. Rowley*, 458 U.S. 176 (1982), ruled on the question "What is meant by the Act's requirement of a 'free appropriate public education?' " The case arose when parents of Amy Rowley, a deaf student, contested the appropriateness of the educational program provided her by the Hendrick Hudson School District. Amy had minimal residual hearing and was an excellent lip reader. After meeting with her parents, and prior to her entering school, it was decided to place her in a regular kindergarten class where she would have supplemental assistance. She was to be provided with an FM hearing aid which would amplify words spoken into a wireless receiver by the teacher and other students during classroom activities. Amy successfully completed kindergarten and per the law was prescribed a new IEP for her first-grade year. The Individual Education Plan (IEP) called for her to be mainstreamed in a regular classroom, continue to use the FM equipment and, additionally, receive instruction from a tutor for the deaf for one hour each day and from a speech therapist for three hours a week. Her parents agreed with the IEP but insisted that, additionally, Amy should be provided with a qualified sign-language interpreter, full time, in all her academic classes. The school district officials disagreed maintaining that the child did not need the interpreter.

In reviewing the evidence, the lower court concluded that a "free appropriate public education" must be defined as "an opportunity to achieve her full potential commensurate with the opportunity provided other children." The federal Court of Appeals affirmed but the United States Supreme Court reversed and remanded the decision. The Supreme Court interpreted the Act as requiring that services for handicapped be sufficient to permit the child "to benefit" from instruction, but was not intended to prescribe a substantive standard prescribing a level of education.

In taking issue with the lower court's determinations that "the goal of the Act is to provide each handicapped child with an equal educational opportunity" and to "maximize" each child's potential "commensurate with the opportunity provided other children," the Supreme Court maintained that the lower courts had erred and that there was evidence that Congress "did not intend to achieve strict equality services for handicapped and non-handicapped children...." Rather, according to the Court, the intent was to merely provide "a basic floor of opportunity consistent with equal protection."

As to how and by whom the "basic floor" is to be defined, the Court said that the Act expressly charges states with the responsibility of providing teachers, administrators, and programs and practices appropriate for education of the handicapped. The Act requires that state and local educational agencies in cooperation with the parents or guardian of the child would decide on the appropriateness of the educational services to be offered, but where there is disagreement the Act vests the authority for final determination in the State.

The *Rowley* precedent is now relied on by lower courts in determining appropriate placement and the requirements of the child's IEP. However, to determine what constitutes the basic floor of opportunity as required by *Rowley*, as opposed to placement in programs of maximum service, has become a source of contention between school districts and parents. Importantly, however, the obligation to provide a free appropriate public education does not require an optimal placement that would require the school district to make unreasonable staffing arrangements to accommodate the IEP. *Kevin G. by Robert G. v. Cranston School Committee*, 130 F.3d 481 (1st Cir.1997).

§ 10.46   Procedural Safeguards

As indicated in the *Mills* and *Rowley* cases, proper procedures are a vital aspect in assuring that appropriate educational services are extended to handicapped children. The necessary due process specifications delineated in *Mills* were followed and embellished by the EAHCA in 1975. Section 1415 of that act contains procedures that are mandatory. Most importantly, the procedures specify that parents must be given notice and an opportunity to participate in the development of a child's education program. Inclusive is the requirement that parents be informed of all methods and procedures by which conflicts and grievances may be appealed and resolved. Implicit therein is the assurance that hearings regarding the child's placement will be impartial and unbiased. The law, § 1415, emphasizes this standard of fairness by giving the parent a right to have the hearing conducted by a person who is neither an employee of the school district nor of the state department of education.

As stated in *Rowley*, a reviewing court must make sure that procedures are followed by the district. A school district making a placement decision without reference to the IEP violates the requirements of the law and free appropriate education. On the other hand, if an insignificant procedural error is made not resulting in the child's loss of educational opportunity, the court will decline to "exalt form over substance" by enforcing a technical infraction from the Act's procedural standards.

If the results of the hearing are not to the satisfaction of the parent or the school district, then appeal can be made to the state department of education. During the time in which appeals are taken, the child must remain or "stay put" in his or her "then current" program. As discussed later in this chapter, indefinite suspension during pendency of appeal violates this section of the law. Appeal to either state or federal courts may be taken after a decision has been rendered by the state department of education. *Amanda J. ex. rel. Annette J. v. Clark County School Dist.*, 267 F.3d 877 (9th Cir.2001).

§ 10.47   Individualized Education Program (IEP)

The purpose, of course, of all these procedural safeguards is to ensure to the parent and child that an appropriate individualized educational program (IEP) will be provided. The IEP goes beyond merely providing a place for the child in the public schools, but, more extensively, must design and reduce to writing an educational plan that takes into account the identification of the child's educational needs, the annual instructional goals and objectives, the specific educational programs and services to be provided, and the necessary evaluation procedures to monitor the child's progress. An IEP is "more than a mere exercise in public relations," indeed, it is the "centerpiece of the statute's education delivery system for disabled children." "The term 'individualized education program' means a written statement for each child with a disability developed in a meeting by a representative of the local educational agency or an intermediate educational unit who shall be qualified to provide, or supervise the provision of, specially-designed instruction to meet the unique needs of children with disabilities...."

The IEP statement describing the child's educational goals and specifying required services is developed by a multidisciplinary team. For initial evaluation and placement the IEP team must have as members a school official, the child's teacher(s), parents and other person(s) qualified to interpret evaluation results. Because the IEP must be jointly prepared by school officials and parents and reviewed annually, a condition of possible contention is staged. Contests between parents and school districts over the nature of the IEP have created a plethora of handicapped litigation in recent years, all of which have begun to form a formidable body of case law.

Challenges of IEP evaluations by parents are the source of much litigation. Federal courts are the final arbiters of these IEP disputes. For example, the U.S. Court of Appeals, First Circuit, held against a school board ruling that even though a disabled student did not have academic needs, she was still eligible for special education under IDEA because her disability affected her ability to perform in nonacademic programs of the school. *Mr. I. v. Maine School Administrative District, No. 55*, 480 F.3d 1 (1st Cir. 2007).

Where a student had a qualifying disability (ADHD) and needed special services in lower elementary grades, but thereafter did not need them and he subsequently robbed a school concession stand, the federal court ruled against the parents noting that the boy's behavioral problems were of non-ADHD origins but rather resulted from family problems. *Alvin Independent School District v. Patricia F.*, 503 F.3d 378 (5th Cir. 2007).

A school's IEP team must have the information necessary to evaluate a student. The courts will require it. Frequently, parents or guardians will not cooperate and will hold the student out of school and refuse evaluation. In a case where a grandmother claimed that the reevaluation of a child would harm the child was rejected by the court. The court said that a school must be allowed to evaluate a student if the IEP is to be completed in accordance with IDEA. *Shelby S. v. Conroe Independent School District*, 454 F.3d 450 (5th Cir. 2006).

The U.S. Court of Appeals, Fifth Circuit, has set forth criteria that can assist in determining whether an IEP is reasonably calibrated to provide a meaningful educational benefit as required by IDEA: (a) whether the IEP is individualized on the basis of a student's assessment and performance, (b) whether it is administered in the least-restrictive environment, (c) whether it is provisioned by the principal service providers in a coordinated and collaborative manner, and (d) whether it results in positive academic and non-academic benefits. *Cypress–Fairbanks Independent School Dist. v. Michael F.*, 118 F.3d 245 (5th Cir.1997).

§ 10.471   Material Failure in Implementation of IEP

Minor departures or failures to adhere to an IEP do not necessarily constitute an automatic violation of an IEP. The IDEA requires a "material failure" to implement an IEP before a court will hold against a school district. The IDEA defines a failure to implement in this way: "A material failure occurs when the services a school provides to a disabled child fall significantly short of the services required by the child's IEP." *Van Duyn v. Baker School District*, 481 F.3d 770 (9th Cir. 2007). Too, it should be noted that a school's failure to identify a specific school at which the IEP could be fulfilled constitutes a violation of IDEA. *A.K. v. Alexandria City School Board*, 484 F.3d 672 (4th Cir. 2007).

§ 10.472   IEP Meetings

An IEP procedural violation by the school district may be grounds to entitle parents to receive tuition reimbursement for placement of their disabled child in a private school. *Shapiro v. Paradise Valley Unified School District No. 69*, 317 F.3d 1072 (9th Cir. 2003).

A school district's preparation prior to a predetermination IEP meeting does not invalidate the meeting. The fact that the school district prepares in advance does not imply that the meeting results will be biased. *Nack v. Orange City School District*, 454 F.3d 604 (6th Cir. 2006). See also *N. L. v. Knox County Schools*, 315 F.3d 688 (6th Cir. 2003).

Parents are not entitled to attend "staff meetings" at school where a consultant is engaged to report on IEP determinations. IDEA only requires that parents be given the opportunity to attend IEP team meetings that are called for the specific purpose of determining the appropriate IEP for their own child. *Kings Local School District v. Zelazny*, 325 F.3d 724 (6th Cir. 2003). If parents are not notified by the school district about IEP procedures and timeframes, the parents are not confined by the statutory limitations. For example, where parents were not notified about a 60–day time limit for challenging an IEP, the court held that the parents were not bound. *M. E. and P. E. v. Buncombe County Board of Education*, 72 Fed. Appx. 940 (4th Cir. 2003). Parental consent as to what constitutes a free appropriate public education (FAPE), is not required by IDEA. School districts are only required to comply with the provisions of IDEA to extend adequate opportunities for parental involvement, but schools are not bound by parental refusal to participate in the development of the IEP. *A. E. v. Westport Board of Education*, 251 Fed. Appx. 685 (2d Cir. 2007).

§ 10.48   Related Services

The IDEA requires that school districts provide children with disabilities with supportive services that will meet their educational needs as prescribed by the above-mentioned Individualized Education Program (IEP). Such support services are called "related services" by the Act. A school district is required to provide "related services" to disabled children, but not "medical services." The courts though tend to give broad meaning to related services. See *Antkowiak v. Ambach*, 838 F.2d 635 (2d Cir.1988). The Act defines related services as "transportation and such developmental, corrective, and other supportive services (including speech pathology and occupational therapy, recreation, and medical and counseling services, except that such medical services shall be for diagnostic and evaluative purposes only) as may be required to assist a handicapped child to benefit from special education...." 20 U.S.C.A. § 1401(17).

Federal regulations pertaining to this section of the Act have further defined each of the terms included in "related services." For example, "psychological services" are explained to be "planning and managing a program of psychological services, including psychological counseling for children and parents." 34 C.F.R. § 300.13(b)(8). "Counseling services" are defined as "services provided by qualified social workers, psychologists, guidance counselors, or other qualified personnel." 34 C.F.R. § 300.13(b)(2). Courts have further added their interpretation of other terms, "psychotherapy," for example, *T.G. v. Board of Education of Piscataway*, 576 F.Supp. 420 (D.N.J.1983); "transportation," *Alamo Heights Ind. School District v. State Board of Education*, 790 F.2d 1153 (5th Cir.1986); and "free transportation," *School District of Philadelphia v. Commonwealth, Dept. of Education*, 547 A.2d 520 (Pa.Cmwlth.1988); *Felter v. Cape Girardeau School District*, 810 F.Supp. 1062 (E.D.Mo. 1993). See also *School Board of Pinellas County v. Smith*, 537 So.2d 168 (Fla.App.1989). *Metropolitan Government v. Tennessee Department of Education*, 771 S.W.2d 427 (Tenn.App.1989).

In 1984 the Supreme Court addressed "related services" in *Irving Independent School District v. Tatro*, 468 U.S. 883 (1984). The issue in *Tatro* was the scope of "medical services" that the school district is required to provide. The child requiring medical services had spina bifida, orthopedic and speech impairments, and a neurogenic bladder, which prevented her from emptying her bladder voluntarily. The child's parents maintained that the school was required to provide the necessary catheterization every three to four hours, while the school maintained that this was not the role of the school because it constituted "medical services." The specific question required the Court to interpret the meaning and statutory intent of Congress in requiring "medical and counseling services, except that such medical services shall be for diagnostic and evaluation purposes only as may be required to assist a handicapped child to benefit from special education...." The Court said "Congress plainly required schools to hire various specially-trained personnel to help handicapped children, such as 'trained occupational therapists ... psychologists,'" etc. Thus, the Court concluded that "school nursing services are not the sort of burden that Congress intended to exclude as a 'medical service.'" The Court then set out guidelines that could be used by school districts pertaining to both health and educational needs that fall within the definition of "related services." First, the child must be classified as handicapped and entitled to related services. Second, only those services necessary to aid the handicapped child must be provided. Third, services are to be extended only if they can be provided by a school nurse or other qualified person and do not require the level of knowledge to be performed only by a physician. Fourth, the related service requires "services" and not the purchase of special equipment. Subsequent court decisions have held that "related services" do not extend to requiring the school to hire an in-school nurse to attend to the child's daily medical needs. Conditions so severe as to require constant nursing care go beyond "related services" and fall within the realm of the medical services that school districts are not required to provide. *Detsel v. Board of Education*, 637 F.Supp. 1022 (N.D.N.Y.1986).

Following *Tatro,* litigation continues to more precisely define what constitutes a medical service as opposed to related educational service. The U.S. Supreme Court later held in furtherance of its rationale in *Tatro* that if the disputed service for the child could be performed by someone other than a physician then the school district is obligated to provide the service. *Cedar Rapids Community School Dist. v. Garret F. by Charlene F.*, 526 U.S. 66 (1999). As to where the related services are to be provided, in the public school or in a private school, that is a decision to be made by the public school district. Where parents decided to voluntarily enroll their child in a parochial school, the Court ruled the IDEA regulations give the public school the discretion to make decisions as to manner and extent of services and whether they are to be provided at the public school. *Foley v. Special School District of St. Louis County*, 153 F.3d 863 (8th Cir.1998).

§ 10.49   Placement

Proper placement of the student in a particular program or school is a most important aspect of the individualized educational program (IEP). There may be several options for placement of handicapped students in programs within the public school, but there is also the recognized alternative to placement in a non-public school which has special education facilities. A question arises as to whether the non-public school options must be taken into account when the student's IEP is devised and if failure to do so invalidates the IEP. The United States Court of Appeals for the Fourth Circuit has held that such consideration of private services is not required to have a valid IEP. *Hessler v. State Board of Education of Maryland*, 700 F.2d 134 (4th Cir.1983). The court said "While the federal and state statutory schemes clearly contemplate the use of non-public educational services under the circumstances, we think it clear that such resort is limited to those instances in which public educational services appropriate for the handicapped child are not available."

Further, the court said that just because parents may be able to show that the non-public school program is possibly more appropriate or better than the public school program does not mean that the public school program is necessarily inappropriate. Following the rationale of *Rowley*, this court emphasized that there was no obligation on the part of the school district to provide a handicapped child "all services necessary to maximize his or her potential commensurate with the opportunity provided to other children."

Where it is shown that a placement in a summer school program, in addition to the regular year-long program, prevents the handicapped child from retrogressing educationally, the school district may be required to provide a summer program. The requirement of the Act that personalized instruction be provided to meet individual needs of the handicapped child may possibly require an IEP with summer school as a requisite condition. *Yaris v. Special School District of St. Louis County*, 558 F.Supp. 545 (E.D.Mo.1983). See also *Alamo Heights Ind. School Dist. v. State Bd. of Educ.*, 790 F.2d 1153 (5th Cir.1986).

In *Johnson v. Independent School Dist. No. 4 of Bixby*, 921 F.2d 1022 (10th Cir.1990), the court ruled that the regression recoupment problem should be applied not only to academic problems but also to non-academic ones as well. Non-academic problems such as behavioral and social needs are to be considered in determining extended school year needs.

§ 10.491   Burden of Proof

If parents believe that the IEP for their disabled child is inappropriate then they may request and receive an "impartial due process hearing." 20 U.S.C. § 1415. Such hearings are held before administrative law judges. Procedurally, IDEA requires that parents and guardians be informed about and consent to evaluations of their child. 20 U.S.C. § 1414(c)(3). Parents must be members of IEP teams. § 1414(d)(1)(B). They have a right to access and examine any records relating to their child and to obtain an independent evaluation of their child. § 1415(b)(1). Parents must be given written prior notice of any changes in an IEP § 1415(b)(3) and be given notice in writing of procedural safeguards provided them under the IDEA, § 1415(d)(1). Then, if they are dissatisfied with the IEP, they may seek and obtain a hearing. Too, even though school districts have the legal authority to finally decide on the nature of the IEP, the school districts themselves can seek a hearing to settle an IEP if, for example, a district wishes to change an IEP and the parents do not consent or if they refuse to allow their child to be evaluated. At a hearing, all parties must be accompanied by counsel and may present evidence and cross-examine. If parents prevail, they may receive attorney's fees. § 1415(i)(3)(B).

Yet, Congress did not provide in the Act as to which party bore the burden of proof. In that IDEA is unclear about the burden of proof, the Supreme Court has decided that, simply, the burden of proof must be carried by the party seeking relief. If parents are seeking relief in challenging the IEP, then they must bear the burden of proof. *Schaffer v. Weast*, 546 U.S. 49 (2005).

§ 10.5   PRIVATE SCHOOL FOR CHILDREN WITH DISABILITIES

There are two categories of disabled children in private schools. The first are those disabled children who are placed in private schools following the appropriate IEP determination. These children are in private schools with specially-designed programs to meet their educational needs. The facilities where children are placed by public agencies must be facilities that are state approved. The second category is those children with disabilities who have been placed in private schools based on a unilateral decision by the parents. The question is: Are children placed in private facilities by parents eligible for IDEA services? The IDEA requires a state's plan to have policies and procedures assuring that: "To the extent consistent with their number and location in the State, provision is made for the participation of private school children with disabilities in the program assisted or carried out under this part by providing them with special education and related services."

Also, according to the federal regulation, the local educational agencies are required to "... provide special education and related services designed to meet the needs of private school children with disabilities residing in the jurisdiction of the agency." The local educational agency is not required to pay for the child's education at the private school or facility unless the local educational agency cannot provide the services.

The 1997 Amendments to IDEA provide that where no public school facility is available to meet the child's needs, then the public school district becomes responsible for the tuition and other costs of attendance at a private facility. The 1997 Act allows public school districts to reduce or deny reimbursements to parents who voluntarily and unilaterally place their child in a private school without referral or consent of the public school. Moreover, parents may not recover costs for sending their child to a private school if the child was withheld or made unavailable for the public school to assess and evaluate the child's special education needs.

Yet, all depends on whether the public school placement is appropriate. The U.S. Supreme Court in *Florence County School Dist. Four, et al. v. Carter*, 510 U.S. 7 (1993), decided that if the court finds the public school educational placement is not reasonable, then the public school can be ordered by the court to reimburse the parents for costs. In this case, the state and local educational authorities found that the IEP developed for a child was adequate; the parents disagreed and enrolled her in a private academy. Subsequently, the parents filed suit seeking reimbursement for tuition and other costs. The district court ruled the public school's proposed IEP and educational goals "were wholly inadequate" and failed to meet IDEA requirements. The Supreme Court stated: "This case presents the question whether a court may order reimbursement for parents who unilaterally withdraw their child from a public school that provides an inappropriate education under IDEA and put the child in a private school that provides an education that is otherwise proper under IDEA ... We hold that the court may order such reimbursement and therefore affirm the judgment of the Court of Appeals."

Reimbursement for private school costs was not allowed where the parents moved a child to a licensed nursing facility that was located within the school district where evidence indicated that the move was motivated for non-educational reasons. Regardless, however, for educational reasons or otherwise, parents cannot expect to be reimbursed if they act unilaterally in moving their child to a private school so long as the public school district had provided appropriate educational placement. *Jasa v. Millard Public School District No. 17*, 206 F.3d 813 (8th Cir.2000).

In other words, IDEA provides for a cooperative placement procedure wherein parents, school officials, teachers and others meet, evaluate, and confer in the IEP and placement process. Where parents fail to cooperate with the school district when it attempts to evaluate the child's disabilities and form an IEP, then the parent forfeits any right to reimbursement for costs if they place the child in a private school. *Patricia P. v. Board of Education of Oak Park and River Forest High School District No. 200*, 203 F.3d 462 (7th Cir.2000).

In keeping with rationale of cooperation and pursuant to the 1997 Amendments, at least two federal circuits have directly ruled to refuse parents reimbursement when they took their child from a public school and placed him in a private school without notification or consultation with the public school. *Schoenfeld v. Parkway School District*, 138 F.3d 379 (8th Cir.1998). *See also Tucker by and through Tucker v. Calloway County Board of Education*, 136 F.3d 495 (6th Cir.1998).

§ 10.6 DISABLED CHILDREN IN SECTARIAN SCHOOLS

In *Zobrest v. Catalina Foothills School Dist.*, 509 U.S. 1 (1993), the Supreme Court ruled that it does not violate the Establishment Clause of the First Amendment for a public school to pay for a sign language interpreter to accompany a student to classes at a Roman Catholic High School. The student was provided an interpreter while enrolled in a public school. When the student enrolled of his volition in a sectarian school, he requested the same services. The public school board refused to pay for the interpreter on the grounds that such assistance constituted aid to religion. The Supreme Court held that "the Establishment Clause does not prevent (the school board) from furnishing a disabled child enrolled in a sectarian school with a sign language interpreter in order to facilitate his education. Government programs that neutrally provide benefits to a broad class of citizens defined without reference to religion are not readily subject to an Establishment Clause challenge just because sectarian institutions may also receive an attenuated financial benefit." Thus, the Establishment Clause of the U.S. Constitution poses no obstacle to reimbursement of parochial or religious schools. (See Chapter 5 of this book.)

§ 10.7 DISCIPLINE

The mainstreaming of disabled children has underscored the need for guidelines governing the disciplining of disabled students. Neither Section 504 nor Public Law 94–142 addresses this issue, leaving it to the courts to decipher the legal ramifications involved.

Two provisions of IDEA must be considered when disciplinary action is taken with a disabled student: appropriate education and least-restrictive environment. IDEA mandates that a disabled student be provided a free appropriate public education in the least-restrictive environment. Acceptable environments for the placement of a disabled child range from least restrictive (a regular classroom) to highly restrictive (an institution). However, each environment can be termed "least restrictive" depending on the seriousness of a particular disability and on the student's ability to cope within a specific environment.

Courts have consistently ruled that disabled students must be given special consideration in disciplinary proceedings. Earlier court decisions prohibited expulsion, noting that, under Public Law 94–142, services must be provided through alternative placement in one of the other educational environments offered.

In 1981, expulsion surfaced as an issue when nine mentally disabled students in the state of Florida sued local districts and the state claiming that they had been denied an appropriate education due to expulsion. The court in *S–1 v. Turlington* upheld expulsion as a viable form of discipline to be used with disabled students. The court, however, pointed out that cessation of all educational programs violated the rights of disabled students; consequently, even after expelling a student, services must be provided.

Suspension, on the other hand, has been viewed favorably by the courts as an appropriate disciplinary action for disabled students when it has been determined that misconduct is not related to the student's disability. If it is related to the disabling condition, an alternative or more restrictive placement should be considered rather than suspension or expulsion.

The stay-put provision discussed above raises the question as to whether a child can be excluded from school for an indefinite period of time for dangerous or disruptive conduct growing out of a disability. *S–1 v. Turlington* and other cases left doubt as to whether there was, in fact, a "dangerousness" exclusion implied by the Act. In *Honig v. Doe*, the U.S. Supreme Court resolved the issue by making it clear that a EAHCA (1) confers a substantive right to education on disabled students, (2) prohibits school officials from unilaterally excluding a disabled student from the classroom for dangerous or disruptive conduct for an indeterminate period of time where conduct grows out of a disability, and (3) permits school officials to temporarily suspend a student for up to ten days to protect the safety of others and to provide a "cooling down." During this time, an IEP meeting can be initiated to review the child's placement.

When Congress amended the IDEA in 1997, a major concern, and one of the most contentious of topics, was the disciplining of disabled students. The 1997 amendments and the IDEA regulation allow school personnel to order a change of placement of special needs children in certain situations. The change of placement may be made if the child brings a weapon to school or to a school function or if the child possesses or uses illegal drugs. Under these conditions, the placement can be changed 1) "to an appropriate interim alternative setting, another setting, or suspension, for not more than 10 school days (to the extent such alternatives would be applied to children without disabilities); and 2) to an appropriate interim educational setting for the same amount of time that a child without disability would be subject to discipline, but not more than 45 days. . . . "

The hearing officer who orders the interim alternative educational placement must have determined that maintaining the current placement would cause harm to the student or others, that the current placement is inappropriate, and that the school has made an effort to minimize the risk with supplementary aids and other services.

When a disciplinary action is required, a manifestation determination review is also required. This review is to decide if the inappropriate behavior of the child is related to his or her disability. If after the review "the behavior of the child with a disability was not a manifestation of the child's disability, the relevant disciplinary procedures applicable to children without disabilities may be applied to the [disabled] child in the same manner in which they would be applied to children without disabilities." Even if the child's inappropriate behavior is not a manifestation of his or her disability, the child must receive a free appropriate education. Therefore, when an IDEA child is suspended or expelled, services may not be terminated. See *Farrin v. Maine School Administrative District No. 59*, 165 F.Supp.2d 37 (D.Me.2001).

§ 10.8 ACQUIRED IMMUNODEFICIENCY SYNDROME (AIDS)

One of the many legal issues emerging from the dread of AIDS retrovirus is whether children so infected can be excluded from school. AIDS cases have been litigated under IDEA, the Rehabilitation Act of 1973, Section 504 (29 U.S.C.A. § 794), and under the Due Process and

Equal Protection Clauses of the U.S. Constitution. A threshold question is whether an AIDS child may be defined as a "handicapped individual" under Subsection 504 of the Rehabilitation Act of 1973. Under this law a person is handicapped if he or she has "a physical impairment" which substantially limits major life activities, has a record of impairment, or is regarded as having an impairment as provided in 29 U.S.C.A. § 707(7)(B). In *Doe v. Dolton Elementary School District No. 148*, 694 F.Supp. 440 (N.D.Ill.1988), the court said that AIDS constituted impairment under Section 504. The rationale supporting this conclusion was based on the U.S. Supreme Court ruling in *Arline*, wherein the Court said that handicapped individuals may include "not only those who are actually physically impaired but also those who are regarded as impaired and who as a result 'are substantially limited in a major life activity.' " Simply having the virus may be considered a handicapping condition, thus, any person infected with the AIDS virus may be handicapped under the meaning of Section 504.

Another issue with AIDS students is whether they are covered by the IDEA. In the case of AIDS students, the category that would most closely fit is "other health impaired children." AIDS is not listed as an example of an acute or chronic health problem by the IDEA. In October of 1984, the Department of Education addressed the applicability of EAHCA (IDEA) to AIDS victims. The department stated that AIDS is not considered to be "handicapped" as a term defined in EAHCA (IDEA) unless the child needs special education. The opinion states: "Children with AIDS could be eligible for special education programs under the category of 'other health impaired,' if they have chronic or acute health problems which adversely affect their educational performance."

The IDEA would apply to AIDS victims only if the virus adversely affects their educational performance. If a child is seropositive or a "healthy carrier," then he or she is not covered under IDEA, but if the child becomes an AIDS victim and this diminishes his or her educational performance, then the IDEA must be enforced to meet the needs of the child.

The courts have unanimously upheld the right of an AIDS child to attend school. A California court held that a child infected with the AIDS virus could not be excluded from regular school programs because the school board could not prove that he was not "otherwise qualified." The school board was, also, unable to prove that the child could possibly spread the AIDS virus to other children even though the infected child had a record of aggressive behavior and had bitten another child. *Thomas v. Atascadero Unified School District*, 662 F.Supp. 376 (C.D.Cal.1986).

§ 10.81 Parents Rights

The question has arisen as to whether the parent of a disabled child has independent enforceable rights under IDEA. The Supreme Court has ruled that they do. Such rights emanate from the clear wording of the IDEA that states: "All children with disabilities have available to them free appropriate public education" and "that the rights of children with disabilities and *parents* of such children are protected (emphasis added)." (20 U.S.C. § 1400(d)(1)(A)(B) By this and other provisions, according to the Court, parents have a "recognized legal interest in their child's education and upbringing." Parents have a substantive stake in all aspects of the IEP proceedings and in the formulation of their child's educational program. Parents, thereby, have an independent and separate statutory interest in legal proceedings involving their disabled child. Therefore, parents are entitled to serve without legal counsel in prosecuting claims under IDEA on their own behalf. *Winkelman v. Parma City School District*, 550 U.S. 516 (2007).

§ 10.9 ATTORNEY'S FEES

Prior to 1986 there was no provision for attorneys' fees to be awarded to successful parents in litigation over provision of educational services for a disabled child. In that year Congress enacted the Handicapped Children's Protection Act (HCPA) (P.L. 99–372), amending the EAHCA to enable the courts to award attorney's fees. The act authorized the awards to be made for litigation that was either filed or still pending as of July 3, 1986.

The U.S. Court of Appeals for the Sixth Circuit has held that Section 1988 of HCPA establishes that the courts may award the attorney for parents who prevailed in the litigation "reasonable fees" to be calculated according to the prevailing market rate in the relevant community, regardless of whether the plaintiff is represented by private or non-profit counsel. *Eggers v. Bullitt County School District*, 854 F.2d 892 (6th Cir.1988). In a case where parents obtained an emergency stay-put order requiring that the student stay in school until graduation, such did not constitute a victory in the trial; therefore, the parents could not obtain attorney's fees. *Board of Educ. of Oak Park v. Nathan R.*, 199 F.3d 377 (7th Cir.2000).

Attorney's fees may be awarded by the court for legal work done even though the dispute ends in an out-of-court settlement, prior to trial, in which the school district assumes the special education obligation originally sought by the plaintiff parents. *Masotti v. Tustin Unified School District*, 806 F.Supp. 221 (C.D.Cal.1992). Attorney's fees were awarded in an Ohio case where a dispute between parents and school district was settled prior to a hearing. *Moore v. Crestwood Local School District*, 804 F.Supp. 960 (N.D.Ohio 1992).

§ 10.91 Monetary Damages

Congress did not intend the child's entitlement to a *free* education to turn upon her (or his) parent's ability to 'front' its costs; nevertheless, federal legislation does not provide for money damages to be awarded to parents of disabled students when they prevail in court challenges. Where school officials do not violate any civil or equal protection rights but merely fail to provide the student with an IEP under the IDEA, no money damages will be awarded for physical or emotional harm. *Smith v. Philadelphia School District*, 679 F.Supp. 479 (E.D.Pa. 1988). Disabled children, however, may seek recovery by bringing a civil rights suit against local school boards. *Edward B. v. Brunelle*, 662 F.Supp. 1025 (D.N.H.1986).

CHAPTER 11

STUDENT SEX DISCRIMINATION

§ 11.1 INTRODUCTION

Education in America reflects the norms of society; if society is unjust, then the educational system is likely to be also. Societal standards have historically assumed that women and men should play different and carefully delineated roles. Cultural stereotypes of males and females spilled over to the schools where boys played interscholastic athletics and girls were the cheerleaders or majorettes. Athletic activity by girls was generally confined to intramural sports or to physical education classes. The women's rights movement of the 1970s has had an important influence on the schools. Today women are advised to participate in school programs, enter occupations which were formerly male enclaves, to enter colleges and graduate, and to pursue careers in professional schools once reserved for men only.

In recent years, legislation and court decisions have sought to eradicate gender discrimination in our schools and to the extent possible in society at large. Sex discrimination among students in public schools is prohibited by the Equal Protection Clause of the Fourteenth Amendment of the U.S. Constitution and Title IX of the Education Amendments of 1972.

§ 11.2 EQUAL PROTECTION OF SEXES

The first major modern case involving gender discrimination was *Reed v. Reed*, 404 U.S. 71 (1971), in which the United States Supreme Court struck down a state statute because it gave preference to the male over the female and as such was held to violate the Equal Protection Clause. The Court, however, did not elevate sex classifications to the special category of constitutional classes, such as race, requiring strict judicial scrutiny of legislative actions when challenged under federal Equal Protection. Under Equal Protection where race is concerned, the state at one time must show a compelling interest in classifications; where sex is concerned, the state need only to show that its actions are rational and not arbitrary or capricious. Now, gender discrimination occupies a kind of in-between constitutional status which requires that the state bear the burden of showing that its acts are not arbitrary or irrational, but does not rise fully to the status of a fundamental right that would require that the state bear the burden of showing that its acts are, in fact, compelling and absolutely necessary to effectuate the common interests of all the people.

It was in a later case in which the Supreme Court appeared to add more significance to sex as a classification when it held, in *Craig v. Boren*, 429 U.S. 190 (1976), "that classification by gender must serve important governmental objectives and must be substantially related to achievement of those objectives." In this case it appears that the Court established a separated, albeit, intermediate, category of judicial scrutiny to cases involving sex discrimination. Instead of the state showing simply that its classification by sex is rational, it must now show that the classification "serves important governmental objectives." Thus, the state must bear a greater burden in justifying an act which classifies persons based on gender. What this means is that actions by a school district which treat students differently because of their sex must bear the burden of showing that the rule furthers an "important governmental objective." Whether the rule will stand depends on the interpretation of what constitutes an "important" objective.

The Seventh Circuit has held that a student could maintain an equal protection claim of discrimination on grounds of both gender and sexual orientation. The student had been abused by fellow students because he was homosexual, he was regularly called a "faggot," hit and spit upon, and he was subjected to a mock rape by other boys. A school official failed to intercede and said that "boys will be boys" and he should "expect" such behavior from fellow students since he was gay. The court held that the school officials were not entitled to qualified immunity due to their violation of equal protection based on the student harassment by fellow students. *Nabozny v. Podlesny*, 92 F.3d 446 (7th Cir.1996).

§ 11.21 Admission of Females

Various discriminatory practices apparently acceptable to the majority in society filtered into the schools. Higher admission standards for female than for male applicants to a public preparatory high school violate the Equal Protection Clause. *Berkelman v. San Francisco Unified School District*, 501 F.2d 1264 (9th Cir.1974). In another case, a federal district court in Massachusetts held that the admission policy at the Boston Latin School violated equal protection because it set a different test cutoff score for boys and girls. *Bray v. Lee*, 337 F.Supp. 934

(D.Mass.1972). Here the school in attempting to maintain a 50–50 balance in the number of boys and girls had established separate cutoff scores. The method used for each group was to simply count down from the highest test score in each of the two groups of applicants, boys and girls, until they had accepted the total number necessary to maintain a balanced enrollment. The court held that this type of admissions policy violated equal protection because it created "prejudicial disparities" based on sex.

§ 11.22   Athletic Teams

Gender classifications which deny participation to female students may violate equal protection. The courts have generally held the Equal Protection Clause requires high school females be allowed to compete in non-contact sports. Some federal and state courts have ruled that denying a female the right to participate in a contact sport, such as football, violates the equal protection clause of the Fourteenth Amendment. One rationale has been that the exclusion of girls from contact sports in order to protect them from injury is not related to a government objective justifiable under the Fourteenth Amendment. *Darrin v. Gould*, 540 P.2d 882 (Wash.1975); *Leffel v. Wisconsin Interscholastic Athletic Association*, 444 F.Supp. 1117 (E.D.Wis.1978).

On the other hand, the courts have generally ruled that it does not deny equal protection to refuse to allow males to compete on female teams. *Clark v. Arizona Interscholastic Assoc.*, 695 F.2d 1126 (9th Cir.1982). See also *Rowley v. Members of the Board of Education*, 863 F.2d 39 (10th Cir.1988). In *Clark*, the court considered the governmental reasons for denying males the right to compete on female teams. Among the objectives was the desire of the school to offer girls the opportunity to participate in interscholastic sports, an opportunity not previously extended with all male teams. To allow males to participate in female sports and to possibly crowd girls out of their own sports activities would have defeated the school's purposes in creating such opportunities for females. These objectives were legitimate and important; therefore, they withstood the equal protection test as enunciated in *Craig v. Boren*, supra, as serving important governmental objectives. In *Kleczek v. Rhode Island Interscholastic League, Inc.*, 612 A.2d 734 (R.I.1992), the court denied a male student the opportunity to participate on a girls' field hockey team. The reason was given that gender issues were to be reviewed under the intermediate scrutiny standard as opposed to the strict scrutiny standard which places an obligation on the government to have a compelling reason for the rule. The court accepted as reasonable that the rule excluding males from female sports was to promote safety and the preservation of interscholastic competition in high school athletics. See also *B.C. v. Board of Educ., Cumberland Regional School District*, 531 A.2d 1059 (N.J.Super.1987) denying a male student's request to play on a girls' hockey team.

In a Minnesota case, a state athletic association league rule was challenged because it forbade girls' participation in the boys' interscholastic athletic program either as a member of a boys' team or as a member of a girls' team competing against boys. Two girls where denied the opportunity to participate as members of boys' skiing and cross-country running teams. No teams in these sports were provided for girls by their schools. The court said that in evaluating state actions under the Equal

Protection Clause, the courts were to consider three criteria: (1) the character of the classification, (2) the individual interest affected by the classification, and (3) the governmental interest asserted in support of the classification. In evaluating the facts of the case against these criteria, the court concluded, first, that the discrimination was based on sex and as such was subject to examination by the courts as a legitimate controversy. Secondly, the interests denied were educational benefits that should be for all students. In particular, the court said, "discrimination in education is one of the most damaging injustices women suffer. It denies them equal education and equal employment opportunity, contributing to a second-class image. . . . Discrimination in high school interscholastic athletics constitutes discrimination in education." Thirdly, the court queried the high school athletic league in determining its interest in maintaining the separation of the sexes in the sports activities. The league maintained that physiological differences between males and females made it impossible for girls to equitably compete with males. The court refused to accept this rationale observing that evidence had been presented indicating that there was widely differing athletic ability within the classes of men and women, possibly as wide as between the classes of men and women. The record showed the schools had, in fact, adopted no cut policies allowing all male students, no matter how untalented, to participate in these same non-contact sports. On this basis the court had no alternative but to declare the rule unconstitutional. *Brenden v. Independent School District 742*, 477 F.2d 1292 (8th Cir.1973). However, gender classifications may be analyzed under the more strict scrutiny standard if a state constitution is found to impose a more rigorous test than does the federal Equal

Protection Clause. Such is the situation in Massachusetts. Using this higher standard, a Massachusetts state court determined a male must be allowed to participate on the girl's team. *Attorney General v. Massachusetts Interscholastic Athletic Association*, 393 N.E.2d 284 (Mass.1979).

§ 11.3 TITLE IX

The Education Amendments of 1972, 20 U.S.C.A. §§ 1681–1683, contained Title IX, the popular law that forbade discrimination based on sex. Title IX prohibits discrimination not only for athletics and other extracurricular activities but also for financial aid, testing, curricular offerings, pregnancy and marital status. In 1984 in *Grove City College v. Bell*, 465 U.S. 555 (1984), the U.S. Supreme Court interpreted the section of Title IX which states "any education program or activity receiving federal financial assistance" to mean that the specific program must be receiving federal funds for Title IX to apply. In other words, federal funds provided to an education program would be subject to Title IX restrictions only if the alleged discrimination occurred in the specific program that actually received the federal funds. This program-specific approach obviously excludes interscholastic athletic programs because they do not receive federal funding.

In response to *Grove City*, Congress passed the Civil Rights Restoration Act of 1987. This Act specified that Title IX applied to the entire institution if any program within the institution was a recipient of federal funding. Also, in *North Haven Board of Education v. Bell*, 456 U.S. 512 (1982), the Supreme Court determined Title IX not only includes students but also employees and that

Title IX is enforceable through the Office of Civil Rights (OCR) in the Department of Education. In *Cannon v. University of Chicago*, 441 U.S. 677 (1979), the U.S. Supreme Court held that Title IX created a private remedy under which an individual could challenge discriminatory acts. Before *Cannon*, Title IX had been interpreted as establishing legal redress resulting only in termination of federal funds. The Supreme Court said: "Title IX was patterned after Title VI of the Civil Rights Act of 1964. Except for the substitution of the word 'sex' in Title IX to replace the words 'race, color, or national origin' in Title VI, the two statutes use identical language to describe the benefitted class." Therefore, an individual had a right to litigate under Title IX to seek enforcement of the Act. Further, in *Franklin v. Gwinnett County Public Schools*, 503 U.S. 60 (1992), the U.S. Supreme Court interpreted Title IX to cover sexual harassment based on the same standards that sexual harassment is covered under Title VII, 1964 Civil Rights Act. Title VII prohibits sexual harassment based on *quid pro quo* harassment, involving conditioning of benefits on sexual favors and "hostile environment" which relates to an abusive environment. As will be noted later, punitive damages were not available under *Cannon*; these would come later by court interpretation in the *Franklin* case.

Title IX has proven to be a more potent and effective force than the Equal Protection Clause to challenge sex discrimination in the schools. For example, a rule of an athletic association or a high school may violate Title IX but not be offensive to the Equal Protection Clause. The statute itself provides in Section 901(a) "No person in the United States shall, on the basis of sex, be excluded from participation in, be denied the benefits of, or be subjected to discrimination under any education program or activity receiving federal financial assistance...." Title IX is not without limitations; however, there are certain exceptions for religious schools if the act is contrary to religious tenets.

§ 11.31 Enforcement of Title IX

Until 1992 when there was sex discrimination in a school district, the plaintiff could only request that the federal funding be removed or suit could be filed under a private right of action as per *Cannon*. There were no money damages available for the first 20 years of Title IX and there was therefore a paucity of litigation. In 1992 in *Franklin v. Gwinnett County Public Schools*, supra, the Supreme Court drastically changed the enforcement of Title IX and other anti-discrimination statutes by allowing monetary damages for intentional violations of Title IX.

In *Franklin* a female student was sexually harassed by a teacher. The student said the teacher "... engaged in sexually-oriented conversations ... forcibly kissed her on the mouth ... [and] subjected her to coercive intercourse." School officials were aware of the sexual harassment but took no action. The student filed an action against the school board for monetary damages and the U.S. Supreme Court held damages were available under Title IX for intentional violations of the law. The Court noted that without damages the student would basically have no remedy for her injury.

§ 11.32 Comparability

Regulations pursuant to Title IX permit institutions to offer separate team sports, but are not intended to require boys' teams to be opened to girls. Teams, however, must be offered on a "comparable" basis for students of both sexes taking into account the interests and abilities of both sexes; "an institution would be required to provide separate teams for men and women in situations where the provision of only one team would not 'accommodate the interests and abilities of both sexes.'" *O'Connor v. Board of Education of School District 23*, supra.

Some of the standards that are reviewed to determine if the teams are comparable are:

1. Whether the selection of sports and levels of competition effectively accommodate the interests and abilities of both sexes;

2. A provision of equipment and supplies;

3. Scheduling of games and practice times;

4. Travel and per diem allowances;

5. Opportunity to receive coaching and tutoring;

6. Assignment and compensation of coaches and tutors;

7. Provision of locker rooms, practice and competitive facilities;

8. Provision of medical and training facilities and services.

§ 11.33 One Sex Teams

Regulations under Title IX (§ 86.41) provide for operation of separate sports where selection of teams is based on competitive skill or the activities involve a contact sport. Where a team is offered for one sex but not for the other, members of both sexes must be allowed to try out for the team offered unless the sport involved is a contact sport. In Colorado, a high school girl sued because she was denied a chance to participate on a boys' soccer team, a contact sport. A court found that denial of the girl's request violated the Equal Protection Clause even though it may not have violated Title IX. *Hoover v. Meiklejohn*, 430 F.Supp. 164 (D.Colo.1977). In this case, the court said that "the failure to establish any physical criteria to protect small or weak males from injurious effects of competition with larger and stronger males destroys the credibility of the reasoning urged in support of the sex classification ... and there is no rationality in limiting this patronizing protection to females."

A group of female students filed suit against the Kentucky High School Athletic Association and the Kentucky State Board of Elementary and Secondary Education for violating equal protection and Title IX because they had not established fast-pitch softball for females. This diminished the ability of females to compete for college fast-pitch softball athletic scholarships. The court said: "The statute itself does not require gender balance. *See* 20 U.S.C.A. § 1681(b). (The statute states: '[n]othing contained in subsection (a) of this section shall be interpreted to require any educational institution to grant preferential or disparate treatment to the members of one sex on account of an imbalance which may exist with respect to the total number of percentage of persons of that sex participating in or receiving the benefits of a federally-supported program or activity in comparison with the total number or percentage of persons of that sex in any community, ...'); ... In certain instances, separate teams for males and females are allowed (*see* 34 C.F.R. § 106.41(b) (1998)), permitting separate sports teams for males and females where selection for the team is based on competitive skill or is a contact sport." *Horner v. Kentucky High School Athletic Association*, 206 F.3d 685 (6th Cir.2000). See also *Communities for Equity v. Michigan High School Athletic Association*, 178 F.Supp.2d 805 (W.D.Mich.2001). The court found that the Athletic Association had violated equal protection and Title IX by scheduling female athletic seasons and tournaments during non-traditional and less advantageous times of the academic year than boys seasons and tournaments.

Disparities in facilities between boys' baseball and girls' softball programs has been held to violate Title IX. *Landow v. School Bd. of Brevard County*, 132 F.Supp.2d 958 (M.D.Fla.2000). The Florida court later approved a plan to build two new softball fields and said the plan "... constitutes an adequate and effective remedy for the gender equity violations ..." *Landow v. School Board of Brevard County*, 2001 WL 311307 (M.D.Fla. 2001).

Yet another example of application of Title IX was found where a girl who had been an all-state football kicker in high school tried out for the Duke University team. She was the only woman who had ever tried out and she was informed that she made the team. She was listed as a player and participated in drills although she did not get to play in any games. The following year she was denied the right to attend summer camp and was not allowed to dress for games or sit on the sidelines. She filed a Title IX sex discrimination suit. The U.S. Fourth Circuit ruled that once Duke had opened up football tryouts to girls, it could not discriminate on the basis of sex. *Mercer v. Duke University*, 190 F.3d 643 (4th Cir. 1999).

§ 11.34　Sexual Harassment Under Title IX

As mentioned above, sexual harassment is covered under Title IX. Defining sexual harassment is difficult, but basically it constitutes "the unwanted imposition of sexual requirements in the context of a relationship of unequal power." This characterization of sexual harassment is applicable to the teacher/student relationship, wherein there exists an exploitation of a power relationship to gain sexual favors. A teacher quite obviously holds power over a student by being in a position to affect the student's grades, academic attainments, and career choices. Title IX, therefore, seeks to prohibit unwelcome sexual behavior by any party who is in an inherently unequal position in relation to another.

As noted above, two basic categories of behavior constitute sexual harassment under Title IX. The first is *quid pro quo* harassment by which the teacher, administrator, or other person in power attempts to compel submission to sexual demands by conditioning rewards or punishment upon the student's acquiescence or lack thereof. The second category, hostile environment, encompasses behavior that causes the educational environment to become hostile, offensive, or intimidating to the student as a result of the harassment, and it may be manifested in the teacher's mistreatment of the student solely due to gender.

§ 11.35   Student-to-Student Harassment

In 1992 the Supreme Court in *Franklin v. Gwinnett County Public Schools*, supra, changed the landscape of Title IX. As mentioned earlier, there were no money damages available under Title IX before *Franklin*. The plaintiff could only request that federal funding be removed or suit could be filed under a private right of action as established in *Cannon* for injunctive relief.

Shortly after the *Franklin* litigation, substantial numbers of cases began to appear involving peer-to-peer sexual harassment in the schools. In these cases, plaintiffs claimed that the schools are liable for damages when students sexually harass other students. The theory supporting such allegations was premised on the plaintiffs proving that a hostile environment existed.

The peer-to-peer harassment of students was found to violate Title IX in *Davis v. Monroe County Board of Education*, 526 U.S. 629 (1999). The court concluded that student-to-student harassment violates Title IX "... but only where [the school district] acts with deliberate indifference and the harassment is so severe that it effectively bars the victim's access to an educational opportunity or benefit."

After *Davis*, federal courts have on a case-by-case basis sought to determine when there is actual "deliberate indifferences" by school officials in failing to protect students who claim to be victims of sexual harassment. In *Davis*, the Supreme Court advanced a three-part test to be applied by the courts. First, plaintiff must show that there was, in fact, sexual harassment by peers. Second, school officials or teachers must have had "actual knowledge" of the harassment. Third, the harassment must be so pervasive, severe, and objectively offensive that it deprives the victim of access to educational opportunities. (*Davis*, 1999).

Following the *Davis* test, in 2007, the U.S. Court of Appeals, First Circuit, held that "Title IX does not make an educational institution the insurer either of a student's safety or of a parent's peace of mind." *Fitzgerald v. Barnstable School Committee*, 504 F.3d 165 (1st Cir. 2007). A remedy in damages may lie for a plaintiff student under Section 1983 of the Civil Rights Act. *Fitzgerald v. Barnstable School Committee*, 129 S.Ct. 788 (2009). Further explanation was given in another decision by the U.S. Court of Appeals, Seventh Circuit. In this case a kindergarten girl alleged by "vague and unspecific" testimony that a kindergarten boy jumped on her and classmates and tried to kiss them and repeatedly unzipped his pants. The school responded immediately, assigned the boy to detention and sent him to the school psychologist. The court held that the school was not deliberately indifferent. The court observed that young children will frequently interact in ways unacceptable to adults, but such interaction does not necessarily rise to the level of a statutory offense. The court reasoned, "Simple acts of teasing and name-calling among students" do not normally result in a denial of educational opportunity, the third element in the *Davis* test. *Gabrielle M. v. Park Forest–Chicago Heights School District 163*, 315 F.3d 817 (7th Cir. 2003). Similarly, the U.S. Court of Appeals, Eleventh Circuit, held that where students are not denied access to educational programs and their grades and participation in school are unaffect-

ed, then a Title IX peer-to-peer claim of sexual harassment will fail. Simple acts of "teasing and mere name-
calling" will not result in school district liability. *Hawkins v. Sarasota County School Board,* 322 F.3d 1279
(11th Cir. 2003).

§ 11.36 Deliberate Indifference

The deliberate indifference test expanded on in *Davis*
was established by the Supreme Court in 1998 in *Gebser
v. Lago Vista Independent School District,* 524 U.S. 274
(1998). In this case a high school student was having a
sexual relationship with a teacher. A police officer discovered the teacher and student having sexual intercourse
in a car. The court in *Gebser* ruled that monetary damages were available under Title IX if the school district
knew about the harassment and acted with "deliberate
indifference." The Court said that a lower standard
would leave the school district that received federal funds
liable not for official actions but for independent actions
of employees. "Consequently, in cases like this one that
do not involve official policy of the recipient entity, we
hold that damages remedy will not lie under Title IX
unless an official who at minimum has authority to
address the alleged discrimination and to institute corrective measures on the recipient's behalf has actual
knowledge of a discrimination in the recipient's programs and fails adequately to respond." "[F]or actual
notice (knowledge) to exist, an agent of the school district must be aware of the facts that indicate a likelihood
of discrimination."

Pursuant to the *Gebser* and *Davis* liability standard, a
school district was found to be deliberately indifferent
where a girl over several years was repeatedly proposi-
tioned, groped, threatened, and stabbed in the hand; the
male student-perpetrator removed her shirt, pulled her

hair, took his pants off and told her he would have sex with her. *Vance v. Spencer County Public School District*, 231 F.3d 253 (6th Cir.2000). Thus, the test of "deliberate indifference" becomes the key to determining where liability exists on the part of the school officials or the school district. School districts would be well-advised to provide in-service sensitivity training regarding sexual harassment for both teachers and school administrators that includes documentation of warnings and warning signs of such behavior between employees to employees, employees to students, and students to students. See also *Murrell v. School Dist. No. 1, Denver, Colo.*, 186 F.3d 1238 (10th Cir.1999).

In another example of deliberate indifference, a student was sexually abused by a teacher over a period of years and subsequently sued the school district. The principal had been told the offending teacher was a pedophile and advised to watch his behavior. This warning had come from a former student who had been molested. Later a librarian informed the principal he observed the student sitting on the teacher's lap. The molesting teacher told the principal it was a "father-son chat." The evidence, therefore, was of such magnitude to indicate that the principal had been deliberately indifferent. The superintendent and personnel director who did not know of the situation were found not to have acted with deliberate indifference. *Baynard v. Malone*, 268 F.3d 228 (4th Cir.2001).

Thus, in order to avoid liability for deliberate indifference, school officials must act quickly and decisively in instituting measures that will protect the victim of alleged sexual harassment. Whether the situation involves sexual harassment allegations of teacher-to-student

(*Henderson v. Walled Lake Consolidated Schools*, 469
F.3d 479 (6th Cir. 2006)), or peer student-to-peer student, the *Davis* test applies.

CHAPTER 12

CIVIL LIABILITY

§ 12.1 INTRODUCTION

One of the most frequently expressed concerns of teachers and school administrators is their potential liability. When can they be sued and, if so, what are the chances of having to pay substantial damages out of their own meager earnings? In addressing these questions, this chapter is divided into two sections: (1) common law torts and (2) constitutional torts. The first section deals with common law torts, since they more commonly come into play with school litigation in which teachers are involved.

§ 12.2 WHAT IS A TORT?

Tort is a term applied to a wide variety of civil wrongs for which a court will afford a remedy to the injured party in the form of money damages. Torts are civil wrongs of person against person as opposed to person against the state, as in a crime. In a tort action, the injured party brings an action in law to recover compensation for damage suffered; while with a crime, the state brings criminal proceedings to protect the interests of the public against the wrongdoer. A tort is to be distinguished from a breach of contract in that no special agreement exists between the parties. With a tort the person's rights are created by common law and not by the condition of a contract.

The word "tort" is a French term derived from the Latin "torquere," meaning twisted, which in English became a common synonym for "wrong." A tort may be committed by either an act or an omission to act which violates a person's right as created by law. While most are aware that to directly harm someone is deserving of damages, the more indirect nature of harm caused by an omission or failure to act creates a less discernible action. At school, the teacher and the student are placed in a special legal relationship where, if danger occurs, the teacher may, by virtue of this special relationship, be required to act to prevent harm to the student. Failure to act accordingly may result in a tort of omission.

Torts may be classified into three basic groups: (1) intentional interference, (2) strict liability, and (3) negligence. Virtually all of tort law in schools can be divided into actions for injuries caused by intentional acts and those for negligence.

§ 12.3   INTENTIONAL INTERFERENCE

Intentional torts come about as a result of voluntary action by the defendant. The defendant must intend to bring about a certain result which invades the interests of another. In schools, the most common types of intentional torts are assault and battery. Assault and battery brought as a tort is a civil action, a corresponding criminal action of assault and battery may be brought for the same incident. This section deals with assault and battery as a civil tort.

§ 12.31 Assault and Battery

Technically, a defendant may be liable if the plaintiff is placed in fear and apprehension of immediate physical contact. To hold a weapon in a threatening position, to chase in a hostile manner, or shake a fist under another's nose may all constitute assault. The key to establishing assault is the intent of the defendant and the fear of imminent harm by the plaintiff. No assault exists if the defendant did not intend to harm the plaintiff; there is no such thing as negligent assault. On the other hand, there is no assault if the plaintiff is not aware of the physical threat. If a person brandishes a gun over the head of a sleeping person, there is no assault.

In order for an assault to exist, there must be an unequivocal appearance of an attempt to do some immediate physical injury to the person of another. The act must be a display of force or menace of violence of such a nature as to cause reasonable apprehension of immediate bodily harm. For example, where a man said, "Were you not an old man I would knock you down," the court held there was no assault. There was no assault because the old man had no reason to expect immediate harm. Therefore, the intentional tort of assault may be consummated by an act which, while not involving physical contact, places a person in immediate fear of physical attack.

While assault is apprehension, battery is the actual physical contact. Assault and battery generally go together, but it is possible for each to exist without the other. For example, if a plaintiff was struck from behind and was not aware of the impending attack, battery is present, but not assault.

Assault and battery in schools are most often found in actions for excessive punishment of pupils. As discussed elsewhere in this book, teachers and school administrators have the authority by virtue of the doctrine of *in loco parentis* to administer reasonable corporal punishment where permitted by state statute or regulation. This means that the teacher-student relationship is a special one in law, and by virtue of this relationship teachers have a privilege or an immunity which protects them against liability so long as they act within their normal and reasonable prerogatives in the school. If, though, punishment is excessive, malicious, or in violation of school regulations, then the teacher or administrator may be subject to an assault and battery action by or on behalf of the pupil. The school's privilege and its attendant authority extend to all pupil offenses which directly affect the decorum and conduct of the school, whether on school property or not.

One court has explained the teacher's privilege with regard to criminal battery in this way. "Teachers under the authority of school boards are authorized by law to use reasonable force to maintain good conduct in classes and on school property. Teachers are invested with the prerogative, and indeed obligation, to hold students accountable for their actions. If corporal punishment is required, and allowed by state statute, to fulfill this responsibility, then no criminal battery can accrue if the punishment is reasonable and not excessive." Where a misbehaving student was grabbed by his jacket collar by a teacher and either tripped or was forced to the floor, the court said that the teacher acted reasonably under the circumstances and no battery had occurred. *Young v. St. Landry Parish School Board*, 759 So.2d 800 (La.App. 1999).

The privilege and the immunity that a teacher possesses as a shield against liability cannot be defeated without a demonstration that a student's injury resulted from actual malice of the teacher. *Crisp County School System v. Brown*, 487 S.E.2d 512 (Ga.App.1997).

Another court observed that minor bruises could be expected from a hit or a swat on the posterior and that discoloration of the skin or soreness was not sufficient to establish excessiveness to constitute assault and battery. A teacher, however, should not be misled into believing that the courts will tolerate any degree of severity. (See Chapter 8, Student Discipline—Child Abuse.)

Where a teacher took a student alone into a vacant schoolroom and claimed to have given the student a "severe shaking," bruises on the student's chest and stomach, apparently fist marks, belied the teacher's testimony and the teacher was held to be liable for battery. *Thomas v. Bedford*, 389 So.2d 405 (La.App.1980).

§ 12.32   False Imprisonment

A teacher may wonder if a student could institute an action for false imprisonment for staying after school or being confined to a certain schoolroom or space as punishment. False imprisonment is an unlawful restraint of one's physical liberty by another. A cause of action for false imprisonment must be sustained by the plaintiff showing two things: first, that detention or restraint was against his or her will and, second, that the detention or restraint was unlawful.

The key word here is "unlawful." Certain persons are immune from liability because they have a special legal relationship with the person who is restrained. Judicial officers, attorneys, physicians, parents, and school teachers, generally, have such legal status. School teachers, acting *in loco parentis*, have the authority to place reasonable restraints on students' physical liberty. The word "reasonable" is a necessary qualifier since the teacher and even the parent could restrict a child's freedom to an extent exceeding the bounds of their special privilege. To be reasonable, detention must be relatively brief in terms of minutes or a very few hours, and such infliction must be in good faith, without malice, for the best interests of the student and/or the school. *Fertich v. Michener*, 11 N.E. 605 (Ind.1887).

In a Michigan case the court said, "[The] principal was engaged in [a] discretionary act in keeping students in his office, and had individual governmental immunity from action for false imprisonment resulting in keeping student in [the] office, absent allegations that [the] principal was not acting in [the] course of [his] employment or that he maliciously or intentionally falsely imprisoned student." *Willoughby v. Lehrbass*, 388 N.W.2d 688 (Mich. App.1986).

§ 12.4 STRICT LIABILITY

Cases of strict liability are almost nonexistent in public school litigation. Strict liability may, though, occur where injury is done yet there is the inability to establish "fault." An establishment of fault requires that a causal connection be proven between an act and the injury. Where, however, there is no specific act, *per se*, or definable chain of events causing the injury, damages for the traditional negligence tort cannot prevail. This problem is particularly acute where hazards or ultra-hazards to individuals or the public have been created. In such instances, on occasion, courts have allowed the claim of strict liability in the theory that "he who breaks must pay" or that the person (or corporation) best able to pay for an injury must bear the burden. Within the schools, it is conceivable that hazards subject to strict liability could be found in inherently dangerous activities.

A rare example of such a claim was litigated in Illinois in 1986 where a child was injured at school while jumping on a trampoline. The plaintiff alleged that "the trampoline was an *abnormally dangerous* instrumentality" (emphasis added). Illinois state law provides you must be held strictly liable under two theories: (1) unreasonably dangerous defective products and (2) ultra-hazardous activities. The trampoline met neither of these standards and the injury was caused by the manner of its use. *Fallon v. Indian Trail School*, 500 N.E.2d 101 (Ill.App.1986). Strict liability is an area of tort law that has very little impact on teacher or school administrator liability.

§ 12.5   NEGLIGENCE

The most common tort action against teachers and school administrators is negligence. Negligence torts are neither expected nor intended as opposed to the intentional tort whose result is contemplated at the time of the act. Negligence is conduct falling below a legally established standard which results in injury to another person. It is failure to exercise due care when subjecting another to a risk or danger which causes harm.

An accident is by definition unavoidable and thus does not constitute negligence, but in many instances what first appears to be an accident may be traced to someone's negligent act. Children are well known for their accident propensities and courts are well aware of this, yet teachers must be on constant guard to prevent avoidable injuries to students. Where an injury could have been prevented by a teacher or an administrator, what may appear to be an accident becomes the tort of negligence.

§ 12.51   Standard of Conduct

That which is negligence in one circumstance may not be in another. No definite result can be predicted in an action for negligence. Each case must stand on its own set of facts as applied to a rule of law. The basic rule, which is the key to negligence, is the standard of conduct of the defendant. The appropriate standard of conduct is determined by a balancing of the risks, in light of the social value of the threatened interest and the probability and extent of harm, against the value of the interest which the actor is required to protect. *Restatement of Torts*, pp. 291–293.

This balance between the threatened harm and the utility of the actor's conduct is not, in most cases, easy to determine. In attempting better definition, the courts have developed the reasonableness theory requiring that for negligence to exist injury must have occurred from the exposure of another to "unreasonable risk." The reasonableness test has been personified in the "reasonable person."

§ 12.52   The Reasonable Person

The reasonable person is hypothetical; a community ideal of human behavior whose conduct under the same or similar circumstances is regarded as the measure of reasonable behavior, "a fictitious person who never has existed on land or sea." William L. Prosser, *Law of Torts* (West Publishing Company, 1955), p. 124. The reasonable person has been portrayed by different courts as a prudent person, a person of average prudence, a person of ordinary sense using ordinary care and skill, and as a reasonably prudent person. He or she is an ideal, a model of conduct and a community standard. The nature of the reasonable person, although a community ideal, varies in every case. His or her characteristics are (1) the physical attributes of the defendant, (2) normal intelligence, (3) normal perception and memory with a minimum level of information and experience common to the community, and (4) such superior skill and knowledge as the actor has or holds himself or herself out as having. As can be seen, the reasonable person formula changes with different factual situations because of the attributes or deficiencies of the defendant and because of peculiarities of beliefs, values, and customs of the individual community.

The reasonable person then has the same physical characteristics as the actor himself and the acts in question are measured accordingly. Correspondingly, the man who is crippled is not held to the same standard as the man with no physical infirmities. The courts have also made allowances for the weaknesses or attributes connected with the sex and age of the individual. The courts have not, however, been so lenient with individuals who have mental deficiencies. The courts have traditionally held that a person with lower mental ability than an average person must adjust and conform to the rules of society. Where a person is actually insane, a more convincing argument can be made for allowing for the particular incapacity but that also depends on the situation.

One such case illustrating this point occurred when a junior high pupil entered school and shot and killed the principal and wounded a teacher and two students. The student was ruled criminally insane, but the wounded teacher and student filed a civil action in tort. The court found that although a person was criminally insane, civil liability in damages was an appropriate remedy. The court said that "American courts have unanimously chosen to impose liability on an insane person rather than leaving the loss on the innocent victim." *Williams v. Kearbey*, 775 P.2d 670 (Kan.App.1989).

§ 12.53   A Reasonably Prudent Teacher

Teachers are specially educated and trained to teach and work with children and young adults. Teachers hold college degrees and are certified in educational methodologies. As such, teachers hold themselves out to the public as possessing superior skills and understanding of educational processes. By virtue of these attributes teachers may be held to a higher standard of conduct than the ordinary person without commensurate education and training. The teacher's required conduct in tort law may be that of a reasonably prudent teacher in the same or similar circumstances rather than the lesser standard of merely a reasonably prudent person.

Too, the teacher has the additional responsibility of standing *in loco parentis*; a Vermont court has said that a teacher's "relationship to the pupils under his care and custody differs from that generally existing between a public employee and a member of the general public. In a limited sense the teacher stands in the parents' place in his relationship to a pupil ... and has such a portion of the powers of the parent over the pupil as is necessary to carry out his employment. In such relationship, he owes his pupils the duty of supervision...." *Eastman v. Williams*, 207 A.2d 146 (Vt.1965).

This view is apparently taken by most courts. Some, though, hold that a teacher should not bear this additional burden. Where this view prevails the teacher is required to exercise only the reasonable prudence of any normal person.

§ 12.6   ELEMENTS OF NEGLIGENCE

The nature of negligence is best explained in four component parts. These are: (1) a duty on the part of the actor to protect others against unreasonable risks, (2) a failure on the part of the actor to exercise a standard of care commensurate with the risks involved, and (3) the conduct of the actor must be the proximate or legal cause of the injury. A causal connection must exist between the act and the resulting injury. The fourth is that there must be an injury, actual loss, or damage that resulted from the act.

§ 12.61   Duty

A person has a duty to abide by a standard of reasonable conduct in the face of apparent risks. The courts generally hold that no duty exists where the defendant could not have reasonably foreseen the danger of risk involved. A duty owed by one person to another intensifies as the risk increases. In other words, the duty to protect another is proportional to the risk or hazard of a particular activity. In school functions where risks are greater to school children, a teacher has an increased level of obligation or duty to the children. For example, whenever a teacher has children perform a dangerous laboratory experiment, he or she has a greater obligation for the children's' safety than where he or she is merely supervising a study hall. One judge has explained the duty requirement in this way. "Every person is negligent when, without intending any wrong, he does such an act or omits to take such a precaution that under the circumstances he, as an ordinary prudent person, ought reasonably to foresee that he will thereby expose the interest of another to an unreasonable risk of harm. In determining whether his conduct will subject the interest of another to an unreasonable risk of harm, a person is required to take into account ... the surrounding circumstances ... and to use such judgment and discretion as is exercised by persons of reasonable intelligence under the same or similar circumstance." *Osborne v. Montgomery*, 234 N.W. 372 (Wis.1931).

A person is negligent when, by affirmative act, he injures another. However, the question often arises as to whether a person can be liable for failure to act at all. Generally the law holds that a person is not liable for an omission to act where there is no definite relationship between the parties. In other words, no general duty exists to aid a person in danger. For example, even though there is a moral duty, no legal duty exists for a bystander to aid a drowning person.

Where teachers and students are concerned, however, the situation is quite different. The greater duty of the teacher invested by the *in loco parentis* standard compels the teacher to take affirmative action to protect students. Thus, teachers may be liable for an omission to act as well as for a negligent affirmative act.

An example of an action raised because of an alleged omission was litigated in a case where a student told several friends that she intended to kill herself and the information was relayed to a guidance counselor. The counselor questioned the girl who denied the statement. Yet, later the girl committed suicide in a murder suicide pact with another 13 year old. There had earlier been much discussion at school about teen suicides. The question before the court was whether the counselor owed a duty to inform the parents of the suicidal statements. The court said, "We hold that school counselors have a *duty* to use reasonable means to attempt to prevent a suicide when they are on notice of a child or adolescent student's suicide intent." The case was remanded to the lower court to determine if the counselor had breached her duty. *Eisel v. Board of Education*, 597 A.2d 447 (Md.1991).

§ 12.62   Standard of Care

A standard of care must be exercised commensurate with the duty owed. A legally recognized duty or obligation requires the actor to conform to a certain standard of care as the foreseeable risk involved in an act increases. The standard of care of auto mechanics shop teachers for protection of youngsters is generally greater than that of the school librarian. This is, of course, true because the risk of injury involved in handling power tools, machinery, and electrical equipment is much greater than the risk of being injured while reading a book.

The standard of care which a teacher owes a student assumes an extra duty to keep the children secure from injury. Teachers have a "special responsibility recognized by common law to supervise their charges." *Miller v. Griesel*, 308 N.E.2d 701 (Ind.1974). It is further well settled that the amount of care which the teacher owes the student increases or decreases with the relative maturity or immaturity of the student. One court has commented that even with students of 17 or 18 years of age, a teacher's care must be quite high, particularly where students are in groups "where the herd instinct and competitive spirit tend naturally to relax vigilance." *Satariano v. Sleight*, 129 P.2d 35 (Cal.App.1942).

While standards of care may differ among teachers, differences may also be found among other persons in society. Children and aged persons have generally been given substantially more leeway in their activities than is allowed a normal adult. While both children and aged persons are liable for their torts, they are not held to the same standard as are others without impairments of age. While it is difficult to pinpoint precise standards to determine the reasonableness of a child because of the great variations in age, maturity and capacity, the courts nevertheless have established a rough standard as a guideline. As the age, intelligence, and experience of the child increases, a commensurate increase in the standard of care is required of the child. A child is generally held to a standard of care of a reasonable child of the same age, intelligence, and experience in the same or similar circumstances.

Some courts have established an arbitrary cutoff age below which a child cannot be held liable for tort. Authorities generally agree though that such arbitrary limits are not the best standard. No one can deny that, under certain circumstances, a child of six or even five years could conceivably be guilty of negligence. Some courts have said that the rule providing for a specific age cutoff, usually at six or seven years of age, is arbitrary and open to objection because one day's difference in age surely cannot determine whether a child is capable of negligence.

At any rate, children of school age are almost always capable of negligence. Thus, each child at school, as well as the teachers and administrators, may be negligent if their standard of conduct falls below that of a reasonably prudent person, of their age, physical attributes and knowledge, in the same or similar circumstances.

§ 12.63   Proximate or Legal Cause

"Proximate cause" or "legal cause" is the sequential connection between the actor's negligent conduct and the resultant injury to another person. The *Restatement of Torts* explains the necessity of adequate causal relation in this way: "In order that a negligent actor shall be liable for another's harm, it is necessary not only that the actor's conduct be negligent toward the other, but also that the negligence of the actor be a legal cause of the other's harm."

In order for proximate or legal cause to exist, there must first be a duty or obligation on the part of the actor to maintain a reasonable standard of care. In such cases, the courts require that the defendant's conduct be the legal or proximate cause of the injury. In most negligence cases, however, the courts will not refer to proximate cause but will rely solely on the duty or obligation of the defendant and the standard of conduct required to avoid liability. Proximate cause as a criterion of liability has been used most often where some doubt is present as to whether the injured person was within the zone of obvious danger.

Courts require that the negligence of the defendant must be the "substantial" cause of the harm to the plaintiff, substantial enough to lead a reasonable person to conclude the act is indeed the cause of injury. There must be an unbroken chain between the act and the resulting injury. If the negligence is not a substantial factor in producing the harm, then there is no liability.

The actor's negligent act must be in continuous and active force up to the actual harm, and the lapse of time must not be so great that contributing causes and intervening factors render the original negligent act to be an insubstantial or insignificant force in the harm.

Therefore, a teacher may be relieved of liability where an intervening act results in a pupil's injury. In a case illustrating this point, a teacher went home after school leaving three young boys unsupervised in her classroom. The student found a small knife left in the unlocked teacher's desk drawer and one student was cut rather severely. The teacher's leaving the boys alone in the room was adjudged not to be the proximate cause of the injury. *Richard v. St. Landry Parish School Board*, 344 So.2d 1116 (La.App.1977).

Proximate cause tends to overlap with the question of duty and serve in some cases as a corollary to an intervening act. Prosser has noted the elusive nature of proximate cause, thusly: " 'Proximate cause' ... has been all things to all men. Having no integrated meaning of its own, its chameleon quality permits it to be substituted for any one of the elements of a negligence case when decision on that element becomes difficult...." Prosser, § 42.

§ 12.64   Injury or Actual Loss

A defendant is not liable for injury unless he has, in fact, caused the injury. Similarly, a defendant is not liable for damages unless the plaintiff shows that he has actually suffered an injury or can show actual loss or damages resulting from the act. Nominal damages cannot be obtained where no actual loss can be shown or has occurred.

Damages for an injury may be assessed against one or more persons. If the harm suffered was caused by more than one person, then damages may be apportioned among the feasors. Also, if more than one harm is present and the harms and damages can be distinguished, there will be apportionment among the defendants.

§ 12.7   DEFENSES FOR NEGLIGENCE

Teachers or school administrators may employ one or more of several defenses if an action is brought against them in tort. In all cases involving negligence, the defendant may seek to show that the plaintiff's injury was caused by mere accident and not by anyone's fault. It may be to show, too, that no duty was owed or that there was an intervening act which broke the causal chain between the act and the injury. Or, it may be maintained that the plaintiff simply could not foresee the injurious result. These, though, are not strictly speaking defenses, but instead are elements of the tort which the plaintiff must establish in order to have a case. Assuming that foreseeability, duty, standard of care, and so forth are established by plaintiff, then defendant must respond with what are classically known as tort defenses; they are: (1) contributory negligence, (2) comparative negligence, (3) assumption of risk, (4) act of God, (5) immunity, and (6) last clear chance.

§ 12.71 Contributory Negligence

Contributory negligence involves some fault or breach of duty on the part of the injured person, or failure on his or her part to exercise the required standard of care for his or her own safety. The injured party through personal negligence and fault contributes to his/her injury. In other words, contributory negligence is conduct on the part of the injured party which caused or contributed to the injury and which would not have been done by a person exercising ordinary prudence under the circumstance. This is sometimes referred to as the "all or nothing" rule meaning that if the plaintiff is shown to be negligent at all, then defendant is completely absolved from liability. *Funston v. School Town of Munster*, 849 N.E.2d 595 (Ind. 2006), *The Law of Torts*, William L. Prosser (West Publishing, 1971), defines contributory negligence as "... conduct on the part of the plaintiff ... which falls below the standard to which he is required to conform for his own protection.... [A]lthough the defendant has violated his duty, has been negligent, and would otherwise be liable, the plaintiff is denied recovery because his own conduct disentitles him to maintain the action. In the eyes of the law both parties are at fault...."

As previously pointed out, a child is capable of negligence, and his failure to conform to a required standard of conduct for a child of his age, physical characteristics, sex, and training will result in the court assigning fault to his actions. If an injured child is negligent and his or her negligence contributes to the harm, then a defendant teacher, who is also negligent, may be absolved from liability. However, since a child is not expected to perform with the same standard of care as an adult, teachers have more difficulty in showing contributory negligence than if the plaintiff were an adult. A child is by nature careless and often negligent, and knowing this, a teacher should allow for an additional margin of safety when dealing with students. This is especially true with younger children. Contributory negligence is much less reliable as a defense when dealing with children than it is with adults. In fact, courts have said that where a child is concerned, the test to be employed is whether the child has committed a gross disregard of safety in the face of known, perceived, and understood dangers.

In earlier cases, if a plaintiff's negligence or fault contributed to his or her injury, the court would normally bar recovery of any damages at all. This rule, which prevents recovery no matter how "slight" the plaintiff's negligence, has more recently been almost entirely abandoned by the "substantial factor" rule. That is, plaintiff's negligence must be a substantial factor in causing his or her own injury or defendant will be liable anyway. Some courts have held that complete barring of any damages because of contributory fault is perhaps a little drastic and have, therefore, sought to prorate damages based on the degree of fault of each of the parties. This results in what is known as damages for comparative negligence, discussed below.

§ 12.72   Comparative Negligence

As previously pointed out, where contributory negligence on the part of the plaintiff is shown, the defendant is often absolved from all liability. This, some courts and legislatures have felt, works a hardship on the negligent plaintiff who suffers injury but can recover nothing from the negligent defendant. This concern for the injured party has led legislatures in some states to enact statutes to determine degrees of negligence and allow recovery based on the relative degree of fault. While the specific provisions of "comparative negligence" statutes vary from state to state, the concept works this way: If the plaintiff's fault is found to be about equal to the defendant's, then the plaintiff will recover one-half the damages and must bear the remainder of the loss. If the plaintiff's negligence amounted to one-third of the fault and the defendant's two-thirds, then the plaintiff could recover two-thirds of the damages, or damages may be apportioned more than two ways. For example, where a six-year-old child was killed by an automobile while crossing an intersection where a guard was normally posted, the court ruled that the percentage of comparative fault of the automobile driver was 50%, for Orleans Parish School Board it was 25%, and the City of New Orleans Police Department was 25%. *Barnes v. Bott*, 615 So.2d 1337 (La.App.1993). In states with "comparative negligence" statutes, the idea is carried forth that the plaintiff, even though he is partly to blame for his own harm, will not be totally barred from recovery. Today, over one-half the states have adopted comparative negligence in some form.

In some instances courts have not waited for legislatures to shift from contributory to comparative negligence. For example, the Florida Supreme Court in 1973 decided that it was within the province of judicial authority to make the change. In so doing the court said: "Whatever may have been the historical justification for it [contributory negligence], today it is almost universally regarded as unjust and inequitable to vest an entire accidental loss on one of the parties whose negligent conduct combined with the negligence of the other party to produce the loss." *Hoffman v. Jones*, 280 So.2d 431 (Fla.1973).

§ 12.73   Assumption of Risk

Another defense against negligence is assumption of risk which, if pleaded and proved by the defendant, will absolve the defendant from liability. The theory here is that the plaintiff in some manner consents to relieve the defendant of his duty or obligation of conduct. In other words, the plaintiff by expressed or implied agreement assumes the risk of the danger and thereby relieves the defendant of responsibility. The defendant is simply not under any legal duty to protect the plaintiff from normal risks. The plaintiff with knowledge of the danger voluntarily enters into a relationship with the defendant, and by so doing agrees to take his own chances.

Important to this defense is the plaintiff's knowledge and awareness of the danger. Basically, assumption of risk is plaintiff's voluntary consent to encounter a known danger. Unlike contributory negligence, which requires only unreasonable conduct on the part of the plaintiff, assumption of risk requires voluntary consent or a showing that plaintiff's state of mind was such that the danger was known to him.

The courts have generally established that the participant in athletic events, whether intramural or interscholastic, assumes the risk of the normal hazards of the game when he participates. This also applies to spectators attending sports or amusement activities. Spectators assume all the obvious or normal risks of being hurt by flying balls, fireworks explosions, or the struggles of combatants. For example, where a boy playing basketball was injured when his arm went through a glass pane in a door immediately behind the basketball backboard, the court said that the boy had not assumed the risk of such an injury because he did not know the glass in the door was not shatterproof. *Stevens v. Central School District No. 1*, 270 N.Y.S.2d 23 (1966). However, another court held that a boy had assumed the risk when he suffered a broken neck in a football game. "Assumption of risk in competitive athletics is not an absolute defense but a measure of the defendant's duty of care." Players who voluntarily participate in extracurricular sports assume the risks to which their roles expose them but not risks which are concealed or unreasonable. *Benitez v. New York City Board of Ed.*, 541 N.E.2d 29 (N.Y.1989).

The school's duty is to protect the student from "unassumed, concealed or unreasonable risks." Where a student voluntarily agreed to wrestle an opponent in a heavier weight class and was injured and sued the school for damages, the court ruled for the school because the student had assumed the risk. *Edelson v. Uniondale Union Free School District*, 631 N.Y.S.2d 391 (1995). Students also assume the normal risks of other highly physical activities such as cheerleading. No liability will accrue to the school or coach so long as the coach provides proper instruction and does not expose the participants to risks that are beyond their level of experience. *Aaris v. Las Virgenes Unified School District*, 75 Cal.Rptr.2d 801 (App.1998).

Essential to the doctrine of assumption of risk is that the plaintiff have knowledge of the risks; if he or she is ignorant of the conditions and dangers, then risk is not assumed. If plaintiff does not take reasonable precautions to determine the hazards involved, the risk is not assumed, and contributory negligence may be present instead. However, neither a participant nor a spectator assumes the risk for negligence or willful or wanton conduct of others. For example, a spectator at an athletic contest does not assume the risk of the stands falling down at a football game nor is risk assumed by attending a baseball game where a player intentionally throws a bat into the stands and injures a spectator. Only those hazards or risks normally associated with the activity are assumed. *Stowers v. Clinton Central School Corporation*, 855 N.E.2d 739 (Ind. Ct. App. 2006).

§ 12.74 Exculpatory Notes

Release forms or permission notes to obtain parents' permission for students to participate in certain school activities have been utilized by many school districts in an effort to exculpate the school or teachers from liability should a student be injured. Such instruments have been viewed to have value as evidence of assumption of risks of more dangerous than normal school undertakings. Yet, such permissions by parents to waive liability for their children have not been completely satisfying for many legal authorities because the nature of tort law itself does not provide for the parent to waive the right of a child to recover damages for an injury. Nor do such releases modify the duty of a school official or teacher to act reasonably in protecting the student. The waiver or permission given by the parent is presumed to be some sort of contract, the *quid pro quo*, for the child's participation in the school activity.

According to the Supreme Court of Washington, exculpatory releases by parents are not only legally ineffectual, but for school districts to require them is invalid as against public policy. This court says that such attempts to gain immunity against liability by public agencies violates good public policy because the parents and children as members of the public, who are seeking the public service of education, are placed under a kind of coercion and control of the school district, the provider of public service. In this court's opinion, the party invoking the exculpation, the school, possesses a decisive advantage of bargaining strength against any member of the public (parent and/or child) who seeks the services. *Wagenblast v. Odessa School District*, 758 P.2d 968 (Wash. 1988).

Because the legality of this kind of agreement is questionable, some commentators have concluded that such permission notes are therefore worth very little. On the other hand, of late, courts have begun to give weight to such release forms as evidence that there may be a valid parental and student assumption of risk that can, in fact, absolve the school district from liability. *Aaris v. Las Virgenes Unified School District*, 75 Cal.Rptr.2d 801 (App.1998).

Some courts that have upheld the validity of exculpatory notes address the other side of the argument. In one case where a cheerleader was injured rehearsing a pyramid formation, the court upheld a consent note as a valid waiver of liability and stated, "Our views with respect to the permissibility of requiring releases as a condition of voluntary participation in extracurricular sports activities, and the enforceability of releases signed by parents on behalf of their children for those purposes, are also consistent with and further the public policy of encouraging athletic programs for the Commonwealth's youth.... To hold that releases of the type in question are unenforceable would expose public schools, who offer many of the extracurricular sports opportunities available to children, to financial costs and risks that will inevitably lead to the reduction of those programs." *Sharon v. City of Newton*, 769 N.E.2d 738 (Mass.2002).

Following the rationale of this court, other Massachusetts courts have consistently enforced release agreements that immunize parties from future liability for negligent acts. *Cormier v. Central Mass. Chapter of National Safety Council*, 620 N.E.2d 784 (Mass.1993). In 2008, the Appeals Court of Massachusetts held that a broadly-worded release agreement for a school carpentry class was valid. In this instance the student handbook indicated that students were required to sign the school's exculpatory agreement as a condition of enrollment in the class that released "all" school instructors and employees from "all responsibility" in case of an accident during the course of instruction. The court rejected the student's argument that the agreement applied only to "unforeseen mishaps." *Kennedy v. North Bennet Street School*, 72 Mass. App. Ct. 1112 (2008).

In another jurisdiction, North Dakota, exculpatory notes were approved as waivers of liability. In this North Dakota case a child was injured in a bicycle accident on the elementary school property while participating in an after-school program. The court held that a waiver and release which was clear and unambiguous signed by the child's mother was a valid exoneration. *Kondrad v. Bismarck Park District*, 655 N.W.2d 411 (N.D.2003).

§ 12.75   Act of God

Man cannot, of course, be held responsible for injuries caused by natural elements or acts of God. No liability will ensue if the injury caused to a student is the result of a tornado, lightning, earthquake, volcano, etc. One should be very sure, however, that sufficient precautions are taken to protect students if natural calamities are foreseen.

When games or practices are conducted out-of-doors, coaches should be especially cognizant of weather conditions, such as thunderstorms. A coach is not normally liable if a child is struck by an unexpected burst of lightning, but liability may well result if the weather conditions are ignored and students are allowed to continue to play when lightning strikes repeatedly in the vicinity.

§ 12.76   Immunity

Immunity from tort liability is used in different contexts. Immunity is generally conferred on (1) national and state governments unless abrogated by statute; (2) public officials performing judicial, quasi-judicial, or discretionary functions; (3) charitable organizations granted immunity in some states; (4) infants under certain conditions; and (5) in some cases, insane persons.

Governmental or sovereign immunity is an historical and common law precedent which protects a state agency against liability for its torts. The defense of immunity may be invoked to protect the public school district against liability. The immunity defense is available for acts of negligence. Some states have ruled that such immunity is only available for ordinary negligence and not gross negligence. *Lentz v. Morris*, 372 S.E.2d 608 (Va.1988).

Teachers as well as others are liable for their own torts beyond the normal privilege and immunity in their capacity to control the conduct of students; in most states, however, school districts, as state entities, are not subject to liability for an action in tort. A general rule of law is that government is immune from tort liability unless the legislature or the courts specifically abrogate the immunity. In other words, common law theory maintains that government cannot be sued without its consent. A school district is an arm of the state and as such may have immunity in tort. The doctrine of governmental immunity originated with the idea that "the King can do no wrong" and manifests itself today in the sovereign immunity of government in general.

Legal historians claim that sovereign immunity, as it applied to torts of the King, did not become common law until the 16th century. At that time, it was maintained that the King was not liable for his torts or for the torts of his ministers. Most agree that the transition was made from "the King can do no wrong" to "the government can do no wrong" in 1788 in the case of *Russell v. The Men Dwelling in the County of Devon*, 100 Eng.Rep. 359 (1788). Governmental immunity evidently crossed the ocean to Massachusetts and became American law in 1812 in the case of *Mower v. The Inhabitants of Leicester*, 9 Mass. 247 (1812).

The courts in the United States that have sustained the immunity principle with regard to school districts have relied primarily on five criteria: (1) school districts have only those powers granted by the legislature; if the legislature has not given the school district authority to be sued in tort, then it is beyond the district's legal powers; (2) payment of tort claims is an illegal expenditure of public funds since the public receives no benefit; (3) abolition of immunity would cause a multiplicity of cases putting a financial burden on the school; (4) the doctrine of *respondeat superior*, where the master is liable for acts of his servant, does not apply to public school districts; and (5) immunity must be abolished by the legislature, not the courts.

The doctrine of governmental immunity has been severely criticized by many courts. The leading case attacking the concept is an Illinois case where a pupil was injured in a school bus accident and sued the school district. *Molitor v. Kaneland Community Unit District No. 302*, 163 N.E.2d 89 (Ill.1959).

In *Molitor*, the court said: "The whole doctrine of governmental immunity from liability for tort rests upon a rotten foundation. It is almost incredible that in this modern age of comparative sociological enlightenment, and, in a republic the medieval absolutism supposed to be implicit in the maxim, 'the King can do no wrong,' should exempt the various branches of the government from liability for their torts, and that the entire burden of damage resulting from the wrongful acts of the government should be imposed upon the single individual who suffers the injury, rather than distributed among the entire community constituting the government, where it could be borne without hardship upon any individual, and where it justly belongs."

Yet, in Illinois today immunity of school districts has been restored by the legislature in the Tort Immunity Act; thus, a school district is entitled to immunity for negligent and improper supervision of students by a teacher. *Henrich v. Libertyville High School*, 683 N.E.2d 135 (Ill.App.1997).

Each state has its own laws and judicial precedents regarding immunity from tort. Some states have abrogated immunity, others retain immunity, while others have abrogated immunity either partially or wholly depending on whether the school district is performing a proprietary or a governmental function. In other states, immunity is in force unless a school board has purchased liability insurance, in which case the school district waives its immunity not to exceed the amount of the insurance policy. *Daniel v. City of Morganton*, 479 S.E.2d 263 (N.C.App.1997).

In Connecticut there exists an interesting twist to the general rules of governmental immunity called the imminent harm-identifiable exception. Under this provision a school district may be liable if a child is injured where conditions exist where a reasonable person would expect an injury to occur. This exception was invoked and the district was held liable where a second-grade student, unsupervised, ran down a hallway and into a wire mesh window. *Purzycki v. Town of Fairfield*, 708 A.2d 937 (Conn.1998).

§ 12.77   Save–Harmless Laws

This view has been slowly adopted by several state legislatures as well as by the courts. In Florida, for example, the state legislature abolished immunity of school districts and municipalities and, secondarily, enacted a save-harmless provision which protects teachers and other school and governmental employees against liability up to a specified limit of damages.

Certain other states along with Florida have enacted save-harmless laws; these include Connecticut, Iowa, Massachusetts, New Jersey, Oregon, New York, and Wyoming. The wording of the New York statute is typical; it reads in part: "... it should be the duty of each board of education, trustee or trustees ..., to save harmless and protect all teachers, practice or cadet teachers, and members of supervisory and administrative staff or employees from financial loss arising out of any claim, demand, suit, or judgment by reason of alleged negligence or other act resulting in accidental bodily injury to any person within or without the school building, provided such teacher, practice or cadet teacher, or member of the supervisory or administrative staff or employee, at the time of the accident or injury was acting in the discharge of his duties within the scope of his employment...."

Such provisions are tantamount to liability insurance policies against personal liability of teachers, administrators and others, including student teachers, so long as they are acting within the scope of their employment. Where the amount of damages which a school district is authorized to pay is limited by statute, as it is in Florida at $100,000, then the teacher or other school employee is well advised to supplement the state efforts by obtaining personal liability insurance. This is particularly true where the teaching takes place in high risk areas such as shops, chemistry classes, physical education or coaching activities. Of course, in those states which have not abrogated immunity nor have a save-harmless law, the entire burden of an action in tort rests on the shoulders of the teacher, administrator, or other employee, personally.

§ 12.78   Bullying

Much has been said recently regarding bullying in schools. School teachers and administrators have traditionally had to deal with students who intimidate and are physically aggressive toward others. Intimidation may be psychological as with cyber bullying (See Chapter 8.51) or may simply be more primitive forms where a student or students corporally encroach less physically able students. Bullying may be singular or in groups, as with gang formation.

Bullying in various forms has in some contexts been considered a rite of passage in schools as with the English public (private) schools of *Tom Brown's School Days* at Rugby, Eton, Winchester and the like. But it has only been lately that parents of bullied students have conceived of the idea of making the school legally responsible and subject to damages. Parents and their attorneys have taken various avenues of legal redress, including complaints that are based on tort law, civil rights laws and constitutional laws. (See Constitutional Torts in this chapter below.) In one unreported case that was settled out of court, the attorney for plaintiff, bullied girls, claimed that a constitutional right was violated in a state where education is considered a fundamental right. The matter was not litigated, so no precedent was set.

The incidence of bullying appears to vary by race and ethnicity and is more frequent among boys in primary and middle schools than in high schools. [Richard Lawrence, *School Crime and Juvenile Justice, 2d edition* (New York: Oxford University Press 2007), p. 20.] Several state legislatures, including those in Illinois, Minnesota, New Jersey, Oregon and Washington, have enacted anti-bullying laws. School principals have broad discretion in handling pupil control and bullying. (*Albers v. Breen*, 806 N.E. 2d 667 (Ill. App.Ct. 2004). Moreover, a school principal may have immunity from tort liability for exercise of her discretion in handling of student offenses such as bullying.

The question, of course, arises: Is the teacher, school official or school district liable if bullying is not prevented and someone is injured. Standard tort precedents normally apply to bullying situations; that is, the school teacher or administrator must have been able to reasonably foresee that a student would be harmed by another student and took no corrective action. In New York it has been held that while schools have a duty to adequately supervise students, such a duty does not make the school teachers and administrators insurers of the safety of students. Schools, school teachers or administrators, will not be held liable for incidences that unexpectedly occur without prior knowledge or foreseeability. (*Smith v. Half Hollow Hills School District*, 349 F.Supp.2d 521 (E.D.N.Y. 2004). The fact that there is no foreseeable harm nor that a teacher is "insensitive to a situation" will not make the teacher, principal or school district liable in damages. Further, liability will not accrue simply because a school does not have a bullying policy. *Jasperson v. Anoka–Hennepin Independent School District, No. 11*, 2007 WL 3153456 (Minn. Ct. App. 2007).

The issue of foreseeability with regard to bullying is a matter of evidence in each case. Where a student was assaulted by a student who had a reputation for minor misconduct, improper language, horseplay, and had been suspended for fighting, the court ruled that such facts did not in and of themselves establish the necessary foreseeability required to hold the school liable in damages. Testimony by staff of the school was given to the effect that the offending student was not viewed as a bully or a disciplinary problem. The court in holding for the school district observed that the school is not required to "follow the student around the entire day" in anticipation of an assault on another student where foreseeability is so tenuous. (*Aratari v. Leetonia Exempt Village School District*, 2007 WL 969402 (Ohio Ct. App. 2007).

Claims against schools for failure to appropriately deal with bullying may arise as constitutional matters or have some basis in federal statutory law. For example, if a parent complainant can successfully attach bullying to a child's disability, and the Individuals with Disabilities Act (IDEA) can be involved and damages sought through 42 U.S.C. § 1983, then there may possibly be a viable damage claim. However, a factual situation may be difficult to conjure. For example, in a case where parents of a small boy with attention deficit hyperactivity disorder (ADHD) claimed that he had been bullied and harassed by classmates and the school did nothing to prevent it, the federal district court examined the connection between federal constitutional and statutory law. The parents based their claim on Fourteenth Amendment equal protection and due process as well as on the student's rights under IDEA. The district court in holding for the school district concluded that the U.S. Constitution creates no affirmative right to government protection. It only creates rights against "government offenses" against the individual, thereby rejecting both the equal protection and due process claims. Further, the district court evidence did not show that the plaintiff boy was improperly treated due to his disability. On appeal, however, the federal circuit court required the district court to reconsider the facts based on an allegation that the boy was not given a "free appropriate public education" under the IDEA, and the court further required reconsideration of the state law negligence claims. Thus, with the proper alignment of facts under IDEA with bullying, there may be some possibility of a successful damage claim. (*Smith v. Guilford Board of Education*, 226 Fed. Appx. 58 (2d Cir. 2007).

The bottom line with regard to the legalisms of bullying is that: first, schools are responsible to act reasonably in the exercise of their *in loco parentis* status; second, the common law rules of tort law apply, a duty, standard of care, foreseeability and reasonableness; third, courts will provide administrators and students with broad discretion in the conduct of the school; fourth, schools, as corporate entities, and/or school administrators and teachers generally have a qualified or conditional privilege that protects them against liability unless their standard of care to protect students is not commensurate with the duty owed; fifth, schools, school administrators and teachers are vulnerable to liability if they are "indifferent" or "deliberately indifferent" to the plight of a bullied child; sixth, complaints of bullying beyond tort liability may possibly gain traction by plaintiffs if a state or federal statute or constitutional violation can be substantiated. In this regard, the effects of state bullying statutes have yet to be explored by the courts.

§ 12.79 Statutory Teacher Protection

Both state statutes and common law seek to provide public school teachers and staff with some assurance that they will not be held liable in damages in performance of their duties to provide students with a safe and educationally efficient learning environment. Without such legal support few persons would venture into the realm of teaching and school administration.

One seldom mentioned provision for such protection is the omnibus No Child Left Behind (NCLB) Act (20 U.S.C. § 6731–38). This part of the law, the Coverdell Teacher Protection Act, reinforces state laws that protect teachers and staff from liability when they control student behavior that may be harmful to other students or good order in the school. As with common law and state statutory provisions, the school, teachers, and staff will not suffer liability if the control over students is exercised "within the scope of the teacher's or staff member's employment." The federal Coverdell law provides that teachers and staff will not be held liable so long as they act in conformance with law "in furtherance of efforts to control, discipline, expel, or suspend a student or maintain order or control in the classroom or school," and that the teacher or staff member does not act with gross negligence, reckless misconduct, willful or criminal misconduct or flagrant disregard for the student's rights. This provision of NCLB prohibits punitive damage awards against a teacher or staff member unless they have "clear and convincing evidence that the harm was proximately caused by an act or omission of such teacher that constitutes willful or criminal misconduct" or constitutes flagrant indifference to the student's rights.

§ 12.8   EDUCATIONAL MALPRACTICE

Several courts in recent years have issued opinions on cases that fall under a general classification of educational malpractice. Such cases are not a separate area of law, but rather represent an expansion of the traditional tort law concept as applied to the educational setting. Basically, educational malpractice is an attempt to apply tort law to educational outcomes in such a way as to compensate a student in damages for knowledge deficiencies allegedly created by some substandard treatment of the student during the educational process.

Evidence to support an allegation of intentional tort would seem to be very difficult to support unless one could show that an educator, for some malicious purpose, set out to prevent a child from obtaining an education. The possibility of maintaining an action for intentional tort was recognized by a Maryland court when it stated: "It is our view that where an individual engaged in the educational process is shown to have wilfully and maliciously injured a child entrusted to his educational care, such outrageous conduct greatly outweighs any public policy considerations which would otherwise preclude liability so as to authorize recovery." *Hunter v. Board of Education*, 439 A.2d 582 (Md.1982).

The more common application of tort to redress a student's educational deficiencies is found in negligence. Here it is maintained that educators failed to act reasonably in administering to a student's educational needs. Such actions, though, have met with little or no success as the courts have established an imposing array of precedents denying students damages. The courts have generally denied such remedies for three reasons: "the absence of a workable rule of care against which defendant's conduct may be measured, the inherent uncertainty in determining the cause and nature of any damages, and the extreme burden which would be imposed on the already strained resources of the public school system to say nothing of the judiciary."

The first reason given is related directly to the tort of negligence. But this type of action involved several legal questions including the following. How can a court enunciate a standard of care without a clear determination of the actual duty owed the student? Does the educator have a duty to fill the vessel of the student's mind with a given amount of knowledge, and if the vessel remains half-full, does the educator, student, parent, or society bear the blame? *Donohue v. Copiague Union Free School District*, 391 N.E.2d 1352 (N.Y.1979).

The problem of delineating an actionable duty was recognized by a California court in *Peter W. v. San Francisco Unified School District*, 131 Cal.Rptr. 854 (App.1976), when it explained: "The 'injury' claimed here is plaintiff's inability to read and write. Substantial professional authority attests that the achievement of literacy in the schools, or its failure, is influenced by a host of factors which affect the pupil subjectively, from outside the formal teaching process, and beyond the control of its ministers. They may be physical, neurological, emotional, cultural, environmental; they may be present but not perceived, recognized but not identified."

In such a situation, the court could not find that the student had suffered injury within the meaning of negligence law, nor could it identify a workable "rule of care" that could be applied. Neither could the court find a causal relationship between any perceived injury and the alleged negligent commission or omission by the defendant. From these cases, one must conclude that courts are not enthralled with the entire notion of educational malpractice as a general and viable action. Education does not adapt well to the factual situations normally found in medical or other malpractice litigation where the certainty of cause and effect is more demonstrable in evidence that can be laid before a court.

§ 12.9 CONSTITUTIONAL TORTS

Although the foundation of constitutional torts is grounded in the Civil Rights Act of 1871, codified as Title 42 of the United States Code, Section 1983, the majority of litigation is of recent origin. The basic concept extends personal liability to public officials who violate the statutory or constitutional rights of an individual, such as a student or teacher.

The statute was enacted during the Reconstruction Era after the Civil War to protect the rights of blacks and was commonly referred to as the Ku Klux Klan Act. In March of 1871, President Grant sent a message to Congress requesting they use their power under the Fourteenth Amendment to pass legislation to protect individuals from state officials who were abusing their power and violating the natural rights of those individuals. The President further pleaded that legislation was needed to protect the life, liberty, property, and enforcement of laws at all levels of government. Congress responded by passing the 1871 Civil Rights Act which states: ''Every person who, under color of any statute, ordinance, regulation, custom, or usage, of any State or Territory, subjects, or causes to be subjected, any citizen of the United States or other person within the jurisdiction thereof to the deprivation of any rights, privileges or immunities secured by the Constitution and laws, shall be liable to the party injured in an action at, law, suit in equity, or other proper proceeding for redress.'' 42 U.S.C.A. § 1983.

This statute was the subject of very little litigation from the time of passage until the 1960s. With the expansion of the civil rights movement, this Act was used as a weapon to hold state officials personally liable if they violated the rights of another.

§ 12.91   Definition of Person

The Act provides that liability for damages may be had against "every person" who infringes on the rights of another. Initially, the word "person" applied to the individual who deprived another of a civil right, but it did not include an institution, such as a city or a school district. In *Monroe v. Pape*, 365 U.S. 167 (1961), the Supreme Court determined policemen were personally liable as individuals, but the City of Chicago was not a person and, therefore, was not liable. Some 17 years later in *Monell v. New York City Department of Social Services*, 436 U.S. 658 (1978), the Supreme Court overturned *Monroe* and declared the word "person" included local government or institution.

§ 12.92   Absolute Immunity

The Supreme Court, in a series of cases, determined that absolute immunity was available as a defense for prosecutors in initiating and presenting the state's case, *Imbler v. Pachtman*, 424 U.S. 409 (1976), and state legislators, *Tenney v. Brandhove*, 341 U.S. 367 (1951).

§ 12.93   Qualified or Conditional Immunity

Prosecutors and legislators have absolute immunity; therefore, it may appear other state officials have absolute immunity. But in *Scheuer v. Rhodes*, 416 U.S. 232

(1974), the Supreme Court declared the Governor of Ohio and other state officials have only qualified or conditional immunity. Qualified or conditional immunity from civil liability means individuals would not be liable as long as they are acting clearly within the scope of their authority for the betterment of those they serve. If they venture outside the scope of their authority, and, in doing so, violate someone's rights, then they may be personally liable. The Supreme Court granted qualified immunity to the superintendents of state hospitals in *O'Connor v. Donaldson*, 422 U.S. 563 (1975) and for local school board members in *Wood v. Strickland*, 420 U.S. 308 (1975).

§ 12.94 Good Faith Immunity

Although individuals may assert good faith as a defense in a constitutional tort action, a municipality has no immunity and may not assert a good faith defense. *Owen v. City of Independence*, 445 U.S. 622 (1980).

§ 12.95 Actual and Punitive Damages

Generally, actual damages will be allowed, but not punitive damages. The Supreme Court "... had indicated that punitive damages might be awarded in appropriate circumstances in order to punish violations of constitutional rights ...," *Carey v. Piphus*, 435 U.S. 247 (1978). "... but it never suggested that punishment is as prominent a purpose under the statute as are compensation and deterrence." *City of Newport v. Fact Concerts, Inc.*, 453 U.S. 247 (1981).

CHAPTER 13

STUDENT RECORDS, DEFAMATION, AND PRIVACY

§ 13.1 INTRODUCTION

By the very nature of the educational process, educators are constantly dealing with sensitive matters involving students' private and personal affairs. Schools routinely collect and process information that can materially affect the student's life and prosperity. Personal information that is carelessly released may attach a stigma to a student's image in the community or may detract from the student's success in both future education and employment. The incorrect recording of a grade or idle gossip in inappropriate places can permanently cast a damaging shadow over one's reputation.

The law protects the student in three ways: First, school districts are required to handle and process student records in a careful and prescribed manner by federal statute, failure of which can result in the loss of federal funds. A number of states also have statutes mandating procedures in protecting the student's right of privacy. Second, students are protected through judicial precedents which form the law of defamation. Third, the student has a right of privacy at common law against invasion of privacy.

§ 13.2 THE FAMILY EDUCATIONAL RIGHTS AND PRIVACY ACT (FERPA)

The federal Family Educational Rights and Privacy Act (FERPA) of 1974, commonly known as the Buckley Amendment, prescribes standards for schools to follow in handling student records. 20 U.S.C. § 1232g. Parents are given the right to inspect all records that schools maintain on their children and are extended the opportunity to challenge the accuracy of the records. Parents must consent before the school can release the student's records to agencies outside designated educational categories. Consent may also be given by the student, in lieu of the parent, to release his or her own records upon the attainment of age 18 or upon entry to postsecondary school. School districts which do not follow the required procedures risk losing federal funds administered by the United States Department of Education. A school may release the records to the parent(s) of a dependent student if such parent(s) are financially supporting the student as provided under the Individual Revenue Code of 1986.

§ 13.21 Pre–FERPA

Before FERPA, students at times had difficulty in obtaining access to their school records. This was true, in spite of the fact that some courts had held that parents had a right of access to records unless such access was detrimental to the public interest. This right was explained by a New York court in 1961 when it ruled that "absent constitutional, legislative, or administrative permission or prohibition, a parent had the right to inspect the records of his child maintained by school authorities as required by law." *Van Allen v. McCleary*, 211 N.Y.S.2d 501 (1961). This court's rationale was based on the common law rule that a person with an interest in public records is entitled to inspect them.

In other cases, students were upheld in their attempts to have items removed from their records or communicated to third parties. In each instance, however, litigation was required to obtain redress for the parent or the student. School districts were generally without precedents of law or other guidelines on which they could rely. The Buckley Amendment thereafter introduced a required uniformity to the handling of student records both among school districts and institutions of higher education.

§ 13.22   Requirements of FERPA

Under the Family Educational Rights and Privacy Act (FERPA) each school district is required to publish a pupil records policy. Parents and students over age 18 must receive annual notification of this policy. The Act requires that each agency or institution establish procedures for granting access to school records within a reasonable period of time after the parental request. The reasonable period of time cannot exceed 45 days. The Act provides that "directory" information, date and place of birth, major field of study, participation in activities and sports, weight and height of members of athletic teams, dates of attendance, degrees and awards and most recent educational institution attended by the student, may be released by the school district without written consent of parents. But the Act also provides the school district must give notice of what categories are included in directory information. After the public notice, a parent may inform the school "... that any or all of the information designated should not be released without the parent's prior consent." Parental consent is not required for release of education records to: (1) other school officials and/or teachers in the school system who have legitimate educational interests, (2) officials of other schools or school systems in which the student seeks to enroll upon the condition that the student's parents are notified of the transfer of records, are given a copy, and have an opportunity to challenge the record, (3) authorized representatives of government including state education authorities, (4) financial aid officers in connection with a student's application for financial aid, (5) state and local officials collecting information required by state statutes adopted before November 19, 1974, (6) organizations conducting studies for, or on behalf of, educational agencies if personal identification of students is destroyed after no longer needed for the study, (7) accrediting organizations, (8) parents of a dependent student as defined by statute, and (9) the Secretary of Education for the purpose of maintaining regulations pertaining to the health and welfare of the student.

The policy of the school district must also accommodate other requirements of the act including several musts:

1. Records of individual students, containing "personally, identifiable information," must be kept confidential and cannot be released by the school without written consent of the parent or consent from the student if the student is over the age of 18.

2. Parents and guardians of students under age 18, and those students over 18 must have the right to inspect all school records concerning that student.

3. The school district record-keeping system must be described in sufficient detail for parents to locate their child's records.

4. School district staff members with access to student records must be identified by title.

5. Each child's file must include a record of access, which must be signed by each staff member whenever they withdraw that student's file.

6. Parents must have a right to appeal anything in a student's file that is considered incorrect, and if the school is not willing to delete the challenged material, the parents may request a hearing and/or provide a written statement to be attached to the challenged material.

In addition, treatment records "made or maintained by a physician, psychologist, or other recognized professional or paraprofessional acting in his or her professional capacity or assisting in a paraprofessional capacity" and used in the treatment of an eligible student may be excluded from the definition of "education records" in federal law and are not automatically accessible to the student.

An exception to the student record act (FERPA) is recognized for disclosures that were required by state statutes before enactment of the act. Further, "personal notes" that are defined as "not education records" are exempted from parental access. Personal notes are notes kept by an individual, such as a guidance counselor, to "jog the memory" when the child is counseled at a later date. These personal notes are not accessible to other school staff members and are available only to substitutes of the original note-writers.

In an IDEA suit where parents claimed that the child was denied a free and appropriate education, one of the issues the parents claimed was that FERPA had been violated. The assertion was that the classroom teacher had destroyed personal notes about the child at the end of the year. The court said the "personal notes" did not constitute "educational records" under FERPA. *J.P. v. West Clark Community Schools*, 230 F.Supp.2d 910 (S.D.Ind.2002). "FERPA was adopted to address systematic, not individual, violations of students' privacy by unauthorized releases of sensitive information in their educational records." *Jensen v. Reeves*, 45 F.Supp.2d 1265 (D.Utah 1999). "FERPA does not protect information which might appear in school records but would also be 'known by members of the school community through conversation and personal contact.' Congress could not have constitutionally prohibited comment on, or discussion of, facts about a student which were learned independently of his school records." *Frasca v. Andrews*, 463 F.Supp. 1043 (E.D.N.Y.1979). See also *Daniel S. v. Board of Education of York Community High School*, 152 F.Supp.2d 949 (N.D.Ill.2001).

Grades under the federal statute may only be challenged to insure they are not inaccurate, mathematically incorrect or do not reflect what the grader intended. *Tarka v. Cunningham*, 917 F.2d 890 (5th Cir.1990).

§ 13.23 No Child Left Behind Act of 2001

Both the No Child Left Behind Act and the National Defense Authorization Act for Fiscal Year 2002 "... requires high schools to provide military recruiters, upon request, access to secondary school students and directory information on those students." Even if the Local

Education Agency (LEA) does not disclose "directory information" under FERPA, which currently under FERPA is a LEA prerogative, it must still provide military recruiters access to secondary names, addresses and telephone listings. Parents must be given the opportunity to opt-out of providing directory information by the LEA. This information will be used specifically for armed service recruiting and informing students of scholarship opportunities. (Letter signed by Rod Paige, Secretary of Education, and Donald H. Rumsfeld, Secretary of Defense, October 9, 2002.)

§ 13.24   Individual Right to Damages

The redress for a plaintiff claiming that a school district violated provisions of FERPA is limited to injunctive relief by the courts and/or to the denial of federal funds to the school district. The question has also arisen as to whether a school district that had violated FERPA could be required by the courts to pay money damages to an aggrieved student or parent. This question has been answered in the negative by the U.S. Supreme Court in *Gonzaga University v. Doe*, 536 U.S. 273 (2002).

This case arose from an incident where administrators of Gonzaga University, a Catholic institution, overheard students discussing alleged sexual misconduct of another student, one John Doe. Later, when John Doe applied for his state teacher's certificate, the university declined to recommend him because of a lack of moral character. Doe sued the university for damages under FERPA and Section 1983 of the Civil Rights Act, 42 U.S.C. § 1983. The Supreme Court held that FERPA does not create enforceable individual rights. Parents and students may complain to the United States Department of Education

Family Policy Compliance Office (FPCO) regarding violations of the Act, but FERPA confers no direct private right of action to sue for damages. Chief Justice Rehnquist's opinion for the Court pointed out that nondisclosure provisions of FERPA "fail to confer enforceable rights." He said that the language of FERPA, unlike that of Title VI of the Civil Rights Act of 1964 and Title IX of the Education Amendments of 1972, only denies federal funds to the college or school district for improper disclosure of a student's records, and that such determination is to be made by the U.S. Secretary of Education and does not permit a private cause of action whereby a student or parent could bring an individual action for damages.

§ 13.25 Parental Rights

A natural parent has the right to review a student's records unless prohibited by a court order such as a divorce decree. In a case where a natural mother claimed a right, under FERPA, to her child's records, the parents were divorced and the court had given the father "the right to make all decisions regarding the child's health and safety while in his care during the school year." The court cited the implementing FERPA regulation which "specifically addresses the question of non-custodian parent's rights under the statute: 'An educational agency or institution shall give full rights under the Act to either parent, unless the agency or institution has been provided with evidence that there is a court order, state statute, or legally binding document relating to such matters as divorce, separation, or custody that specifically revokes these rights.' 34 C.F.R. § 99.4. In other words, the extent of [the parent's] rights under FERPA must be determined with reference to the rights [the parent] retained under the decree. The divorce decree clearly states that all legal rights over education lie with the father. The decision to bring a FERPA hearing to challenge the content of [the student's] records certainly falls within the authority given to the natural father to make educational determinations on behalf of [the student].... It is not necessary ... for the custody decree to state explicitly that it revokes 'FERPA rights,' nor recite the litany of all possible rights that have been abrogated. It is enough that the court determined that [the parent] no longer has authority to make decisions related to the education of her daughter. [The parent's] right to seek a hearing to challenge the content of her daughter's academic files has therefore been 'specifically revoked' within the meaning of the regulation." *Taylor v. Vermont Department of Education*, 313 F.3d 768 (2nd Cir.2002).

§ 13.26   Posting of Grades

It is a common practice to post student grades on the school door or to list them in other ways. In a recent case where a parent sought to compel a board of education to release all student grades in a third-grade class containing 75 students, the court held that disclosure of test scores, if scrambled and with names deleted, would sufficiently protect the privacy of students as required under FERPA. In this case the parents wanted to compare scores and were not interested in the grades being in any particular order. Relying on this rationale, it appears that teachers and school officials can continue to post grades so long as they cannot be identified by individual.

In a New York case, a conflict was created between the parent's right to view public records under the state's Freedom of Information Law, or public records act, and FERPA. The public records act requires school districts to release public information, while FERPA requires that school districts keep individual, personal student information private except upon request of the student's parent. This conflict was resolved by the definition of what is public as opposed to that which is private and personal. According to this decision, information that is not personally identifiable may be released under public records acts. *Kryston v. Board of Education, East Ramapo, etc.*, 430 N.Y.S.2d 688 (1980).

§ 13.27   Student–Graded Work

Can a teacher have students grade other student's papers or does FERPA prohibit such classroom practices? In answer to this question, the U.S. Supreme Court in a unanimous decision ruled that FERPA does not prohibit the practice of peer grading. *Owasso Independent School District No. I–011 v. Falvo*, 534 U.S. 426 (2002). The Court reasoned that student-graded work does not constitute an "education record" as material "maintained" by an educational institution or a person "acting for" the institution. The Court noted that student papers are not "maintained" by the institution and that students are not persons "acting for" the institution in maintaining educational records. The Court further pointed out that a contrary interpretation of FERPA "would impose substantial burdens on teachers across the country" in that it "would force all instructors to take time, which otherwise could be spent teaching and in preparation, to correct an assortment of daily student assignments."

Too, the Court narrowed the definition of "education records" to exclude student grades that had not yet been collected and recorded in the teacher's grade book. The decision, however, left open the question as to whether the teacher's grade book itself constitutes an "education record" under FERPA. Too, the Court did not decide whether a teacher's practice of calling out student grades in class is an impermissible release of records in violation of the Act.

§ 13.3 DEFAMATION

Anyone, a teacher, administrator, parent, or student, is capable of incurring liability by defaming other persons. Words are defamatory if they impute to another dishonesty, immorality, vice or dishonorable conduct which engenders an evil opinion of one in the minds of others in the community. Defamation is generally understood to be injury by calumny or by false aspersion of another's reputation. Defamation is anything which tends to injure one's character or reputation. Where school employees were dismissed from their positions and subsequently claimed that the dismissal had effectively defamed them, the Court rejected their claims because the events and statements surrounding the dismissals were "neither scurrilous nor inflammatory" so as to cause damage or subject them to ridicule. *Brammer–Hoelter v. Twin Peaks Charter Academy*, 81 F.Supp.2d 1090 (D.Colo.2000).

The distinction between "criticism" and "defamation" is that criticism is addressed to public matters and does not follow a person into his or her private life. A true critic never indulges in personal ridicule but confines his or her comments to the merits of the particular subject matter under discussion.

Defamation is not itself a legal cause of action but encompasses two causes, the twin torts of libel and slander. Libel is written defamation and slander is spoken. Speaking defamatory words to a newspaper reporter may ultimately involve both slander and libel if the speaker intends his words to "be embodied forthwith in a physical form" and the words do, in fact, appear in a newspaper article. *Tallent v. Blake*, 291 S.E.2d 336 (N.C.App.1982).

§ 13.31 Libel

Libel is an accusation in writing or printing against the character of a person which affects his or her reputation and tends to hold him or her up to shame or disgrace. *Stevens v. Wright*, 179 A. 213 (Vt.1935). Libel must be false, unprivileged, and malicious to be actionable. Publication is required for libel to exist. This does not mean publication in the mass media, but may be constituted by written communication which tends to harm one's reputation in the community. A note written to a third party or a secretary typing and reading a letter may constitute publication.

Communication sufficient to establish libel may be conveyed by sign, mark, movie reel, videotape, picture, or effigy. The communication may be actionable if it holds a person up to ridicule, contempt, disgrace, obloquy, or shame in the eyes of the community.

§ 13.32 Slander

Slander is the speaking of base and defamatory words tending to create an unfavorable impression in the mind of a third party. To constitute slander there must be conveyance by words of disparagement of character of one to a third party. Plaintiff must show that there was a third party communication. Words spoken only to the offended party cannot constitute slander. If a third party overhears defamatory words, slander may be established.

There are two types of slander, slander *per se* and slander *per quod*. Words which in and of themselves, without extrinsic proof, injure one's reputation are defamatory *per se*. Defamation *per se* does not require proof of actual damage. With defamation *per se*, the plaintiff's cause of action is complete when he or she proves that the words have been articulated and conveyed. The plaintiff is not required to prove actual injury or out-of-pocket monetary loss, but rather must merely show that the words were of such a kind as to impair one's reputation or standing in the community or to cause personal anguish, suffering or humiliation. The plaintiff need not prove that he or she suffered special harm of direct loss.

Under American common law today, an action for defamation *per se* will lie without proof of special harm (damage) where there exists (1) imputation of a criminal offense punishable by imprisonment, or imputation of guilt of a crime involving moral turpitude; (2) imputation of venereal or other loathsome or communicable disease; (3) imputation of conduct, characteristics, or a condition incompatible with proper conduct of lawful business, trade, or profession, or a public or private offense; and/or (4) imputation of unchastity of a woman.

If the plaintiff is unable to bring his or her case under one of these categories, he or she must resort to proving special harm or actual damages by the communication of defamation *per quod*. Defamation *per quod* requires that the plaintiff prove actual damage. The plaintiff must show that publication of the defamation was the legal cause of special harm. The distinction between defamation *per se* and *per quod* may rest on whether a crime is imputed. For example, the law holds that it is defamation *per quod,* and special damages must be proven if the words imputed to a teacher appear to harm the teacher's reputation but do not relate to conduct of a crime, moral turpitude, unchastity, or damage the teacher in his or her profession. To say that a male teacher seduced a female student would, of course, be defamation *per se*. On the other hand, where a defendant had accused a headmaster of committing adultery with the school custodian's wife, the court found that the words had not been uttered in the context of the school nor in reference to the plaintiff as schoolmaster, and thus, the charge could not be defamation *per se*. A showing of special and actual damage was necessary, a burden the plaintiff could not sustain. Yet because a teacher's reputation among students and the community is so vital to performance of his or her professional responsibilities, it is easy to see how, in the majority of cases, false imputations against a teacher could fall into the category of defamation *per se*.

In an interesting case where a ninth-grade student worked part-time as a maintenance worker for his school system, and he later learned, after graduation, that a school board member had said that "he was such a bad worker that we had to fire him," the student, who wanted to become a teacher, sued the school board member for slander. The trial court granted a summary judgment motion for the board member because the graduate, when asked during deposition if he believed his reputation had been harmed, answered in the negative, saying "[a]t the present time, no." Based on this information the trial court concluded that there had been no damage to him. The appeals court, in upholding the trial court's decision, pointed out that a statement is defamatory if it tends to harm the reputation of another person in a way that lowers the estimation of the person in the community. There was no evidence that such denigration of the graduate had transpired and, in such case, slander is not actionable without proof of actual damages. In short, the Court applied the *per quod* standard in rejecting the graduate's complaints. *Janusz v. Olen*, 610 N.W.2d 511 (Wis.App.2000).

§ 13.33   Public Officials/Public Figures

Since *New York Times v. Sullivan*, 376 U.S. 254 (1964), a 1964 United States Supreme Court decision, the law of defamation as it pertains to freedom of speech and press has changed considerably. This case, and subsequent ones, holds the interest of the publisher to be of vital importance to a free and informed society. In *Sullivan*, a paid advertisement in the *New York Times* signed by a number of prominent individuals criticized the behavior of the Montgomery, Alabama, police in dealing with racial unrest. The police chief, Sullivan, claimed that the derogatory reference to police behavior amounted to defamation of him personally. The Alabama State Supreme Court held that the publication was libel *per se* and that the *New York Times* was liable for one-half million dollars without the plaintiff showing special damage or fault on the part of the *Times*.

The U.S. Supreme Court reversed the lower court, holding that the guarantee of free speech under the First Amendment prohibits a *public official* from recovering damages for a defamatory falsehood relating to his *offi-*

cial conduct, unless he proves that the statement was made with malice and that the statement was made with knowledge that it was false or in reckless disregard of whether it was false or not. This protection extended to both the newspaper and to the private persons who paid for the advertisement and signed it. Plaintiffs in the case were unable to show that the *New York Times* actually had knowledge of the falsity of portions of the statement. A major question is whether the individual is a public official. The determination is made on a case-by-case situation. The Supreme Court in *Sullivan* said, "We have no occasion here to determine how far down into the lower ranks of government employees the 'public official' designation would extend for purposes of this rule, or otherwise to specify categories of persons who would or would not be included."

Shortly after the *Sullivan* case, the U.S. Supreme Court expanded the definition of *"public officials"* to include *"public figures"* in *Curtis Publishing Co. v. Butts*, 388 U.S. 130 (1967). Butts, a former University of Georgia football coach, was accused by a major news magazine of giving away football secrets to the University of Alabama football coach. The Supreme Court concluded that public figures who commanded "a substantial amount of public interest at the time of publications in question" were subject to the same burden of proof as public officials. A public figure is someone who injects himself into an ongoing public controversy and tries to impact the outcome of that controversy. Thus, the plaintiff must show malice and knowledge of or reckless disregard for the falsity of the publication. The law requires proof of knowledge or conscious indifference to falsity when imputations are made denigrating either public officials or public figures.

Where a private person is offended by the press, liability may be incurred by merely showing that the statement was untruthful, not that it was made with malice nor that the newspaper knew that it was false so long as liability is not imposed without *fault*. Whenever liability is imposed against the press for false publication, the damages must be limited to the actual injury sustained; general or punitive damages are not available.

The courts are split as to whether a teacher is a public official with a slight majority ruling they are not. This is a most important issue since teachers do not need to prove malice if they are not public officials. As stated in *Sullivan,* "a public figure may not recover damages for a defamatory falsehood without clear and convincing proof that the false statement was made with 'actual malice'— that is, with knowledge that it was false or with reckless disregard of whether it was false or not." Imputations against a teacher by the student press would be actionable if the teacher shows that the student publisher was at fault by directing the defamation toward the teacher. Similarly, students cannot attack other students or school administrators personally without potential consequences. Yet, a former school board member running in a school board election is considered to be a public figure under the *Sullivan* precedent. *Fisher v. Larsen*, 188 Cal.Rptr. 216 (App.1982).

The courts are split on whether a school principal is a public official. In *Ellerbee v. Mills*, 422 S.E.2d 539 (Ga. 1992), the Supreme Court of Georgia ruled a high school principal "... is not a public official under the standard of *New York Times, Co. v. Sullivan* ..." nor is he a public figure as defined by *Gertz v. Robert Welch, Inc.*, 418 U.S. 323 (1974). The principal was found not to be a public figure in *McCutcheon v. Moran*, 425 N.E.2d 1130 (Ill.App.1981); *East Canton Educ. Assoc. v. McIntosh*, 709 N.E.2d 468 (Ohio 1999); *Goodwin v. Kennedy*, 552 S.E.2d 319 (S.C.App.2001); *Beeching v. Levee*, 764 N.E.2d 669 (Ind.App.2002). This conclusion is in contrast to *Johnson v. Robbinsdale Ind. Sch. Dist. No. 281*, 827 F.Supp. 1439 (D.Minn.1993), where the court found an elementary principal to be a public figure. The *Johnson* court decision is in agreement with *Palmer v. Bennington School Dist.*, 615 A.2d 498 (Vt.1992); *Kapiloff v. Dunn*, 343 A.2d 251 (Md.App.1975); *Reaves v. Foster*, 200 So.2d 453 (Miss.1967); and *Junior–Spence v. Keenan*, 1990 WL 17241 (Tenn.App.1990). *State v. Defley*, 395 So.2d 759 (La.1981); *Andreucci v. Foresteire*, 1998 WL 1184151 (Mass.Super.1998); and *Jee v. New York Post Co., Inc.*, 671 N.Y.S.2d 920 (1998).

§ 13.34 Truth

Defamation constitutes harm of reputation by denigrating a person in the minds of others by falsehood. Falsification is the basic ingredient of the tort of defamation. It follows then that conveyance of truth is not defamation. In some states, courts have held that truth is a defense for libel only when published with good motives and justifiable ends. *Farnsworth v. Tribune Co.*, 253 N.E.2d 408 (Ill.1969) ruled that a person will not be allowed to resurrect a long forgotten mistake of another and republish it. The prevailing view is, though, that truth of a defamatory statement affords a complete defense to defamation regardless of whether ill will or malice is present. "One who publishes a defamatory statement of fact is not subject to liability for defamation if the statement is true." *Restatement 2d, Torts*, § 581A (1977).

Under common law tort where the plaintiff is a private person, a defamatory statement is presumed to be false and the defendant must prove that the statement was true. The burden of proof is on the defendant.

As explained above, if the plaintiff is a "public official" or "public figure," the burden of proof shifts. The "public person" must present clear and convincing proof to the court that defendant published false, defamatory information with knowledge of its falsity or with reckless disregard for the truth. Thus, if a teacher has been the brunt of a defamatory statement, then the burden of proving truth is on the defendant because a teacher is generally a private person. If, for example, a parent or student published defamatory information about a teacher, the burden would be on the parent or student to prove the statement is true.

One may conceive of a situation where a teacher could be a public figure if he or she had won fame for some reason, but this is generally not the case. Such fame may be localized; however, several courts have ruled high school coaches are public figures because of the athletic publicity. So long as the teacher does not acquire the status of a public personage, the burden of proving truth would be on the defendant if the publication did harm to the teacher.

§ 13.35 Absolute Privilege

Public policy requires that certain persons or officials in society be afforded absolute privilege against liability for defamation. Judges, attorneys, witnesses in court, legislators, and certain other public officials are vested with absolute protection for utterances or writings which are given in the course of conduct of public affairs and include: (1) judicial proceedings, (2) legislative proceedings, and (3) executive proceedings. See Laurence H. Eldredge, *The Law of Defamation* (The Bobbs–Merrill Company, Inc., Charlottesville, Va.), pp. 339–532.

§ 13.36 Teachers Have a Conditional Privilege

Courts have found it necessary to extend limited privileges to other persons in society where the public interest requires such protection. Such *conditional* or *qualified* privileges are extended to teachers and school administrators as well as to other public servants who are charged with duties which require them to handle sensitive information, which is important not only to the individual but to the public generally. Rationale for such protection may be stated as follows: "In order that the information may be freely given, it is necessary to afford protection against liability for misinformation given in an appropriate effort to protect or advance the interest in question. If protection were not given, true information that should be given or received would not be communicated because of fear of the persons capable of giving it that they would be held liable in an action of defamation if their statements were untrue." *Restatement 2d, Torts*, § 592A at 258, Topic 3, Scope Note.

The degree of protection afforded by the conditional or qualified privilege is determined by the courts in weighing on "one hand society's need for free disclosure without fear of civil suit, and, on the other hand, an individual's right to recover for damage to his reputation.…" *Weissman v. Mogol*, 462 N.Y.S.2d 383 (1983).

The conditional privilege negates any presumption of implied malice emanating from the defamatory statement and places the burden on the plaintiff to show proof of actual malice. *Weissman v. Mogol*, supra. One can easily see that teachers would be hesitant to convey any information at all about students if no privilege existed. Without such conditional privilege, school reports, both academic and disciplinary, would hold great potential for legal actions against teachers.

In order for the privilege of the teacher or administrator to withstand challenge, the communication must have been made (1) in good faith, without malice, and within the scope of the students, teachers, or public's interest in the good conduct of the school; (2) in the honest belief that the information conveyed was true, with knowledge that any communication brought about a student was made with reasonable and probable grounds; and (3) in response to a legitimate inquiry by one with the right to know about a student's educational or personal qualifications, the answer must not go beyond that which is required to satisfy the inquiry.

§ 13.37   Parents Have a Conditional Privilege

Parents have a conditional or a qualified privilege to speak publicly before a school board regarding teacher's instruction of his or her children. It is within the right of parents to oversee their children's education to make statements pertaining to a teacher's competency or inefficiency in the classroom. If, however, the statements are untrue and made with "actual or express malice, then the privilege is destroyed." *Nodar v. Galbreath*, 462 So.2d 803 (Fla.1984).

In a case where a parent, who was also a teacher, informed the school principal about male teachers allegedly fondling girl students, the court said the teacher/parent had a qualified privilege. No malice was found because the parent/teacher had been told by girls of the alleged events and written statements were obtained to that effect. *Desselle v. Guillory,* 407 So.2d 79 (La.App. 1981).

§ 13.38 Teachers, Malice and Truth

Malice is indicated where the defendant conveys false information which is not reasonably germane to the subject matter of the occasion; then the scope of the conditional privilege has been exceeded. For example, a teacher's privilege does not extend to communication about a student's personal love life outside of school if it has no bearing on his or her school conduct. In such instances, technically, a teacher does not abuse his or her privilege but, instead, exceeds the protection of the privilege. Volunteering excessive information not bearing on the school's or the student's interests is hazardous. For a court to deduce malice "requires at a minimum that the statements were made with reckless disregard for truth." *Hugger v. Rutherford Institute,* 94 Fed. Appx. 162 (4th Cir. 2004).

Where a teacher conveys erroneous information about a student but believes the communication is truthful then the privileged occasion of the teacher will not be foregone. Statements by teachers must be motivated by a desire to protect the interest of the student or the school and, if so taken, then an honest belief that the communication is true will be protected. The fact that the teacher is unintentionally mistaken is, in this case, immaterial.

Too, the teacher may be compelled to show that reasonable or probable grounds were available to support the truthfulness or belief in the truthfulness of the communication.

§ 13.39   Teacher's Legitimate Inquiry

Legitimate inquiry regarding a student's educational performance may be made by other teachers, school administrators within the same school or school districts, as well as by educational and employment agencies outside the school or school district proper. The Buckley Amendment (FERPA) discussed above in this chapter gives good guidelines in this regard. At common law, a teacher is protected if communication is given in response to proper inquiry.

If information were to be given about a student to a third party who had no legitimate interest in the student, then, if the communication is defamatory, the teacher may be liable. Thus, a teacher may abuse and lose the conditional privilege by carelessly releasing false information about students.

§ 13.4   RIGHT OF PRIVACY

A legal question of privacy, however, may arise beyond statute or common law defamation. Invasion of privacy may be a separate and independent tort. As a new area of law, invasion of privacy has come into focus in recent years from hundreds of cases which have emerged in which a person's privacy has been invaded and their private lives have become subject to unwanted public exposure.

According to Prosser in his *Handbook of the Law of Torts* (3rd ed. 1964), Ch. 22, p. 832, the common law right of privacy is "not one tort, but a complex of four. The law of privacy comprises four distinct kinds of invasion of four different interests of the plaintiff, but otherwise have almost nothing in common except that each represents an interference with the right of the plaintiff 'to be let alone.' " The four different kinds of invasion of privacy are: "(a) unreasonable intrusion upon the seclusion of another, ... (b) appropriation of the other's name or likeness, ... (c) unreasonable publicity given to the other's private life, ... (d) publicity which unreasonably places the other in a false light before the public, ..." *Restatement 2d, Torts*, § 652A, 1967. Invasion of the right of privacy may result from any of the four or there may be overlapping or concurrent invasion.

The law of privacy was relied on by plaintiffs in a Maryland case where parents claimed that the release of their child's psychological records to another school upon transfer subjected the child to unreasonable publicity and unreasonably placed her in a false light before the public. *Klipa v. Board of Education of Anne Arundel County*, 460 A.2d 601 (Md.App.1983). Parents had asked that the girl's records be transferred, but had specifically requested that the psychological portion of the records not be sent. Parents had signed a consent form to transfer the records in which no reference was made to psychological records. The school psychologist had agreed not to send the psychological records, but due to a clerical error of another employee, the records were mailed anyway.

The court in ruling for the defendant school district held that the fact that parents had signed a consent form for the records, but had not specifically released the psychological records, was irrelevant because the school district had no legal obligation to obtain parental consent for the transfer. The evidence made it clear that the records were mailed directly to the principal of the school to which the girl transferred and were delivered by him to the custody of the chief school guidance counselor; thereafter, the records remained under lock and key. Further, no evidence was presented which indicated that the student was exposed to unwarranted publicity. In applying the four legal conditions under which invasion of privacy can occur, the court found that there was no invasion of something secret, secluded or private, as required by the first and second types of invasion. The school had validly obtained the information in the first instance. There was no publicity as required under the third and fourth types of invasion and there was no falsity or fiction involved as required under the third kind of invasion. Neither was the information used for the defendant's advantage as is required by the fourth condition. On the contrary, the information regarding the student's psychological background and prior behavioral pattern was vital and necessary for the school to plan for an appropriate educational program and to address the student's social and emotional needs.

CHAPTER 14

STUDENT TESTING

§ 14.1 INTRODUCTION

The state has the authority to set standards for promotion and graduation in public school programs and to establish criteria by which students are to be evaluated. One of the most commonly used criteria is, of course, some type of examination. Boards of education have the right, if not a positive duty, to develop reasonable means to determine the effectiveness of their educational programs, with respect to all individual students to whom they issue diplomas, and that tests are a reasonable means of accomplishing this purpose. *Brookhart v. Illinois State Board of Education*, 697 F.2d 179 (7th Cir. 1983). Public schools may set standards and require adherence to those standards. *Bester v. Tuscaloosa City Board of Education*, 722 F.2d 1514 (11th Cir.1984).

§ 14.2 JUDICIAL REVIEW OF STUDENT EVALUATIONS

The courts have been reluctant to substitute their judgment in academic matters for that of school officials. The United States Supreme Court has distinguished between judicial review of academic and disciplinary measures taken by school authorities saying that "Courts are particularly ill-equipped to evaluate academic performance." *Board of Curators, University of Missouri v. Horowitz*, 435 U.S. 78 (1978).

The inappropriateness of judicial intervention in student evaluations has long been documented by judicial precedent. In 1913 a Massachusetts court refused to substitute its judgment for that of school authorities who had not allowed a student to continue in school because of his poor academic performance. "The care and management of schools which is vested in the school committee includes the establishment and maintenance of standards for the promotion of pupils from one grade to another and for their continuance as members of any particular class. So long as the school committee acts in good faith their conduct in formulating and applying standards and making decisions touching this matter is not subject to review by any other tribunal." *Barnard v. Inhabitants of Shelburne*, 102 N.E. 1095 (Mass.1913).

Pupil evaluation is essential to the conduct of schools, and testing is considered to be an appropriate means of determining educational effectiveness of the school and the achievement of the pupil. Unless the school enunciates a level of academic attainment for the student and measures student progress toward that level, "no certification of graduation can have any meaning whatsoever." *Brookhart v. Illinois State Board of Education*, supra.

Accordingly, the reluctance of the Courts to substitute their judgments for those of teachers, administrators, and publicly elected school board members is a basic tenet of judicial philosophy, even though examples to the contrary are legion. The enunciated policy of nonintervention by the courts, however, normally remains the rule where schools act rationally pursuant to a legitimate academic purpose and a fundamental constitutional right of a student is not denied. For a student to sustain a claim against a school board for academic decisions such as denial of promotion because of failure on tests or grades, the student must document a cognizable constitutional loss. A student's mere showing that he or she was not promoted does not constitute such a loss. *Erik V. By and Through Catherine V. v. Causby*, 977 F.Supp. 384 (E.D.N.C.1997).

The general view of the courts was set out in *Gaspar v. Bruton*, 513 F.2d 843 (10th Cir.1975), where it was said that "the courts are not equipped to review academic records based upon academic standards within the particular knowledge, experience, and expertise of academicians.... The court may grant relief, as a practical matter, only in those cases where the student presents positive evidence of ill will or bad motive." See also *Clements v. Nassau County*, 835 F.2d 1000 (2d Cir.1987).

§ 14.3 LIMITATIONS ON THE SCHOOL

A child's constitutional rights, however, may place limitations on the school's prerogatives in employing tests as standards of academic attainment. In recent years states have used competency tests to gauge students' progress. Such tests have been employed as the criterion by which students are advanced, remediated, or placed in special educational programs. Courts have always exercised their power to overturn the determinations of school boards where a student could show that an academic decision was arbitrary or capricious or was motivated by bad faith or ill will unrelated to academic performance. The burden of proof, however, has heretofore been on the plaintiff to show that the action was taken without due regard for the welfare of the student. The Due Process and Equal Protection Clauses of the

Constitution have been applied to competency tests when a student's movement from grade to grade would be affected or when graduation would be delayed or denied.

However, there is probably a difference in the judicial view of actual graduation versus the graduation ceremony. An Alabama court apparently concluded that the physical walking across the stage at graduation is not a constitutionally protected interest. Thus, participating in a graduation ceremony and receipt of a diploma may not be the same in the eyes of the courts. *L.I. by Wanda I. v. Montgomery County School Board*, No. CV–98–A–597–N (N.D.Ala.1998).

§ 14.4   COMPETENCY TESTS

Recent state legislation requiring educational accountability for minimal competency tests has been the impetus for litigation challenging testing. The purpose of such test legislation is to assure that (a) students have mastered certain skills, (b) students with deficiencies have been identified, and (c) students are provided the appropriate types of classroom instruction. Passage of a minimum competency test means that a student has reached the prescribed level of proficiency on a series of skills.

Legislation requiring competency tests generally assumes that tests are an appropriate method of measuring the attainment of the required skills. Such tests have been used as the prerequisite for obtaining a high school diploma, promotion from grade to grade, and placement of students in remedial programs. The failure to progress normally through school or the denial of a diploma may be of such importance as to invoke strict judicial scrutiny if the student's constitutional rights are threatened. The constitutional rights which may be at stake include substantive due process and/or equal protection. *Debra P. v. Turlington*, 644 F.2d 397 (5th Cir.1981).

§ 14.5 STUDENTS' DUE PROCESS INTERESTS

The United States Supreme Court has made it clear that a high school diploma is of such personal importance that its denial may be tantamount to denial of "liberty or property" under the Fourteenth Amendment. The Court observed in *Board of Regents v. Roth*, 408 U.S. 564 (1972), that property interests are not bestowed lightly. "To have a property interest in a benefit, a person clearly must have more than an abstract need or desire for it. He must have more than a unilateral expectation of it. He must, instead, have a legitimate claim of entitlement to it." The property interest must be founded on a state-created benefit which is available to all persons in the same circumstance. Such interests emanate from "rules and understandings that secure certain benefits and that support claims of entitlement to those benefits."

A person's interest in receiving a public education is beyond a mere "unilateral expectation," it is essential to success in today's society. A high school diploma is a means to social and economic mobility. Also, the high school diploma is a prerequisite to admission to higher education. Thus, public education which culminates in the all important diploma may be viewed as an entitlement to every citizen. However, even though a person has a property interest in public education and, ultimately, in a high school diploma, this interest can be denied if a student does not perform to expectations. Public education and the diploma can be denied by following judicial requirements of procedural due process.

The Supreme Court in *Board of Curators of the University of Missouri v. Horowitz*, 435 U.S. 78 (1978), refused to extend procedural due process rights to a medical student before she was dismissed from school because of less than adequate clinical performance. The Court stated: "Academic evaluations of a student, in contrast to disciplinary determinations, bear little resemblance to the judicial and administrative fact-finding proceedings to which we have traditionally attached a full-hearing requirement. In *Goss*, the school's decision to suspend the students rested on factual conclusions that the individual students had participated in demonstrations that had disrupted classes, attacked a police officer, or caused physical damage to school property. The requirement of a hearing, where the student could present his side of the factual issue, could under such circumstances 'provide a meaningful hedge against erroneous action.' The decision to dismiss respondent [Horowitz], by comparison, rested on the academic judgment of school officials that she did not have the necessary clinical ability to perform adequately as a medical doctor and was making insufficient progress toward that goal. Such a judgment is by its nature more subjective and evaluative than the typical factual questions presented in the average disciplinary decision. Like the decision of an individual professor as to the proper grade for a student in his course, the determination whether to dismiss a student for academic reasons requires an expert evaluation of cumulative information and is not readily adapted to the procedural tools of judicial or administrative decision-making."

"Under such circumstances, we decline to ignore the historic judgment of educators and thereby formalize the academic dismissal process by requiring a hearing. The educational process is not by nature adversary; instead, it centers around a continuing relationship between faculty and students, 'one in which the teacher must occupy many roles—educator, adviser, friend, and, at times, parent-substitute.' ... In *Goss*, this Court concluded that the value of some form of hearing in a disciplinary context outweighs any resulting harm to the academic environment. Influencing this conclusion was clearly the belief that disciplinary proceedings in which the teacher must decide whether to punish a student for disruptive or insubordinate behavior may automatically bring an adversary flavor to the normal student-teacher relationship. The same conclusion does not follow in the academic context. We decline to further enlarge the judicial presence in the academic community and thereby risk deterioration of many beneficial aspects of the faculty-student relationship."

Failure of student academic expectations comes in many forms. Where high school students photocopied significant portions of paper from reference sources and were charged with plagiarism, they were given zeros for the project and suit was launched. The Court ruled that the students had not established that any protected property or liberty interests were involved. Citing *Horowitz*, the Court stated "The judiciary should exercise even greater restraint in cases involving academic discipline in contrast to expulsions or suspensions." *Zellman v. Independent School District No. 2758*, 594 N.W.2d 216 (Minn.App.1999).

While the Supreme Court has answered the question of whether procedural due process applies in academic matters, it did not address the substantive due process issues. In 1985 this question was answered. The Court stated: "In ... *Horowitz* ... we assumed, without deciding, that federal courts can review an academic decision of a public educational institution under a substantive due process standard." The Court assumed that the student had a substantive property right under the due process clauses to continued enrollment. This right could not be taken away for an arbitrary reason, but "... university faculties have a wide range of discretion in making judgments as to academic performance of students." *Regents of University of Michigan v. Ewing*, 474 U.S. 214 (1985).

The courts, however, have held that the nature of substantive due process review does not apply to subjective judgments about academic qualifications.

§ 14.6 EQUAL PROTECTION RIGHTS

Beyond due process, students are also entitled to constitutional protection against unjustified discrimination. If a test is racially discriminatory, its use is violative of the Equal Protection Clause of the Fourteenth Amendment. In 1967, a federal judge in Washington, D.C., held that the use of tests for "tracking" of students was unconstitutional. *Hobson v. Hansen*, 269 F.Supp. 401 (D.D.C.1967). The court had found that the use of tests to assign students to ability groups resulted in black students being relegated to lower curricular levels and little opportunity was provided them to improve their position by moving upward from level to level. The court concluded with regard to testing that "teachers acting under false assumptions because of low test scores will treat the disadvantaged student in such a way as to make him conform to their low expectations ... creating a self-fulfilling prophecy based on false assumptions that black students are intellectually inferior."

A similar decision in California in 1972 found that the use of non-validated I.Q. tests to evaluate students for placement in classes for the educable mentally retarded violated federal statutes and the equal protection clauses of the United States and California Constitutions. The school administrators could not show that there was a relationship between the I.Q. tests and the intellectual capabilities of the black students. *P. v. Riles*, 343 F.Supp. 1306 (N.D.Cal.1972).

In 1984 the Ninth Circuit reversed the decision on the federal and state constitutional issue but affirmed on statutory grounds. *Larry P. By Lucille P. v. Riles*, 793 F.2d 969 (9th Cir.1984). The court stated that " ... provisions of the Rehabilitation Act and the Education for All Handicapped Children Act [were violated] (1) by not insuring that the tests were validated for the specific purpose for which they were used, and (2) by not using the variety of statutorily mandated evaluation tools." To determine whether the children's rights under Title VI of the 1964 Civil Rights Act were violated, the court applied the "discriminatory *effect* analysis." A disproportionate number of black children were placed in the EMR class and the school could not prove the disproportionate placements were required by an educational necessity.

The court found that there was no proof of discriminatory intent which would be required to establish a violation of constitutional rights.

§ 14.61　Effect vs. Intent

The *Hobson* and *Larry P.* cases, referred to above, rested on the judicial assumption that if the "effect" of a test was to create a racially disparate placement of students, the use of the tests was unconstitutional unless school officials could show that the test measured what it was supposed to measure, was not biased, and was required by an educational necessity.

However, in the United States Supreme Court in 1976, *Washington v. Davis*, 426 U.S. 229 (1976), established a higher standard than a mere effect test to be applied when analyzing a constitutional violation. According to *Davis*, the plaintiff must prove discriminatory intent. In this case the Court upheld a written test of verbal knowledge used to select recruits for the District of Columbia police force even though the test resulted in disqualification of a much higher percentage of black applicants than whites. The Court found that racially disparate results alone were not enough to invalidate selection based on test scores for a constitutional violation. The standard adopted by the Court was one of "intent"; plaintiffs must show that government has a racially discriminatory intent or purpose in order to have the test set aside. (See Chapter 15, Teacher Tests.)

§ 14.62　Academic Grouping

In applying the intent test of *Davis*, the courts have held that school achievement tests may be constitutionally appropriate academic tools for actually measuring achievement. The U.S. Court of Appeals for the Eleventh Circuit has held that the use of achievement tests for the purpose of academic grouping does not violate the Equal

Protection Clause. *Georgia State Conference of Branches of NAACP v. State of Georgia*, 775 F.2d 1403 (11th Cir.1985).

"[T]he practice of achievement grouping is not, *per se*, unconstitutional. Under proper circumstances, courts have approved the practice. Indeed, in some cases, courts have directed the use of special groups, particularly where concentrated remedial counseling is required to overcome language difficulties." The mere fact that scholastic achievement tests result in the placement of a disproportionately greater number of white students than black in advance placement courses does not indicate racial discrimination. If a school district has operated a unitary school system and can, thus, show that the ability grouping is not caused by past discrimination, then the black students' rights are not violated. *Montgomery v. Starkville Municipal Separate School District*, 854 F.2d 127 (5th Cir.1988).

§ 14.7 VALIDITY OF TESTS

In 1978, the Florida Legislature enacted a law requiring that public school students pass a functional literacy examination in order to receive a high school diploma. Shortly afterward students challenged the test maintaining that it violated both the due process and equal protection clauses of the Fourteenth Amendment. A federal district court held for the students and enjoined the use of the test to withhold diplomas until the 1982–83 school year. *Debra P. v. Turlington*, 474 F.Supp. 244 (M.D.Fla.1979). On appeal the Fifth Circuit Court of Appeals affirmed the lower court's findings. *Debra P. v. Turlington*, 644 F.2d 397 (5th Cir.1981). The Circuit

Court, however, remanded the case for further factual findings on two key issues: (a) the instructional validity of the test (the Florida Student State Assessment Test, Part II) and (b) the vestiges of racial discrimination questions.

The validity issue was succinctly stated by the court as being whether the "test is a fair test of that which was taught." Accordingly, if the test was not fair, then it could not be rationally related to a legitimate state interest and therefore would be violative of the Equal Protection Clause. The state presented evidence showing that the subjects tested paralleled the curricular goals of the state. Instructional programs of all the school districts addressed the skills for which the test was designed and the state-approved instructional materials were used in all districts to implement the state prescribed curricular objectives. Further, local school districts reported that the skills required to pass the test were included in their curriculum and that a substantial number of public school teachers responded to a questionnaire and stated that they actually taught the prescribed curriculum. The court held that this intensive verification of instructional validity was sufficient to withstand constitutional challenge.

The court rejected the plaintiff's argument that the state must show that each teacher, individually, actually teaches the prescribed curriculum. "What is required," the court said, "is that the skills be included in the official curriculum and that the majority of the teachers recognize them as being something they should teach." *Debra P. v. Turlington*, 564 F.Supp. 177 (M.D.Fla.1983). The court further elaborated, in rejecting plaintiff's contentions, that "It strains credibility to hypothesize that teachers, especially remedial teachers, are uniformly avoiding their responsibilities at the expense of their pupils."

Tests that are not validated for the purpose for which they are used may violate the Equal Protection Clause or Title IX of the 1972 Education Amendments. This was the situation in New York where the Scholastic Aptitude Test (SAT) was used to award scholarships to college. Such use of the test was challenged by female students who claimed that the test discriminated because females won disproportionately fewer scholarships. The legislature defended the use of the test by maintaining that the tests were a valid means of determining superior high school achievement. The court held for the female students. Upon examining the evidence, the court found that the SAT had been statistically validated to predict college academic performance, but had never been validated as a means of past high school academic achievement. The court in holding against the state ruled that the state must show that the SAT does, in fact, measure high school performance if the test is to be used as a device to reward such performance. Without showing such a relationship, the test is invalid. *Sharif v. New York State Education Department*, 709 F.Supp. 345 (S.D.N.Y.1989).

§ 14.71 Race and Tests

Concerning the vestiges of racial discrimination issue, the court in *Debra P.* had originally deferred the effective date of the test until 1983 because Florida public schools had not been fully integrated until 1970, and the court wanted to assure that all black students would have had the opportunity to attend integrated schools for a full twelve years. With regard to racial segregation, the court enunciated the rule that the use of a particular test "can be enjoined only if it perpetuates the effects of past school segregation or if it is not needed to remedy those effects." In applying this standard, the court was unable to find that the tests were offensive to equal protection; on the contrary, because the tests identified students who did not have the necessary skills and provided remedial instruction for them, the court was of the opinion that use of the basic literacy test was an important factor in eradicating vestiges of past racial discrimination.

Thus, competency tests are acceptable instruments to measure student performance, even if the effect is for higher percentages of black students than white to fail. According to *Debra P.,* however, the state must be prepared to go to substantial lengths to document the validity of the tests given, and provision must be made for those students failing the test to be given remedial assistance in overcoming their deficiencies.

The Equal Protection and Due Process Clauses of the Fourteenth Amendment and Title VI of the Civil Rights Act of 1964 have been invoked by minority students in challenging state testing programs. In recent years, post-*Debra P.*, the courts have been reluctant to upset state testing regimes and, too, states have generally been guarded and very cognizant of possible deleterious effects of tests on children of minority groups. For example, a question of racial discrimination arose in Texas where the Texas Assessment of Academic Skills (TAAS) has been administered throughout the decade of the 1990s to measure student mastery of a state prescribed curriculum. In order to graduate from high school, each student is required to pass the tenth grade test level. The plaintiffs showed that minority children failed the test at much higher rates than did white students. The court, however, excused this disparity by accepting evidence that the minority students were rapidly narrowing the passing-rate gap. Too, the state provided targeted, concentrated educational remediation for those students who failed the test. The court concluded that the difference in test scores between white and minority students did not constitute a severe disparate impact sufficient to violate Title VI. Concerning due process, the Court found that the exam was reliable in that it measured what it purported to measure and further that it met accepted standards of curricular validity. *GI Forum v. Texas Education Agency*, 87 F.Supp.2d 667 (W.D.Tex.2000).

As yet the United States Supreme Court has not ruled on the extent of the burden which a state must bear in showing test validity for students. The range of options at this time extend from the strict adherence to the intent standard, as espoused in *United States v. South Carolina*, supra, where the state must merely show that its test is rationally related to a legitimate state objective, to the more restrictive standard of *Debra P.* where the state must bear a substantial burden of proof to document instructional validity and to show that the test does not perpetuate and augment the vestiges of racial discrimination.

CHAPTER 15

TERMS AND CONDITIONS OF TEACHER EMPLOYMENT

§ 15.1 INTRODUCTION

In order to qualify for employment as a public school teacher, a person must be certified or licensed by the state. Certification signifies that an individual is competent to teach and must be obtained before a person has capacity to contract as a teacher. *Keatley v. Mercer County Board of Education*, 490 S.E.2d 306 (W.Va.1997). The assurance of teacher competency is a necessity if children are to be subject to compulsory attendance laws. If the state compels children to attend school, then it is logical, and indeed rational, that the children be supervised and taught by qualified or certified teachers.

§ 15.2 CERTIFICATION

Education is a state responsibility; consequently, certification differs in each state depending on the statutory provisions and regulations. Each state has the responsibility for certification or decertification (revocation of license) and in normal circumstances this responsibility is delegated to the State Board of Education and/or the Department of Education. These agencies administer the certification process and promulgate rules and regulations. The certification process is generally less involved than decertification. A teacher who is decertified has a right to know the cause of revocation and the opportunity for a hearing since constitutional issues may be present and generally are a factor.

Most states require that all teachers have a college degree as a condition precedent to certification. Some states have made provisions for qualified or conditional certification where teachers have completed only a specified number of college units that have to be upgraded within a specified period of time. College credits usually are required in the subject area (i.e., history) in which the teacher plans to teach. Concomitantly, states usually require the appropriate professional curriculum and methodology classes. In addition to higher education training, states require that individuals aspiring to be teachers be of: (1) good moral character, (2) a specified age (usually 18 or older), and (3) a citizen of the United States, or if not already a citizen, the applicant must intend to become a citizen. Some states require pledging loyalty to the constitutions of the state and United States. In recent years, some states have instituted a teacher examination. All states approve the content of Teacher Education programs conducted by colleges and universities. If individuals meet all of the state established standards, then they are eligible for certification or licensing, and the certifying body may not arbitrarily or capriciously refuse certification.

Some states require further academic training after initial certification in order to maintain certification, while other states endorse teachers for life. If certification requirements are changed, grandfather clauses often cover those already certified and the new regulations apply to new applicants only.

In most states, certifying agencies are vested with discretionary authority. This discretion is particularly important when applying the elusive standard of moral conduct or appropriate and good behavior. In one case, an Oregon policeman was convicted of breaking and entering and grand larceny. After serving his term, he completed all the college requirements to apply for a teaching certificate but was denied. The crux of the question was whether he had overcome his questionable past. State certification standards required that an individual be of good moral character. It was the determination of the State Board of Education that he had not overcome his past indiscretions and therefore he was denied certification. The courts generally refuse to question the discretion of a Board's decision unless it can be shown that the board members acted arbitrarily or capriciously. *Bay v. State Board of Education*, 378 P.2d 558 (Or.1963).

Similarly, a New York appellate court upheld the New York City Board of Education's denial of an application for a teaching license for a person who had been convicted nine years earlier for a felony of selling cocaine. The court said that the board had appropriately considered whether there was a nexus between the offense and the teacher license sought. In determining that there was a direct and negative relationship between the role of a teacher and a drug conviction, the court upheld the licensing board's denial of the license. Moreover, the court pointed out that whether to grant or deny the teaching license was within the sole discretion of the board, and the court was without authority to intervene. *In the Matter of Arrocha v. Board of Educ. of City of New York*, 712 N.E.2d 669 (N.Y.App.1999).

§ 15.21 Teacher Tests

In recent years states have reinstituted examinations as conditions for certification with several states employing the National Teacher Examination. Some teachers have objected, maintaining that the "effect" of the tests is to exclude a higher percentage of blacks than of whites. These tests do not violate the Fourteenth Amendment if they were not designed with the "intent" to discriminate. To challenge a test under the Fourteenth Amendment, teachers must bear the burden of proving discriminatory intent. Teacher tests have also been challenged under Title VII, Civil Rights Act of 1964, and have been upheld if the state can show that they are reasonably related to the knowledge needed to teach. In a key decision dealing with Title VII, the court said: "[a]lthough the NTE was not designed to evaluate experienced teachers, the State could reasonably conclude that the NTE provided a reliable and economical means for measuring one element of effective teaching—the degree of knowledge possessed by the teacher." *United States v. State of South Carolina*, 445 F.Supp. 1094 (D.S.C.1977).

In other litigation involving the testing of teachers, the Texas legislature passed a law which required all teachers and administrators to pass an examination to continue certification. The test was challenged claiming it (1) impaired the contracts of the educators who were already certified and (2) violated due process. The court held a teaching certificate is not a contract; therefore, the federal constitutional prohibition against impairment of contracts was not violated. Accordingly, the court concluded that a teaching certificate is a license subject to future reasonable restrictions by the state. With regard to due process, the court said teachers who failed the test may retake the test and appeal to a state commission before revocation of their certificate. The court concluded that such provision gave the teachers ample due process. *State v. Project Principle, Inc.*, 724 S.W.2d 387 (Tex.1987).

§ 15.22 Alien Teachers

Can states legally deny teacher certification to persons who are not citizens of the United States? The answer is "yes." A New York statute provided that a teaching certificate would be denied any individual who was not a United States citizen or who had not manifested an intention to apply for citizenship. In 1979, the United States Supreme Court upheld the New York statute. In doing so, the Court relied on a 1978 case which upheld the exclusion of individuals who wanted to be policemen because of the special nature of the governmental obligation. *Foley v. Connelie*, 435 U.S. 291 (1978). The Supreme Court held that the State of New York had a rational governmental interest in requiring teachers to be either citizens or be in the process of becoming naturalized citizens. *Ambach v. Norwick*, 441 U.S. 68 (1979).

§ 15.23 Nonrenewal of Certificates

States have the authority to issue limited term teaching certificates and to require that additional qualifications be acquired if the teachers want to renew their credentials. Where a group of teachers' term of certification ended and they were required to pass an assessment test for renewal, several failed the test and subsequently sued claiming a right to receive damages for denial of property without due process of law. The Supreme Court of Georgia held against the teachers, ruling that they had no substantive property interest in nonrenewable teaching certificates and that the fact that their certificates had expired did not constitute a taking of their property without due process. *State Board of Education v. Drury*, 437 S.E.2d 290 (Ga.1993).

In 1993 the Governor of Massachusetts signed into law an Education Reform Act, and pursuant thereto the state board promulgated a regulation that requires math teachers in low scoring schools and math teachers not certified in math, but teaching math, to take an assessment test. Results of the test were used as diagnostic tools in providing individual professional development plans. The Court ruled the regulations were within the Board's authority and did not violate equal protection or the due process rights of the teachers who were required to take the test. *Massachusetts Federation of Teachers v. Board of Education*, 767 N.E.2d 549 (Mass.2002).

Too, as observed above, teacher certificates are not considered contracts unless there is some provision in the law or contract instrument that indicates that the state and individual teacher have created an agreement that is in fact contractual in nature. If such exists, then the state cannot unilaterally take away the certification. Yet such conditions do not normally exist and without them, certificates are not contracts and reasonable conditions for retaining certification can be added as need arises.

§ 15.24   Revocation of Certificates

Teaching certificates may be revoked for unprofessional conduct, which may include the violation of state law, false swearing to loyalty oaths, incompetency, child abuse, and immorality. If a state seeks to revoke a license or decertify a teacher, it may consider not only classroom ability and performance but also outside activity. Recent precedents indicate that state teacher licensing agencies are becoming more assertive in decertifying teachers.

Although teachers may have their certificates revoked for good and valid reasons, the revocation may not be for an unconstitutional reason. It is unconstitutional to deny teachers freedom of speech or expression unless the actions of the teacher disrupt the educational process. Reasonable questions related to job performance must be answered by teachers.

Teaching certificates, therefore, may be revoked, but only for serious offenses that are detrimental to students or the teaching profession. There must be a *nexus* between the outside activity and the performance of teaching duties. The general rule of law is that a teacher cannot be dismissed for behavior of nonschool activity unless such activity can be shown to be detrimental to the conduct of the school. For example, where a female teacher was convicted of first degree criminal mischief for ramming her car into the car of her husband's lover, the Supreme Court of Oregon ruled for the teacher, holding that the conviction did not "render (the teacher) unqualified to perform her professional duties" because her crime did not bear a demonstrable relationship to her ability to perform school duties. There was no nexus. Absent a link or nexus the state licensing agency is without authority to remove certification from a teacher. *Teacher Standards and Practices Commission v. Bergerson*, 153 P.3d 84 (Or.2007). Concerning "nexus," a West Virginia court has set down the rule as follows:

"A rational nexus exists between a teacher's off-duty conduct and his or [her] duties as a teacher in at least two circumstances: (1) if the conduct directly affects the performances of the occupational responsibilities of the teacher; or (2) if, without contribution on the part of the school officials, the conduct has become the subject of such notoriety as to significantly and reasonably impair the capability of the particular teacher to discharge the responsibilities of the teaching position." *Powell v. Paine*, 221 W.Va. 458, 655 S.E.2d 204 (2007) and *Rogliano v. Fayette County Board of Education,* 176 W.Va. 700, 347 S.E.2d 220 (1986).

The following are examples of such serious nature that have led to revocation of teaching certificates. Certification was revoked where a classroom teacher physically attacked the district superintendent and the superintendent was cut, bloodied and bruised, *Everett v. Texas Education Agency*, 860 S.W.2d 700 (Tex.App.1993); a "transcript of victim's trial testimony describing rape [by the teacher] was sufficient evidence of teacher's immorality and misconduct in office to support license revocation," *Ulrich v. State*, 555 N.E.2d 172 (Ind.App.1990); where a teacher falsified welfare records for six years and received approximately $43,000 in welfare benefits, *Stelzer v. State Bd. of Ed.*, 595 N.E.2d 489 (Ohio App. 3 Dist.1991); and where a male teacher engaged in sexual conduct with male students certification withdrawal was deemed appropriate, *Stedronsky v. Sobol*, 572 N.Y.S.2d 445 (1991). Valid reasons for revocation include improperly coaching students on tests of basic skills. *Professional Standards Commission v. Smith*, 571 S.E.2d 443 (Ga. App.2002). Too, revocation of a certificate was found to be appropriate where a teacher accessed pornographic internet websites on the school computer, *Stueber v. Gallagher*, 812 So.2d 454 (Fla.Dist.Ct.App., 5th Dist. 2002). The California Supreme Court upheld the decertification of a teacher who belonged to a "swingers" club and engaged in public sexual acts with numerous men and had appeared on television in disguise, espousing nonconventional sexual behavior. *Pettit v. State Board of Education*, 513 P.2d 889 (Cal.1973).

Reporting child abuse to a state Department of Children and Family Services, as required by statute, is not discretionary. Teachers who know of incidences of child abuse and do not report them may have their teaching certificates revoked. *Pagani v. Meriden Board of Education*, 2006 WL 3791405 (D.Conn. 2006) and *A. G. ex rel. K.C. v. Autauga County Board of Education*, 506 F. Supp. 2d 927 (M.D. Ala. 2007).

§ 15.3 LOCAL BOARD PREROGATIVES FOR EMPLOYMENT

Teacher certification does not guarantee employment. State legislatures delegate the authority to employ personnel to local school boards. Although the final authority over employment rests with the school board, some states provide that a school board may employ personnel only if the superintendent has recommended the person to the board for employment. Wide latitude is vested in the board so long as the board does not violate one's constitutional or statutory rights such as sex, race, or religion, or if the board acted arbitrarily, capriciously or in bad faith.

§ 15.31   Certification as a Minimum Standard

A local school board may promulgate reasonable rules and regulations relating to employment even though the teacher has already met minimum certification standards. A board may require additional training more advanced than that required for certification, such as having a Master's degree before employment. Also, a board may require a teacher to take additional courses or be involved in staff development training after employment. A teacher may be required, as a part of the employment relationship, to obtain higher levels of academic training as long as the school board policy requirements are not discriminatory.

§ 15.32   Residency Requirement

A board may require a teacher to establish residency in the school district. In recent years, urban school districts have utilized this authority to prevent mass movement of teachers out to the suburbs. Teachers have challenged the residency requirements as violation of their liberty rights. The courts have upheld the policies as rational. The courts have accepted the school boards' rationale that teachers who live in the district have a better understanding of the students and the community and, therefore, are more likely to be committed to the school district and more involved in community activities. They also would be local taxpayers and, therefore, more personally interested in the quality of education offered in the districts. Some school districts have established policies that allow teachers who lived outside of the district prior to the implementation date of the residency policy to be exempt from the policy. These ''grandfather'' provisions have been attacked by new teachers claiming discrimination, but the courts have upheld the policies as reasonable if they are applied in a nondiscriminatory manner. *Wardwell v. Board of Education*, 529 F.2d 625 (6th Cir.1976); *McClelland v. Paris Public Schools*, 742 S.W.2d 907 (Ark.1988).

§ 15.33   Outside Employment

Some school boards have formulated policies forbidding teachers to engage in other employment during the school year. The courts have given wide latitude to local school boards in establishing such employment rules and have upheld these policies. Such policies though must be applied uniformly and consistently to all teachers in like classification.

§ 15.34   Health and Physical Requirements

Within the boundaries of federal and state statutes and regulations, a local school board may adopt reasonable health and physical condition requirements for teachers. These standards are generally viewed favorably by the courts if they are applied uniformly. But a board has to be especially cognizant of the protections and prohibitions with regard to those persons who may be classified under various federal and state provisions as disabled. Health and physical requirements must be rationally related to job performance and should not be promulgated to disenfranchise otherwise qualified persons. In a New York case, the court said "From this constitutional authority the right of government agencies to adopt such 'health' standards may be inferred provided such standards are reasonably and rationally related to ability to perform...." *Parolisi v. Board of Examiners of the City of New York*, 285 N.Y.S.2d 936 (1967). In another case shedding light on this issue, a teacher was advised to visit a dentist to improve the condition and appearance of his teeth, and he was also advised to lose weight and develop adequate body tone. The teacher sued and the court ruled the superintendent had taken no steps to compel compliance with the suggestions; therefore, no rights were violated. The teacher was, though, required to undergo a physical examination as authorized by statute. *Mermer v. Constantine*, 520 N.Y.S.2d 264 (1987).

§ 15.35 Assignment of Teaching Duties

A school board generally has the authority to transfer and assign teachers to best benefit the educational program of the school district. Such assignments are contingent on the certification of the teacher. If a teacher is certified to teach in the primary grades, then the teacher may only be assigned to primary courses. A teacher has no right to demand a particular grade or teaching position within a school district. A local board may adopt reasonable rules and regulations regarding transfer, but once established they cannot be violated. To transfer a teacher for purposes of punishment or to make life so uncomfortable as to force the teacher's resignation is, of course, considered to be arbitrary and violative of the teacher's rights.

In a case illustrating the extent of school board prerogative, a court ruled that a guidance counselor who refused to supervise the school campus before school could be dismissed for refusing to obey the request. *Jones v. Alabama State Tenure Commission*, 408 So.2d 145 (Ala. Civ.App.1981). In contrast, a West Virginia court has ruled that librarians and guidance counselors could not be used on a regular basis as substitute teachers but could only be assigned as regular substitutes for a reasonable time if a financial emergency existed. *Randolph County Bd. of Ed. v. Scalia*, 387 S.E.2d 524 (W.Va.1989).

§ 15.36 Extracurricular Duties and Activities

In the absence of specific contractual terms, a school board may assign reasonable extracurricular duties to a teacher. These duties may constitute such responsibilities as supervising study halls, directing a school play, coaching intramurals, conducting field trips and supervising athletic events. School officials may not assign bus driving duty, crossing guard duty or janitorial duties to teachers. Such duties are not reasonably related to the professional responsibilities of teachers. Extracurricular assignments must be related to the instructional activities for which the teacher is certified.

§ 15.4 RIGHT TO REMAIN SILENT

In *Beilan v. Board of Public Education*, 357 U.S. 399 (1958), the United States Supreme Court ruled that a teacher must answer questions posed by school officials if the questions are relevant to the terms of employment. In this case, the teacher was dismissed because of refusal to answer relevant questions posed by the school superintendent regarding teaching responsibilities.

However, questions posed by a legislative committee or in a judicial proceeding may not be used as a basis for dismissing teachers. *Board of Public Education School District of Philadelphia v. Intille*, 163 A.2d 420 (Pa.1960). Any questions asked must be balanced against the teacher's constitutional rights. The United States Supreme Court has recognized the unique position and interest teachers have in speaking out on issues that are matters of public concern. Thus, the political rights and prerogatives of teachers are protected and any state or local encroachments on those political freedoms are unconstitutional. *Pickering v. Board of Education*, 391 U.S. 563 (1968).

§ 15.5 CONTRACTS

A teacher contract contains the basic elements of regular contract law. The basic elements for a valid contract are: (1) offer and acceptance; (2) competent parties; (3) consideration; (4) legal subject matter; and (5) proper form. Each of these elements pertaining to teacher contracts is elaborated below.

§ 15.51 Offer and Acceptance

Only a school board may make a valid offer to contract with a teacher. The offer has to be made to the teacher and within a reasonable time; the teacher may only accept the offer that has been tendered. If a school board tenders an offer for a specific salary and the teacher accepts the offer but requests the salary be increased, then there is no valid offer and there cannot be a valid acceptance. In essence, the teacher has made a counter offer. There has been no meeting of the minds as to conditions and terms of the contract; thus, no contract can be formed without further action by the school board.

§ 15.52   Competent Parties

Both parties must have the legal capacity to contract. A school board is a legal party under the authority vested in it by the legislature. A person is not legally competent to contract as a teacher if he/she is without certification. Thus, certification makes a teacher competent to contract.

§ 15.53   Consideration

Consideration is an essential element of a contract. By definition, consideration is something of value received for performing an act or service for another party. In most teacher contracts, consideration constitutes the paying of a salary for the teaching services rendered. Consideration may be divided into three categories: (1) a valuable; (2) a good; and (3) a promise for an act. A teacher's salary falls into the category of "a valuable." An example of good consideration would be love and affection; although important to teaching, is not normally considered to be applicable to a teaching contract. This category is normally not found in public school board transactions. The third category may be a promise to act for good consideration.

§ 15.54   Legal Subject Matter

The contract must be for a legal subject matter. Contracting for a teacher to teach a prescribed curriculum would fall in this category. If a board enters into a contract that is not of legal subject matter (such as conducting rooster fights or selling drugs) or is beyond the scope of its authority, the contract would be invalid or voidable.

§ 15.55   Legal Form

The contract must be in the legal form required by state statutes or regulations. Most states require contracts to be written and to include specific provisions. However, there are instances when an oral agreement may be legally binding. Teacher contracts, however, must be in writing, approved in public action by the board, and recorded in its minutes.

§ 15.6   TENURE

Tenure is a privilege bestowed upon the teaching profession by the legislature. This privilege may be prospectively altered by legislative action, but not by local school boards. In 1927, the Indiana legislature used the word "contract" in the tenure statute, and this created a contract between the tenured teachers and the state. The United States Constitution, Article I, Section 10, provides that the obligation of a contract may not be impaired, and the United States Supreme Court invoking this provision ruled that subsequent Indiana legislatures could not alter the contractual relationship. If a tenure statute is written so as not to create a contractual relationship, it may be altered or abolished by the state legislature. *Indiana ex rel. Anderson v. Brand*, 303 U.S. 95 (1938).

If, however, tenure is not interpreted to be a contract between the state and the individual, but rather an agreement conditioned upon the teacher's maintenance and upgrading of teaching skills, then a school district may be justified in the nonrenewal of a tenured teacher's contract. In the case where a teacher persistently refused to comply with her district's continuing education requirements and over the years forfeited salary rather than obtain the training, the school district finally threatened her with dismissal if she did not satisfy the requirements. She did not and was fired. The teacher sued claiming denial of Equal Protection, and the U.S. Supreme Court, finding no merit to the teacher's claims, ruled for the school district. The Court reasoned that there was no denial of Equal Protection because all the teachers were equally obligated to acquire the continuing education credits, and the school district's rationale for such training was related to the district's objective of maintaining a qualified teaching force. *Harrah Independent School District v. Martin*, 440 U.S. 194 (1979).

Many reasons have been given as to why tenure was established. Some of these are: (1) to remove political abuse from the profession; (2) to prevent arbitrary interference by boards; (3) to provide a permanent, competent teaching force; and (4) to protect the competent, experienced professional, thereby providing job security.

Most states have established statutory provisions which grant tenure, or continuing contracts. These statutes provide that a teacher, after serving a specified probationary period, cannot be removed from a position unless the school board has established good and just cause and provided the teacher with procedural due process. The specific causes for removal vary from state to state depending on the statutory language, but include such causes as immorality, insubordination, incompetence, misconduct, neglect of duty, or other good and just cause. (See Chapter 17, Teacher Dismissal.) Generally, the tenure statutes provide specific procedures that must be followed before a teacher may be removed. Tenure is a statutory right and not a constitutional right.

Once tenure is granted, a "property" right is created, and by virtue of that right, procedural due process is required before removal.

Before teachers are awarded tenure status they must serve a probationary period. States require from two to five years of probation, with the majority of states requiring three years. After serving the specified period, a local school board has the discretion of granting tenure or not renewing the probationary teacher's contract. If a school board chooses not to renew a probationary teacher's contract during the probationary period, the board is not required to give reasons unless statute so requires. Even if reasons are given by the board, and they are not constitutionally impermissible reasons, the board has no obligation to provide the teacher with a removal hearing.

Tenure may or may not be transferred from district to district within a particular state depending on the construction of the state statute. Some states allow at the discretion of the local school board the granting of tenure immediately upon moving from one district to another. In other states, an experienced teacher may be required to serve a partial probationary period such as one year rather than a full probationary period of three years.

Tenure is granted for teaching and not for extracurricular assignments such as coaching. Supplementary contracts have been interpreted by the courts to be outside tenure statutes. This rule, though, is not uniform. Not only are teaching positions encompassed by tenure laws, but statutes in a number of states provide tenure status for administrative personnel such as principals, assistant superintendents, superintendents and others.

§ 15.7 REDUCTION IN FORCE

In recent years, in many districts, there has been a decline in the student population. This has necessitated a corresponding reduction in the number of professional employees. As mentioned previously, teachers and other professionals who have acquired tenure may be dismissed for reasonable cause only. Where there are declining enrollments, teachers may be laid-off as a result of a work force reduced. Legitimate reduction in force may be caused by such factors as enrollment decline, fiscal restraints, reorganization, or elimination of positions or programs. Most state tenure laws provide local school boards the flexibility to reduce the work force due to financial exigency. The local school board has within its discretion the authority to adopt procedures to reduce the work force, absent contractual obligations created by statutory or collective bargaining agreements.

§ 15.71 Rationale for Reduction in Force

The courts will look closely at whether or not a reduction in force is necessary or rather is an attempt to circumvent statutory protections of employees. Whether a board has a real financial exigency requiring lay-off becomes an essential question. The burden is upon the board or institution to establish that a financial exigency exists. In *American Association of University Professors v. Bloomfield College*, 322 A.2d 846 (N.J.Super.1974), Bloomfield College abolished tenure for all faculty then dismissed 11 tenured faculty members. The union requested that the college sell a golf course to obtain funds for re-employment. The court found that the college had a true financial crisis and need not dispose of assets to obtain funds to continue faculty employment.

§ 15.72 Positions to Be Eliminated

After it has been determined that a financial crisis exists, school boards then must decide who and what positions are to be eliminated. In the absence of statutory or collective bargaining provisions, tenured teachers are in most states given priority over non-tenured teachers in consideration of dismissal. Seniority is generally given substantial weight. However, there have been some court decisions to the contrary in which other standards besides seniority have been upheld. The courts, though, require that these standards be rational, job related, and established prior to the incident of their implementation. *Underwood v. Henry County School Board*, 427 S.E.2d 330 (Va.1993).

A board in deciding which positions are to be eliminated may not act in an arbitrary or capricious manner. A board cannot abolish a position, terminate the employee, then transfer the responsibilities of the former employee to another position. This type of shift in responsibilities may circumvent tenure laws, and if it does is illegal.

§ 15.73 Intent of the Board

A board must act in good faith and may not terminate a teacher under the guise of need to reduce the teaching force. Some cases have arisen over whether a true financial exigency existed or whether the teacher's position was eliminated because of some teacher action that offended the board. In *Zoll v. Eastern Allamakee Community School District*, 588 F.2d 246 (8th Cir.1978), a teacher had written letters to a local paper criticizing the school board. A jury determined the real reason for elimination of the position was something the teacher had said. The board was unable to show that a financial crisis existed and because the teacher had been outspoken, the court suspected that the dismissal was motivated by the teacher's speech and not financial exigency. Thus the teacher prevailed. In *Hagarty v. Dysart–Geneseo Community School District*, 282 N.W.2d 92 (Iowa 1979), the court said "... we could not countenance a subterfuge by which an unscrupulous school board would use a fictitious necessity for staff reduction as a pretext for discharging a teacher."

§ 15.74 Seniority Displacement

As previously mentioned, generally, tenured teachers take precedence over non-tenured teachers in reduction in force. School board rules, however, may provide for "bumping" procedures if reduction in force is necessary. In the absence of such rules, a school board generally would take into consideration not only seniority but also certification. If a teacher is certified in a specific area where teachers are needed, then he or she may be able to replace someone with less seniority.

CHAPTER 16

CONSTITUTIONAL RIGHTS
OF TEACHERS

§ 16.1 INTRODUCTION

Teachers' lives and activities have always been subject to close public scrutiny. Because teachers are entrusted with the responsibilities of educating the children and legally stand *in loco parentis*, they are expected to be role models for youth. In earlier times, teachers' contracts included provisions that prohibited the use of alcoholic spirits, smoking, and in many cases required dismissal of female teachers who had the temerity to get married while employed as a teacher. There were also other restrictions forbidding attendance at theaters, dating, keeping late hours, and divorce. In some instances, teachers were required to teach Sunday School and per- haps more importantly, teachers were also prohibited from speaking out on political issues that might be construed as criticism of individuals in authority.

§ 16.2 TEACHERS' FREEDOMS OF SPEECH AND EXPRESSION

In the formative stages of our constitutional develop- ment, public employment was viewed as a privilege and not a right. The basis for this logic, that public employees could not fully retain their political freedoms while hold- ing public employment, was justified by Justice Holmes' in his often-quoted assertion, in 1892, that "The petitioner may have a constitutional right to talk politics, but he has no constitutional right to be a policeman." Many earlier cases involving public school teachers followed this philosophy, holding that the contract provisions between the board and the teacher could prohibit the exercise of various rights and freedoms by teachers; and, if the teacher violated the provisions of the contract, even though they were repressive of the teacher's rights, dismissal would be upheld.

Although the courts were generally split and relatively uncertain as to the personal freedoms of teachers, the privilege-right dichotomy continued for many years. Where teachers did prevail, the courts based their conclusions on common-law reasonableness and not on constitutional rights or freedoms. It did not clearly reach to constitutional rights and freedoms until 1968.

§ 16.3 *PICKERING* AND TEACHER POLITICAL FREEDOM

The watershed case in application of constitutional standards to teacher employment came in 1968 in *Pickering v. Board of Education*, 391 U.S. 563 (1968), wherein the U.S. Supreme Court held that freedom of speech, while not absolute in all circumstances, is nevertheless sufficiently strong to require the state to show a "compelling state interest" in order to overcome a teacher's right to speak out on issues of public concern. In so doing the Court equated the teachers' right of free speech with that of other members of the general public to criticize and comment on public policies and issues. Any lingering doubt about the legal dichotomy of privileges versus rights was extinguished by this case.

In *Pickering* the Supreme Court said that "a teacher's exercise of his right to speak on issues of public importance may not furnish the basis for his dismissal from public employment." In this particular case a teacher sent a letter to a local newspaper attacking a proposed tax increase by the Board of Education. The letter contained partially erroneous information and the teacher was dismissed by the board because the letter "impugned" the "motives," "honesty" and "integrity" of the board and administration. The Court, acknowledging that a balance must be maintained regarding such political activity, gave the following guideline: ". . . It cannot be gainsaid that the State has interests as an employer in regulating the speech of its employees that differ significantly from those it possesses in connection with regulation of the speech of the citizenry in general. The problem in any case is to arrive at a balance between the interests of the teacher, as a citizen, in commenting upon matters of public concern and the interest of the State, as employer, in promoting the efficiency of the public services it performs through its employees."

The Court pointed out that a school board may be justified in dismissal of an employee if the statements or activities are of such a nature as to be detrimental to the actual operation of the schools. The Court found that the facts in *Pickering* did not indicate that the teacher's activity was inhibitive in any manner to the educational performance of the school. It was not shown that the teacher's letter had any impact on the proposed tax increase nor was it shown that the false statements were made recklessly or knowingly. The Court said: "On such a question free and open debate is vital to informed decision-making by the electorate. Teachers are, as a class, the members of a community most likely to have informed and definite opinions as to how funds allotted to the operation of the schools should be spent. Accordingly, it is essential that they be able to speak out freely on such questions without fear of retaliatory dismissal."

§ 16.31   Teacher Speech and the *Connick* Rule

After *Pickering*, the courts developed a flexible rule that provided for balancing the public's interests against the private interest of the employee in each circumstance. This balancing, however, did not remove all state restraint on teacher activities; on the contrary, the courts have reflected a strong belief that because of their sensitive position in the classroom, teachers must be held accountable for certain activities both internal and external to the school.

The balancing of interests with regard to freedom of speech was given new clarity by the U.S. Supreme Court in *Connick v. Myers*, 461 U.S. 138 (1983). *Connick* explains that First Amendment free speech is protected when the employee speaks out on "matters of public concern." According to *Connick*, speech or expression exercised by a public employee concerning matters of private or personal interest and not as a citizen upon matters of public concern is not protected by the First Amendment.

Connick and *Pickering* combined to form a free speech test that is a two-step process. First, the initial inquiry is whether the speech is a matter of public concern; in this regard *Connick* states: "When employee expression cannot be fairly considered as relating to any matter of political, social, or other concern to the community, government officials should enjoy wide latitude in managing their offices, without intrusive oversight by the judiciary in the name of the First Amendment."

Second, if the speech is found to be a matter of public concern, the court then must apply the *Pickering* balancing test. The interest of the public employee as a citizen in commenting on matters of public concern must be weighed against the interests of the state, as an employer, to promote effective and efficient public service.

Thus, the Court will evaluate whether the speech of the teacher is primarily made in the teacher's role as a citizen or as an employee of the school, *Urofsky v. Gilmore*, 216 F.3d 401 (4th Cir.2000). Too, speech is protected if it is exercised regarding matters of public concern. *Klug v. Chicago School Reform Board of Trustees, District No. 299 Trustees*, 197 F.3d 853 (7th Cir.1999).

Drawing the line between a public concern and a private one has been a principal issue confronting the courts since *Pickering* and *Connick*. For example, one teacher speaking out at a school board meeting regarding the tenure of another teacher was held to be a matter of public concern, *Piver v. Pender County Board of Education*, 835 F.2d 1076 (4th Cir.1987), as was a letter of complaint written by teachers to a state education agency concerning a local school district's delay in implementing a federal program. *Southside Public Schools v. Hill*, 827 F.2d 270 (8th Cir.1987). Yet, even when an issue of public concern is at stake, a school district or other government agency may restrict speech of an employee if it is detrimental or disruptive to the school environment. The U.S. Supreme Court explains that there is a difference between free speech applied to government as employer as opposed to government as sovereign. Government control over the speech of its own employees can be more restrictive than over speech of the public in general. *Waters v. Churchill*, 511 U.S. 661 (1994). The Supreme Court in *Waters* said that: "The government cannot restrict the speech of the public at large just in the name of efficiency. But where the government is employing someone for the very purpose of effectively achieving its goals, such restrictions may well be appropriate."

The Court further explained that the extra power that government possesses in regulating the speech of its employees emanates from the government's mission in being charged by law with the responsibility for conducting government business. School districts as government agencies employ teachers and other personnel to carry out that mission. If the employee, in the exercise of a free speech, inhibits the operation of the schools or induces conditions that inhibit the operation of the school, or causes inefficient or ineffective performance, then the exercise of speech may be curtailed. *Waters*, supra.

Of course, whether the teacher's exercise of speech has, in fact, been detrimental to the school is always a central question. School board members frequently feel that any disagreement with their policies is by their very nature harmful to the conduct of the school. Courts are not, however, likely to agree or to cast a broad net in this regard and tend to give relatively little credence to such perceived detriments. Therefore, a teacher's speech or expression regarding a matter of public concern will normally be given the benefit of the doubt; *Connick* is instructive in this regard.

Connick explains that the speech test of the public employee can be summarized as follows: (1) public speech is a fundamental constitutional right, and allegations regarding teacher dismissal for exercise of freedom of speech place the burden of proof on the state (or school board); (2) public speech can be denied if the interests of the state outweigh the interests of the employee in the exercise of that right; (3) public speech involving matters of public concern imposes an extensive burden on the part of the state to justify denial, in which case the state must "clearly demonstrate" that denial was necessary in order to prevent "substantial interference"; (4) speech involving private concerns involves a relatively low standard of proof by the state to justify dismissal, one that a school board can easily sustain by showing minimally that the exercise of speech can be reasonably believed to undermine authority, disrupt decorum, or harm working relationships.

§ 16.311   The *Garcetti* Test

In 2006, the U.S. Supreme Court in *Garcetti v. Ceballos,* 547 U.S. 410 (2006) further explained the public employer/employee freedom of speech relationship. In *Garcetti*, the Court built on the *Pickering* and *Connick* precedents by enunciating what it called the "pursuant to duty" test. Under this test, the public employer can control the speech of an employee if the employee's statements are made pursuant to their public duties. In other words, public employees do not have unfettered freedom of speech to speak out on matters of internal consequence in the conduct of their public employment. To explain, the Court said: "We hold that when public employees make statements pursuant to their official duties, the employees are not speaking as citizens for First Amendment purposes, and the Constitution does not insulate their communications from employer discipline." (*Garcetti v. Ceballos*, 547 U.S. 410 (2006)). The meaning of *Connick* and *Garcetti* is, therefore, quite clear. The exercise of speech by a public employee about policies or activities of the public office are subject to public employer control. For schools, this means that a principal who criticizes policies of the superintendent and school board may possibly place her or his job in jeopardy. Justice Kennedy in *Garcetti* explained the freedom of speech rights of public employees in this way:

> "So long as employees are speaking as citizens about matters of public concern (*Pickering*), they must face only those restrictions that are necessary for their employers to operate efficiently and effectively (*Connick*) ... [However], [g]overnment employers, like private employers, need a significant degree of control over their employee's words and actions [because] without it, there would be little chance for the efficient provision of public services." (*Garcetti*) *(Case names added)*

In view of *Connick* and *Garcetti*, teachers and school administrators are well-advised not to publicly criticize school policy in a way that could be detrimental to the operations of the school. One federal court, in taking a very restrictive view of teachers' free speech rights, has said that a "school system does not 'regulate' teachers' speech as much as it hires that speech." In that regard, teachers must teach the prescribed curriculum and cannot use the classroom as a forum to express personal viewpoints, even of public concern, that is outside the curriculum content as prescribed by the school board. This court rejected the teacher's claim that 'academic freedom' gave her a special forum to express her views. *Mayer v. Monroe County Community School Corp.*, 474 F.3d 477 (7th Cir. 2007). Similarly, a special education teacher was held not to have a constitutional right to arrange for special psychological services for a student beyond that prescribed by the student's Individualized Education Program (IEP). The court said that the teacher's scheduling of the student's therapy sessions and other assistance was a school matter, not a matter of public concern, and thus the teacher did not have a speech or expression right to undertake it. *Montanye v. Wissahickon School District*, 218 Fed. Appx. 126 (3d Cir. 2007).

Many times the facts of a case require that the court draw a fine line between matters of public concern and those matters that concern only the operations of the school. Speech concerning a school teacher's job is not of public concern. Neither are teacher complaints about the principal, lack of teacher aides, teacher workloads, or staffing levels matters of public concern. However, speech by teachers regarding school officials' misdeeds and impropriety are of public concern and is protected. *Brammer–Hoelter v. Twin Peaks Charter Academy*, 492 F.3d 1192 (10th Cir. 2007).

The U. S. Court of Appeals, Fifth Circuit, has explained the *Garcetti* rule as employing a "balancing test" that weighs the employer's interests against the employee's rights of speech and expression. In a case where a football coach/athletic director took it upon himself to castigate the business manager and school principal because they had not funded a tournament entry fee for the school teams, the court held that his speech was not protected. The coach had also instituted a campaign against what he called "discriminatory funding." The court found that the totality of the coach's crusade was centered in daily fiscal operations of the school, was not a matter of public concern and was, therefore, not protected speech. *Williams v. Dallas Independent School District*, 2007 WL 504992 (5th Cir. 2007).

School administrators, in particular school principals, must be particularly wary of criticizing policies of the school superintendent and school board. Principals at times will be caught up in competition among schools in a district and become overly adversarial regarding their own school's budgets or programs. In one extreme case in Florida, a school principal became so antagonistic toward the superintendent and the school district funding policies that he, contrary to the superintendent's orders, sought to bolt the school district and turn his school into a charter school. As could be expected, his contract as principal was not renewed and he sued. The court ruled that the principal's conduct was not protected, and that his widely-publicized effort to convert the school to a charter school involved school matters and was "part and parcel of his official duties." *D'Angelo v. School Board of Polk County, Florida*, 497 F.3d 1203 (11th Cir. 2007). (See also *Deschenie v. Board of Education of Central Consolidated School District No. 22*, 473 F.3d 1271 (10th Cir. 2007).

Thus, teachers and school administrators should be well aware of the balance of their individual prerogatives as employees as against their rights and interests as citizens. They must be able to discern between school operational matters and external matters of public concern. The Supreme Court in *Garcetti* restated and summarized the test as follows:

"Employers have heightened interests in controlling speech made by an employee in his or her professional capacity, official communications, creating a need for substantive consistency and clarity. Supervisors must ensure that their employees' official communications are accurate, demonstrate sound judgment, and promote the employees' mission . . ."

That is the test against which administrators and teachers must measure their exercise of freedom of speech and expression.

§ 16.32 Dismissal When Constitutional Issues are Involved

A board may dismiss or not renew a teacher's contract even if constitutional protections are involved if there are other valid and legitimate reasons for termination. In other words, if a board, in deciding to dismiss a teacher, would have reached the same decision, even if the free speech issue had not occurred, then dismissal would not have infringed on the constitutional rights of the teacher. This rule is called the *mixed motive test* where there are both constitutional and non-constitutional issues involved. Under this test where several motives may have contributed to an employee's dismissal, the court will seek to determine whether the "motivating factor" for the dismissal was the employee's exercise of a constitutional right or was the "motivating factor" found to be some action by the employee that had no constitutional import.

In *Mount Healthy City Sch. Dist. Bd. of Ed. v. Doyle*, 429 U.S. 274 (1977), a non-tenured teacher telephoned a local radio station and criticized a dress and appearance policy unilaterally issued to teachers by the administration. The teacher, Doyle, was also involved in a number of other incidents such as a physical altercation with another teacher, an argument with school cafeteria em-

ployees, swearing at students and making obscene gestures to female students. Doyle's contract was subsequently not renewed and he requested the reasons for
non-renewal. In response to Doyle's request, the superintendent referred to "a notable lack of tact in handling
professional matters which leave much doubt as to your
sincerity in establishing good school relationships," then,
he specifically referred to the radio station incident and
the obscene gesture incident. The teacher challenged the
dismissal as violative of his First and Fourteenth Amendment rights. The Sixth Circuit Court of Appeals reasoned
that the telephone call was a matter of public concern
and therefore protected free speech and it also was the
major reason for Doyle's dismissal. The United States
Supreme Court remanded the case back to the lower
court to determine if the board had substantial and
legitimate reasons for not renewing Doyle's contract,
other than those of protected free speech. "A borderline
or marginal candidate should not have the employment
question resolved against him because of constitutionally
protected conduct. But that same candidate ought not to
be able, by engaging in such conduct, to prevent his
employer from assessing his performance record and
reaching a decision not to rehire on the basis of that
record, simply because the protected conduct makes the
employer more certain of the correctness of its decision."

This mixed motive test articulated in *Doyle* was used
in *Connick* discussed above. In *Connick*, a public employee (Assistant District Attorney Sheila Myers), when informed she would be transferred to another area in the
district attorney's office, opposed the personnel decision.
In response, Myers passed out a questionnaire to other
fellow assistant district attorneys, soliciting information
about office morale and pressure to work in political

campaigns. Myers was told the questionnaire constituted insubordination, and her employment was terminated. The Supreme Court upheld Myers' dismissal, finding that the matter was basically of a personal nature and not a matter of public concern of any particular weight or magnitude. Though one question on Myers' question-naire did fall under the rubric of "public concern," Myers' First Amendment interest was outweighed by the disruptive nature of the other questions. The beliefs by the state that Myers' actions would disrupt the office, undermine authority, and destroy the close working rela-tionships within the office were reasonably taken in view of the evidence. The fact that Myers issued the question-naire immediately after the transfer dispute lent weight in balancing the scales on behalf of the state that her actions were of a personal nature and not a matter of public concern. In so holding, the Court rejected Myers' contention that the state must bear the burden of clearly demonstrating that the discharge was necessary because the speech "substantially interfered" with the operation of the office.

§ 16.33   Rule of Causation

The mixed motive test can also be explained in terms of causation. The principal aspect of the *Mt. Healthy* case that becomes decisive in teacher dismissal or non-reten-tion cases is whether the teacher's exercise of speech or expression was the cause of the school board's action against the teacher. The court will ask whether the teacher's exercise of the constitutional right to speak out on matters of public concern was the cause or motivating factor or "played a 'substantial' part in the decision not to rehire" or to dismiss. Stated another way, the court must be satisfied that the "employee is placed in no worse a position than if he had not engaged in the conduct."

In such free speech cases, the burden of proof is placed upon the teacher to show that his conduct was constitutionally protected and that this conduct was a "substantial factor" or the "motivating factor" in the school board's decision to dismiss or not rehire him. If the teacher carries this burden to the court's satisfaction, then the board must show by "a preponderance of the evidence that it would have reached the same decision ... even in the absence of the protected conduct." *Mt. Healthy*, supra.

§ 16.34   Private Criticism

A teacher's freedom of speech is protected in private communication with an employer. In *Givhan v. Western Line Consolidated School District*, 439 U.S. 410 (1979), a junior high school English teacher met privately with the principal and criticized the policies of the school on racial discrimination. The principal alleged that the criticism involved "petty and unreasonable demands and were presented in an insulting, loud, hostile and arrogant manner." The Fifth Circuit Court of Appeals upheld the dismissal, citing *Pickering*, supra, and *Mount Healthy*, supra. The U.S. Supreme Court reversed the decision and rejected the argument that the First Amendment did not protect the teacher's private criticism of the school principal. A teacher's First Amendment rights are not lost when the teacher " ... arranges to communicate privately with his employer rather than to spread his views before the public." The court refused to grant a lesser protection to private speech than to public speech, but emphasized that the teacher could be dismissed if either private or public speech impeded the proper performance of classroom duties. It was recognized that public speech is contingent upon content, whereas the impact of private speech might be judged on the time, place, and manner of the comments.

§ 16.35 Political Activity

Pickering, as discussed above, tells us that teachers may speak out on political issues as citizens. Political rights are protected by the First Amendment. Thus, a school administrator may not use punitive measures such as transferring, dismissing or demoting a teacher for protected political activities. On the other hand, a teacher may not be involved in political activities which disrupt the educational process. A school board may reasonably expect a teacher not to use his or her position to promote a particular political outcome, or to use the classroom for partisan political purposes, or to be involved in any activity that will interfere with or disrupt the educational environment of the school, or detract from job performance.

Following *Pickering*, the general rule prevails that public employees are protected from retaliation for their exercise of speech if the speech relates to a matter of public concern. If the matter is one of public concern, then the court will determine whether the employee's interest outweighs that of the public employer (the school board) in promoting an efficient public service. *Jones v. Collins*, 132 F.3d 1048 (5th Cir.1998).

A California court upheld the suspension of a teacher for using the classroom for political activity. *Goldsmith v. Board of Education*, 225 P. 783 (Cal.App.1924). The teacher chose to comment on the election of the superintendent and said, "I think he would be more helpful to our department than a lady, and we need more men in our schools. Sometimes your parents do not know one candidate from another; so they might be glad to be informed. Of course, if any of you have relatives or friends trying for the same office, be sure and vote for them."

It goes without saying that a plaintiff teacher claiming retaliation for an exercise of speech of public concern must show that he did in fact speak out on an issue of public concern in the first place. Where a local newspaper published an unfavorable article about dust and fumes from a school construction project which caused minor illnesses to students and teachers, and the principal believed the teacher had contacted the reporter and called her to his office, the teacher denied contacting the reporter and the principal reassigned the teacher's extra-curricular responsibilities for which she was paid extra. The Court said that the First Amendment protects public employees from retaliation when they speak out on matters of public concern. Since the teacher denied contacting the reporter and the principal had no proof, then no issue of free speech actually took place. Therefore, the Court found for the school board simply because no constitutional right can be denied if no speech has occurred. *Fogarty v. Boles*, 121 F.3d 886 (3d Cir.1997).

A teacher's expression of political views is not unlimited, however, and cannot be so aggressive as to exploit the obvious considerable power and influence over students in the restricted environment of the school. Where a school district advised employees that state law prohibited school districts from sponsoring and distributing partisan election campaign material on school grounds, a representative of the teacher's union objected and suit was filed. The court in holding for the school district pointed out that teachers represented the school district in the classroom and that it was not unreasonable to restrict their wearing of campaign buttons in the classroom because school authorities must have the power to disassociate the school district from political controversy and the appearance of approval of political messages. *California Teachers Association v. Governing Board of San Diego Unified School District*, 53 Cal.Rptr.2d 474 (App.4th Dist.1996).

Some states have passed legislation modeled after the Federal Hatch Act which prohibits participation in partisan politics. *United States Civil Service Commission v. National Ass'n of Letter Carriers*, 413 U.S. 548 (1973). The United States Supreme Court in *Broadrick v. Oklahoma*, 413 U.S. 601 (1973) upheld an Oklahoma statute prohibiting public employees from participating in partisan politics. These statutes usually limit activities such as direct fund raising for partisan candidates, becoming a candidate, starting a political party, or actively managing a campaign.

§ 16.36 Political Office

It is well settled that a teacher, as a citizen of the United States, has a right to run for political office, but there is a difference between the right to run for public office and the right to continue public employment after being elected. Common law provisions stipulate that a public employee may not hold positions simultaneously that are incompatible, and may not have a conflict of interest, or be in violation of the separation of powers of government. These prohibitions have been determined to be of "compelling state interest," and, therefore, do not infringe on the basic political rights of teachers. Whether or not a teacher may hold political office and serve as a teacher depends on these provisions and individual state statutes. Some states have "conflict of interest" statutes which provide that teachers may not serve as a state legislator while employed as a public teacher. But, if a state does not have a statutory provision prohibiting teachers from serving in the legislature, then, the courts have held, they may serve.

§ 16.4 PERSONAL APPEARANCE

School boards have promulgated dress codes, not only for students, but sometimes for teachers as well. These regulations have sometimes been challenged as violations of teachers' rights of free speech, expression, privacy and liberty. There is a distinct difference between the privacy rights of a governmental employee and the privacy rights of a member of the general public. The United States Supreme Court in *Kelley v. Johnson*, 425 U.S. 238 (1976) ruled that hair-grooming of police officers could be regulated. "The constitutional issue to be decided by the courts is whether petitioner's determination that such regulations should be enacted is so irrational that it may be branded 'arbitrary' and therefore a deprivation of respondent's 'liberty' interest in freedom to choose his own hairstyle."

Similarly, where a Louisiana school board expanded its student dress code to prohibit employees from wearing beards, *Domico v. Rapides Parish School Board*, 675 F.2d 100 (5th Cir.1982), the Fifth Circuit Court of Appeals recognized the liberty interest of the individual in choosing how to wear his hair. Yet, this court ruled that the school board had made a rational determination in establishing the rule as "... a reasonable means of furthering the school board's undeniable interest in teaching hygiene, instilling discipline, asserting authority, and compelling uniformity." This court clearly distinguished a difference between high school and college environments where hair regulations of faculty and students, in institutions of higher education, could not be justified, absent exceptional circumstances.

In *Miller v. School District No. 167, Cook County, Illinois*, 495 F.2d 658 (7th Cir.1974), the Seventh Circuit Court held that a school board "... undoubtedly may consider an individual's appearance as one of the factors affecting his suitability for a particular position. If a school board should correctly conclude that a teacher's style of dress or plumage has an adverse impact on the educational process, and if that conclusion conflicts with the teacher's interest in selecting his own life style, we have no doubt the interest of the teacher is subordinate to the public interest."

The Second Circuit Court in *East Hartford Education Association v. Board of Education, etc.*, 562 F.2d 838 (2d Cir.1977), recognized the liberty interest of an individual's personal appearance, but said that these liberty interests are "less weighty" than those of "procreation, marriage, and family life." The school board had instituted a rule requiring male classroom teachers to wear a jacket, shirt and tie and female teachers a dress, skirt, blouse and pantsuits except where other teaching assignments would require more appropriate apparel, i.e., gym teachers. To this the court responded, "[w]e join the sound views of the First and Seventh Circuits, and follow

Kelley by holding that a school board may, if it wishes, impose reasonable regulations governing the appearance of the teachers it employs."

§ 16.5   RIGHT OF PRIVACY

The word "privacy" is not mentioned in the Constitution nor in the Bill of Rights, yet the right of privacy is so basic and fundamental to individual freedom that it is assumed to emanate implicitly from the Constitution.

Justice Douglas in *Griswold v. Connecticut*, 381 U.S. 479 (1965) stated that there is a broad right of privacy which may be inferred from several provisions of the Bill of Rights. He said that the various guarantees of the constitution "create zones of privacy." Justice Douglas elaborated on the areas where privacy is found in the constitution saying that "The right of association contained in the penumbra of the First Amendment is one. . . . The Third Amendment in its prohibition against the quartering of soldiers 'in any house' in time of peace without the consent of the owner is another ... The Fourth Amendment explicitly affirms the 'right of the people to be secure in their persons, houses, papers, and effects, against unreasonable searches and seizures.' The Fifth Amendment in the Self–Incrimination Clause enables the citizen to create a zone of privacy beyond which government may not encroach. The Ninth Amendment provides: 'The enumeration in the Constitution, of certain rights, shall not be construed to deny or disparage others retained by the people.' "

The right of privacy also finds basis in the substance of liberty of the Due Process Clause of the Fourteenth Amendment. This was the basis for the Supreme Court's decision in *Roe v. Wade*, 410 U.S. 113 (1973). The connection between personal privacy and liberty is reinforced by the earlier U.S. Supreme Court precedents of *Pierce v. Society of Sisters*, 268 U.S. 510 (1925), and *Meyer v. Nebraska*, 262 U.S. 390 (1923). It is the confluence and implication of these specified constitutional rights and freedoms that create the penumbras that Justice Douglas spoke of in *Griswold*. Because privacy is a fundamental right, governmental restraint can be justified only by a showing of a "compelling state interest."

A teacher does not have an expectation of privacy in his desk or file cabinet. Moreover, all tests, quizzes and other educational material belong to the school and are not private property of a teacher. *Shaul v. Cherry Valley–Springfield Central School District*, 218 F.Supp.2d 266 (N.D.N.Y.2002). Neither does a teacher's right of privacy protect her (or him) against denial of tenure where the teacher engages in conduct that is detrimental to students or the good conduct of the school. Such was the decision of the U.S. Court of Appeals, Sixth Circuit, which held that a teacher who had been engaged in an alleged "intimate relationship" with a former high school student did not have a right of privacy nor did she have a substantive due process interest as to thwart the school board's denial of tenure for the affair. *Flaskamp v. Dearborn Public Schools*, 385 F.3d 935 (6th Cir. 2004).

§ 16.51 Teacher's Mental and Physical Examinations

A high expectation of privacy exists for teachers and others in their public employment with regard to their health and other personal matters. *Murray v. Pittsburgh Board of Education*, 759 F.Supp. 1178 (W.D.Pa.1991). Yet, the courts have generally upheld school boards in regulating the personal conduct of teachers within reasonable limits. Teachers' invocation of privacy rights have become more frequent in recent years, as schools have required teachers to take tests and be subject to various examinations. In one such case, a federal district judge rejected the privacy claim of a female teacher who refused to submit to a physical examination by a male physician employed by the school district. The court, in holding against the teacher, said that there was no right of privacy at stake, but rather a personal predilection against male physicians. *Gargiul v. Tompkins*, 525 F.Supp. 795 (N.D.N.Y.1981). See also *Hoffman v. Jannarone*, 401 F.Supp. 1095 (D.N.J.1975). In another case, a school principal's privacy claim was found to give way to the public interest where the school superintendent had reason to believe that the principal needed psychiatric attention. The principal had gotten into three near physical altercations with other administrators and a student. *Daury v. Smith*, 842 F.2d 9 (1st Cir.1988). Thus, school districts may require teachers or administrators to be examined to determine their physical, mental or intellectual fitness to teach so long as the tests conducted are reasonable and related to job performance.

§ 16.52   Drug Testing

As observed above, the Fourth Amendment of the U.S. Constitution guarantees privacy of individuals and safeguards against unwarranted and unreasonable search and seizure of their persons, papers, effects, and places where they may expect privacy as against the world. The protection of the Fourth Amendment places a magistrate or a judge between a person and the government. In order for police to search and seize they must first obtain a warrant from a judge issued only after a showing of probable cause that something illegal is secreted in a place controlled by the individual. By imposing a judge between the citizen and the state, the Constitution seeks to ensure against unreasonable search and seizure. Thus, what constitutes reasonableness is the critical issue.

For a warrant to be issued the police must show that the proposed search is reasonable. Reasonableness for a police search is established by the police showing probable cause. Probable cause is not, however, required for school searches; rather, the courts have held that the special and unique nature of the public school, with its obligation to protect children, entitles it to a qualified privilege to conduct warrantless searches. Such searches are justified by a showing of "reasonable suspicion."

Reasonable suspicion is also justification for searches of teachers on school grounds. Where a school district had a zero tolerance policy forbidding drugs, and a police dog sniffed, in a random search of the school parking lot, and found drugs in a teacher's car, the teacher claimed illegal search. The school policy required that anyone suspected of drugs must within two hours consent to undergo urine tests for drugs, and refusal could result in termination of employment. The teacher refused and was terminated. The court said the search "was based upon the probable cause generated by the dog sniff ..." *Hearn v. Board of Public Education*, 191 F.3d 1329 (11th Cir. 1999).

The exigencies of today's society brought on by increased violence and the pervasiveness of drugs has led the courts to consider and approve in certain circumstances "suspicionless searches." The special and limited conditions justifying "suspicionless searches" entail searches of persons who are employed in "safety-sensitive" positions, positions where the use of drugs or alcohol could endanger or seriously harm others. The two leading cases justifying suspicionless searches were decided by the U.S. Supreme Court wherein the government conducted suspicionless drug tests. The first was a situation where railway employees were drug tested, as required by federal regulation if the employees had been involved in an accident. The court said that the testing was compelling because of the public safety. *Skinner v. Railway Executives Association*, 489 U.S. 602 (1989). On the same day that *Skinner* was handed down, the Supreme Court ruled that customs service employees who carried firearms, enforced drug laws and had access to classified information could be required to take random drug tests. The court said drug tests may be allowed if compelling and special government reasons are articulated. *National Treasury Employees Union v. Von Raab*, 489 U.S. 656 (1989).

Thus, testing for drugs and alcohol may be reasonable and justified without particularized suspicion if the search can be expected to have a deterrent effect to incurrence of harm or injury. This means that in certain circumstances an individual's right of privacy can be overcome by a compelling interest of the government in deterring the use of drugs and alcohol in safety-sensitive jobs.

A federal court, in ruling on the validity of suspicionless drug searches of teachers by means of urine analysis, concluded that school teachers are in safety-sensitive positions. The court explained that, "Although the position of school teacher may not fit neatly into the prototypical 'safety-sensitive' position, we do not read the definition of 'safety-sensitive' so narrowly as to preclude application to a group of professionals to whom we entrust young children for a prolonged period of time on a daily basis. Simple common sense and experience with life tells us 'that even a momentary lapse of attention can have disastrous consequences.' " *Knox County Education Association v. Knox County Board of Educ.*, 158 F.3d 361 (6th Cir.1998). However, some courts have disagreed with the *Knox County* holding. See: *American Federation of Teachers v. Kanawha County Board of Education*, 592 F.Supp.2d 883 (S.D.W.Va.2009).

Safety-sensitive suspicionless drug test searches may extend to other school personnel as well. Based on the safety-sensitive rationale, a school custodian has been compelled to submit to urine tests for drugs. The federal court said that the school board's interests in protecting students from drugs were a compelling interest that outweighed the custodian's privacy interests. *Aubrey v. School Board of Lafayette Parish*, 148 F.3d 559 (5th Cir.1998). Too, another federal court has held that a school district policy providing for search of employees under reasonable suspicion of drug or alcohol use was valid and an employee could be directed immediately to have a urine and/or blood test. *Warren v. Board of Education of City of St. Louis*, 200 F.Supp.2d 1053 (E.D.Mo.2001).

§ 16.6 FREEDOM OF RELIGION

All persons have the right of religious freedom as guaranteed by the First Amendment. However, religion, as with other freedoms, is not without limits. For example, in *Palmer v. Board of Education of the City of Chicago*, 603 F.2d 1271 (7th Cir.1979), a teacher refused to carry out certain aspects of the approved curriculum because of personal religious beliefs. The court acknowledged the teacher's right to freedom of belief, but also recognized a compelling state interest in the proper education of all its children. The court stated that education "cannot be left to individual teachers to teach the way they please." Teachers have "no constitutional right to require others to submit to [their] views and to forego a portion of their education they would otherwise be entitled to enjoy." (See Chapter 18, Employment Discrimination.)

A teacher's religious freedom may extend into several aspects of the educational program. For example, if the tenets of a teacher's religion are violated by the Pledge of Allegiance to the American flag, the teacher cannot be compelled to recite the pledge, but, the teacher, in accordance with school board rules, must conduct the pledge ceremony for student participation. Religious freedom of teachers will be sustained by the courts so long as the exercise of the freedom does not encroach on the rights of students or is not deleterious to the good conduct of the school.

A New Jersey court held unconstitutional a teacher-negotiated agreement that allowed for paid leaves of absences for religious believers, but made no allowance for non-believers. According to the court, the rule violated the First Amendment's free exercise clause. *Hunterdon Central High School Board of Ed. v. Hunterdon Central High School Teachers' Ass'n*, 416 A.2d 980 (N.J.Super.1980).

§ 16.61 The 1964 Civil Rights Act and 1972 Amendment (Title VII)

The Civil Rights Act of 1964, Title VII, 42 U.S.C.A. § 2000e et seq., prohibits any employer from discriminating against an individual because of religion. The 1972

Amendment states: "[t]he term 'religion' includes all aspects of religious observance and practice, as well as belief, unless an employer demonstrates that he is unable to reasonably accommodate an employee's or prospective employee's religious observance or practice without undue hardship on the conduct of the employer's business." One of the key questions is, what does an employer need to do to accommodate the religious beliefs of an employee.

In *Ansonia Board of Education v. Philbrook*, 479 U.S. 60 (1986), the employee and employer each proposed a reasonable accommodation. The Supreme Court stated, "An employer has met its obligations under § 701(j) when it demonstrates that it has offered a reasonable accommodation to the employee. The employer need not further show that each of the employee's alternative accommodations would result in undue hardship. The extent of undue hardship on the employer's business is at issue only where the employer claims that it is unable to offer any reasonable accommodation without such *hardship* (emphasis added)."

As to what constitutes "hardship," the issue was addressed in *Trans World Airlines, Inc. v. Hardison*, 432 U.S. 63 (1977). In this case, Hardison, an employee, was working in a maintenance division under a negotiated agreement that allowed employees, with greater seniority, to choose what days they would work. Because of his seniority, Hardison chose not to work on Saturdays, his day of religious observance. Later, at his own request, he was transferred to another work assignment. Hardison had little seniority in his new position, and, therefore, he could not take Saturday off. Hardison challenged the collective bargaining agreement and the seniority rule claiming that his religious beliefs took precedence over such provisions. Justice White said that Title VII did not require TWA "... to carve out special exemptions." "To require TWA to bear more than a *de minimis* cost, in order to give Hardison Saturdays off, is an undue hardship."

Thus, relying on *Hardison* as applicable precedent, it would appear that the burden of proof is on the teacher or individual to establish that religion was a primary determinant in an employment decision. If the teacher sustains the burden and shows the employer's primary motivation was religiously related, then the burden of proof shifts to the school board or employer to show that it made a good faith effort to accommodate the employee and, if this is unsuccessful, then it must be demonstrated that the employer (board) was unable to reasonably accommodate the employee's religious beliefs without undue hardship.

Another case that sheds light on the employer-employee relationship is *Wangsness v. Watertown School District No. 14–4, et al.*, 541 F.Supp. 332 (D.S.D.1982), wherein an employee requested seven days off, without pay, to attend a religious festival. When the request was denied, the employee attended the festival anyway and was as a result discharged from employment. The school board claimed that a qualified teacher could not be found to serve as a substitute during the absence. The teacher, before departing for the festival, prepared lesson plans to be used by a substitute teacher. The court determined that the classes had run smoothly, and no undue hardship was suffered by the board; therefore, the teacher was due equitable relief for a violation of Title VII.

In another similar case, a school district, through a negotiated agreement, provided each teacher with two personal leave days. A Jewish teacher claimed that she needed more than two days to celebrate religious holidays and she emphasized that Christian teachers benefited from the structure of the school calendar citing that school was closed at Christmas and for Easter. Thus, Christian teachers could participate in religious ceremonies without being absent from school. The court ruled the school district's policy did not constitute religious discrimination against Jewish teachers merely because the Jewish teacher was required to occasionally take unpaid leave to accommodate his religious beliefs. The teacher was allowed to take unpaid leave and this was sufficient accommodation. *Pinsker v. Joint District No. 28J*, 735 F.2d 388 (10th Cir.1984).

§ 16.62   Religious Garb

Whether teachers can wear religious garb of any particular church, religious order or society has been an occasional subject of contention over the years. The fact that there is no precise definition as to what constitutes religious dress does not simplify the situation. Yet, some religious dress is readily identifiable and may be of concern because teachers of public school districts, as agents of the state, should not by their various manifestations convey a particular religious belief so as to violate state neutrality toward religion.

A notable case of this type was litigated in Pennsylvania before the turn of the century in which nuns teaching in public schools wore the dress of the Sisterhood of St. Joseph. Pennsylvania state court ruled that the mere wearing of particular apparel did not constitute sectarian teaching and did not inculcate religion, thus such practice was permissible. Moreover, the court found that to deny the wearing of the religious regalia would effectively violate the teacher's religious liberty. *Hysong v. School District of Gallitzin Borough*, 30 A. 482 (Pa.1894).

Later, however, the Pennsylvania legislature prohibited the wearing of religious garb by public school teachers and the act was upheld. The Supreme Court of Pennsylvania found that such a denial was a reasonable exercise of state authority to maintain the secular nature of public schools and to prevent sectarian establishment. The court said in justifying the legislative action that the legislation "is directed against acts, not beliefs, and only against acts of the teacher while engaged in the performance of his or her duties as such teacher." *Commonwealth v. Herr*, 78 A. 68 (Pa.1910).

In a definitive analysis of the issue, the Supreme Court of Oregon held that a teacher's certificate could be revoked for wearing religious garb. The teacher wore white clothes and a Sikh Hindu turban. In so holding, the court observed the legislature had a legitimate objective in maintaining the neutrality of the public schools. While the denial of the wearing of religious garb could be interpreted by some as an impingement on the teacher's personal religious freedom, it could just as logically be maintained the state's condoning of such garb favors a particular religion, and, in fact, places the *imprimatur* of the state behind that particular religious sect. The Oregon court said "the teacher's appearance in religious garb may leave a conscious or unconscious impression among young people and their parents that the school endorses the particular religious commitment of the person (teacher)." *Cooper v. Eugene School District No. 4J*, 723 P.2d 298 (Or.1986).

The issue arose again in Pennsylvania, this time involving a devout Muslim teacher who insisted on wearing traditional Muslim dress. The Pennsylvania statute prohibiting religious attire was again challenged. The teacher claimed discrimination under Title VII of the Civil Rights Act and violation of religious liberty and sought an injunction preventing the school board from enforcing the statute. The U.S. Court of Appeals, Third Circuit, held for the school board ruling that the state had a compelling interest in maintaining religious neutrality in the public schools. With specific regard to Title VII, the court held that the compelling interest of the state in protecting the religious liberty of the public school students in the classroom was clearly an interest of such magnitude to overcome any claimed religious right of the teacher to wear the attire. *United States v. Board of Education for the School District of Philadelphia*, 911 F.2d 882 (3d Cir.1990).

The Pennsylvania and Oregon cases appear to reflect the prevailing view of the courts with regard to teacher religious attire. A contrary opinion, however, is expressed by the Supreme Court of Mississippi where it upheld the right of a teacher to wear an African Hebrew Israelite head-wrap as an expression of religious and cultural heritage beliefs. The Mississippi court said that the wearing of the head-wrap was grounded in a sincerely-held religious belief protected by the First Amendment. *Mississippi Employment Security Commission v. McGlothin*, 556 So.2d 324 (Miss.1990).

CHAPTER 17

TEACHER DISMISSAL

§ 17.1 INTRODUCTION

Conditions of employment are controlled by state statute. Whether a teacher has permanent employment, a
continuing contract, or tenure, the conditions are defined
by legislative enactment. Procedures for nonrenewal of a
probationary teacher or the dismissal of a tenured or
permanent teacher are also determined by statute.

There is a distinction between non-renewals and dismissals. With nonrenewal a probationary teacher is simply not offered a new term of employment at the end of
the contract period. The school board has the discretion
to decide the employee's services are no longer needed.
State statute stipulates the date of notification for the
nonrenewal. Dismissal, on the other hand, occurs within
the term of the contract period, not at the end. A
dismissal may occur during the period of an annual
contract or during the period of tenure or continuing
contract.

With dismissal, a teacher is removed from employment
during a statutory period of probation or during the term
of the permanent contract or tenure. A school board, in
dismissing a tenured teacher, must prove good cause and
afford the individual an opportunity to refute the reasons
for dismissal alleged by the board. To dismiss requires
full procedural process, whereas non-renewals generally

require only that the individual be notified of nonrenewal by a specific time.

Teachers' rights are guaranteed by State and the U.S. Constitutions. The Federal Fourteenth Amendment provides no state shall "... deprive any person of life, liberty, or property, without due process of law...." Also, the First Amendment's protections of speech, expression, religion, and privacy may be invoked in teacher dismissal cases, as may be the Fourth Amendment's search and seizure provision.

§ 17.2   DUE PROCESS OF LAW

As noted more extensively elsewhere in this book, due process of law has two important aspects both of which may affect teacher employment: (1) procedural and (2) substantive. Procedural due process encompasses the actual legal steps that must be adhered to when a court or administrative tribunal holds a hearing to ascertain the guilt or innocence of an individual. Procedural due process itself has been an essential part of Anglo–American law since Magna Charta in 1215. Two elements are essential to procedural due process: (a) fairness of hearing, and (b) an impartial tribunal.

Substantive due process, on the other hand, does not involve the actual hearing process, but, rather, is the extent and nature of the content of due process. The substance of due process emanates from the expanded definition of the terms liberty and property. Liberty is more than simply a right to be free from incarceration, and property rights extend far beyond simply the right to obtain and hold physical property. (See Chapter 3.)

§ 17.21 Procedural Due Process

The basic concept of procedural due process is an opportunity to be heard in a manner that promotes fairness and establishes the accuracy of the charges. Procedural due process is a flexible concept and has been referred to by the courts as "fundamental fairness." An individual has a right to refute the charges brought against him by government before a liberty or property right is taken away. The more serious the deprivation, the more formal the procedure for due process. Therefore, an administrative hearing to remove a teacher from his/her position is not as serious as a criminal offense and would require less stringent procedural due process.

The procedures to be followed in dismissing or not rehiring a teacher are generally specified by statute. Some of the elements of procedural due process are: There must be fair and reasonable notice of the charges; there must be an opportunity for a hearing; the hearing must be conducted by an impartial tribunal; there must be sufficient time to prepare for the hearing; the decision should be based on the evidence presented at the hearing; and there must be an opportunity to appeal a negative decision.

Although the specific elements of hearings may not be specifically set forth, the hearing must adhere to the minimal requirements of fair play to allow the teacher the opportunity to refute the charges. The Supreme Court of Missouri in *Valter v. Orchard Farm School District*, 541 S.W.2d 550 (Mo.1976), suggested these minimal elements for a hearing. They may not necessarily be the same as provided for students since circumstances may be quite different. According to *Valter* the requirements for teachers are:

1.   The opportunity to be heard

2.   The opportunity to present evidence to refute the charges

3.   The opportunity to present witnesses

4.   Representation by legal counsel

5.   The opportunity to cross-examine witnesses

6.   Access to all evidence, such as written reports, in advance

School boards, generally, are the tribunal hearing the evidence and making the decision to dismiss or retain a teacher. This procedure has been challenged as a violation of due process because the school board is said not to be an impartial tribunal; therefore, fundamental fairness of procedural due process is allegedly hindered.

The U.S. Supreme Court addressed this issue of impartiality in *Hortonville Joint School District No. 1 v. Hortonville Education Association*, 426 U.S. 482 (1976). In this case negotiations between teachers and the school board failed to produce an agreeable contract and the teachers went on strike. The teachers claimed the Due Process Clause of the Fourteenth Amendment was violated because the board was not sufficiently impartial. The Supreme Court held that school board members who were public servants and who had no personal or financial stake in the negotiations had no conflict of interest, and, therefore, could constitute an impartial tribunal. In the words of the Court, "[M]ere familiarity with the facts of a case gained by an agency in the performance of its statutory role does not, however, disqualify a decision maker."

§ 17.22   Liberty and Property Interests

Teachers have liberty and property interests, and the extent of these rights has been frequently interpreted by the courts. The United States Supreme Court in *Roth* has observed that liberty and property are "broad and majestic" terms, and society demands that if one of these rights is denied, then due process is required. Property rights have been recognized when the teacher has tenure or a permanent contract as provided by the legislature. Also, the contractual agreement the employee has with the employer is a property right and cannot be breached during the contract period. A property right is created if the individual has a legitimate claim of entitlement to continued employment as created by state law or by the policies and procedures of a local board. *DeMichele v. Greenburgh Central School District*, 167 F.3d 784 (2d Cir.1999).

Liberty interests are involved if the employer stigmatizes the employee and jeopardizes the opportunity for future employment. Stigmatizing the individual's good name or reputation is a violation of a liberty interest and will require due process of law. The following cases are landmarks in establishing and setting the parameters for teacher liberty and property rights.

§ 17.23   *Board of Regents v. Roth*

Roth provides the definitive statement as to the meaning of property and liberty interests. In *Board of Regents v. Roth*, 408 U.S. 564 (1972), a professor was hired by the University of Wisconsin for a fixed term of one academic year. He subsequently was notified his contract would not be renewed for a second year. Wisconsin statute provided that after four years, tenure could be acquired and, at that time, procedural safeguards, such as due process, were by law provided. *Roth* claimed the university had deprived him of his Fourteenth Amendment rights by not giving him reasons for his nonrenewal. He further alleged the true reason for his non-retention was his public criticism of the university administration. The U.S. Supreme Court was presented with the question of whether a probationary teacher, without tenure protection, was entitled to procedural due process for nonrenewal.

The Supreme Court observed that the Fourteenth Amendment requires an opportunity for a hearing if a "property" or "liberty" interest is jeopardized. The Court said: "the range of interests protected by procedural due process is not infinite," but liberty and property are "... broad and majestic terms that are ... purposely left to gather meaning with experience...." "Property interests ... are not created by the Constitution. Rather, they are created, and their dimensions are defined by existing rules or understandings that stem from an independent source such as state law—rules or understandings that secure certain benefits and that support claims of entitlement to those benefits." Property interests of a teacher therefore may be established: (1) by tenure statute, (2) by contract, or (3) if the individual has a legitimate and objective expectation of re-employment. An informal encouragement of a non-tenure teacher by a supervisor does not create an expectation of re-employment vesting a probationary teacher with a property interest in the job. (*Watson v. North Panola School District*, 188 Fed. Appx. 291 (5th Cir. 2006).

With regard to liberty, the Supreme Court in *Roth* said that a liberty interest arises if charges are made against an individual "... that might seriously damage his standing and associations in his community." If, for example, a school district makes charges that would implicate guilt of dishonesty or immorality, then a liberty interest would arise. A charge of dishonesty or immorality would damage one's "good name, reputation, honor, or integrity," and if such were leveled against a teacher, then a hearing to refute the charges would be required. A liberty interest arises if a school district places a "stigma" upon the teacher that forecloses his or her freedom to pursue employment opportunities in the teaching profession. In applying this reasoning, the Supreme Court found, however, that professor Roth had not been deprived of his property or liberty interests and was not entitled to procedural due process.

§ 17.24 *Perry v. Sindermann*

On the same day that *Board of Regents v. Roth* was rendered, the U.S. Supreme Court also handed down *Perry v. Sindermann*, 408 U.S. 593 (1972). This case further elaborated the property rights of individuals engaged in public employment. Sindermann, a teacher, had been employed in the State of Texas college system for ten years, the last four as a junior college professor at Odessa Junior College. His employment had been based on a series of one-year contracts. The college of his current employment, Odessa, had not adopted a tenure system. During his term of employment, Sindermann had had public disagreements with the board of regents, and in particular, he had advocated that the college be expanded to a four-year institution, which was opposed by the governing board. The college board elected not to renew his contract and issued a press release alleging insubordination on the part of the plaintiff. Sindermann brought suit, claiming his nonrenewal was based on his public criticism, a violation of his free speech rights, and he claimed that he should be granted a due process hearing. Although Sindermann did not have a property interest derived from a formal tenure system because the college had none, he claimed *de facto* tenure. To substantiate his claim of *de facto* tenure he pointed out that the faculty handbook stated that as long as the teacher is performing satisfactorily, the administration "wishes the faculty member to feel that he has permanent tenure." In deciding the case, the United States Supreme Court reiterated its statement made in *Roth* that "property" denotes a broad range of interests that are secured by "existing rules and understandings" that may be created by conditions of statute, rules, or regulation. Therefore, the faculty handbook rules constituted a legitimate claim of entitlement which created an objective expectancy of employment on behalf of the plaintiff; he could have reasonably expected to have continued employment. The Court, thus, ruled that Sindermann had a right to procedural due process if his employment was to be terminated.

The *Roth* and *Sindermann* cases established that probationary teachers have no right to a hearing unless they can demonstrate a deprivation of liberty or property interests. A property interest may be established by state statute, policies, rules, or regulations. A property interest may be gained by either direct or *de facto* obligations. A liberty interest may be found where the institution stigmatizes the individual, damaging his good name and reputation.

§ 17.25 Stigmatizing Reasons

A person's constitutional liberty rights are impacted when the state jeopardizes his/her "good name, reputation, honor or integrity," or forecloses the freedom to take advantage of other employment. Courts have ruled that charges such as "immorality, dishonesty, alcoholism" or "lying and/or misrepresentation of facts" were stigmatizing.

The courts have explained in detail how a non-tenured teacher can be stigmatized and entitled to procedural due process in terms of what they call "stigma-plus" claims. This occurs where a plaintiff teacher alleges denial of due process because of loss of reputation that is coupled with the deprivation of a more tangible interest. Such a tangible interest may be the denial of public school employment of which many in the community are aware. According to the U.S. Court of Appeals, Second Circuit, to prevail with a "stigma-plus" claim, the teacher who is not rehired must show three elements to demonstrate deprivation of a due process interest. "First, the plaintiff must show that the school district made stigmatizing statements in response to the plaintiff's statements that call into question the plaintiff's good name, reputation, honor, or integrity. Second, the plaintiff must prove that stigmatizing statements were made public. Third, the plaintiff must show that the stigmatizing statements were made concurrently with, or in close temporal relationship to, the plaintiff's dismissal from the (teaching position)." *Segal v. City of New York*, 459 F.3d 207 (2d Cir. 2006).

§ 17.26 Public Charges

The courts have established that as long as reasons for nonrenewal are not made public, then no stigma or infringement of a liberty interest exists. In *Bishop v. Wood*, 426 U.S. 341 (1976), the U.S. Supreme Court explained what constituted a stigma. In *Bishop*, a probationary policeman was told, in private, by his superior, he would not be re-employed because of his failure to follow orders, his poor attendance, his having and causing low morale among fellow workers and other conduct inappropriate to being a policeman. Testimony indicated that all of the reasons given for his dismissal were false.

The two issues litigated were: (1) whether the employee had a property interest, and (2) if the explanations for dismissal were false, did this deprive the employee of his liberty rights? The Court answered both of these in the negative. The policeman had relied on an ordinance for providing him a property right. The Supreme Court stated, "A property interest in employment can ... be created by ordinance; ... [h]owever, the sufficiency of the claim of entitlement must be decided by reference to state law. The North Carolina Supreme Court has held that an enforceable expectation of continued employment ... can exist only if the employer, by statute or contract, has actually granted some form of guarantee." The U.S. Supreme Court, therefore, accepted the state court's interpretation of a property interest and concluded that the employee "held his position at the will and pleasure of the city." Therefore, no liberty interest had been infringed upon since the reasons for dismissal were communicated in private. Because the reasons were given in private, their truth or falsity was irrelevant and did not create a liberty interest. Therefore, if reasons for dismissal of a probationary teacher are given in private, then no stigma is placed upon the individual and no deprivation of liberty occurs. The Supreme Court stated, "The due process clause of the Fourteenth Amendment is not a guarantee against incorrect or ill-advised personnel decisions of public employees."

§ 17.27 Incompetence, Insubordination, Neglect of Duty

In some cases, non-tenured teachers have sought to have the nonrenewal of their employment overturned by alleging that they have been stigmatized by the district's charges of incompetence, inadequacy, and insubordination. In one such case, *Gray v. Union County Intermediate Education District*, 520 F.2d 803 (9th Cir.1975), an employee was charged with insubordination, incompetence, hostility toward authority, and aggressive behavior. The court stated, "[n]early any reason assigned for dismissal is likely to be to some extent a negative reflection on an individual's ability, temperament, or character. But not every dismissal assumes a constitutional magnitude. The concern is only with the type of stigma that seriously damages an individual's ability to take advantage of other employment opportunities. . . . These allegations certainly are not complimentary and suggest that [the teacher] may have problems in relating to some people, but they do not import serious character defects such as dishonesty or immorality . . . as contemplated by *Roth*." Other courts have held that neglect of duty, failure to maintain discipline, improper teaching techniques, tardiness, and failure to follow orders, do not invoke liberty interests. These reasons for dismissal do not reflect so negatively on the teacher's reputation or honor as to harm the teacher's future employability.

§ 17.28   Stigma of Racism

Accusations of racism may be stigmatizing. In a Minnesota Community College case a non-tenured professor's contract was not renewed, and he claimed he had been stigmatized because of remarks accusing him of being a "racist." Charges of racism had been forwarded to the college by various campus groups, and had been entered into the teacher's personnel file. The Court of Appeals for the Eighth Circuit held that these charges were a deprivation of a liberty interest reflecting on the teacher's reputation and good name. Therefore, a hearing would be required before he could be terminated, despite his non-tenured status. *Wellner v. Minnesota State Junior College Board*, 487 F.2d 153 (8th Cir.1973).

§ 17.29   Emotional Instability

Charges that a teacher lacks mental or emotional stability may attach a stigma. In a 1981 case, a school board announced the reasons for nonrenewal of a teacher were for "... apparent emotional instability, resentment of authority ..." and her failure to follow orders. The court ruled that charges of emotional instability constituted a stigma. The emotional instability charge went beyond job related comments and, thereby, stigmatized the teacher. Such a charge implied a serious personal defect and, therefore, was a violation of the teacher's liberty rights. The other reasons were not found to be stigmatizing. *Bomhoff v. White*, 526 F.Supp. 488 (D.Ariz. 1981).

Similarly, public comment about mental state or psychiatric condition has also been held to stigmatize the teacher. See *Stewart v. Pearce*, 484 F.2d 1031 (9th Cir. 1973).

§ 17.3   BURDEN OF PROOF OF NON–TENURED TEACHERS

If a non-tenured teacher's contract is not renewed and no reasons are given by the board, the teacher's constitutional rights are not offended. If the teacher does not challenge the board and allege denial of a due process right, the board has no responsibility to institute such a hearing of its own volition. An Alabama court, citing *Roth,* stated that the employee must assert himself to protect his rights and institute the process whether school board procedures are established for such procedure or not. *Stewart v. Bailey*, 396 F.Supp. 1381 (N.D.Ala.1975).

If a teacher claims his or her contract has not been renewed because of constitutionally impermissible reasons, the burden of establishing the deprivation rests upon the teacher. The teacher must establish a *prima facie* case that a constitutionally offensive reason was the motivating factor for the non-renewal. If the teacher establishes that an impermissible reason for dismissal is involved, the burden shifts to the school board to show, by a preponderance of evidence, "that [the board] would have reached the same decision as to [plaintiff's] re-employment even in the absence of the protected conduct." *Mount Healthy City School Board of Education v. Doyle*, 429 U.S. 274 (1977). Courts have noted that a non-tenured teacher may be non-renewed for good reasons, no reasons, bad reasons, even false reasons, but not unconstitutional reasons.

§ 17.4 DISMISSAL OF TENURED TEACHERS FOR INCOMPETENCY

Incompetency has been given broad definition by the courts. Legal incompetency may be "want of physical, intellectual, or moral ability; insufficiency; inadequacy; specific want of legal qualifications or fitnesses," (*Webster's New International Dictionary*) *Beilan v. Board of Public Education, School District of Philadelphia*, 357 U.S. 399 (1958). Incompetency generally concerns a fitness to teach encompassing a broad range of factors. The courts have included in the definition of "incompetency" lack of knowledge of subject matter, lack of discipline, unreasonable discipline, unprofessional conduct, and willful neglect of duty. Where incompetency exists, some states' statutes require that teachers be given an opportunity to improve or to remediate themselves. If a statute requires remediation before dismissal for incompetency can be effectuated, the school board must show that remediation was attempted or that the situation was irremediable.

A teacher who has been certified by the state is assumed to be competent and it is the responsibility of the school board to prove incompetency. As long as a school board's actions are not arbitrary or capricious, the courts will generally not interfere. The Fifth Circuit Court of Appeals has stated that "[f]or sound policy reasons, courts are loathe to intrude upon the internal affairs of local school authorities in such matters as teacher competency." *Blunt v. Marion County School Board*, 515 F.2d 951 (5th Cir.1975).

Incompetency may be evidenced by poor classroom decorum. In one instance, a school district dismissed a tenured teacher on grounds of incompetence because she was unable to maintain order in her classroom, the classroom was littered with sunflower seeds, paper, and "junk," and the furniture and walls were covered with graffiti. Moreover, the teacher had not planned her lessons or given students proper directions; the court was, therefore, not hesitant to uphold dismissal for incompetency. *Board of Education of the School District of Philadelphia v. Kushner*, 530 A.2d 541 (Pa.Cmwlth.1987).

The manner of offering evidence in incompetency cases is generally through testimony. Both the quantity and quality of evidence is important. The courts have liberally allowed opinions of principals, curriculum supervisors, and other supervisory personnel to stand as expert testimony. Other testimony by students and parents may be important as well, but the actual observations by supervisors of what transpired in the classroom are very significant. One court said, "This court, in absence of proof of an abuse of discretion, cannot substitute its opinion for the decision of the school board and of the district court where both of these tribunals were presented with substantial evidence upon which to base their decisions." *Frank v. St. Landry Parish School Board*, 225 So.2d 62 (La.App.1969).

As might be expected and with good reason, a Georgia court upheld a school media coordinator's termination for incompetency for videotaping the female student locker room. In this extreme case, the school board was not required to show that the coordinator's incompetency disrupted the school. *Clinch County Board of Education v. Hinson*, 543 S.E.2d 91 (Ga.App.2000).

§ 17.41   Incompetency Not Proven

Teachers, though, cannot be dismissed for incompetency for nebulous and uncertain evaluations. For example, a case on this point reveals the following factual situation: A tenured teacher of 13 years who had received satisfactory evaluations requested and was granted a one-year unpaid leave of absence. The board of trustees instituted a new policy that all teachers seeking positions or teachers seeking voluntary transfers must participate in a structured interview. When the teacher returned from leave, she participated in the structured interviews and did poorly. The trustees dismissed her for incompetency. The court held that after 13 years of apparently satisfactory teaching, the structured interviews were not sufficient to meet the burden of proof necessary to dismiss a tenured teacher. *Trustees, Missoula County School District No. 1 v. Anderson*, 757 P.2d 1315 (Mont. 1988).

A teacher responded to a question about homosexual practices in explicit language after a nurse had shown a video in sex education to a group of fourth-grade boys. The teacher, a male, had been instructed by the nurse to answer the questions as honestly as possible. Since he was a male, the boys would not feel uncomfortable in asking questions. A boy asked how it would be possible for two men to have sex, the teacher graphically explained, whereupon parents complained. The school board dismissed him for incompetency. The court ruled for the teacher since he had a good record for 29 years and had been told to answer the questions by the nurse who conducted the sex education class. A single incident may be of such magnitude or have such consequences that would permanently impair the teacher's ability to perform his duties and would therefore be grounds for dismissal for incompetency. However, one incident of an ill-advised answer did not constitute incompetency so as to impair the ability to teach. *Collins v. Faith School District No. 46–2*, 574 N.W.2d 889 (S.D.1998).

§ 17.42   Failure to Maintain Discipline

Although failure to maintain discipline has been a major factor in dismissing teachers for incompetency, it is usually coupled with other charges. In either case, however, a teacher's inability to control classroom behavior with decorum and maintain a studious atmosphere is good grounds for dismissal. In one case where a teacher's dismissal notification listed 14 specific reasons and included inadequate maintenance of discipline during class, excessive and ineffective use of films, ineffective classroom teaching, and failure to cooperate with school administrators, the court upheld the dismissal because the preponderance of evidence showed that the teacher's students were disruptive, daydreamed in class, wandered around the room, and left the room without permission. The evidence also showed that these same students behaved properly in other classes. *Board of Directors of Sioux City Community School Dist. v. Mroz*, 295 N.W.2d 447 (Iowa 1980).

In Louisiana, a teacher was charged with failure to keep classroom discipline and to prepare lesson plans. The teacher exhibited a negative attitude and did not institute suggested strategies to improve teaching. The failure to maintain discipline was confirmed by the principal, the supervisor of child welfare, the coordinator of special education, and another teacher. The children were allowed to roam around the room and read aloud when the teacher was attempting to read. The assistant principal testified that the teacher did an adequate job and the disciplinary problems arose because of the disparity of student ages in the room. Even so, the court said, "[o]ur review of the record convinces us there is no foundation for holding that the action of the School Board was arbitrary, capricious or an abuse of the Board's discretion." *Mims v. West Baton Rouge Parish School Board*, 315 So.2d 349 (La.App.1975).

§ 17.43   Inappropriate Discipline

Quite obviously, corporal punishment administered in violation of state law may well be valid grounds for dismissal of a teacher. By definition, breaking the law may be directly related to a teacher's fitness to act in a professional capacity. The Nebraska Supreme Court has held that corporal punishment contrary to state statute constitutes "conduct which is unbecoming a member in good standing of a profession," for which a teacher can be dismissed. *Daily v. Board of Education of Morrill County School District No. 62–0063*, 588 N.W.2d 813 (Neb.1999).

Dismissal of a tenured teacher for excessive discipline has also been upheld where it was shown that the teacher punished students by making them stay in the bathroom, pulling their hair, pinching them, and pulling their ears. *Gwathmey v. Atkinson*, 447 F.Supp. 1113 (E.D.Va.1976). Another teacher's dismissal was upheld for incompetency when he administered excessive physical punishment without authority to do so. *Kinsella v. Board of Education, etc.*, 407 N.Y.S.2d 78 (1978).

Inappropriate discipline may take many forms. Where a teacher was dismissed for striking students in the genitals for disciplinary purposes, the court in ruling against the teacher stated the obvious "... a teacher's intentional striking of a student's genitals lacks any positive educational aspect or legitimate professional purpose." *Mott v. Endicott School District No. 308*, 713 P.2d 98 (Wash.1986).

Too, where a school principal bound a student to a desk with a rope and duct tape and placed the student in the doorway for all to see for two hours, the Court agreed with the school board that the action was evidence of incompetence and demotion was a fitting penalty. *Sylvester v. Cancienne*, 664 So.2d 1259 (La.App. 1st Cir.1995).

§ 17.44   Teacher's Ability

Incompetence may also include a lack of knowledge of subject matter, using incorrect English, poor teaching methods, and failure to follow the required pedagogy methodology. For example, the U.S. Court of Appeals for the Fifth Circuit upheld the dismissal of a teacher who had been teaching for 25 years and was discharged for incompetency for using poor grammar, both written and spoken, making spelling errors, including misspelled words on the blackboard, which students copied, having instructional deficiencies in math, English (phonics) and reading, and using poor writing techniques. The teacher also attempted to teach spelling before the children had mastered the alphabet. Three supervisors presented substantial and credible evidence that the teacher lacked the necessary academic skills to teach and was hostile toward criticism aimed at improvement. *Blunt v. Marion County School Board*, 515 F.2d 951 (5th Cir.1975).

In Louisiana, a teacher was held properly discharged for incompetency where the specific charges were made that she could not adapt to the new instructional program and misspelled and mispronounced words. Moreover, she lacked the ability to organize and carry out constructive instructional programs and had serious discipline problems in class. *Jennings v. Caddo Parish School Board*, 276 So.2d 386 (La.App.1973).

As noted earlier, some states, through statute, require that teachers be given a chance to improve or remediate themselves before dismissal. If a state statute requires remediation, the school board must show that a good faith effort has been made to improve the instructional capabilities of the teacher before proceeding with dismissal. In *Gilliland v. Board of Education of Pleasant View*, 365 N.E.2d 322 (Ill.1977), a teacher was charged with incompetency for allegedly ruining pupils' attitudes toward school, lacking rapport with pupils, and giving irregular homework assignments. Charges of cruelty were also alleged because the teacher had grabbed childrens' hair, arms and shoulders, and had hit one child with a book. The teacher claimed she should be allowed to remediate the problems, but the court disagreed and stated "... many causes, when standing alone, may be remediable, whereas those same causes in combination with others may well be irremediable. Here, we think it clear that the combination of a number of causes plus the continuous nature of the conduct were sufficient bases for a finding of irremediability."

Although one act may be remediable, another act may be irremediable, particularly if it is of a nature that offends the senses of the community or endangers the health and safety of children. Where a sixth-grade tenured teacher used high amperage batteries in a cattle prod to discipline children, the court was not convinced that the teacher deserved a second chance and said the "manifest weight of evidence" showed the actions of the teacher were irremediable. *Rolando v. School Directors of District No. 125*, 358 N.E.2d 945 (Ill.App.1976).

§ 17.5 DISMISSAL OF TENURED TEACHERS FOR INSUBORDINATION

Courts have defined insubordination as "constant or continuing intentional refusal to obey a direct or implied order, reasonable in nature, and given by and with proper authority." *In re Proposed Termination of James E. Johnson's Teaching Contract*, 451 N.W.2d 343 (Minn. App.1990); See also *School District No. 8, Pinal County v. Superior Court*, 433 P.2d 28 (Ariz.1967). Some courts have found insubordination in a single incident while other courts have required a constant or persistent course of conduct. Generally, though, insubordination can be substantiated by the seriousness of the single action if the act is of substantial magnitude in bearing on the ability of the teacher to perform his or her duties. Charges of insubordination are not supportable if: "(1) the alleged misconduct was not proved; (2) the existence of a pertinent school rule or a superior's order was not proved; (3) the pertinent rule or order was not violated; (4) the teacher tried, although unsuccessfully, to comply with the rule or order; (5) the teacher's motive for violating the rule or order was admirable; (6) no harm resulted from the violation; (7) the rule or order was unreasonable; (8) the rule or order was invalid as beyond the authority of its maker; (9) the enforcement of the rule or order revealed possible bias or discrimination against the teacher; or (10) the enforcement of the rule or order violated the First Amendment rights to free speech or academic freedom.'' (78 ALR 3d 83, 87).

§ 17.51   Insubordination Not Proven

As observed above, insubordination may be refusal or repeated refusal to follow directions. In a case where a teacher was charged with insubordination for inappropriate punishment of students and allowing card games to be played in study hall, the court ruled that there was no insubordination, though the conduct was highly questionable. Evidence was presented to the court showing that the teacher no longer continued the activities after being admonished by the principal. *Thompson v. Wake County Board of Education*, 230 S.E.2d 164 (N.C.App. 1976), see *Thompson v. Wake County Board of Education*, 233 S.E.2d 538 (N.C.1977).

In another insubordination case a teacher was told not to use J.D. Salinger's "Catcher in the Rye" in his classroom and had agreed not to do so. Later, he started to use the novel again and was requested to meet with the principal concerning the situation. The teacher walked out of the meeting after five minutes and was charged with two counts of insubordination: (1) breaking the previous agreement, and (2) walking out of the conference. The school board upheld the charges and dismissed the teacher. Upon appeal, the court determined the dismissal was too severe. Although the courts will not generally review administrative sanction, in this instance the court found that the dismissal was disproportionate to the offense and was not fair since students were not harmed and there was no indication of lack of fitness to teach. *Harris v. Mechanicville Central School District*, 380 N.E.2d 213 (N.Y.1978).

§ 17.52   Insubordination Proven

Insubordination may be manifested by a teacher's willful disregard for school policies. Certain cases clearly illustrate the point. For example, a teacher with 25 years experience was dismissed for insubordination, neglect of duty and other good cause for showing an R-rated film depicting nudity, sexual activities, drug use and violence in his logic and debate class. The teacher had ignored a school learning resource policy requiring all teachers to provide the school principal with 20 days prior written notice before using a controversial learning resource. The Supreme Court of Colorado in upholding the dismissal observed that the regulation was "reasonably related to a legitimate pedagogical concern" and the teacher's failure to abide by the regulation was insubordination. *Board of Education of Jefferson County School District R–1 v. Wilder*, 960 P.2d 695 (Colo.1998). In another case, a teacher of 24 years requested leave for five days to attend an out-of-state reading conference. The board denied the request whereupon the teacher obtained a well-qualified substitute and attended the conference anyway. The teacher was charged with insubordination and dismissed. The act was held to be irremediable because of the damage done to the faculty and school district by willful violation of a reasonable rule. *Christopherson v. Spring Valley Elementary School Dist.*, 413 N.E.2d 199 (Ill.App. 1980).

Repetition of conduct that is prohibited by school policy may, of course, be grounds for dismissal for insubordination. In such a case a coach was repeatedly told not to let non-certified volunteers coach at games in violation of school policy. The coach did so and the court upheld his dismissal. *King v. Elkins Public Schools*, 733 S.W.2d 417

(Ark.App.1987). See also *Gaylord v. Board of Education, Unified School District No. 218*, 794 P.2d 307 (Kan.App. 1990); *Board of Education of Laurel County v. McCollum*, 721 S.W.2d 703 (Ky.1986).

§ 17.6 DISMISSAL OF TENURED TEACHERS FOR IMMORALITY

Immoral conduct is specified by statute in numerous states as grounds for dismissal of tenured teachers. Although the term "immorality" has been attacked as unconstitutionally vague, *Kilpatrick v. Wright*, 437 F.Supp. 397 (M.D.Ala.1977), it generally has been upheld by the courts, especially when it relates to fitness to teach and where there is a rational nexus between the prohibited activity and the individual's position as a teacher. Immorality may include both heterosexual and homosexual activities, but does not pertain exclusively to sexual activities. In *Horosko v. Mount Pleasant Township School District*, 6 A.2d 866 (Pa.1939), immorality was defined as "[a] course of conduct as offends the morals of the community and is a bad example to the youth whose ideals a teacher is supposed to foster and elevate."

Immorality may be interpreted rather broadly reaching to conduct of teachers that by common judgment reflects on fitness to teach. The scope of immorality is shown by a North Carolina case where a mathematics teacher with 15 years experience brandished a 12–gauge shotgun and a .38 caliber pistol in a town poolroom and was arrested for trespassing. The teacher was dismissed from his teaching position for immorality which is a statutory reason for revocation of a teaching license in that state. The court upheld the school board's dismissal of the teacher finding that the conduct was detrimental to the teacher's ability to effectively serve as a teacher and role model for children. *Barringer v. Caldwell County Board of Education*, 473 S.E.2d 435 (N.C.App.1996). In another case of extraordinary bad behavior, a teacher's dismissal for immorality was sustained by the court where the evidence showed that the teacher had three drunken driving convictions and two convictions for driving without a license. *Zelno v. Lincoln Intermediate Unit No. 12 Board of Directors*, 786 A.2d 1022 (Pa.Cmwlth.2001).

Lying, too, is considered to be immoral. Where a tenured teacher was denied permission to attend a conference, she left anyway, and upon her return submitted a request for excused absences because of illness. The board dismissed her based on immorality. The court upheld the board and said: "questions of morality are not limited to sexual conduct, but may include lying." *Bethel Park School District v. Krall*, 445 A.2d 1377 (Pa.Cmwlth. 1982).

§ 17.61   Sexual Misconduct

§ 17.61a   With Students

Because of the exemplary nature of teaching, the courts have left little question about the seriousness of sexual involvement with students. Teachers must be pure in intent and act when dealing with students. In one instance, a tenured teacher, while on a field trip, tickled and touched female students on various parts of their bodies including between the legs. He was observed lying on a motel bed with one of the female students, watching television. The teacher made sexual remarks and innuendos to the female students and was subsequently dismissed for immorality. Upon being charged with immorality, the teacher responded that the activities were "good-natured horseplay." Later, some students apologized to the field trip coordinator because they considered their behavior was "pretty gross." The teacher, who had enjoyed a reputation as a good teacher with excellent student rapport, contended there was no nexus between his classroom effectiveness and his conduct. The court determined his activities constituted unfitness to teach and his dismissal was upheld. *Weissman v. Board of Education of Jefferson County School District*, 547 P.2d 1267 (Colo.1976).

Another teacher had females sit between his legs, kissed them on the cheek, stuck his tongue in one's ear, and placed his hand on another's breast. Although the teacher testified he did not touch the students, the girls accusations were corroborated by a male student. The court upheld the dismissal as supported by evidence. *Lombardo v. Board of Education of School District No. 27*, 241 N.E.2d 495 (Ill.App.1968). See also *Strain v. Rapid City School Board*, 447 N.W.2d 332 (S.D.1989).

Dismissal for immoral conduct has been upheld where a teacher placed his hand inside the jeans of a student in the area of her buttocks and on another occasion squeezed the breast of a female student. The court determined the conduct to be immoral and irremediable. *Fadler v. Illinois State Bd. of Education*, 506 N.E.2d 640 (Ill.App.1987).

Prior sexual misconduct of a teacher in another school district may be grounds for dismissal from current employment. Where a teacher got a 15–year–old student pregnant and later moved to another teaching position in another state, the new school district in which he was employed, upon gaining knowledge of the earlier situa-

tion, terminated his employment. The teacher challenged
the dismissal arguing that a school district could not take
action against him for an offense he committed in another school jurisdiction. The court disagreed pointing out
that a teacher's prior immoral conduct, and the failure to
disclose the conduct upon his new employment, provided
ample evidence of the teacher's unfitness. *Toney v. Fairbanks North Star Borough School District Board of Education*, 881 P.2d 1112 (Alaska 1994).

Appearances of immoral conduct may be detrimental
to the good conduct of the school and may, therefore,
constitute sufficient grounds for dismissal as statutory
immorality. Where a teacher had a 14–year–old girl come
to his apartment at night without the girl's parents'
permission and then hid the girl from police officers who
came to investigate, the school board dismissed the
teacher for immoral conduct, though no evidence was
presented to indicate any actual physical contact between
the teacher and the girl. The court upheld the dismissal
finding that the teacher's misconduct and poor judgment
created a reasonable concern regarding his moral character. *Hamm v. Poplar Bluff R–1 School Dist.*, 955 S.W.2d
27 (Mo.App. S.D.1997).

§ 17.61b   With Non-students

The courts, when dealing with cases of sexual activity
by teachers with non-students, attempt to determine if
there has been an impact on the teacher's fitness to
teach and whether the activities were public or private.
In a California case, a 48–year–old elementary school
teacher had her life certificate revoked by the State
Board of Education for immorality. The teacher had been
arrested at a private club by an undercover police officer
after he watched her commit three separate acts of oral

copulation, a violation of the California Penal Code. After plea bargaining, the charges were reduced to a misdemeanor, outraging public decency. The teacher and her husband had also appeared previously on television, in disguise, discussing non-conventional sexual life styles. Even though the teacher introduced into evidence her classroom evaluations, which were satisfactory, and a contract from the local board offering to rehire her, the court held that the state board was correct in revoking her certificate. The evidence showed that the sex acts were witnessed by several strangers in a semi-public atmosphere and "[p]laintiff's performance certainly reflected a total lack of concern for privacy, decorum or preservation of her dignity and reputation." The court said a teacher "... in the public school system is regarded by the public and pupils in the light of an exemplar, whose words and actions are likely to be followed by children coming under her care and protection." *Pettit v. State Board of Education*, 513 P.2d 889 (Cal.1973). See also *Ross v. Springfield School District No. 19*, 716 P.2d 724 (Or.1986).

The mores of a small rural community are usually quite different than large metropolitan areas. The norms and expectations of the community have much to do with acceptability of teacher conduct. In a South Dakota case, a teacher's boyfriend moved in to live with her about two months after she became a teacher in a small rural community. The community became aware of the situation and several persons became offended. School officials, trying to stem the initial protest, sought to resolve the situation by talking to the teacher at which time she advised the school officials that her living arrangements were private. The school officials then sought to dismiss her for gross immorality and incompetence. The teacher responded that the dismissal violated her rights of privacy and freedom of association, as well as substantive due process and equal protection of the Fourteenth Amendment. The court ruled for the school board concluding that the state is entitled to maintain a "properly moral scholastic environment" and in this circumstance the dismissal was proper. *Sullivan v. Meade Independent School District No. 101*, 530 F.2d 799 (8th Cir.1976).

§ 17.61c   Unwed Pregnant Teachers

School boards have attempted to dismiss unwed pregnant teachers on charges of immorality and teachers have challenged such actions, basing their claims on right of privacy, denial of due process and equal protection, contravention of Title VII of the 1964 Civil Rights Act, and violation of Title IX of the Education Amendments Act of 1972.

Pregnancy is not proof *per se* of immorality. In a case involving equal protection, a pregnant, unmarried, elementary remedial reading teacher was discharged for immorality because the school board felt that being unwed and pregnant is proof *per se* of immorality. Since the school board offered no proof to support the contentions, the court held the dismissal was in violation of the teacher's equal protection rights. *Avery v. Homewood City Board of Education*, 674 F.2d 337 (5th Cir.1982). See also *Ponton v. Newport News School Board*, 632 F.Supp. 1056 (E.D.Va.1986). (See Pregnancy, Chapter 18.72, Employment Discrimination.)

In another case where the superintendent learned, through rumor, that a teacher was pregnant and unmarried, the school board dismissed her for immorality. "The Board made no findings that [the teacher's] claimed immorality had affected her competency or fitness as a teacher, and no such nexus was developed in the evidence. No 'compelling interest' ... was established by the evidence which would justify the invasion of [the teacher's] constitutional right of privacy." *Drake v. Covington County Board of Education*, 371 F.Supp. 974 (M.D.Ala.1974).

In yet another case where a teacher was dismissed for being pregnant and unwed, but no action had been taken against other pregnant and unmarried teachers who were employed in the district, the court held that the board had acquiesced in allowing unwed pregnant teachers to remain employed and, therefore, was foreclosed from arguing that unwed pregnant teachers were unfit to teach. *New Mexico State Board of Education v. Stoudt*, 571 P.2d 1186 (N.M.1977).

§ 17.62 Homosexuality

Two factors are considered by the courts when a school board takes action to dismiss a teacher for homosexuality: (1) the degree to which the teacher's sexual preferences have become public knowledge; and (2) the recognition that an individual is a practicing homosexual, even if there is no specific act. In matters of sexual misconduct, both homosexual and heterosexual, the courts have attempted to determine if a school board can establish a rational nexus between the private activity and the professional responsibility, and if the private activity manifests an unfitness to teach.

§ 17.62a Public Homosexual Acts

Dismissal of a teacher who had his teaching certificate revoked because he was convicted of disorderly conduct for having touched and rubbed another man's genitalia on a public beach was upheld by a California court because the action demonstrated unfitness to teach. The court held that a nexus did exist between the act and the teacher's professional responsibilities. *Sarac v. State Board of Education*, 57 Cal.Rptr. 69 (App.1967). Where a male teacher was having sex with another male in a booth in an "adult bookstore," the Supreme Court of Oregon stated, "Privacy is a well-known requirement of society for sexual activity. Engaging in sexual intercourse publicly is universally condemned." *Ross v. Springfield School District No. 19*, 716 P.2d 724 (Or.1986).

§ 17.62b   Private Homosexual Acts

Homosexual sodomy in a private home is not a constitutionally-protected privacy right under the U.S. Constitution, and state laws that prohibit such acts are constitutional. *Bowers v. Hardwick*, 478 U.S. 186 (1986). Yet, the courts have held that in determining fitness to teach, there must be a nexus between the homosexuality and teaching and a number of questions must be considered before a teacher can be dismissed: (1) Are the students and other teachers adversely affected? (2) Could one anticipate a high degree of adversity from the situation? (3) Was the conduct or act of a recent nature or substantially in the past? (4) What type of teaching certificate does the teacher hold: elementary, secondary, etc.? (5) Are there any extenuating factors surrounding the situation? (6) What were the motives of the individual? (7) What is the probability of the situation being replicated? and (8) Are any constitutional rights involved? All of these factors are important when considering the teacher's impact on the students and the educational environment, the necessary nexus. The school board must balance the constitutional interests of the teacher against the right to have an orderly and appropriate educational environment for the school children.

The nexus issue is illustrated in a case where a teacher was not a practicing homosexual and had engaged in only one such act, with another teacher, and the state board of education revoked his certificate. The revocation took place three years after the incident and two years after the teacher had voluntarily related the incident to the school superintendent. The court held that the certificate must be restored unless the board could show actual unfitness to teach. *Morrison v. State Board of Education*, 461 P.2d 375 (Cal.1969).

In another case where nexus was shown, a former student told the vice-principal he believed a teacher to be a homosexual. The teacher was dismissed because he was an active member of a homosexual society, had responded to blind advertisements for homosexual company, and had actively sought out other males. The court held that the teacher's homosexuality must be considered within the context of his position as a teacher, the necessary nexus, and it would be unreasonable to assume that his ability as a teacher was not damaged or impaired. The court concluded that the school board does not have to wait for an overt act before exercising fiduciary responsibilities for the children and the school district. *Gaylord v. Tacoma School Dist.*, 559 P.2d 1340 (Wash.1977).

§ 17.63 Transsexuality

The rule of law with regard to transsexuals is the same as with homosexuals, that is, if it is detrimental to the educational environment, the transsexual teacher can be dismissed. Is there a nexus that is detrimental to the teacher's ability to perform normal teaching duties? In one such case, a 54–year–old tenured male elementary teacher, who was married with three children, requested leave for surgery in early spring. Upon returning in May, after surgery, he had become a she. The board, on becoming aware of the situation, had a series of meetings with the teacher, and submitted a proposal to the teacher, including, *inter alia,* teaching electives at the high school and resigning after one more year. The teacher rejected these options. Although testimony presented by psychiatrists conflicted as to the psychological harm the teacher would cause to children in the school, the court concluded that the "... teacher's presence in the classroom would create a potential for psychological harm to the students, the teacher is unable properly to fulfill his or her role, and his or her incapacity has been established within the purview of the statute." The court emphasized the conclusions only related to teaching in that specific district, but expressed no opinion on fitness to teach elsewhere under different circumstances. *In re Grossman*, 316 A.2d 39 (N.J.Super.1974).

§ 17.7 PUBLIC LEWDNESS

Public lewdness is, of course, objectionable behavior in civilized society and is generally presumed to be inappropriate behavior for a school teacher. In a case where a tenured teacher caressed, undressed and made lewd gestures with a mannequin in a well-illuminated vacant lot and the activity became public knowledge and was observed by the school superintendent, the teacher claimed his private conduct constitutionally protected, and his psychiatrist testified that although he had a personality disorder, it would not impair his classroom effectiveness.

The court held that because the actions had already gained notoriety, it was likely the conduct would damage his effectiveness as a teacher and "his working relationship within the educational process." The court said that: "The right to be left alone in the home extends only to the home and not to conduct displayed under the street lamp on the front lawn." *Wishart v. McDonald*, 500 F.2d 1110 (1st Cir.1974).

§ 17.8   CRIMINAL CONVICTION

A number of state statutes provide that teachers can be dismissed for "a felony or a crime of moral turpitude." A felony is "[a] crime of a graver or more atrocious nature than those designated as misdemeanors...." *Black's Law Dictionary, Fourth Edition* (West Publishing Company), p. 744. See *State v. Parker*, 592 A.2d 228 (N.J.1991).

§ 17.81   Felony

It is not necessary for a teacher to be convicted of an offense in order for a school board to dismiss the teacher from employment for the same act. A teacher may be unfit to teach, yet may not have been convicted of a crime. In a case where a teacher was charged with a criminal act of engaging in oral copulation with another man and was acquitted of criminal charges, the school board dismissed the teacher for immorality and unfitness. The state code provided that school boards may dismiss teachers for sex offenses. The court held for the board and said that it was the responsibility of the board to determine the fitness of the employee even if they had been acquitted of criminal charges. The key, again, is whether the act is a detrimental influence on the pupils of the school. *Board of Education v. Calderon*, 110 Cal. Rptr. 916 (App.1973). See also *Matter of Freeman*, 426 S.E.2d 100 (N.C.App.1993).

In a case where a police and school sting operation caught a teacher on video surveillance camera removing pills she thought were Ritalin from the school secretary's desk and slipping them into her pocket, the school board dismissed the teacher for dishonesty, unreliability, and conduct unbecoming a teacher. The teacher was not charged with a crime. The teacher challenged the dismissal claiming the school board had violated various procedures effectively denying her due process rights. The court upheld the school board finding the decision to be neither arbitrary nor capricious. *Lannom v. Board of Education for Metropolitan Government, Nashville and Davidson County*, 2000 WL 243971 (Tenn.App.2000).

Where a teacher was investigated by the police for possessing candid pictures of teenagers that had been taken at his home, the school district removed him from his extracurricular duties yet retained him as a teacher. The police did not charge the teacher with a crime. The teacher sued the school board claiming denial of due process and sought damages. The federal court held that the school board's action was reasonable in light of its obligation to protect the safety of students, particularly in view of the fact that the employee was a teacher and a coach of students who were about the same age of the persons in the photographs. *Montefusco v. Nassau County*, 39 F.Supp.2d 231 (E.D.N.Y.1999).

Guilt of criminal conduct though, itself, may constitute immorality and cause for dismissal. Where a teacher was arrested and charged with two counts of harassment, the teacher was convicted. The teacher had made approximately 35 telephone calls to a board member in the early morning hours; the calls were related to a protracted labor dispute between the board and the teacher's union. The school board brought charges of immorality against the teacher because of the criminal conviction for harassment. The court said "guilty verdict of criminal conduct will support a finding of immorality." *Covert v. Bensalem Township School District*, 522 A.2d 129 (Pa.Cmwlth. 1987).

§ 17.82   Moral Turpitude

Moral turpitude is "[a]n act of baseness, vileness, or depravity in the private and social duties which a man owes to his fellow men, or to society in general, contrary to the accepted and customary rule of right and duty between man and man." (*Black's Law Dictionary,* p. 1160). Moral turpitude is difficult to clearly define because it is premised on the moral standards of the community.

Growing of marijuana in violation of law may constitute moral turpitude. In Florida, revocation of the teaching certificate of two teachers for growing 52 marijuana plants in a greenhouse has been upheld. The court concluded that since teachers are in a leadership capacity, and are obligated to maintain a high moral standard in the community, the possession of marijuana plants, and the ensuing publicity, seriously impaired their abilities to be effective teachers. *Adams v. State, Professional Practices Council*, 406 So.2d 1170 (Fla.App.1981). In an earlier decision, a teacher was found not to be guilty of moral turpitude where he was cultivating only one marijuana plant out of curiosity. *Board of Trustees v. Judge*, 123

Cal.Rptr. 830 (App.1975). Conviction for mail fraud constitutes moral turpitude, justifying revocation of teaching certificate. *Startzel v. Commonwealth*, 562 A.2d 1005 (Pa.Cmwlth.1989).

§ 17.83 Misdemeanor

Teachers may also be dismissed in certain circumstances for misdemeanors. Misdemeanors are "[o]ffenses lower than felonies and generally those punishable by a fine or imprisonment otherwise than in a penitentiary." (*Black's Law Dictionary,* p. 1150). Improprieties in public that reflect on the school, even though relatively minor, may be grounds for dismissal. In a case where a tenured teacher was arrested and charged with "... disturbing the peace by being under the influence of intoxicants, attempting to fight, and display of a gun," his dismissal was upheld for good and just cause, and the board's action was held not to be arbitrary, irrational or unreasonable. *Williams v. School District No. 40 of Gila County*, 417 P.2d 376 (Ariz.App.1966).

§ 17.84 Drugs and Alcohol

Several cases have arisen in recent years where teachers have been dismissed for possession and use of controlled substances. Because state statutes usually do not require dismissal for use of drugs, teachers who have been involved with drugs have, alternatively, been dismissed under statutory provisions for fitness to teach, moral turpitude, immorality, misdemeanor, and felony convictions, plus other good and sufficient cause.

An example is found in Georgia where a tenured teacher was arrested for possession of cocaine, glutethimide, and marijuana and pleaded guilty to violating that state's Controlled Substances Act. Because it was a first offense, the teacher was placed on probation. In order to reduce the impact of bad publicity, she was transferred to two other teaching positions during the remainder of the year. Finally, the board dismissed her for "immorality" and "other good and sufficient cause" based on her guilty plea. The court said, "the proven fact of the teacher's possession of three dangerous drugs is evidence from which 'immorality' may be inferred, even in the absence of criminal purpose or intent." *Dominy v. Mays*, 257 S.E.2d 317 (Ga.App.1979). A similar result was reached in *Chicago Board of Education v. Payne*, 430 N.E.2d 310 (Ill.App.1981).

A different result, however, was reached in a case where a teacher was charged with sale and possession of a controlled substance. The teacher pleaded guilty and was charged by the school board with misconduct. A hearing panel recommended that the teacher merely be reprimanded and the teacher brought suit, claiming the reprimand was excessive. The court felt to simply reprimand the teacher, instead of imposing a more severe penalty, was far too lenient and not commensurate with the teacher's offense. The court remanded the case back to the administrative agency for reconsideration and a determination which would impose a more rigorous penalty on the teacher. The court said, "[T]his penalty is so disproportionate to the misconduct proved by the evidence in the record, an abuse of discretion is manifest and the determination may not stand." *Riforgiato v. Board of Education of City of Buffalo*, 448 N.Y.S.2d 74 (1982).

Use of alcohol, like drugs, also constitutes grounds for teacher dismissal where there is a nexus that is detrimental to the good conduct of the school. In a case in point, the nexus was found where a teacher was frequently absent or late for work, and students and other teachers occasionally noticed alcohol on his breath, and the school board, upon investigation, found that he had been convicted three times for driving while under the influence. The school board dismissed him for immorality and neglect of duty. The teacher sued to claim his unemployment benefits, but the court upheld denial of the benefits finding that his misconduct was willful and directly affected his ability to teach. *Altemus v. Unemployment Compensation Board of Review*, 681 A.2d 866 (Pa.Cmwlth.1996).

§ 17.9 GOOD AND JUST CAUSE

Both common law and statute usually provide for dismissal of tenured teachers for "cause" or "good cause." Where statutes delineate the causes for dismissal, a teacher cannot be dismissed for causes beyond those specified. *People v. Maxwell*, 69 N.E. 1092 (N.Y.1904); *School City of Elwood v. State ex rel. Griffin*, 180 N.E. 471 (Ind.1932). If, however, no causes are specified and the statute merely provides for dismissal for cause, then what constitutes cause is subject to broader interpretation.

Falsification of student test scores in order to achieve state required performance goals is, of course, good cause for dismissal. "Good cause includes any ground which is put forward by the school committee in good faith and which is not arbitrary, irrational, unreasonable, or irrelevant to the committee's task of building up and maintaining an efficient school system." *Hanes v. Board of Education of the City of Bridgeport*, 783 A.2d 1 (Conn. App.2001).

Too, a teacher's dismissed for altering and backdating of student files to make it appear that the school district was in compliance with federal special education laws was cause for dismissal. *Weems v. North Franklin School District*, 37 P.3d 354 (Wash.App.Div. 3 2002).

Where a tenured teacher applied for and received sabbatical leave to pursue graduate work and continued his absence even though he was not admitted to graduate school, the court found the teacher breached his professional responsibilities and such constituted "good cause" for dismissal. *Stansberry v. Argenbright*, 738 P.2d 478 (Mont.1987). "Good cause" has been established supporting dismissal where a tenured teacher (1) cohabitated with a female teacher, (2) used a human fetus in the classroom when discussing abortion, (3) talked about abortion, and (4) spoke to his classes about his personal living arrangements. *Yanzick v. School District No. 23, Lake County, Montana*, 641 P.2d 431 (Mont.1982).

Violation of school policy may constitute "cause." Dismissal of a tenured teacher was upheld for violating a school policy which stated that "the board of education does not encourage corporal punishment." Over a four-year period the teacher had kicked a student, struck another in the face, knocked a female to the floor, and committed other similar acts. *Tomczik v. State Tenure Commission*, 438 N.W.2d 642 (Mich.App.1989).

Refusal to accede to school rules prohibiting teaching of religious beliefs in the classroom may constitute legal "cause" for dismissal. After a tenured teacher was warned numerous times to stop religious activities such as writing "God is truth and truth is God" on the blackboard, the board dismissed him. The teacher did not deny the allegations, and said he would not stop because "he was a Christian and that part of his mission was a sense of evangelism." His actions and refusal to comply with school rules constituted grounds for dismissal. *Rhodes v. Laurel Highlands School District*, 544 A.2d 562 (Pa.Cmwlth.1988).

"Reasonable and just cause" for dismissal has been found where a tenured teacher was discharged for inviting two females from his driver's education class to a party where they drank beer and smoked marijuana. *Barcheski v. Board of Education of Grand Rapids Public Schools*, 412 N.W.2d 296 (Mich.App.1987).

CHAPTER 18

EMPLOYMENT DISCRIMINATION

§ 18.1 INTRODUCTION

The social and political upheavals experienced in the United States after World War II brought about tremendous changes in employment practices. These movements have spawned both federal and state legislation that have attempted to overcome the effects of past discrimination against minorities and to ensure against the re-emergence of discrimination. This chapter discusses precedents grounded in statutes, court decisions, and regulations bearing on race, sex, age, religion, and handicap discrimination that have influenced employment practices in public education.

§ 18.2 RIGHTS IN PUBLIC EMPLOYMENT

Protection against employment discrimination emanates from the federal and state constitutions and statutes. State constitutions and statutes can provide protections greater than those offered by the federal constitution and statutes, but the federal laws establish the groundwork and basic assurances against discrimination.

§ 18.21 Constitution and Statutes

Protection of public employees against discrimination is provided in two principal sources: (1) the Equal Protection Clause of the Fourteenth Amendment, and (2) the federal statutes that are generally referred to as the Civil Rights Act.

The Equal Protection Clause of the U.S. Constitution gives broader and less specific protection while the statutes are sharper honed to address particular types of discrimination. [See: Mack A. Player, *Federal Law of Employment Discrimination In A Nutshell, Fourth Edition* (St. Paul, Minn., West Group, 1999).] The Equal Protection Clause, on the other hand, by being broader in scope, may be invoked to reach discrimination that is not covered by federal statutes. Moreover, the constitutional protections may overlap and encompass statutory discrimination, and redress may be found under either or both.

§ 18.22   The Federal Statutes

The principal federal statutes that form the heart of employment discrimination law are: (1) Title VII of the Civil Rights Act of 1964 (Title VII); (2) the Age Discrimination in Employment Act of 1967 (ADEA); and (3) the Americans with Disabilities Act of 1990 (ADA). These statutes in combination protect against invidious discrimination based on race, color, sex, national origin, religion, age, and individuals with disabilities.

In addition, as noted above, state constitutions and state statutes may have "independent vitality" and offer expanded scope of protections to classes of persons beyond federal law. For example, the California Supreme Court has held that California state law may provide more protection for pregnancy than does federal Title VII. *California Federal Savings and Loan Association v. Guerra*, 479 U.S. 272 (1987).

In addition to these core federal antidiscrimination statutes, there are additional federal statutory provisions that may overlap or complement these basic acts. These are:

1) The Equal Pay Act of 1963 (EPA), which requires that men and women who perform equal work must receive equal pay. EPA had a bit of a different genesis from the three aforementioned Acts in that it was an enforcement provision of the Fair Labor Standards Act.

2) The Immigration Reform and Control Act, which makes it illegal for employers to hire undocumented aliens. This Act guards against discrimination on the basis of national origin as does Title VII, but applies to employers with smaller numbers of employees. Too, the Act reaches beyond Title VII in that it proscribes discrimination on the basis of citizenship, those who are citizens or "intending" to be citizens. (See: *Player*, supra.)

3) The Civil Rights Act of 1866 (42 U.S.C.A., 1981), enacted after the Civil War, extends protection to "all persons the same right to make and enforce contracts as is enjoyed by white citizens." The Act covers all forms of contracts including employment contracts. While the Act was initially intended to apply only to racial discrimination, its scope does include ethnic discrimination. *Saint Francis College v. Al–Khazraji*, 481 U.S. 604 (1987).

4) Title VI of the Civil Rights Act of 1964 (42 U.S.C.A. 2000d), is tied to the distribution of federal funds and is designed to deny such federal assistance on the grounds of discrimination based on race, color, and national origin. Federal funds for "programs or

activities" of institutions may be terminated if discrimination is found to exist, and such overlaps Title VII insofar as employment discrimination may exist in such federally-funded "programs or activities." (See: *Player*, supra.)

5) Title IX of the Educational Amendments of 1972 (20 U.S.C.A. 1681), prohibits discrimination based on sex in any educational "program or activity" receiving federal assistance. Title IX adds sex to the list of proscribed classes of discrimination found in Title VI.

In addition to these Acts, several other federal statutes address unlawful discrimination in particular aspects of employment. These include:

a) The Family and Medical Leave Act of 1993 (FMLA) (29 U.S.C.A. 2601) entitles employees to 12 weeks unpaid leave who have been at that job for at least 12 months. The leave must be granted for needs related to care of spouse, child, or parent; birth or adoption of a child; or of a general serious health condition.

b) The Employee Retirement Income Security Act of 1974 (ERISA) (29 U.S.C.A. 1000) establishes fiscal responsibility for benefit and pension plans.

c) The Veterans Reemployment Rights Act (38 U.S.C.A. 2021) provides persons returning from military leave the right to full reinstatement in their former employment.

d) The Occupational Safety and Health Act of 1970 (OSHA) (29 U.S.C.A. 651) establishes minimum standards for job health and safety and prohibits retaliation against employees who report or complain of unsafe conditions.

§ 18.23 Enforcement of Employment Rights

The federal Equal Employment Opportunity Commission (EEOC) is the principal governmental agency that is charged with enforcement of the various federal employment discrimination statutes. The EEOC was originally created to enforce Title VII, but has since been given the authority to enforce ADEA, the EPA, and the ADA. The EEOC has five functions: (1) complaint processing, investigation and conciliation; (2) litigation to enforce the statutes; (3) interpreting the statutes and regulations; (4) federal employee complaint adjudication, beyond its authority over all other applicable public and private employment; and (5) resolution of complaints by state government employees. (See *Player*, supra, pp. 38–39.)

The EEOC has broad subpoena powers to investigate charges of discrimination and is authorized to file charges in court challenging alleged discrimination. If the EEOC finds evidence of discrimination it may file suit, but if it does not, the party alleging discrimination may obtain a letter of "notice of right to sue" from the EEOC which gives the complainant the legal authority to initiate a private action in court.

Of course, enforcement of constitutional claims, such as challenges to school district, government, employment discrimination, may be taken directly to federal court, pursuant to the Equal Protection and Due Process clauses of the Fourteenth Amendment, if a federal statute falling under the EEOC or other federal agency jurisdiction is not invoked in the complaint.

§ 18.3 EQUAL PROTECTION

The standards under the Equal Protection Clause are not the same as under the various statutory provisions that have been enacted by Congress to eradicate discrimination. The equal protection standard as developed in the school desegregation cases prohibits discrimination that can be ultimately traced to a racially motivated purpose. Remedial action to overcome segregation is not required by the courts under the Equal Protection Clause unless it can be shown that segregation was caused by official actions, the *purpose* and *intent* of which were to discriminate. To show merely that the *effect* of the employer's policy results in adverse impact on racial minorities is insufficient to prove a violation of the Equal Protection Clause.

If plaintiffs cannot show that segregation was a result of discriminatory purpose or intent, the state need only show that its actions were not irrational. On the other hand, if discriminatory intent is shown, the state must bear the burden of showing a compelling reason to act as it did. In contrast, Title VII imposes a more rigorous standard on the state. Under Title VII, Congress provides that where employment practices are concerned, discriminatory intent need not be proved; rather, the plaintiff need only show that the effect of the policy was to discriminate.

§ 18.4 TITLE VI

Title VI of the Civil Rights Act prohibits discrimination in federally-assisted programs based on race, color, or national origin. With Title VI, Congress provided a statutory remedy against discrimination that could be administered by federal agencies in their regulatory capacity. The ultimate enforcement weapon given the federal agencies under this law is the denial of federal funds.

§ 18.5   TITLE VII (RACE)

When Title VII was enacted in 1964, it did not extend to discriminatory employment practices in educational institutions. In 1972, however, the law was amended, eliminating this exemption. As a result, it is now Title VII that is used most often to challenge discrimination in employment in public schools.

An employee who wishes to launch an employment discrimination complaint under Title VII must initiate the action by filing the charge with the Equal Employment Opportunity Commission (EEOC). § 2000 e–5(e)(1). The charge must be filed within a certain time frame as specified, depending on the state from which the claim emanates, either 180 or 300 days after the alleged discriminatory employment action occurred. *Ledbetter v. The Goodyear Tire & Rubber Co., Inc.*, 550 U.S. 618 (2007). If the charge by the employee is not filed in a timely manner, then the employee is foreclosed from filing a subsequent action in court. Further, the Supreme Court has ruled that one filing covering a number of years in which employment discrimination transpired will not be permitted; each incident requires a separate and timely filing with EEOC. (*Ledbetter v. The Goodyear Tire & Rubber Co., Inc.*, 550 U.S. 618 (2007). The Congress changed the law to overturn the *Ledbetter* decision on January 29, 2009. Public Law III–2 (2009).

An area of much importance in applying Title VII has been employee testing for purposes of hiring and promotion. The position of the United States Supreme Court concerning employee testing was enunciated in 1971 in *Griggs v. Duke Power Co.*, 401 U.S. 424 (1971). In this case, the Court found that Title VII of the Civil Rights Act prevented an employer from rejecting black job applicants on the basis of lack of completion of high school or on the results of a general intelligence test. Duke Power Company was unable to show that the general standards it had established were related to job performance. The Court said: "The facts of this case demonstrate the inadequacy of broad and general testing devices as well as the infirmity of using diplomas or degrees as fixed measures of capability. Nothing in the Act precludes the use of testing or measuring procedures, obviously they are useful. What Congress has forbidden is giving these devices and mechanisms controlling force unless they are demonstrably a reasonable measure of job performance."

After *Griggs*, several lower courts invalidated the use of the Graduate Record Examination and the National Teachers Examination because the examinations were not job related. School districts, in these instances, were unable to shoulder the burden of showing job relatedness in the face of the high percentage of black teachers who were disqualified. Under *Griggs*, once the plaintiff shows, under Title VII, that the effect or impact of an employment practice is the cause of racial imbalance, the burden shifts to the defendant to justify the particular practice by showing that the imbalance is justified in terms of job requirements.

In a later testing case, the United States brought suit against the State of South Carolina for alleged violations of Title VII. The allegation was made pursuant to discrimination against minorities who had failed the National Teacher Examination (NTE) which was used to certify teachers and determine salary levels. The plaintiffs claimed there was a disparate racial impact on minorities which violated Title VII. The court determined that since the plaintiffs had established a disparate impact, then it should be determined whether the tests were job related. The government had to establish a rational relationship between the test and the legitimate objectives of government. A group of 456 individuals with professional credentials assessed the content validity of the National Teacher Examination. This group reviewed the curriculum of South Carolina to determine if the test measured what was being taught. "The design of the validity study is adequate for Title VII purposes." The Supreme Court made clear once again that "a content validity study that satisfies professional standards also satisfies Title VII." *United States v. State of South Carolina*, 445 F.Supp. 1094 (D.S.C.1977).

§ 18.51   Disparate Treatment and Disparate Impact

The Supreme Court has attempted to clarify Title VII by creating a distinction between "disparate treatment" and "disparate impact" cases and has explained the two terms in this way: Disparate treatment is the most easily understood type of discrimination. Here, the employer simply mistreats some people because of their race, color, religion, sex, or national origin. "Proof of discriminatory motive is critical, although it can in some situations be inferred from the mere fact of differences in treatment.... Undoubtedly, disparate treatment was the most obvious and Congress had it in mind when it enacted Title VII.... Claims of disparate treatment may be distinguished from claims that stress 'disparate impact.' The latter involves employment practices that are facially neutral in their treatment of different groups but in fact fall more heavily on one group than another and cannot be justified by business necessity.... Proof of discriminatory motive, ... is not required under a disparate impact theory."

Disparate treatment cases generally occur when a plaintiff challenges a particular practice that is detrimental to him or her personally. For example, a faculty member's claim that her promotion in a particular academic department was denied because of bias must be brought as a disparate treatment issue. The nature of the facts does not lend themselves to a showing of impact. On the other hand, disparate impact may be more easily shown in cases involving a number of persons who are affected by a particular employment practice, such as a requirement that all employees pass a test as noted above in the *United States v. South Carolina* case.

When a plaintiff shows evidence to substantiate a claim of disparate impact, the employer must then bear the burden of showing that the particular employment practice was justified as a "business necessity" or that it was "related to job performance."

In 1991 the United States Congress passed the Civil Rights Act of 1991, Public Law 102–166, 105 Stat. 1071. The passage of this act was in response to the perceived weakening of the scope and effectiveness of civil rights protections by the Supreme Court in *Wards Cove Packing Co. v. Atonio*, 490 U.S. 642 (1989). This Act reacted to the *Wards Cove* decision which had placed a greater burden on the plaintiff to prove disparate impact. Congress stated the purposes of the Act were: "(1) to provide appropriate remedies for intentional discrimination and unlawful harassment in the workplace; (2) to codify the concept of 'business necessity' and 'job related' enunciated by the Supreme Court in *Griggs* ... and in the other Supreme Court decisions prior to *Wards Cove* ...; (3) to confirm statutory authority and provide statutory guidelines for adjudication of disparate impact suits under Title VII ... ; and (4) to respond to recent decisions of the Supreme Court by expanding the scope of relevant civil rights statutes in order to provide adequate protection to victims of discrimination."

The 1991 Act provides clarity by making any employment practice unlawful if the plaintiff employee demonstrates that the practice produces an adverse impact on a protected class and that there is an available alternative employment practice that produces a less discriminatory impact (42 U.S.C.A. 2000a–z(K)).

Also, the 1991 Act allowed the plaintiff to recover compensatory and punitive damages under Title VII. The Act, as its basic purpose, was to "strengthen and improve federal civil rights laws, to provide damages in cases of intentional employment discrimination, to clarify provisions regarding disparate impact actions...." This Act includes the rights of victims of sexual discrimination to sue for damages ranging from $50,000 for companies with 100 or fewer workers to $300,000 for employers with more than 500 workers. These damages are recoverable when "unlawful intentional discrimination 'occurred' not [when] a practice is unlawful because of disparate impact."

§ 18.52 *Prima Facie* Case

Because of the difficulties of proving intent, most litigation has been concerned with disparate impact under Title VII. The plaintiffs, in establishing a *prima facie* case must show four basic factors are true: "(i) that he belongs to a racial minority; (ii) that he applied and was qualified for a job for which the employer was seeking applicants; (iii) that, despite his qualifications, he was rejected; and (iv) that, after his rejection, the position remained open and the employer continued to seek applicants from persons of complainant's qualifications." *McDonnell Douglas Corp. v. Green*, 411 U.S. 792 (1973).

These *McDonnell Douglas* standards for establishing a *prima facie* case are flexible. Facts will vary from case to case and specifications for *prima facie* proof will not necessarily be the same in every aspect. "A *prima facie* case under *McDonnell Douglas* raises an inference of discrimination only because we [the Courts] presume these acts, if otherwise unexplained, are more likely than not based on the consideration of impermissible factors." *Furnco Construction Corp. v. Waters*, 438 U.S. 567 (1978).

Therefore, to dispel the adverse inference from a *prima facie* showing, all the employer needs to do is "articulate some legitimate, nondiscriminatory reason for the employee's rejection." *McDonnell Douglas v. Green*, supra. After the employer has articulated some legitimate reason, the plaintiff must be afforded the opportunity to present evidence that this is more than a pretext for discrimination.

§ 18.6 AFFIRMATIVE ACTION

Affirmative action in employment is a voluntary plan adopted by a school district in an effort to remediate past discrimination in that system. The Supreme Court has said that we must be mindful of "this Court's and

Congress' consistent emphasis on 'the value of voluntary efforts to further the objectives of the law.' " Yet, affirmative action in employment, if not justified, may result in unlawful reverse discrimination. The lawfulness of such plans has been tested under Title VII, Title VI, and the Equal Protection Clause.

Title VII attempts to make hiring practices neutral and does not require affirmative action that favors anyone over another. The Act states specifically that "Nothing contained in [Title VII] shall be interpreted to require any employer ... to grant preferential treatment to any individual or any group because of the race, color, religion, sex or national origin of such individual or group...." Under Title VII, affirmative action may, however, be voluntary. In *McDonald v. Santa Fe Trail Transportation Co.*, 427 U.S. 273 (1976), the Supreme Court stated: "Title VII, whose terms are not limited to discrimination against members of any particular race, prohibits racial discrimination in private employment against white persons upon the same standards as racial discrimination against nonwhites."

An *affirmative action* employment plan adopted by a school district will not be unlawful *reverse discrimination* under Title VII if (a) there exists a statistical disparity between the races or sexes in a particular job category, (b) if the institution was guilty of discrimination in the past, (c) the plan does not "unnecessarily trammel" the rights of nonminority employees, (d) the plan does not stigmatize nonminority employees, and (e) the plan is temporary in nature and is scheduled to terminate upon the achievement of a racially or sexually integrated work force.

In an affirmative action challenge taken under Title VII, the plaintiff must prove that the employer did utilize race or sex in making an employment decision. Then the employer must present its rationale for the plan and show that its plans were designed to remedy an under-representation of women or a minority due to past discrimination. *Johnson v. Transportation Agency, Santa Clara County*, 480 U.S. 616 (1987).

The Supreme Court has provided some guidance as to the boundaries between affirmative action and reverse discrimination under the Equal Protection Clause. In *Wygant v. Jackson Board of Education*, 476 U.S. 267 (1986), the school board, because of racial tension in the community, negotiated with the union a new provision in the collective bargaining agreement. This provision allowed tenured non-minority teachers to be laid off before non-tenured minority teachers. The rationale was based on a role model theory. The Supreme Court ruled the agreement violated Equal Protection because the "Board's layoff plan is not sufficiently narrowly tailored. Other less intrusive means of accomplishing similar purposes—such as the adoption of hiring goals—are available." *Wygant* can be distinguished from *Weber*, although both involved collective bargaining agreements. In *Wygant*, a governmental agency, a public school, was involved, whereas in *Weber* all parties were in the private sector. Following *Wygant*, the Court of Appeals, Seventh Circuit, held that a "no minority layoff" clause in a collective bargaining agreement violated both Equal Protection and Title VII. This court found that the plan, which laid off 48 white teachers with greater seniority than black teachers who were retained on the job, constituted an absolute racial preference and was not "narrowly tailored" to serve any remedial affirmative action purpose. *Britton v. South Bend Community School Corporation*, 819 F.2d 766 (7th Cir.1987).

A public school district implementing its own initiated affirmative action plan must establish that the use of race or sex as a criterion for employment must be justified with a showing of a "compelling governmental interest" to show that discrimination existed in the past and the vestiges remain sufficient to support a compelling interest. On the other hand, to merely show that an imbalance between races or sexes exists will not be upheld as compelling. Even an extreme lack of diversity, if taken alone, may not constitute a compelling need to have race-conscious school or college admission criteria. While diversity can be achieved by hiring criteria that take into account education, and experience can be modified in a way to favor minority applicants to achieve diversity, a plan will not be held to be reasonable or compelling if minority applicants who are hired are found to be less qualified or unable to exceed majority employees in performance of duties. *Cunico v. Pueblo School District No. 60*, 917 F.2d 431 (10th Cir.1990).

To accommodate such an end is exceedingly difficult, particularly in view of amendments in 1991 to the Civil Rights Act that makes it an unlawful employment practice "to adjust the scores of, use different cutoff scores for, or otherwise alter the results of employment-related tests on the basis of race, color, religion, sex or national origin." 42 U.S.C.A. 2000a–2(*l*).

An employment plan designed by a school district to create greater diversity violates Title VII if it unduly trammels the interests of white employees, if it allows hiring, rehiring or permits dismissals based on ratios of blacks to whites. *Britton v. South Bend Community*

School Corp., 819 F.2d 766 (7th Cir.1987). If employees have virtually identical qualifications and layoffs are necessary, then race cannot be used as the criterion to determine who goes and who stays. The school district must use racially-neutral criteria such as seniority as the basis for the decision; it cannot use race. *Taxman v. Board of Education, Township of Piscataway*, 91 F.3d 1547 (3rd Cir.1996).

Thus, use of suspect classifications such as race or national origin are suspect and anytime they are used as an employment criterion the school district must be prepared to show how such use is a compelling state interest and not merely rational from an educational and/or racial diversity perspective. See *Adarand Constructors, Inc. v. Pena*, 515 U.S. 200 (1995). Even an extreme historical lack of diversity, if not a result of *de jure* segregation, will be insufficient to justify use of race as a criterion. *Hopwood v. Texas*, supra.

Thus, it appears that affirmative action plans to achieve diversity may be found to be discriminatory if they are justified only on very broad grounds of correcting discrimination alone and/or are too vague to serve the specified remedial purpose of removing the vestiges of past discrimination. If a plan is not merely to create greater diversity but, rather, is to remediate past discrimination, there must be convincing evidence of prior discrimination by the particular governmental unit, and "[s]ocietal discrimination alone is insufficient to justify a racial classification."

§ 18.7 SEX DISCRIMINATION

Sex-based discrimination in affecting working conditions, compensation, prerequisites for employment, and work-related benefits has been of such magnitude historically that Congress responded by passing legislation to prohibit such discrimination. Lawsuits have been filed under the Equal Protection Clause of the Fourteenth Amendment, the Equal Pay Act of 1963, Title VII of the Civil Rights Act of 1964, and Title IX of the Education Amendments of 1972, challenging such sex discrimination.

§ 18.71 Title VII

Sex discrimination in employment is prohibited by Title VII. In part, the Act provides that it shall be unlawful for an employer "to fail or refuse to hire or to discharge an individual or otherwise to discriminate against any individual ... because of such individual's race, color, religion, *sex* or national origin." The plaintiff is required to show, as with racial discrimination, that: (1) he or she is a member of a class protected by Title VII; (2) he or she applied and was qualified for the position; (3) despite such qualifications, plaintiff was rejected; and (4) after plaintiff's rejection, the position remained open and the employer continued to seek similarly qualified applicants. If plaintiff sustains this *prima facie* case of sex discrimination, then the burden falls on the defendant to show the employment decision was based on a legitimate nondiscriminatory reason.

A school board may be subject to damages for sexual harassment under Title VII if administrators or supervisors knew or should have known of the alleged misconduct but did not take appropriate action to remediate the situation. The employer must take immediate corrective action. *Engel v. Rapid City School District*, 506 F.3d 1118 (9th Cir. 2007).

If a teacher establishes a *prima facie* case of discrimination, the school board must show that its rationale for the employment decision was based on nondiscriminatory reasons. Where a school board defended its decision not to promote a black female teacher on the subjective factors of her "lack of interpersonal and management skills which are necessary for an administrator to have" as well as "abrasive" personality, the court found that these reasons "articulated legitimate nondiscriminatory reasons" for the board's decision. If a plaintiff establishes by direct evidence that an employer acted with discriminatory intent, the defense will fail unless the employer can show "that the same decision would have been reached absent illegal motive." Where a female plaintiff presented direct evidence of discrimination, the board's defense in showing that "she would not have been promoted if she were a man" provided the defendants with a complete defense to plaintiff's charges. In other words, the employment decision must be gender neutral, or that gender was irrelevant to the determination. *McCarthney v. Griffin–Spalding County Board of Education*, 791 F.2d 1549 (11th Cir.1986).

In order for plaintiffs to prevail in sex discrimination suits, they must show that the discrimination resulted in some "adverse employment action." This means that there must be evidence presented by the plaintiff that there was "a materially adverse change in the terms of employment." A material adverse action may involve a transfer, hiring, firing, reassignment with lesser duties, loss of income or benefits, failure to promote, etc. Denial of tenure is an adverse employment action if the plaintiff can show that the denial was based on sex discrimination. *Shohadaee v. Metropolitan Government of Nashville and Davidson County*, 150 Fed. Appx. 402 (6th Cir. 2005).

In a case where a woman was rejected in her application to become the boys' basketball coach and the pay was greater than the girls' coach position, the federal court, in ruling for the woman, held that the evidence indicated the woman was denied the job because she was a woman, and that there was an adverse employment action because she would have received a pay raise if she had been hired as the boys' coach. *Fuhr v. School District of City of Hazel Park*, 364 F.3d 753 (6th Cir. 2004).

With sex discrimination, the court must determine, based on proof, the determinants of the employer's decision. Was the decision based on considerations that were legitimate, illegitimate, or a mixture of the two? The Supreme Court in considering the dilemma of a mixture of the two has held that the language of Title VII which states, in part, *"because of* such individual's sex," means if the evidence is insufficient to discern the causal significance between legitimate and illegitimate considerations, then the court must conclude that the employment decision was made "because of" sex. According to the Court, plaintiffs should be spared the extremely difficult burden of precisely distinguishing causality as to the employer's motives. In this way Title VII "forbids employers to make gender an indirect stumbling block to employment opportunity." The Supreme Court has concluded with regard to the plaintiff's burden of proof that "[i]t is difficult for us to imagine that, in the simple words 'because of' Congress meant to obligate plaintiff to identify the precise causal role played by legitimate and illegitimate motivations in the employment decisions she challenges. We conclude, instead, that Congress meant to obligate her to prove that the employer relied upon sex-based considerations in coming to its decision." *Price Waterhouse v. Hopkins*, 490 U.S. 228 (1989).

Sexual stereotyping is prohibited. The employer cannot have different standards or demand different levels of performance for one gender but not the other. The courts have ruled that a no-children rule applied only to women, and discharging a female for extra-marital relations, but tolerating it for male workers, violated the law. *Phillips v. Martin Marietta Corp.*, 400 U.S. 542 (1971); *Thomas v. Metroflight, Inc.*, 814 F.2d 1506 (10th Cir.1987).

In the *Price–Waterhouse* case, supra, a female was refused a partnership in an accounting firm. The individual was described as "macho," "overcompensated for being a woman," and "a lady using foul language." She was also advised to "walk more femininely, dress more femininely, wear make-up, have her hair styled and wear jewelry" to improve her chances for a partnership. The Court held this to be sex discrimination, that of measuring a female against male-perceived expectations.

§ 18.72 Pregnancy

Discrimination based on pregnancy is prohibited under the Pregnancy Discrimination Act of 1978 (PDA), an amendment to Title VII, 42 U.S.C.A. § 2000e(k). Pregnancy while protected under Title VII, as amended by PDA, is not considered to be a disability under American Disabilities Act (ADA). The PDA has been interpreted, however, to require employers to treat pregnancy as any other disabling illness. PDA prohibits sex discrimination against women who are pregnant, have recently given birth, have secured abortions, have refused to have abortions, or have contemplated abortions. *Turic v. Holland Hospitality, Inc.*, 85 F.3d 1211 (6th Cir.1996). Health and leave benefits extended to employees for disabling illnesses must also be extended to pregnancy. Proof in establishing discrimination applies to pregnancy allegations in the same manner as to other aspects of Title VII. Plaintiffs must establish a *prima facie* case of disparate treatment and, if successful, the institution must articulate legitimate nondiscriminatory reasons for the employment decision.

The U.S. Supreme Court has held that "... Congress intended the PDA (Pregnancy Discrimination Act) to be a floor beneath which pregnancy disability benefits may not drop—not a ceiling above which they may not rise." Therefore, the PDA does not prohibit employment practices that favor pregnant women. *California Federal Savings and Loan Association v. Guerra*, 479 U.S. 272 (1987).

§ 18.73 Benefits

With regard to sex discrimination, actuarial tables used by insurance companies indicate that females live longer than males. Because of this fact, females have either been charged more at the initial pay-in stage of pension plans or receive smaller monthly payments at the pay-out stage. These types of programs have been challenged as a form of sex discrimination under Title VII. The U.S. Supreme Court held in *Manhart* in 1978 that a pension plan that required female employees to make larger contributions than males for equivalent monthly benefits upon retirement violated Title VII because the difference in treatment was based strictly on sex. *Los Angeles Dept. of Water and Power v. Manhart*, 435 U.S. 702 (1978).

The State of Arizona developed a different approach with the differential at the pay-out as opposed to the pay-in stage. Employees were offered a deferred annuity plan and could select from three options: (1) a single lump-sum payment upon retirement, (2) payments at a specified amount for a fixed period of time, or (3) monthly annuity payments for the remainder of the employee's life. The first two options treated males and females equally and therefore were not in dispute. The third option was determined by sex-based mortality tables and therefore in violation of Title VII. All benefits provided by an employer must be gender neutral. *Arizona Governing Committee v. Norris*, 463 U.S. 1073 (1983).

§ 18.74 Equal Pay Act

Sex discrimination is prohibited by the Fair Labor Standards Act of 1938 as amended in 1963 to include what is commonly called the Equal Pay Act. The intent of the Act was to eliminate discrimination in wages based on sex where equal work, equal skills and effort are performed under the same working conditions, 29 U.S.C.A. § 206(d)(1). The Act provided for exceptions when differential pay is based on: (1) a seniority system; (2) a merit system; (3) where quantity and quality of production is a factor; and (4) where pay differences are based on any factor except sex.

Title VII of the Civil Rights Act of 1964, 42 U.S.C.A. § 2000e–2(h), was amended to incorporate the Equal Pay Act. The language of Title VII is similar to that of the Equal Pay Act, except that race, color, religion and national origin as well as sex is covered. Title VII provides: it is not unlawful to provide different compensation, "or different terms, conditions, or privileges of employment pursuant to a *bona fide* seniority or merit system, or a system which measures earnings by quantity or quality of production or to employees who work in different locations, provided that such differences are not the result of an intention to discriminate because of race, color, religion, sex or national origin," 42 U.S.C.A. § 2000e–2(h). The EPA has been interpreted to permit more pay if responsibility is greater. Where it was shown that a college male basketball coach had greater responsibilities than the coach of the female team because the men's team generated more revenues and, therefore, had more public relations duties, the court agreed that there could be a pay differential. *Stanley v. University of Southern California*, 13 F.3d 1313 (9th Cir.1994).

When a claim of unequal pay for equal work is litigated, the standard is essentially the same for the Equal Pay Act and Title VII. "To establish a claim of unequal pay for equal work a plaintiff has the burden to prove that the employer pays different wages to employees of opposite sexes for equal work on jobs the performance of which requires equal skill, effort and responsibility, and which are performed under similar working conditions." *Odomes v. Nucare, Inc.*, 653 F.2d 246 (6th Cir.1981); see *Corning Glass Works v. Brennan*, 417 U.S. 188 (1974). It was not the intent of Congress that the jobs must be identical. To effectuate the Equal Pay Act and its remedial remedies, "only substantial equality of skills, effort, responsibility and working conditions is required." *Odomes*, supra. The Equal Pay Act (EPA) prohibits employers from paying employees of opposite sexes a different rate for performing similar work. *Buntin v. Breathitt*

County Board of Education, 134 F.3d 796 (6th Cir.1998). Working conditions need not be exactly "equal" but only "similar." "Equal work" does not mean "comparable work" nor "identical work"; rather, "equal" means the job duties are "substantially equal." (See *Player*, supra, p. 186.) Whether the work is equal must be established on a case-by-case basis.

§ 18.75 Title IX

In 1972, Title IX of the Education Amendments was enacted to prohibit sex discrimination in educational programs or activities receiving federal funds. Title IX was closely patterned after Title VI of the Civil Rights Act of 1964. Title IX in its original form stated: "No person in the United States shall, on the basis of sex, be excluded from participation in, be denied the benefits of, or be subjected to discrimination under any educational program or activity receiving Federal financial assistance...."

Because Title IX is patterned after Title VI and covers students in educational institutions, some courts ruled that Title IX did not cover employees. But the Supreme Court, in *North Haven Board of Education v. Bell*, 456 U.S. 512 (1982), stated, "[W]hile section 901(a) does not expressly include or exclude employees within its scope, its broad directive that 'no person' may be discriminated against on the basis of gender includes employees as well as students."

Further controversy over the application of Title IX occurred as a result of the federal government's requirement that a private college, Grove City College, supply assurance of compliance. The college refused, and the United States Department of Education cut off the stu-

dents' federal financial assistance. The U.S. Supreme
Court in *Grove City College v. Bell*, 465 U.S. 555 (1984),
held that Title IX applied only to "programs" receiving
federal assistance and not to the entire institution. Under a narrow interpretation of the statute, the Court held
that the college was obliged to submit assurance of
compliance for the office responsible for administration
of student federal financial aid only, and not for the
college as a whole.

This decision was the impetus for the Congress to
amend Title IX with the Civil Rights Restoration Act of
1987, 20 U.S.C.A. § 1687, correcting the loophole identified in the Grove City case. Effectively, Grove City not
only narrowed the coverage of Title IX, but of Title VI of
the Civil Rights Act of 1964, § 504 of the Rehabilitation
Act of 1973, and the Age Discrimination in Employment
Act of 1975 as well. The Civil Rights Restoration Act of
1987 restored institution-wide application of these laws.

The Act now provides that the entire institution or
system is covered and not just the program receiving
federal assistance. If federal aid is distributed to any part
of a public school district, the entire school system is
subject to compliance requirements. Private education
corporations are also covered if they receive federal funding.

In 1992 in *Franklin v. Gwinnett County Public
Schools*, 503 U.S. 60 (1992), the Supreme Court drastically changed the enforcement of Title IX and other anti-
discrimination statutes by unanimously allowing monetary damages for intentional violations of Title IX. Until
Franklin there was very little litigation under Title IX,
but since *Franklin* there has been an explosion of cases.
Monetary damages are available to the plaintiff; however,

in 1998 in *Gebser* the U.S. Supreme Court ruled that an award for damages would not be allowed in a Title IX case unless a school official with the authority to address the discrimination had actual knowledge of the situation and failed to do anything about it. The failure to act on the part of the school official must amount to what the courts have termed "deliberate indifference." If there is deliberate indifference on the part of the school officials, then damages may be awarded to the plaintiff. *Gebser v. Lago Vista Independent School District*, 524 U.S. 274 (1998).

§ 18.76 Sexual Harassment

Employees are protected from sexual harassment in the workplace by Title VII of the Civil Rights Act of 1964 and Title IX, Education Amendments of 1972. Sexual harassment may range from verbal innuendo to an overt act, and the definition must be broad enough to encompass the diversity of behavior. In 1980 the Equal Employment Opportunity Commission (EEOC) promulgated regulations prohibiting sexual harassment. These regulations state: "Harassment on the basis of sex is a violation of Sec. 703 of Title VII. Unwelcome sexual advances, requests for sexual favors, and other verbal or physical conduct of a sexual nature constitute harassment when (1) submission to such conduct is made explicitly or implicitly a term or condition of an individual's employment, (2) submission to or rejection of such conduct by an individual is used as a basis for employment decisions affecting such individual, (3) such conduct has the purpose or effect of unreasonably interfering with an individual's work performance or creating an intimidating, hostile, or offensive working environment." The U.S.

Supreme Court has held that same-sex harassment is protected by Title VII. *Oncale v. Sundowner Offshore Services, Inc.*, 523 U.S. 75 (1998). See also: *Burlington Northern and Santa Fe Railway Company v. White*, 548 U.S. 53 (2006).

The EEOC guidelines suggest two types of sexual harassment, *quid pro quo* and *non quid pro quo*. The United States Supreme Court in *Meritor Savings Bank, FSB v. Vinson*, 477 U.S. 57 (1986), the leading case on sexual harassment, provides definition: "[T]he guidelines provide that sexual conduct constitutes prohibited 'sexual harassment,' whether or not it is directly linked to the grant or denial of an economic *quid pro quo*, where 'such conduct has the purpose or effect of unreasonably interfering with an individual's work performance or creating an intimidating, hostile, or offensive working environment *[non quid pro quo].*' "

The Supreme Court in a 1993 case found that a hostile or abusive environment is determined by examining a number of factors and the frequency with which they occurred. These include the severity of the conduct, whether it was physically threatening or humiliating and whether it interferes with the employee's work performance. The Court also said, "To be actionable under Title VII as 'abusive work environment' harassment, conduct need not seriously affect the employee's psychological well-being or lead the employee to suffer injury, so long as the environment would reasonably be perceived, and is perceived, as hostile or abusive. . . ." Title VII does not require the employee to prove they have actually been harmed psychologically or otherwise. *Harris v. Forklift Systems, Inc.*, 510 U.S. 17 (1993).

The EEOC guidelines further provide that an employer is held responsible "[f]or its act and those of its agents and supervisory employees with respect to sexual harassment regardless of whether the specific acts complained of were authorized or even forbidden by the employer and regardless of whether the employer knew or should have known of their occurrence."

Also, an employer is held responsible for acts of sexual harassment between fellow employees where the employer "knows or should have known of the conduct, unless it can show that it took immediate and appropriate corrective actions." In 1992 the U.S. Supreme Court in *Franklin v. Gwinnett County Public Schools*, supra, ruled that a student may collect monetary damages for sexual harassment. Since Title IX covers employees as well as students, then an employee can hold an employer liable for damages under Title IX if sexual harassment occurs in the work place. The *Gebser* ruling comes into play where damages are concerned; that is, in order to obtain damages, the plaintiff must show that an official of the school district, with authority to address the situation, had actual knowledge of the offense and treated the plight of the plaintiff with "deliberate indifference." *Gebser v. Lago Vista*, supra.

§ 18.761 Retaliation

As observed above, Title IX protects against sex discrimination, and "retaliation" is an attendant-viable action for damages. A private right of action for damages may be had by a complainant that sustains allegations of harassment. *Gebser v. Lago Vista Independent School District*, 524 U.S. 274 (1998). Retaliation as a separate action is, by definition, an intentional act, a form of "discrimination" that emanates from the aggrieved being treated differentially because of sex. *Olmstead v. L.C.*, 527 U.S. 581 (1999). The Supreme Court has said that:

" . . . retaliation is discrimination 'on the basis of sex' because it is an intentional response to the nature of the complaint, an allegation of sex discrimination." *Jackson v. Birmingham Board of Education*, 544 U.S. 167 (2005). Thus, retaliation against a person by a school district because of a complaint of sexual discrimination alleged by that person "constitutes intentional discrimination on the basis of sex in violation of Title IX." (*Jackson v. Birmingham Board of Education*, 544 U.S. 167 (2005)). The Supreme Court has clearly ruled that even though "retaliation" is not mentioned in the language of Title IX, it nevertheless is an implicit violation. The Court reasoned that reporting of incidents of sex discrimination is essential if protection is to be realized. "Indeed," the Court says, "if retaliation were not prohibited, Title IX's enforcement scheme would unravel . . . Without protection from retaliation, individuals who witness discrimination would likely not report it . . . , and the underlying discrimination would go unremedied."

Retaliation claims for damages are available to persons who suffer adverse employment action due to their reporting of discrimination against school districts. The leading precedent on the subject was established in a case where a girls' basketball coach complained that the girls' team was discriminated against in the provision of athletic funds by a school district. The Supreme Court held that even though the coach was only an "indirect victim" of the monetary loss of sex discrimination, he nevertheless was the "direct" victim of the retaliation by the school when it subsequently gave him negative evaluations and removed him as girls' coach. (*Jackson v. Birmingham Board of Education*, 544 U.S. 167 (2005)). Therefore, retaliation by a school district against a third party for reporting sex discrimination against another may result in the indirect victim prevailing and gaining compensation in damages.

§ 18.77 Sexuality

Some states and municipalities have passed statutes or ordinances which prohibit discrimination on the basis of sexual orientation. These are defined as heterosexuality, homosexuality, or bisexuality. Homosexuality is not defined by the Rehabilitation Act of 1973, the American Disabilities Act, or other federal statutes. The American Disabilities Act specifically excludes from protection homosexuality, transvestism and transsexualism, pedophilia, exhibitionism, gender identity disorders, compulsive gambling, and substance-use disorders resulting from illegal drug use. See *DeSantis v. Pacific Tel. & Tel. Co., Inc.*, 608 F.2d 327 (9th Cir.1979), and *Ulane v. Eastern Airlines*, 742 F.2d 1081 (7th Cir.1984).

§ 18.8 RELIGIOUS DISCRIMINATION

Employees' religious rights and freedoms are protected by both the First Amendment of the U.S. Constitution and Title VII of the Civil Rights Act of 1964, as amended in 1972.

The Civil Rights Act of 1964, Title VII, prohibits any employer from discriminating against an individual because of religion. The 1972 Amendment states: "The term 'religion' includes all aspects of religious observance and practice, as well as belief, unless an employer demonstrates that he is unable to reasonably accommodate an employee's or prospective employee's religious observance or practice without undue hardship on the conduct of the employer's business." The Supreme Court in 1989 ruled that religion not only includes organized faiths such as Baptist, Judaism, etc., but also "moral or ethical beliefs as to what is right and wrong which are sincerely held with the strength of traditional religious views, ... The fact that no religious group espouses such beliefs or the fact that the religious group to which the individual professes to belong may not accept such belief will not determine whether the belief is a religious belief of the employee or prospective employee." *Frazee v. Illinois Dept. of Employment Security*, 489 U.S. 829 (1989). Title VII protects atheists from discrimination because of the absence of religious beliefs, *EEOC v. Townley Engineering & Mfg. Co.*, 859 F.2d 610 (9th Cir.1988), but political beliefs are not included under the act. The act exempts religious organizations and religious corporations, also religion can be a *bona fide* occupational qualification. A professor of Catholic Theology must be a Catholic; therefore, this is a *bona fide* occupational qualification (BFOQ). *Pime v. Loyola University of Chicago*, 803 F.2d 351 (7th Cir.1986).

A primary question emerges as to what the employer must do to reasonably accommodate the religious beliefs of an employee. In *Trans World Airlines, Inc. v. Hardison*, 432 U.S. 63 (1977), the Supreme Court addressed this issue. Hardison, the plaintiff employee, challenged a company rule, claiming violation of Title VII, which prevented him from observing Saturday as his religious holiday. The U.S. Supreme Court held for the airline and said that Title VII did not require the company "to carve out special exemptions" to accommodate one's religious beliefs. To require the company, in this case Trans World Airlines, "to bear more than a *de minimis cost*" in order to give Hardison Saturdays off is an undue hardship.

As with other aspects of Title VII, the burden of proof to show religious discrimination is borne by the plaintiff who must show that the employer's decision was religiously related. If the plaintiff sustains this burden, then the employer must in turn show that the encroachment on the employee's religious beliefs could not be reasonably accommodated without undue hardship to the employer. The issue of religious discrimination frequently conjures strange situations; the magic rock episode in Missouri is one such example. Here an apparently rather innocent second-grade teacher failed to receive a renewal of her contract from the school board because of pressure from religious fundamentalists. The evidence indicated that the teacher had a game she played with the second graders where they would rub a magic rock and make positive statements about themselves. The idea presumably was to help the children to have confidence and feel good about themselves and others. The religious fundamentalists objected and applied sufficient pressure to terminate the teacher's employment. The court ruled against the school board finding that the nonrenewal of the teacher's contract was religiously motivated and was, therefore, in violation of Title VII. *Cowan v. Strafford R–VI School District*, 140 F.3d 1153 (8th Cir.1998).

Employees' work schedules have also come in conflict with religious worship in other cases. In one such case a teacher was dismissed because of absence from the job, without permission, to attend a religious festival. The teacher had arranged for a substitute teacher, instructed the substitute on lesson plans, and so on, and the classes had in fact run very smoothly. The court determined that to accommodate the teacher resulted in no undue hardship to the school and rendered judgment for the teacher.

Wangsness v. Watertown School Dist. No. 14–4, 541
F.Supp. 332 (D.S.D.1982).

In a similar case, the court held that it is a violation of
one's freedom of religion to compel an employee to
choose between employment and religion. The court said:
"... [A]n employer who punishes an employee by placing
the latter in a position in which he or she must ignore a
tenet of faith in order to retain employment violates"
Title VII. *Pinsker v. Joint District No. 28J, etc.*, 554
F.Supp. 1049 (D.Colo.1983).

In *Ansonia Board of Education v. Philbrook*, 479 U.S.
60 (1986), the Supreme Court ruled a school board had
met its obligation under Title VII when it offered a
reasonable accommodation to the teacher. The employee
presented his preferred plan which would have given him
three additional days of paid leave for religious meetings.
The school district need not accept the employee's preferred plan but may present its own plan as long as it
reasonably accommodates the teacher.

§ 18.9   AGE DISCRIMINATION

The federal government passed the Age Discrimination
in Employment Act (ADEA) in 1967. This Act prohibited
discrimination against individuals who are at least 40,
but less than 70 years of age. The Act was amended in
1986, striking out the language "but less than 70 years
of age." The effect of the amendment is to remove the
maximum age limitation applicable to employees who are
protected under the Act. The Act applies equally to all
governmental employees, with the exception of firefight-
ers and law enforcement officers, who, by virtue of the
rigors of their job requirements, are considered separate-

ly. The Act prohibits discrimination with respect to hiring, discharging, compensation, terms and conditions, privileges, retirement, and demotion. The ADEA is modeled after Title VII and, therefore, the courts have held that complaints of parties alleging age discrimination will be evaluated under judicial precedents of Title VII.

Two cases decided by the Supreme Court are important in understanding mandatory retirement statutes and age discriminations. In the first case, *Massachusetts Board of Retirement v. Murgia*, 427 U.S. 307 (1976), the Court upheld a Massachusetts statute requiring uniformed state police to retire at age 50. The Court held that government employment was not a fundamental constitutional right or age a suspect classification. Therefore, the Court required that the government show a rational interest to support its policy and not bear the higher burden of showing a compelling interest to support the policy if a fundamental constitutional right was involved. Because the purpose of the statute was to assure physical preparedness by having younger troopers patrolling the highways, the policy was not unconstitutional. The rationale that younger policemen are more physically capable and can provide better protection to all of society was held to be a proper and reasonable societal objective.

In the other case, again using the rational interest test, the Supreme Court upheld a statute requiring Foreign Service employees to retire at age 60. The Court said: "Congress ... was legitimately intent on stimulating the highest performance in the Foreign Service by assuring that opportunities for promotion would be available despite [the] limits on [the] number of personnel in the Service, and plainly intended to create [a] relatively small, homogeneous and particularly able corps of foreign service officers. . . ." *Vance v. Bradley*, 440 U.S. 93 (1979). This the Court found to be an acceptable objective.

Whether a *bona fide* occupational qualification (BFOQ) exemption is allowed under the ADEA depends on how narrowly the employer fashions the exemption. In *Western Air Lines, Inc. v. Criswell*, 472 U.S. 400 (1985), the U.S. Supreme Court established a two-part test for evaluating an employer's exemption. First, the job qualifications must be reasonably necessary to the essence of the business; and second, the employer must be "compelled to rely on age as a proxy for a safety-related" job qualification by showing that there exists a factual basis for believing that all persons over a specified age are incapable of performing the duties in a safe and efficient manner, or that it is "impossible or highly impractical" to deal with older employees on an individual basis.

This test was applied to a rule for eight school bus drivers. A lower federal court ruled that to broad-brush all persons of 65 and older as incapable was inappropriate when the entire group of drivers was such a small number that all could have been evaluated separately. *Tullis v. Lear School, Inc.*, 874 F.2d 1489 (11th Cir. 1989).

Thus, the reasonableness of an exemption can be largely determined by the practicality of application and efficacy of implementation. An employer may not require all employees over a certain age, such as 60, to take a mental and physical test unless all workers are given the test. *Shager v. UpJohn Co.*, 913 F.2d 398 (7th Cir.1990). Standard of performance must be applied to all age groups.

The courts have held that the party claiming age discrimination will be evaluated under the same factors as established for race discrimination. If the action is a private, non-class action, "the complainant has the burden of establishing a *prima facie* case, which he can satisfy by showing that (i) he belongs to a special minority; (ii) he applied and was qualified for a job the employer was trying to fill; (iii) though qualified, he was rejected; and (iv) therefore, the employer continued to seek applicants with complainant's qualifications." After establishing a *prima facie* case, the burden shifts to the employer who must articulate legitimate, nondiscriminatory reasons for not employing the individual or individuals.

Damages may be awarded to plaintiffs under ADEA by the courts against the offending school district if the district is not considered by applicable precedents to be arms of the State. *Narin v. Lower Merion School District*, 206 F.3d 323 (3rd Cir.2000).

§ 18.10   DISCRIMINATION AGAINST THE DISABLED

In 1990 the Congress enacted the Americans with Disabilities Act of 1990 (ADA). In expanding on the Vocational Rehabilitation Act of 1973, § 504, which was conditioned on the receipt of federal funds, the new ADA covers all employees, in the public and private sector, who work for companies with 15 or more employees.

The ADA covers virtually all aspects of society, including transportation, public accommodations, telecommunications, and other areas. The Act's coverage is categorically delimited to exclude coverage of illegal drug use and defines "disability" as excluding "(1) transvestism, transsexualism, pedophilia, exhibitionism, voyeurism, gender identity disorders not resulting from physical impairment, or other sexual behavior disorders; (2) compulsive gambling, kleptomania, or pyromania; or (3) psychoactive substance-use disorders resulting from current illegal use of drugs."

The focal point of employee litigation by disabled persons continues to be the Vocational Rehabilitation Act of 1973, § 504. Section 504 is violated if a disabled person is denied a position "solely by reason of his handicap." "The standards for determining the merits of a case under Section 504 are contained in the statute. First, the statute provides that the individual in question must be an 'otherwise qualified handicapped individual'; second, the statute provides that a qualified handicapped individual may not be denied admission to any program or activity or denied the benefits of any program or activity . . . solely on the bases of handicap." If an individual is not otherwise qualified, he or she cannot be said to have been rejected solely because of handicap.

Pursuant to this Act, the Supreme Court has held tuberculosis is a physiological disorder covered by § 504. If a person is "otherwise qualified" to work, then the handicapping condition cannot be the grounds for dismissal. The Court said that "[a]n otherwise qualified person is one who is able to meet all of a program's requirements in spite of his handicap." *School Board of Nassau County v. Arline*, 480 U.S. 273 (1987).

In a recent case that helps define the extent of protections of this statute, two school van drivers who were insulin-dependent diabetics were demoted to aide positions at a lower rate of pay because of their illness. It was determined that they were not "otherwise qualified" under Section 504 because of safety. The court stated, "Section 504 of the Rehabilitation Act provides that 'no otherwise qualified individual with a disability ... shall ... be excluded from the participation in, be denied the benefits of, or be subjected to discrimination under any program or activity receiving Federal financial assistance' solely by reason of her or his disability. An otherwise qualified individual is one who, with reasonable accommodation, can perform the essential functions of the position in question without endangering the health and safety of the individual or others. In determining what kinds of accommodations are reasonable, courts are permitted to take into account the reasonableness of the cost of any necessary workplace accommodation, the availability of alternatives therefore, or other appropriate relief in order to achieve an equitable and appropriate remedy. An unreasonable accommodation is one which would impose undue hardship on the operation of the program in question." *Wood v. Omaha School District*, 25 F.3d 667 (8th Cir.1994).

The exact definition of what constitutes a "disability" under ADA has come under contention in several court decisions. The U.S. Supreme Court provided clarity to definition of disability in the *Toyota* case (2002) wherein an employee claimed the physical condition called carpal tunnel syndrome that she developed on the job constituted a disability under ADA. Toyota had reassigned the employee but she claimed that the new tasks also caused neck and shoulder pain. The issue before the Court was whether this condition constituted a "disability" defined by the ADA as "a physical or mental impairment that substantially limits one or more of the major life activities of such individual." If the condition of plaintiff could be brought within that definition, then Toyota's failure to accommodate the disability would have constituted discrimination under the ADA. *Toyota Motor Manufacturing, Inc. v. Williams*, 534 U.S. 184 (2002). The Supreme Court relying on the definitions of EEOC under the Rehabilitation Act noted that "walking, seeing, hearing, and performing manual tasks are examples of major life activities." The evidence before the Court indicated that the employee could manage basic life tasks outside the workplace. The Court held that "disability" does not hinge entirely on whether the employee has difficulty in performing her special job tasks, but further to come within the definition of disability the employee must show that she was severely restricted in performing manual tasks related to major life activities. Under the *Toyota* test an employee's condition will be defined as an ADA "disability" not only on the basis of inability to perform certain occupation-related tasks but further whether the employee can manage to perform basic life tasks outside the workplace. Thus, the *Toyota* test is a subjective standard that must be decided based on the circumstances of each case.

§ 18.11 FAMILY AND MEDICAL LEAVE ACT OF 1993

In 1993 the U.S. Congress passed the Family and Medical Leave Act (FMLA), 29 U.S.C.A. § 2601. The purpose of the Act is "to balance the demands of the workplace with the needs of families, to promote the stability and economic security of families, and to promote national interest in preserving family integrity." Also, the Act is designed to "entitle employees to take reasonable leave for medical reasons for the birth or adoption of a child and for the care of a child or parent who has a serious health condition."

The FMLA applies to both public and private sector employees. Private employers must have 50 or more eligible employees at any one site to be included under the Act. There is a special section for schools stating eligible employees of any "local educational agency" and "any private elementary or secondary school" are covered. In order to be eligible, an employee, which includes part-time, must have worked at least one year, providing that at least 1250 hours of service were completed during the year immediately preceding the start of leave.

The employee may request leave for the birth or adoption of a child. This provision expires one year after the birth, adoption, or care of a seriously ill child, parent, or spouse. The term "child" includes biological, adopted, foster, step-child, or legal ward, with focus on the actual provider of care. The leave to which an employee is entitled is up to 12 weeks of unpaid leave within any 12–month period. The leave may be taken intermittently, an occasional day leave, or a reduced work week. Leave generally requires agreement and coordination with the employer unless it is a "medical necessity."

The FMLA has a section that addresses employees who are "principally in an instructional capacity" which impacts schools. This provision is where an employee requests leave which is "foreseeable based on planned medical treatment" and the employee would be on leave for more than 20% of the total working days during the instructional period. If this is the case, the employer may require the leave either to be taken for a particular duration not to exceed the planned medical treatment or transfer to a temporary alternative position. This is based on the need for instructional continuity. There are also rules for leave near the end of the academic term which are designed not to jeopardize the instructional integrity of the class.

INDEX

References are to Pages

563

†